OUR LIFE
AND
PSYCHOLOGY

S. K. Mangal
Formerly Principal, Professor and Head
Department of Post Graduate Studies & Research
C.R. College of Education, Rohtak

Shubhra Mangal
Formerly Principal, Professor and Head
Department of Post Graduate Studies & Research
CRS College of Education, Noida

STERLING

STERLING PUBLISHERS (P) LTD.
Regd. Ofice: A1/256 Safdarjung Enclave, New Delhi–110029.
Cin: U22110DL1964PTC211907
Mobile: +91 82877 98380/+91 120–6251823
e-mail: mail@sterlingpublishers.in
www.sterlingpublishers.in

Our Life and Psychology

ISBN 978 93 93853 12 7

Printed and Published in India by

Sterling Publishers Pvt. Ltd.,
Plot No. 13, Ecotech–III, Greater Noida–201306, U. P. India

Preface

The book is necessarily meant for serving the needs of class XII students of the schools affiliated to CBSE and Board of School Education of the other states. In its inclusion of the subject matter of the discipline Psychology and style of presentation, it has a unique distinction for being credited with some of its basic features given below:

- Being divided into well-organized nineteen chapters, the text has been presented in a quite engaging style involving simple language properly graspable on the part of the readers and users of the text.
- Each chapter of the text begins with the laying out of the learning objectives.
- Covering each and every aspect of the prescribed syllabi of the Boards of School Education, especially CBSE, the authors have properly kept in view the selection of the contents for each chapter.
- The key concepts used in the chapters have been presented through the box material provided in different chapters.
- After having discussion about a unit or sub-unit of the chapter, it has been summarised in the form of a box material entitled "To Sum Up"
- For the benefit of readers, the text has been adequately illustrated with examples, diagrams and tables.
- The evaluation is an integral part of the teaching-learning process. Keeping this fact in view as well helping students in getting prepared for their examination, assessment questions in the form of Essay, Short answer and Objective types have been given at the end of each chapter.
- Relevant references and suggested readings have been provided in the name of bibliography at the end of the text for helping students and teachers who need to go into depth and gain desired insight into the topics in hand.
- For the benefit of the students, the discussion about carrying and reporting of the various psychological experiments has been carried out in the last chapter of the text (chap 19).

With all such inclusion as well as style of presentation, it is hoped that the text in its presented form will serve more useful purposes in meeting the requirements of not only class XII students belonging to the various schools of our country, but will also be able to provide a basic structure to those who study psychology at the graduation or post-graduation stages of their higher education; or for those who opt for psychology as an optional paper for their Indian or provincial civil services and other competitive examinations.

With all good wishes for the brilliant career to its readers,

S.K. Mangal
Shubhra Mangal

Mother's Day
May 8, 2022

Contents (In Brief)

Contents

List of Figures

List of Tables

1

Individual Differences or Variations in Human Beings

Learning Objectives

After going through this chapter, you will be able to:

- Explain the meaning of the term individual differences
- Tell about the types or varieties of individual differences
- Name the different subcategories of Physiological and Psychological differences in which people differ from each other
- Discuss about the distributions of individual differences among the population
- Throw light on the various causes or determinants of individual differences
- Know about the methods of assessing individual differences among individuals

Meaning of the Term Individual Differences

There seems to be no end to the variations, deviations and differences present among the creations of the Almighty in the form of living or non-living. We can see different types of soils, rocks, stones around us on this very earth. The quality and characteristics of the water we drink varies from place to place and region to region. Such variations and differences are equally prevalent among the living beings as well. We can see uncountable number of varieties among plants, insects, birds and animals on the earth. Some are named as fruits, some as vegetables, some as pulses or some as grains depending upon their common or varying characteristics. It is true that there are some characteristics common or otherwise, that help in grouping a class of objects or living beings in one category or species and thereby also separating them from others. It helps us in differentiating and distinguishing a particular type of living or non-living being from others. As a result, we can confidently say that this particular bird is a crow and this is a parrot or a peacock.

However, with such classification or grouping, it should not be assumed that members of the same species are all alike in all aspects. Apparently all cows, buffaloes, parrots and peacocks may seem to be alike on account of their common resemblance as well as qualities and characteristics peculiar to their species. However, a cow is not the same as others. In spite of having all the common qualities and characteristics unique to its species, all cows differ from one another in so many aspects.

As a conclusion, it must be clearly understood that whatever lies around us in the form of non-living or living, beings differ from each other in so many aspects. These differences and variations become more intense and remarkable as we draw closer to human beings as one of the ultimate creation of the Almighty in the history of evolution. We as human beings quite distinctly differ in size, shape, appearance, speed of reaction and innumerable other aspects of our personality make-up and behaviour. Among us, some are healthy and jolly while others are weak and irritable. Some are blue-eyed and black-haired while others have black eyes and red hair. Some are known as girls or women while others are termed as boys or men. Some learn quickly and others slowly, some remember well while others forget, some respond quickly and others slowly. In this way, no one among us is just same as another. The sons and daughters of the same parents or even identical twins are not exactly similar to each other. Every one of us is a typical human being in oneself.

Though alike in some aspects, we are definitely different in so many ways. We, in spite of belonging to a common species known as human beings, have our own individuality which contributes towards the variance and differences found in us. It is these differences that are entitled as "individual differences" in the languages of sociology and psychology. It is a very simple and practicable meaning of the term "Individual differences". However, let us try to know something more about it in order to build up a definition. For this purpose, let us begin with the citation of two different explanations given for this term in the "Dictionary of Education" by Carter B. Good. (1959, p. 172).

1. Individual differences stand for "the variations or deviations among individuals in regard to a single characteristic or a number of characteristics."
2. Individual differences stand for "those differences which in their totality distinguish one individual from another."

Individual Differences: The differences among individuals that distinguish or separate them from one another and make them an unique individual in themselves.

The above two dictionary meanings of the term individual differences, now, can help us in building a workable definition with reference to our discussion earlier in this chapter:

The differences among individuals, that distinguish or separate them from one another and make one as an unique individual in oneself, may be termed as individual differences.

Types or Varieties of Individual Differences

Whatever physical or physiological differences among human beings, they may be generally grouped or classified in two broad categories, namely (i) physical or physiological differences and (ii) psychological differences.

Here are the differences falling in the first category - Physical or physiological differences among us, are related with the differences created on account of the differences or variations in terms of physical or physiological make-up of our bodies. As examples of these differences we may cite the differences existing among us in relation to differences in height, weight, colour of the skin and eyes, somatic structure, bodily systems and their functioning, physical growth and development, motor skills and abilities etc.

On the other hand, the differences falling in the second broad category-psychological differences among us are related with the differences created on account of the psychological make-up or conditions lying within ourselves or in our environment. As examples of these differences we may cite the differences existing among us in relation to the possession of the differences in our mental or cognitive development, socialisation and social development, morality and character development, aesthetic sense and artistic ability, mental or intellectual potentialities, interests and aptitudes, attitudes, beliefs and opinions, value system and self-concept, levels of aspiration, study habits and achievements, acquisition of psychomotor skills, learning skills and abilities including the status of learning performance and the overall development in our personality.

In this way, the two broad categories or classifications of individual differences can be divided into certain specific sub-categories exemplified and stated as below:

1. **Physical differences:** Individuals differ in height, weight, colour of skin, colour of the eyes and hair, size of the hands and heads, arms, feet, mouth and nose, length of waist line, structure and functioning of internal organs, facial expression, mannerism of speech and walk, hair style, and other such native or acquired physical characteristics.
2. **Mental Differences:** Individuals differ in intellectual abilities and capacities like reasoning and thinking powers, power of imagination, creative expression, and concentration, etc., In the field of equipping with IQ, we may find tremendous differences between individuals. On the basis of these differences they are usually classified as idiot, imbecile, moron, border line, retarded, normal, bright, superior and genius.
3. **Difference in motor ability:** There exist wide differences among the individuals with regard to their motor capacities such as reaction time, speed of action, steadiness, rate of muscular movements, manual dexterity and resistance to fatigue etc.
4. **Differences in achievement:** Differences exist in achievement and in knowledge level even among individuals who had almost same amount of intelligence and had been subjected to equal amount of schooling and experiences.
5. **Emotional Differences:** In some individuals, positive emotions like love, affection, and amusement etc., are more prevalent, whereas in others negative emotions like fear, anxiety, anger, aggression, etc., are more powerful. Individuals also differ in the manner, they express their emotions. Some are emotionally stable and mature while others are emotionally unstable and immature. In this way, there exist wide emotional differences among individuals.

6. **Differences in interests and aptitudes:** There exist great variations among individuals in relation to the specific tastes and interests. Some take interest in meeting people, attending social functions, picnics and excursions, others feel happy in solitude, avoid social gatherings and are interested in meditation or enjoy the company of books. In a similar way, people are found to have different aptitudes. In this concern, while some may have mechanical aptitude, others may possess scholastic, musical or artistic aptitudes.
7. **Differences in attitudes, beliefs and opinion:** Individuals are found to possess varying attitudes towards different people, groups, objects and ideas. Their attitudes may be positive, negative or somewhat indifferent in nature. Similarly they may also differ in respect of their beliefs, opinion and ideas. Some may believe in one thing, others in the other. Some are conservatives, and rigid while the others may be progressive, liberal and dynamic.
8. **Learning differences:** Individual differences are found in the field of learning also. Some learn more easily and are able to make use of their learning more comfortably than others. For some one method or style of learning or memorisation is more suitable while the other may not adjust with it and are more comfortable with some other methods. In the same way, suitability of leaning environment also depends upon the individual nature of the learners. Thus, there are wide individual differences among the individuals in relation to their learning.
9. **Differences in Psychomotor Skills:** Individuals are found to differ with regard to development and acquisition of one or more types of skills. These difference are observable right from an early age in children. Some are very quick, efficient and methodical in performing physical tasks like jumping, running, skipping, hopping, galloping, climbing, dancing, swimming, reading, writing, drawing, catering, copying, drawing, handling laboratory equipment and working tools, experimenting, computing, surveying, measuring, sketching, stitching, sewing, cooking, washing, dry-cleaning, etc. However, others may not be so efficient and competent and be quite unfamiliar or fail in performing these skilled tasks.
10. **Differences in Level of Aspirations:** To achieve or acquire something, the most essential requirement is to have an aspiration for its achievement. While we all as human beings are endowed with an inner urge of aspiration, we differ with regard to its level. While many of us demonstrate a very high level of aspiration for achieving things in our lives, a good large number is also found to have a very low level of aspiration for achieving or avoiding failure.
11. **Differences in Self-concept:** The self-concept about the self, reflects the images, considerations or judgment about one's abilities and limitations usually held by an individual not only for projecting himself before others but also for estimating his self in his own eyes. Thus in simple words, what one thinks of him may be referred to as his concept about his self. The individuals may be found to differ much from each other in the possession of self-concept. In this concern, while some people may have a poor or negative estimate about their self, and the others may have a strong and favourable concept about themselves.
12. **Differences in Social and Moral development:** Individuals differ in respect to their social and moral development. Some are found to be adjusted properly in the social situations and lead a happy social life, while others are socially handicapped, unsocial or antisocial. Similarly people may differ with respect to their moral development and imbibing of moral sense and ethical values. Accordingly, where some of us are materialistic, others may lean more towards the social, cultural, moral, spiritual or human values in their life at one occasion or the other.

All the above-mentioned varieties of individual differences lead us to conclude that as a whole the personality of an individual is unique in itself. In all the dimensions and aspects of behaviour and personality traits the individuals differ from each other and thus no one can be said to be exactly alike to one or the other.

To Sum Up

Individual differences among human beings may be grouped into two broad categories, one related with the physical or physiological make-up of our bodies and the other related with the psychological make-up consisting of one's intelligence, interests, attitudes, aptitudes, emotional, social and moral development, etc.

Distribution of Individual Differences

It might be clear now that we all differ from one another in one way or the other in so many aspects.

However, at this point the question may emerge as to how much are we likely to differ, what should be the range or limitations of the difference existing among us? Do these variations or differences follow some pattern? How these differences are distributed over a large segment of population?

Let us seek answers for such questions.

The answers to all such questions lie in the fact that distributions of almost all the things in nature follow the pattern of a normal curve. Height, weight, beauty, wealth, intelligence and similar other attributes of our personality are distributed in our population in a normal way. Let us discuss, what does this normal distribution mean? For this, let us take simple practical instances from our day-to-day life. We find that most of us are quite average in terms of the possession of the attributes of our personality. As a result you will find that majority of us possess average weight, height, wealth, beauty and intelligence etc. There are very few who are too fat or too thin. Similarly while we seldom come across beauties like Noor Jahan, Padmavati or Cleopatra, we also rarely find extremely ugly figures. Mostly there are normal or average beautiful figures all around us. This is equally applicable to the distribution of intelligence. Most of us have normal intelligence with IQ ranging between 90 and 100. Person having IQs more than 140 or 150 (Genius) as well as possessing IQs less than 60 or 40 (Imbeciles) are rarely found.

In this way, it can be easily concluded that most of us or majority of us are average or normal in terms of the possession of all the attributes of our personality. How many of us are above or below average in a given population can be understood with the help of a distribution pattern shown by a normal curve. Let us try to draw such a normal curve on the basis of hypothetical data related with the distribution of the achievement scores (as attribute of the personality) over a given population of the examinees.

To obtain a large sample of population of the examinees, let us approach the Central Board of School Education (CBSE) for the record of the last year class XII annual examination arranged serially according to their roll numbers. Out of this huge data we can randomly select the total marks scores of 10,000 students for our study. Let us now calculate the average score or mean value of the sample. For this purpose, we will add individual total marks of these 10,000 students and then divide it by 10,000 for getting mean or average score value for the sample. If we try to analyse the total marks earned by this population of 10,000, we will find that majority of them have either earned the mean average score or lie quite near to this value. There are very few who have earned distinction marks or got very low marks. In case we try to plot the total marks (scores) earned by these 10,000 students on a sheet of graph paper by taking scores on X-axis and no. of students earning these scores (frequencies) on Y-axis, we can have a bell-shaped curve like below (shown in figure 1.1).

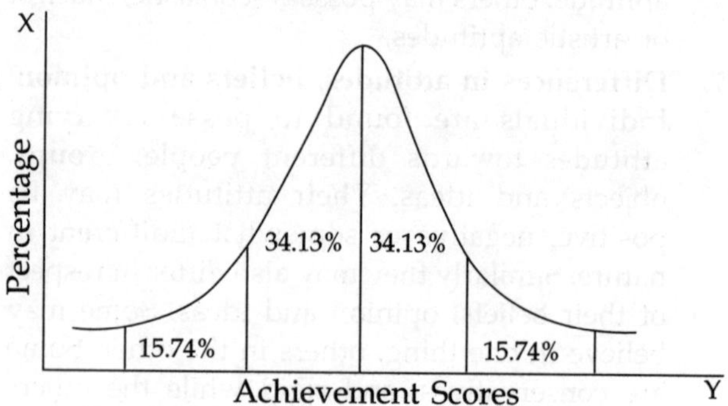

Fig. 1.1: The distribution of achievement scores in a population of examinees.

Let us analyze the pattern of distribution of achievement scores in the population of examinees.

1. As revealed by this curve, we can locate the majority, 34.13% + 34.13%, *i.e.,* 68.26% of the students either getting marks equal to the mean average value or lying quite near to this value. This sub-population of 6826 out of 10,000 thus can be declared as normal, *i.e.,* the students who possess normal or average academic achievement abilities.
2. The curve shows that there are 15.74% of the students who have earned more marks than the average. This 15.74% sub-population of the students, *i.e.,* 1574 out of 10,000, is named as above average in terms of their academic achievements. A similar percentage, *i.e.,* 15.74% of the students, also lies on the other side of the mean value. It shows that there are 15.74% students *i.e.,* 1574 out of 10,000, who have got lesser marks than the average value. These students are named as below average or sub-normal in respect to their academic achievement in class XII final examination.
3. The normal curve thus can portray the pattern of distribution of an attribute in a given population. Here it has demonstrated that out of 10,000, the majority 68.26%, *i.e.,* 6826 out of 10,000 consists of averages. There are only 15.74%, *i.e.,* 1574 out of 10,000 who are below

average and a similar percentage 15.74%, *i.e.,* 1574 out of 10,000 are labelled as above average.

As a consequence, we may easily conclude that individual differences among us always follow the pattern of a normal curve.

It is true that we do differ from each other and no two people are alike, However, majority of us, *i.e.,* 68.26% are quite average, which means they possess average typical value in terms of the possession of personality attributes. A very few of us deviate too much from this average value, depending on which we are termed as quite above or below than the averages or normal.

Divisions as such referred above in the form of averages, below averages, above averages etc. help us in discovering some sort of commonalities emerging out of so much diversity and variation in individual differences. It may further help in the task of ability grouping, homogeneous grouping etc. for tailoring the need of individualised instructions.

To Sum Up

Distributions of all types of individual differences among human beings follow the pattern of a normal curve. This means that the majority among us consists of averages or is normal in terms of the possession of all the attributes of our personality. Only a few of us deviate too much from this average value for being designated as exceptional

Causes or Determinants of Individual Differences

We differ from each other in so many ways but why? What is that which is responsible for such differences and variations among us? Are these differences present right from the birth or even conception among the individuals or do they creep up after wards? Psychologists and sociologists have tried to seek answers to these questions through their studies and researches. In conclusion they have declared that whatever differences in the individuals seem to exist can be clearly attributed to the varieties in hereditary endowment or environmental stimulation or both.

Firstly, it can be observed that people belong to different heredity stock and are thus bound to differ in native endowments and characteristics. These native endowments, abilities and capacities provided by heredity decide the path of the progress and development of an individual. In a way heredity provides the limits of one's growth and development in various dimensions and aspects of one's personality and thus variations in hereditary characteristics cause differences among individuals. Heredity, not only contributes directly towards the differences in individuals with respect to the colour of the skin, eyes and shape, composition and working of various internal as well as external bodily organs, but also makes contributions indirectly by creating differences in the individuals in relation to sex, intelligence and other specific abilities.

Secondly, if we try to consider environmental influences and stimulation experienced by the individuals, right from their conceptions in the wombs of their mothers, we can come to the conclusion that no two individuals in the universe get exactly the same environment. Definitely there happens to be a difference with respect to the stimulation received by the individuals from their respective internal as well as external environments.

The differences in environmental stimulation and influences in the womb of the mother, varying conditions at the time of the birth and nutrition as well as care received by the infants at the early age, differences in the amount and nature of schooling, socio-economic status of the family, race, caste and nationality, education of the parents, peer group relationships and so many other physical, emotional, mental or social environmental stimulation bring lot of differences in the personality characteristics and behaviour patterns of individuals.

In this way, heredity and environment both seem to be contributing towards the individual differences. However, nothing can be said about the relative importance of these two factors in connection with the creation of individual differences. Hence, it is difficult to say whether heredity or environment is exclusively responsible for the differences between Ram and Shyam or Gita and Sita. Unless they are identical twins (with different names) they have a different heredity and some of the differences between them are attributable to this. They certainly have somewhat different environment even if living in the same home or reading in the same school and enjoying same privileges and getting similar nourishment and educational facilities. Any part of the difference—physical and psychological—is thus attributable to the differences in their environments.

Consequently, the difference between different individuals is normally attributable to both heredity and environment and thus, we should always keep in mind the hereditary characteristics and traits of the individuals as well as the physical, social and psychological stimulation they receive from their peculiar environments in looking towards the cause of differences between them.

To Sum Up

Causes of individual differences found in human beings may be attributed to their hereditary endowment as well as to the environmental stimulation. However, their impact and role in creating such individual differences is so interwoven and intermingled that it is quite reasonable to conclude that both hereditary and environmental forces are responsible for generating as well as perpetuating all these differences.

Assessment of Individual Differences

How much and to what extent, the individuals differ from each other with respect to their one or the other physical/physiological or psychological aspects, it can be ascertained only with the application of the suitable assessment method or devices used for this purpose. The assessment or detection of the differences related to former category -physical and physiological differences is made by making use of one or the other physical devices, scales and instruments such as using measuring scales for the measurement of height and weight, or functioning of the internal organs with the help of one or the other sophisticated medical appliances. For the purpose of ascertaining or detecting individual differences among the individuals with regard to their one or the other psychological variables or personality attributes such as intelligence (general and emotional), creativity, interests and aptitudes, attitudes, achievement or performances, adjustment, and personality as a whole we may make use of the specially designed assessment devices, tests and techniques. We will be discussing the use of such assessment devices in respect to measuring of a number of such personality attributes in the different chapters of this text along with the necessary description of the nature and functioning of these psychological abilities or personality attributes.

To Sum Up

Assessment of Individual differences–physical and psychological can be made with the help of the suitable measuring devices. In the case of measuring physical or physiological differences among the individuals we make use of one or the other physical devices, scales and instruments. On the other hand, the use of specially developed psychological method or tests is made for the assessment of the differences related to one or the other psychological attributes.

ASSESSMENT QUESTIONS

Section I: Essay Type Questions

1. Define the term individual differences and tell about its meaning.
2. What do you understand by the term individual differences? Discuss about the different types or varieties found in the human beings.
3. Name the different subcategories of physiological and psychological differences, in which people differ from each other and discuss any four of them in detail.
4. What do you understand by the term distributions of individual differences among the population? Discuss.
5. What are individual differences? Throw light on the various causes or determinants of individual differences.
6. How can we assess different types of individual differences existing among the individuals? Tell about the possible means and ways applied for this purpose.

Section II: Short Answer Type Questions

1. Provide a definition of the term individual differences.
2. Name the broader categories in which individual differences of the human beings are usually classified.
3. Name any five types or varieties of individual differences existing among the individuals in the form of physical and psychological differences.

4. What do you understand by the normal distribution of the individual differences existing among the people?
5. "Intelligence is normally distributed". What does it convey?
6. Name any three environmental factors that works as the causes or determinants of individual differences.
7. Name any five causes of individual difference lying within the individuals.
8. Name three methods or techniques used in the assessment of individual differences among the people.

Section III: Objective Type Questions

1. Examine the following statements and tell about their correctness.
   (i) Individuals differences among the individuals are caused on account of the differences in their personality traits
   (ii) Differences in their heredity endowments bring these individual differences
   (iii) Situational or environmental factors are the real cause of these individual differences
   (a) Only (iii) is true
   (b) (ii) and (iii) are true
   (c) Only (i) is true
   (d) All are true
2. Which one of the following is not used as the method or technique of assessing individual differences among the individuals?
   (a) Psychological tests
   (b) Weighing machine
   (c) Astrology
   (d) Observation

Answers

1. (d) 2. (c)

2

Intelligence–Nature, Theories and Measurement

Learning Objectives

After going through this chapter, you will be able to:

- Define the term intelligence
- Tell about the meaning and nature of intelligence
- Mention about some established facts about intelligence
- Point out the misconceptions about intelligence
- Name and categorize the theories of intelligence as factor and cognitive theories of intelligence
- Discuss about the various Factor theories named as (i) Unitary Theory, (ii) Anarchic Theory or Multifactor Theory, (iii) Spearman's Two Factor Theory, (iv) Thurstone's Group Factor Theory, and (v) Guilford's Theory Involving a Model of Intellect
- Discuss about the various Cognitive Theories of Intelligence named as (i) Cattell and Horn's Theory of Intelligence, (ii) Sternberg's Information Processing Theory of Intelligence, (iii) Planning Attention–Arousal and Simultaneous–Successive (PASS) Model of Intelligence, and (iv) Howard Gardner's Theory of Multiple Intelligence
- Throw light on the nature and use of various types of intelligence tests for the measurement of intelligence named as (i) Individual Verbal Intelligence Tests, (ii) Individual Performance Intelligence Tests, (iii) The Group Verbal Intelligence Tests, and (iv) The Group Non-Verbal Intelligence Tests
- Tell about the concept of Culture–Fare and Culture Biased Tests
- Explain and discuss about the concept of Mental Age and Intelligence Quotient (IQ)
- Throw light on the ways of classifying individuals on the basis of their IQs
- Discuss about the limitations or abuses of intelligences tests.

Introduction

In contrast to animals, man is considered to be endowed with certain cognitive abilities, which make him a rational being. He can reason, discriminate, understand, adjust and face a new situation. Definitely, he is superior to animals in all such aspects of behaviour. But human beings themselves are not all alike. There are wide individual differences. A teacher easily discovers these differences among his pupils. Some learn with a good speed while others remain lingering too long. There are some who need only one demonstration for handling the tools properly while for others, even the repeated individual guidance brings no fruitful result.

What is it that causes one individual to be more effective in his response to a particular situation than another? No doubt, interest, attitude, desired knowledge, skill, etc. count towards this achievement. But still there is something that contributes significantly towards these varying differences. In Psychology, it is termed 'Intelligence'. In ancient India, our great Rishis named it 'Viveka'.

Nature and Meaning

Since time immemorial, attempts have been made to have understanding about the meaning and nature of intelligence. Let us get acquainted with the nature and meaning of intelligence by throwing light on the following aspects:

- Meaning and Definition of Intelligence
- Some established facts about Intelligence
- Misconception about Intelligence

Meaning and Definitions of Intelligence

As discussed earlier, in a day-to-day conversation, an individual is said to be intelligent in proportion as he is successful in meeting general life situations. What is there in intelligence that contributes towards this success is a question which has been attempted by psychologists in different ways resulting in so many varied definitions. Below, we give some of these important definitions.

Woodworth and Marquis (1948. p. 33): "Intelligence means intellect put to use. It is the use of intellectual abilities for handling a situation or accomplishing any task."

Stern (1914, p. 3): "Intelligence is a general capacity of an individual consciously to adjust his thinking to new requirements. It is a general mental adaptability to new problems and conditions of life."

Terman (1921): "An individual is intelligent in proportion as he is able to carry on abstract thinking."

Wagnon (1937, p. 40): "Intelligence is the capacity to learn and adjust to relatively new and changing conditions."

David Wechsler (1944, p. 3): "Intelligence is the aggregate or global capacity of an individual to act purposefully, to think rationally, and to deal effectively with his environment."

What is Intelligence?

Intelligence is the configuration or composition of the mental or cognitive abilities helpful in one's

- learning
- dealing with abstraction
- adjusting or adapting to self and environment
- solving actual life problems and thus leading a happy and well-contented life

Analysis of these Definitions

Above, we have given some definitions. More of such definitions can further be cited. All these definitions, when taken separately, give an incomplete picture because they partly emphasize that—

(*a*) intelligence is the ability to learn,

(*b*) it is the ability to deal with abstraction,

(*c*) it is the ability to make adjustment or to adapt to new situations.

The definition given by Wechsler seems to combine all three viewpoints presented above but this definition too has come under criticism due to difference of opinion among psychologists. Several attempts have been made to reach some general agreement but all have been in vain. However, the British psychologists are said to have reached some measures of agreement regarding a suitable definition of intelligence.

To them intelligence consists of the ability

(*a*) to see relevant relationships between objects or ideas, and

(*b*) to apply these relationships to novel situations.

It makes us conclude that intelligent behaviour is divided into two categories—theoretical and practical, abstract and concrete. The theoretical operations make an individual capable of facing and solving the actual life-problems and making adjustments to the environmental situations. If we try to analyse the factor which determines the success of an individual's activities, we can by all means say that cognitive or mental abilities have a dominant role to play in the success or failure. "Intelligence," as Rex and Margaret Knight have put it "*is the factor that is common to all mental abilities.*" (1952, p. 124). Therefore, the judgement about intelligence can ever be taken with the evaluation of the task one performs, how he reacts and responds to a situation. In this way, if we try to come to the practical ground, we can define intelligence as below:

Intelligence consists of an individual's mental or cognitive abilities which help him solve his actual life-problems and lead a happy and well-contented life.

Some Established Facts about Intelligence

1. **The relation of intelligence with nature and nurture :** There have been too many attempts on the part of psychologists to weigh the relative importance of nature and nurture. The conclusion of their studies reveals, that intelligence is the product of heredity and environment. Both are necessary for the intellectual growth of an individual; neither can be considered more necessary than the other.
2. **Distribution of intelligence:** There are individual differences with regard to the distribution of intelligence in nature like wealth, health, etc. This distribution is a normal distribution in nature and governed by a definite principle that is "the majority of the people are at the average, a few very bright and a few very dull."
3. **Growth of intelligence:** As the child grows in age, so does the intelligence as shown by intelligence tests. Now the question arises—at what age does this increase cease? The age of cessation of mental growth varies from individual to individual. However, in majority of cases, intelligence reaches its maximum, somewhat at the age of 16 or 20 in the individual. After that, the vertical growth of intelligence ceases. But the horizontal growth—accumulation of knowledge and acquisition of skills—continues throughout the life-span of an individual.
4. **Intelligence and sex differences:** Various studies have been conducted to find out whether

women are less intelligent than men and vice versa. The result of these researches hangs in one way or the other. In some of the cases, no significant difference has been found. Therefore, it is proper to think that difference in sex does not contribute towards difference in intelligence.

5. **Intelligence and racial or cultural difference:** Whether a particular race, caste, or cultural group is superior to others in intelligence—the hypothesis has been examined by so many research workers. In the U.S.A. it has been a burning problem for centuries. The results of earlier studies which take the Whites to be a superior race in comparison to the Black-Americans have been questioned. Now it has been established that intelligence is not the birth-right of a particular race or group. The 'bright' and the 'dull' can be found in any race, caste or cultural group and the differences which are found can be explained in terms of environmental influences.

Misconception about Intelligence

There are a number of misconceptions prevalent about the nature and concept of intelligence. For the clarification, let us be clear that what is not meant by intelligence.

1. Intelligence is not knowledge, though acquisition of knowledge depends, to a great extent, on intelligence and vice versa.

What Intelligence is Not

- Intelligence is not synonymous to knowledge
- Intelligence is not limited to memory
- Intelligence is no guarantee against abnormal behaviour, backwardness, and delinquency.

2. Intelligence is not memory. Every intelligent person may have a dull memory and vice versa.
3. Intelligence is no guarantee against abnormal behaviour, backwardness and delinquency in spite of the fact that it is one of the major factors contributing towards achievement, adjustment and character formation.

To Sum Up

Intelligence may be considered as a sort of mental energy, an aggregate or global mental capacity of an individual for helping him in coping with his environment in terms of adaptation and dealing with novel situations as effectively as possible. It has many established facts regarding its nature like—(i) the distribution of intelligence in the population follows the properties of the normal distribution, (ii) It is a joint product of heredity and environment, and (iii) Differences in sex, race or culture do not create differences in intelligence etc.

Theories of Intelligence

With the help of definitions of intelligence, we can be able to understand how intelligence operates, what type of behaviour of an individual makes him intelligent or unintelligent. But these do not tell us about the structure of intelligence or in other words, the different components or elements involved in one's intelligence. The theories of intelligence propagated by psychologists from time to time have tried to answer this question. These theories can be grouped under two heads, namely, factor theories and cognitive theories. Let us now discuss the theories of intelligence falling into these two broad categories-Factor and Cognitive

Factor Theories of Intelligence

Let us try to discuss some of these theories below:

Unitary Theory

This theory holds that intelligence consists of one factor: simply a fund of intellectual competency, which is universal for all the activities of the individual. A man who has vigour can move so much to East as to the West in a similar way if one has a fund of intelligence, he can utilize it in any area of his life and can be as successful in one area as in the other depending upon his fund of intelligence. But in actual life situations, the ideas propagated by this theory do not fit well. We find that the children who are bright in Mathematics may, despite serious interest and hard work, not be so good in Civics. A student very good in conducting Science experiments does not find himself equally competent in learning language. This makes us conclude that there is nothing like one single unitary factor in intelligence. Therefore, the unitary theory stands rejected.

Unitary theory: A Factor theory of intelligence insisting that intelligence consists of only one single factor, i.e., simply a fund of intellectual competency which is universal for all the activities of the individual.

Anarchic Theory or Multi-Factor Theory

The main propagator of this theory was E.L. Thorndike. As the name suggests this theory considers intelligence a combination of numerous separate elements or factors, each one being a minute element of some ability. So, there is no such thing as general intelligence (a single factor) and there are only many highly independent specific abilities which go into different tasks.

> **Anarchic or multi-factor theory:** A Factor theory of intelligence insisting that one's intelligence consists of numerous separate elements or factors, each one being a minute part or component of an intellectual activity.

In this way, Monarchic and Anarchic theories hold the two extremes. Just as we cannot assume good intelligence, a guarantee of success in all the fields of human life, we cannot also say with certain specific type of abilities one will be entirely successful in a particular area and completely unsuccessful in the other areas. Actually, as Gardner Murphy puts it, *"There is a certain positive relationship between brightness in one field and brightness in another and so on."* (1968, p. 358). This brings us to the conclusion that there should be a common factor running through all tasks. The failure to explain such phenomena gave birth to another theory, named Spearman's two factor theory.

Spearman's Two-Factor Theory

This theory was advocated by Spearman. According to him every different intellectual activity involves a general factor 'g' which is shared with all intellectual activities and a specific factor 's' which it shares with none.

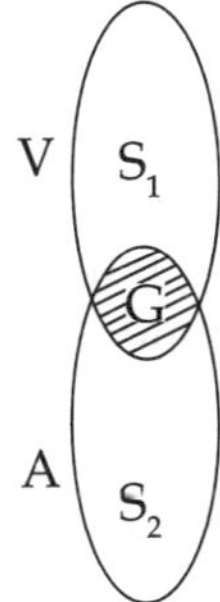

Fig. 2.1: Spearman's Two Factor Theory

In this way, he suggested that there is something which might be called general intelligence, a sort of general mental energy, running through all the different tasks but in addition to this general factor there are specific abilities, which make an individual able to deal with particular kinds of problems. For example, an individual's performance in Hindi is partly due to his general intelligence and partly to some kind of specific ability in language which he might possess *i.e.,* $g + s1$ *or* in Mathematics his performance will be due to $g + s2$; in drawing it will be due to g + s3 and so on and so forth. The factor g (in lesser or greater degree) will enter in all specific activities. The total ability or intelligence of such an individual (symbolized as A), thus, will be expressed by the following equation schedule.

$$g + s1 + s2 + s3 + \ldots = A.$$

This two-factor theory of Spearman has been criticized on various grounds. The main reasons are given below:

> **Spearman's two-factor theory:** A Factor theory of intelligence asserting that there are two types of factors working in one's intelligence namely, the general intelligence (common to all the different cognitive tasks) and specific intelligence (quite specific to a specific task).

(a) Spearman said that there are only two factors expressing intelligence but as we have seen above there are not only two but several factors (g, s1, s2, s3 … etc.).

(b) According to Spearman each job requires some specific ability. This view was not proper as it implied that there was nothing common in the jobs except a general factor and professions such as those of nursery, compounders and doctors could not be put in a group. In fact the factors *s1,s2 , s3, s4,…*etc. are not mutually exclusive.

They overlap and give birth to certain common factors. This idea of overlapping and grouping has given origin to a new theory called Group Factor Theory.

Thurstone's Group Factor Theory

For the factors not common to all of the intellectual abilities, but common to certain activities comprising a group, the term 'group factor' was suggested. Prominent among the propagators of this theory is L.L. Thurstone. While working on a test of primary mental abilities, he came to the conclusion that certain mental operations have in common a primary factor which gives them psychological and functional unity and which differentiates them from other mental operations. These mental operations constitute a group factor. So, there are a number of groups of mental abilities each of which has its own primary factor. Thurstone and his associates have differentiated nine such factors. They are:

- Verbal factor (V): concerns with comprehension of verbal relations, words and ideas.
- Spatial factor (S): involved in any task in which the subject manipulates an object imaginatively in space.
- Numerical factor (N): ability to do numerical calculations, rapidly and accurately.
- Memory factor (M): involving the ability to memorize quickly.
- Word Fluency Factor (W): involved whenever the subject is asked to think of the isolated words at a rapid rate.
- Inductive reasoning factor (RI): ability to generalize through specific examples.
- Deductive reasoning factor (RD): ability to make use of generalized result.
- Perceptual factor (P): ability to perceive objects accurately.
- Problem-solving ability factor (PS): ability to solve problems independently.

The group factor theory: A Factor theory of intelligence advocating that our intellectual activities can be categorized into certain specific groups and each of these groups is governed by a special type of intelligence component known as a group factor. Thurstone and his associates (the main propagator of the theory) have pointed out nine such group factors as the constituents of one's intelligence.

The weakest link in the group factor theory was that it discarded the concept of common factor. It did not take Thurstone very long to realise his mistake and to reveal a general factor in addition to group factors.

Guilford's Theory Involving a Model of Intellect

J.P. Guilford and his associates have developed a model of intellect on the basis of the factor analysis of several tests employed for testing intelligence of the human beings. They have come to the conclusion that any mental process or intellectual activity of the human being can be described in terms of three basic dimensions or parameters known as operation (the act of thinking or way of processing the information), contents (the terms in which we think or the type of information involved) and products (the ideas we come up with *i.e.,* the fruits of a thinking).

Each of these parameters — operations, contents and products — may be further subdivided into some specific factors or elements. As a result, operations may be subdivided into 5 specific factors, contents into 5 and products into 6. The interaction of these three parameters, according to Guilford, thus results into the 5 x 5 x 6 = 150 different elements or factors in one's intelligence. In a figural form, these 150 factors or independent abilities of the human beings along with the basic parameters and their divisions can be represented through a model named as Guilford's Model of Intellect or Intelligence (See figure 2.3).

Guilford's Model Of Intelligence

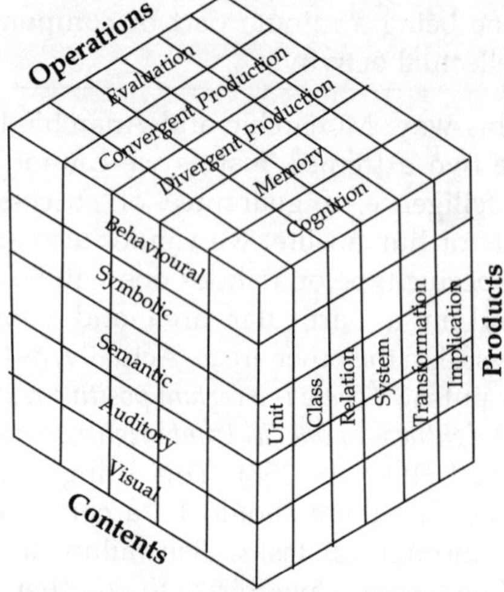

Fig. 2.2: Guilford's three dimensional model of the structure of the intellect (Guilford, 1982)

(Note: The model depicted above in figure 2.2 proposes that intelligence consists of 150 independent abilities that result from the interaction of five types of contents, five types of operations and six types of products)

What is implied by these contents, operations and products can be understood through the following brief description:

Contents (The Type of Information involved)

Figural (visual) — The properties of stimuli we can experience through the visual senses *e.g.* colour, size, shape, texture and other visual characteristics of figure.

Figural (Auditory) — the properties of stimuli we can experience through the auditory senses *e.g.* voice and sound.

Symbolic — numbers, letters, symbols, designs.

Semantic — the meaning of words, ideas.

Behavioural — the actions and expressions of people.

Operations (The Way of Processing the Information)

Cognition — recognizing and discovering.

Memory – retaining and recalling the contents of thought.

Divergent production – producing a variety of ideas or solutions to a problem.

Convergent production – producing a single best solution to a problem.

Evaluation – taking decisions about the nature of the intellectual contents or gathered information whether it is positive or negative, good or, bad, etc.

Guilford's theory of Intelligence: A Factor theory put forward by J.P. Guilford and his associates lay down a model of intellect involving three interrelated basic parameters – operations, contents and products for explaining the structural composition of human intelligence.

Products (The results obtained through Operations)

Units – Individual pieces of information limited in size *e.g.* a single number, letter or word.

Classes – groups of units of information related to each other on the basis of some common characteristics involving a higher order concept (*e.g.* men + women = people).

Relations – a connection between concepts.

Systems – an ordering or classification of relations.

Transformation – altering or restructuring intellectual contents.

Implication – making inferences from separate pieces of information.

In this way according to Guilford's model of intellect, there are 150 factors operating in one's intelligence. Each one of these factors has a trigram symbol, *i.e.,* at least one factor from each category of three parameters has to be present in any specific intellectual activity or mental task.

Let us illustrate this basic fact with an example. Suppose a child is asked to find out the day of the week on a particular date with the help of a calendar. In the execution of this mental task he will need mental operations like convergent thinking, memory and cognition. For carrying out these operations, he has to make use of the contents. In this particular case, he will make use of semantics, *i.e.,* reading and understanding of the printed words and figures indicating days and dates of a particular month in the calendar. By carrying out mental operation with the help of contents he will finally arrive at the products. The day of the week to which the date in question refers, represents the factor known as "relations". He may further transform and apply this knowledge to identify the days for contiguous dates or vice-versa.

To Sum Up

Factor theories of intelligence try to explain the structural composition of our intelligence by pointing out specifically its different factors. Unitary theory, the oldest theory in this regard, for example holds that intelligence consists of only one single factor, i.e., simply a fund of intellectual competency which is universal for all the activities of the individual. Quite contrary to this, multifactor theory insists that one's intelligence consists of numerous separate elements or factors, each one being a minute part or component of an intellectual activity. Spearman's two-factor theory asserts that there are two types of factors working in one's intelligence namely, the general intelligence (common to all the different cognitive tasks) and specific intelligence (quite specific to a specific task). The group factor theory advocates that our intellectual activities can be categorized into certain specific groups and each of these groups is governed by a special type of intelligence component known as a group factor. Thurstone and his associates (the main propagator of the theory) have pointed out 9 such group factors as the constituents of one's intelligence. Guilford's theory put forward by J.P. Guilford and his associates lay down a model of intellect involving three interrelated basic parameters – operations, contents and products for explaining the structural composition of human intelligence.

Cognitive Theories of Intelligence

Apart from the above-mentioned theories of intelligence grouped as factors theory of intelligence psychologists have also propagator number of theories explaining the mechanism of human intellect grouped as cognitive theories of intelligence. Here at present we would like to discuss in this chapter a few of such important theories named as below:

- Cattell and Horn's Theory of Intelligence
- Sternberg's Information Processing Theory
- Planning Attention-arousal and Simultaneous -successive Model of Intelligence
- Howard Gardner's Theory of Multiple Intelligence.

Cattell and Horn's Theory of Intelligence

Cattell and Horn (1965, 1966) proposed a theory of intelligence by distinguishing between two types of intelligence, i.e., *fluid intelligence* and *crystallized intelligence.* Although viewed as different and distinct, these two types of intelligence intermingle and interact to produce overall intelligence.

Fluid intelligence is considered to be the mental capacity of an individual, which is required for learning and problem solving. It is dependent on neurological development and is relatively free from the influences of education and culture. In other words, it is derived more from biological and genetic factors and is less influenced by training and experience. This type of intelligence is put to use when facing new and strange situations requiring adaptation, comprehension, reasoning, problem solving and identifying relationships, etc. It reaches full development by the end of an individual's adolescence.

Cattell and Horn's theory: A Cognitive theory of intelligence stating that intelligence is made up of two types of intelligence—fluid intelligence (derived more from biological and genetic factors and relatively free from the influence of education and culture) and crystallized intelligence (acquired fund of general information).

Crystallized intelligence, on the other hand, is not a function of one's neurological development and therefore is not innate or unlearned like fluid intelligence. Rather, it is specially learned and is, therefore, dependent on education and culture. It involves one's acquired fund of general information consisting of knowledge and skills essential for performing different tasks in one's day-to-day life. It can be identified through one's fund of vocabulary, general knowledge of the world affairs, the knowledge of customs, traditions and rituals, manner of behaving in the society, handling of machines and tools, craftsmanship and art, computation and keeping of accounts and various other such tasks requiring knowledge, experience and practice.

Thus, while fluid intelligence is characterized by a relatively high degree of culture, education, experience and training-free performances in abstraction, thinking, reasoning and imagination, crystallized intelligence is known for its evolution through experience, training and interaction with one's environment over a number of years. That is why it is found to continue to increase throughout one's life span.

Sternberg's Information Processing Theory of Intelligence

Robert Sternberg is distinctively known for his information processing theory of intelligence popularly named as 'Triachic Theory of Intelligence'. According to him there are three basic types of intelligence.

A. Component or Analytical intelligence (analysis of information to solve problems)
B. Experiential or Creative intelligence (using prior knowledge as information in problem solving and creating new ideas)
C. Contextual or Practical intelligence (using intelligence to adapt to environmental demands or practically using cognition in doing day-to-day work).

Let us know about them.

Componential or Analytical Intelligence

This type of intelligence demonstrated by an individual reflects how an individual relates to his internal world. It is demonstrable through the capacity of an individual to analyse the available information for sorting out a way of solving a problem or performing a given cognitive act. People of such intelligence perform excellently on the standard intelligence tests and in displaying rational behaviour. Sternberg believes that componential or analytical Intelligence is based on the joint operations of three types of components namely (i) meta-components (ii) performance components and (iii) knowledge acquisition components of intelligence.

Meta-components control, monitor and evaluate cognitive processing going in one's mind. They prepare a theoretical ground work for the execution of a task in the form of analysis of the problem, selection of the strategies, monitoring of the possible solutions and interpretation of the feedback about performance etc. In fact, as a higher order process, they carry out executive functions and decide what the performance and knowledge components will do. Their contribution helps the performance and knowledge components to carry out the responsibilities enshrined on their shoulders.

Performance components execute the directions and strategies provided by the meta-components. They are the action centres and thus represent the actual mental processes used for the execution or completion of a cognitive act such as problem solving. Cognitive processes associated with this component enable one to encode stimuli, hold information in short-term memory, make calculations, perform mental calculations, mentally compare different stimuli, retrieve information from long-term memory etc. Performance components go beyond meta-components, in that they perform the function also of weighing the merit and or consequences of actions in comparison to other options rather than simply identifying options.

Knowledge-acquisition components represent the mental processes used in gaining and storing new knowledge, *i.e.*, the ability to learn new information in order to solve a potential problem or doing a cognitive act. This type is much more abstract and may or may not be directly related to a current problem-solving task (Driscoll, 2001). The strategies you use to help memorize things exemplify the processes that fall into this category.

Experiential or Creative intelligence

This component of intelligence focuses on experience. It is involved in using the past experience creatively to solve new problems. Thus, experiential intelligence is reflected in creative performance. Persons who are high in this component quickly find what information is crucial in a given situation, and how the information is to be used to reach the target. This is the kind of intelligence shown by many scientific genius and inventors such as Einstein, Newton, Freud, C.V. Raman and J. C. Bose or artists and cartoonists like Michael Angel and R.K. Laxman.

Sternberg's information processing or Triachic theory: A cognitive theory of intelligence adopting information approach and advocating that there are three basic types of intelligence involved in one's cognitive or problem-solving behaviour, named as.

- Component or Analytical intelligence
- Experiential or Creative intelligence
- Contextual or Practical intelligence

Contextual or Practical Intelligence

This type of intelligence is associated with the contextual aspect or practical application of one's intelligence and reflects how one relates to the external world about him or her. In its basic operation it involves the ability to grasp, understand and deal with the practical management of day-to-day life affairs, *i.e.*, how to get rid of trouble, how to face the environmental demands, and how to get along with society. Sternberg (1985) has termed it as "mental activity directed toward purposive adaptation to, and selection and shaping of, real world environments relevant to one's life."

In seeking purpose or goals of his life, thus one has to make use of his contextual intelligence working in a real way in that particular context or situation. For this purpose, his practical intelligence may persuade him for *(a)* adaptation to present environment *(b)* selection of a relatively favourable environment instead of the existing one, and (c) modifying the present environment to fit to one's skills, needs, and value.

Contextual or practical Intelligence can be said to be intelligence that operates in the real world. Sternberg believes this kind of practical intelligence is tacit knowledge or street smartness. It consists of all of the important information about practical reality of the world about which one is taught neither in schools nor in colleges. According to him, tacit knowledge is more important for success than the obvious "bookish" knowledge. The standard IQ tests are unable to tap contextual or practical intelligence. In measuring this facet, not only mental skills but attitudes and emotional factors that can influence intelligence are also measured.

Howard Gardner's Theory of Multiple Intelligence

Howard Gardner of Harvard University proposed a cognitive theory of intelligence in the name of "Theory of Multiple Intelligence". His theory first appeared in his 1983 book "Frames of Mind: The Theory of Multiple Intelligences". Believing in the natural phenomenon of individual differences found in the human beings, he strongly asserted that people in general possess different kinds of minds and intellectual capacities to learn, remember, perform and function in the different types of life situations. Therefore, it is quite absurd to assume a single type of intelligence or intellectual current flowing in the minds of the human beings. Rather, there are multiple sets of varying intelligences owned by the people depending upon their hereditary and environmental composition. Every one of us possesses a unique set of multiple intelligences that distinguishes us from one another.

What are Multiple Intelligences?

Gardner tried to give a broad base to the concept of intelligence and its measurement by providing a multiple frame. He suggested that human intelligence or cognitive competence can be better described as a set of an individual's multiple abilities, talents and mental skills related to a multiple number of domains of knowledge in a particular cultural setting. Elaborating his pluralistic view of intelligence, further, he concluded that there are seven independent types of intelligence that grow and develop differently in different people, depending upon their hereditary characteristics or environmental experiences. These different types of intelligence named as multiple intelligences by Gardner were outlined as below.

1. Linguistic-Verbal Intelligence
2. Logical-Mathematical Intelligence
3. Spatial Intelligence
4. Musical Intelligence
5. Bodily-Kinaesthetic Intelligence
6. Intrapersonal Intelligence
7. Interpersonal Intelligence

Let us learn about these intelligences one by one.

1. *Linguistic-verbal intelligence:* This type of human intelligence is responsible for all kinds of linguistic competence-abilities, talents and skills, available in human beings. It can be best broken down into components like syntax, semantics and pragmatics as well as more school-oriented skills such as written or oral expression and understanding. This type of intelligence is most visible in professionals like lawyers, lecturers, writers and lyricists, and a number of other professionals exploiting linguistic intelligence.

   The individuals loaded with this type of intelligence may be seen to demonstrate the features like below.
   - Good at remembering written and spoken information
   - Enjoys reading and writing
   - Good at debating or giving persuasive speeches
   - Able to explain things well
   - Often uses humour when telling stories

2. *Logical-mathematical intelligence:* This type of intelligence is responsible for all types of abilities, talents and skills in areas related to logic and mathematics. It can be broken down into components like deductive reasoning, inductive reasoning, scientific thinking including solving of logical puzzles, carrying out calculations and the like. Professionals like mathematicians, philosophers, physicists, etc. are found to exhibit this type of intelligence in abundance. The individual possessing this intelligence may be seen to demonstrate the following features in a good amount.
   - Excellent problem-solving skills
   - Enjoys thinking about abstract ideas
   - Likes conducting scientific experiments
   - Good at solving complex computations

3. *Visual-spatial intelligence:* This type of intelligence is concerned with the abilities, talents and skills involving the representation and manipulation of spatial configuration and relationship. Many of us as adults make use of this kind of intelligence in the sphere of our work. For example, painters may be seen to demonstrate spatial intelligence through their use of space when applying pigments to a canvas. This is also true of professionals like land surveyors, architects, engineers, mechanics, navigators, sculptures and chess players – who are found to rely upon the spatial intelligence in their own way. Individuals having this type of intelligence have been found to possess the following characteristics in a good amount.
   - Enjoy reading and writing
   - Good at putting puzzles together
   - Good at interpreting pictures, graphs and charts
   - Enjoy drawing, painting and the visual arts
   - Recognize patterns easily

4. *Musical intelligence:* This type of intelligence covers the abilities, talents and skills pertaining to the field of music. It may be well demonstrated through one's capacity for pitch discrimination, sensitivity to rhythm, texture and timbre, ability to hear themes in music; and in its most integrated forms, the production of music through performance or composition. It is visible in a quite large proportion in professionals like musicians and composers. The individuals possessing this type of intelligence may be seen to demonstrate the following features in a good amount.
   - Enjoy singing and playing musical instruments
   - Recognize musical patterns and tones easily
   - Good at remembering songs and melodies
   - Rich understanding of musical structure, rhythm and notes

5. *Bodily-kinaesthetic intelligence:* This type of intelligence is concerned with the set of abilities, talents and skills involved in using one's body or its various parts to perform skilled and purposeful movements. A child may be seen to demonstrate such intelligence in moving expressively in response to different musical and verbal stimuli or bending different body parts in organised sports. Among professionals, dancers, athletes and surgeons may be seen to demonstrate a high degree of bodily-kinaesthetic intelligence in their respective

fields. The individuals possessing this type of intelligence may be found to imbibe the following features in a good amount.

- Good at dancing and sports
- Enjoy creating things with their hands
- Excellent physical coordination
- Tend to remember by doing, rather than hearing or seeing

6. *Intrapersonal intelligence:* This type of intelligence consists of an individual's abilities to enable him to know his self. It includes knowledge and understanding of one's own cognitive strengths, styles and mental functioning, as well as one's feelings, range of emotions and skills to utilize one's fund of knowledge in practical situations. In brief, intrapersonal intelligence helps an individual to understand his own self by providing an insight into his total behaviour – what he feels, thinks or does. It is, therefore, said to be the most private of the intelligences that a person possesses. On account of its secret and private nature, the access to this type of intelligence in an individual is available only through self-expression, *i.e.,* language, music, visual art and similar other forms of expression. In our practical life, this type of intelligence is demonstrated by yogis, saints and masters of Zen. The individuals possessing this type of intelligence may be found to have the following features in a good amount.

7. *Interpersonal intelligence:* The counterpart of intrapersonal intelligence in one's cognitive structure is interpersonal intelligence. It consists of the abilities to understand individuals other than one's self and one's relations to others. In addition, it includes the ability to act productively, based on the understanding of others. The knowledge and understanding of others is the quality that is needed for social interactions in one's day-to-day life. In practical life, this type of intelligence is most visible among psychotherapists, teachers, sales people, politicians and religious leaders. The individuals having this typing intelligence may be found to possess the following features in a good amount.

- Good at communicating verbally
- Skilled nonverbal communicators
- See situations from different perspectives
- Create positive relationships with others
- Good at resolving conflict in groups
- Good at analysing their strengths and weaknesses
- Enjoys analysing theories and ideas
- Excellent self-awareness
- Clearly understands the basis for their own motivations and feelings

In addition to the seven intelligences discussed above, Gardner in the later years of his research study arrived with his "eighth intelligence" named as naturalistic intelligence. Now Gardner's theory of multiple-intelligence is known to consist of eight intelligences instead of the seven as laid down earlier. Throwing light on his 'eighth intelligence' Gardner writes as under "The naturalist intelligence refers to the ability to recognize and classify plants, minerals, and animals, including rocks and grass and all variety of flora and fauna. The ability to recognize cultural artefacts like cars or sneakers may also depend on the naturalist intelligence. Some people from an early age are extremely good at recognizing and classifying artefacts. For example, we all know kids who, at 3 or 4, are better at recognizing dinosaurs than most adults."

According to Gardner, thus individuals who are high in this type of intelligence are more in tune with nature and are often interested in nurturing, exploring the environment and learning about other species. These individuals are said to be highly aware of even subtle changes to their environments.

The individuals having such type of intelligence may be found to possess the characteristics like below in a good amount.

- Interested in subjects such as botany, biology and zoology
- Good at categorizing and cataloguing information easily
- May enjoy camping, gardening, hiking and exploring the outdoors
- Does not enjoy learning unfamiliar topics that have no connection to nature

Gardner's theory of Multiple intelligence: A Cognitive theory of intelligence advocating that one's intelligence consists of seven independent types of intelligence (developing differently in different people) named as:

- Linguistic Verbal Intelligence
- Logical-Mathematical Intelligence
- Visual-Spatial Intelligence
- Musical Intelligence
- Bodily Kinaesthetic Intelligence
- Interpersonal intelligence
- Intrapersonal Intelligence

Planning Attention–Arousal and Simultaneous –Successive (PASS) Model of Intelligence

Based on the information processing approach, this model of intelligence has been developed by J.P. Das, Jack Naglieri, and Kirby (1994). Basically it has its roots in Alexander Luria's (1966, 1973) work on modularization of brain functions and studies in cognitive psychology involved in promoting a different look at intelligence.

According to this model, any intellectual activity or task performed by us is processed through the coordination of the different cognitive functions carried out by the different neurological systems/ functional units of our brain. We may name these functions as (i) Arousal or paying attention, (ii) Simultaneous processing, (iii) Successive processing, and (iii) Planning.

Let us know about these cognitive functions and the parts of the brain responsible for carrying out these functions.

Arousal or paying attention

It is the first element involved in the execution of an intellectual task on our part. In the process of information processing it is the information that we need as input for getting it processed further on our part for getting the desired output or conclusion. We can avail it by making us alert (having a proper level of arousal) and getting focused for paying needed attention on the targeted stimuli. Hence the first and foremost activity needed for the execution of an intellectual task is to ensure focusing on the relevant stimuli by maintaining a proper arousal level and alertness on our part.

The functional unit of our brain responsible for carrying out this important function–proper attending to the relevant stimuli lying in our environment consists of the combined efforts of the two brain areas named as (i) the frontal lobe and (ii) the lower parts of the cortex. In addition, some help is also available through the involvement of the parietal lobes for this purpose.

Simultaneous processing and successive processing

Both these processes jointly represent the task of the processing of information available with regard to the stimuli attended at the first stage. Accordingly, they help us in encoding, transforming and retaining the information attended and gathered at the first stage. The areas of our brain responsible for carrying out these functions lie in the posterior region or the back of the brain. Here where, the task of simultaneous processing is mainly carried out with the courtesy of functioning of the occipital and the parietal lobes, the task of successive processing is said to be the outcome of the functioning of our frontal–temporal lobes. Let us see what happens in the tasks of simultaneous and successive processing.

- The task of *simultaneous processing* is found to help us first in perceiving and determining the relationship among different concepts, items and segments or pieces of information and then integrating them into meaningful pattern or whole unit of the information for our proper comprehension and use. In this way it can help us in grasping and comprehending the meaning and relationship between the given abstract figures, abstract piece of literary presentations etc. such as recognizing, triangles and rectangles in the circular figures and vice versa.
- On the other hand, successive processing proves helpful to us in the tasks of organizing given separate items, or pieces of information in a successive or sequential way so that the recall of one leads to the recall of another such as remembering a sequence of words or actions exactly in the order in which they had just been presented or learning and remembering of the digits and alphabet in a successive and sequential way.

PASS Model of Intelligence: A model of intelligence advocating that any intellectual activity performed by us is processed through the coordination of the different cognitive functions carried out by the different neurological systems/ functional units of our brain, named as:
- Planning
- Arousal or paying attention
- Simultaneous processing
- Successive processing

Planning

The areas of our brain responsible for carrying out the planning associated activities are mainly located in the front part of our brains, the frontal lobe. With the help of this feature or element of one's intelligence, all that which is attended, and processed at the first and second stages and now available as output is put to action in terms of planning for the achievement of the targeted goals or solution of the faced problems. Therefore, the activities carrying out at this stage are exclusively associated with the thinking about the possible courses of actions controlling and organizing behaviour, selecting and constructing strategies, and monitoring performance. Accordingly, in view of attaining the desired objectives or solutions of the problems the possible course of action in terms of planning suitable strategies are properly chalked out and implemented in their correct order. It is then followed by an evaluation work evaluating what has been done in terms of failure or success in achieving the set target. In case there remains some deficiency, then the work of re-planning is done by setting out the new strategies and implementing them afresh for reaching the target.

Actually, all of these four processes mentioned above are highly interactive and dynamic in nature. It is true that a particular type of cognitive functioning is carried out by them, but the sequence of their occurrence is not rigid or fixed. We can start or end up with planning according to the needs of situation in the performance of one or the other intellectual activity.

The theoretical framework of one's working intelligence discussed above, has helped Das and his associates to develop a measuring instrument named as Cognitive Assessment System (CAS). It provides an assessment of intellectual functioning redefined as four brain-based cognitive processes (Planning, Attention, Simultaneous and Successive), providing information about cognitive strengths and weaknesses in each of the four processes in a quite different way other than arrived through the use of conventional verbal and non-verbal tests.

To Sum Up

The theories designated as Cognitive theories of intelligence include the theories like Cattell and Horn's theory of intelligence, Sternberg's information processing theory and Gardner's theory of multiple intelligence that try to describe the mechanism of human intellect in terms of certain fundamental cognitive processes. In this regard Cattell and Horn's theory of intelligence states that intelligence is made up of two types of intelligence-fluid intelligence (derived more from biological and genetic factors and relatively free from the influence of education and culture) and crystallized intelligence (acquired fund of general information).

On the other hand, *Sternberg's information processing theory of intelligence* makes use of the information processing approach for explaining the individual's cognitive or problem-solving behaviour. It outlines our mental functioning as definite steps explaining what we do with information from the time we perceive it till the time we finish using it to solve our problem.

In the sequence of Cognitive theories of intelligence, the theory named as Gardner's *theory of multiple intelligence,* while challenging the notion of general intelligence, insists that there are seven independent types of intelligence (developing differently in different people) ranging from linguistic and logical-mathematical abilities to intrapersonal and interpersonal abilities.

A modern theory of intelligence presented through *Planning Attention-Arousal and Simultaneous-Successive (PASS) Model of Intelligence* is also based on the information processing approach. It emphasizes that any intellectual activity performed by us is processed through the coordination of the different cognitive functions carried out by the different neurological systems/ functional units of our brain. We may name these functions as (i) Planning, (ii) Arousal or paying attention, (iii) Simultaneous processing, and (iv) Successive processing.

Measurement of Intelligence

We are only familiar with that intelligence of an individual which is manifested by him on an intelligence test or tests. Psychologists have devised so many such tests for the measurement of intelligence.

Classification of Intelligence Tests

1. As far as the administrative point of view is concerned the intelligence tests can be classified into two broad categories namely—
   - (a) *Individual Test*: In which only one individual are tested at a time.
   - (b) *Group Test*: In which a group of individuals are tested at a time.
2. Another way of classifying the intelligence tests is based on the form of the test. Accordingly there are two types of tests:
   - (a) *Verbal or Language Tests:*

     These tests make use of language. Here the instructions are given in words (either in written or oral form or both). Individuals are required to use language as well as paper and pencil for giving the responses. The test content is loaded with verbal material.

(b) *Non-Verbal and Non-Language Tests:* These tests involve such activities in which the use of language is not necessary. The use of language is eliminated from test content and response except in giving directions. The typical examples of such non-verbal tests are Performance Tests. The principal characteristics of these tests are given below:

(a) Test contents of these tests are in the form of material objects.

(b) What an individual has to do is indicated by the tester either through oral instructions or by pantomime or signs.

(c) Individual's responses depend upon what he does or performs rather than by anything he says or writes.

(d) Generally these tests are individual tests. As Dr. Filial observes, *'These cannot be used as group tests, chiefly because it is necessary to supervise the individual testee at work and give him necessary direction."* (1972, p. 265).

If we try to have a final picture of all the types of tests of intelligence we will have to keep in view both the ways of classifying them as mentioned above. All these types of intelligence tests can be represented – diagrammatically as follows:

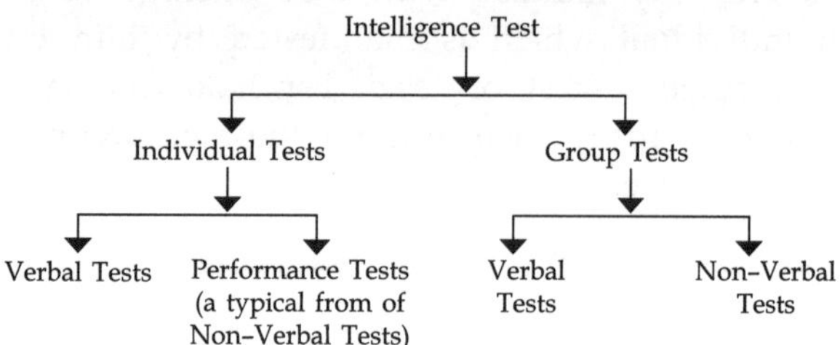

Fig. 2.3: Types or classification of Intelligence Tests

Now we will discuss these types one by one.

Individual Verbal Tests

The tests involving the use of language and administered to an individual at a time belong to this category. As an example of such tests we can quote Stanford-Binet Scale. It is the revised form of the Binet-Simon test. Binet Tests have been adopted in India too. The first such attempt was made by Dr. C.H. Rice in 1922 when he published his "Hindustani Binet Performance Point Scale." This was an adaptation of the Binet test along with some performance tests in addition. The State Manovigyan Shala of Uttar Pradesh has made a Hindi Version of Stanford Binet test. This test is divided into several age-groups and named as Budhi Pariksha Anooshilan. The other common Verbal Individual Intelligence test (used in India) is Samanya Budhi Pariksha (Pt. 1 and 2). This test is an Indian adaptation of the well-known test of William Stephenson. It has been prepared by State Bureau of Educational and Vocational Guidance, Gwalior (M.P.).

Individual Performance Tests

As mentioned earlier, the complete non-verbal or non-language tests of intelligence for testing an individual at a time, falls into this category. Here the contents and responses in the form of performance and language are not used at all. In these tests the items which require responses in terms of motor activities are included. Generally, the activities, on which the performance of an individual is tested, are of the following types:

(*i*) *Block building or cube construction:* Where the subject is asked to make a structure or design by means of blocks or cubes supplied to him. The examples of the tests, involving such type of activities are Merrill Palmer Block Building, Koh's Block Design Test, Alexander's pass-along Test etc.

(*ii*) *To fit the blocks in the holes:* Test material of such type provides numerous blocks and a board in which there are holes corresponding to these blocks. The subject has to fit the blocks in these corresponding holes (in the board). Examples are Seguin Form Board Test and Goddard Form Board Test.

(*iii*) *Tracing a maze:* Test material consists of a series of mazes of increasing difficulty, each printed on a separate sheet. The subject is required to trace with pencil, the path from entrance to exit. Porteus Maze Test is an example involving such types of activities.

(*iv*) *Picture arrangement or picture completion:* In picture arrangement test the task is to arrange in series the given pictures whereas in picture completion test the subject is required to complete the pictures with the help of given pieces cut of each picture. The Healy pictorial completion test is a good example of such test which provides a good estimate of the intelligence of the subject without making use of language.

As seen above, these tests try to emphasize upon one or the other types of performance. Instead of using one or two tests a group of performance tests, organised either into a scale or battery, are used for a comprehensive picture of an individual's mental ability. In India too, the attempts for constructing such batteries have been made. Dr. Chander Mohan Bhatia's work, in this regard, deserves special mention. He has developed a battery of performance tests known as 'Bhatia's Battery of Performance Tests'.

The Group Verbal Intelligence Tests

The tests requiring the use of language and applied to a group of individuals at a time fall under this category. These are available in sufficient numbers. In India too, attempts have been made to construct such tests. Some of the popular tests of this nature are:

1. C.I.E. Verbal Group Test of Intelligence (Hindi) constructed by Prof. Uday Shankar.
2. The Group Test of General Mental Ability (Hindi) constructed by Dr. J.S. Jalota.
3. Group Test of intelligence (Hindi), prepared by Bureau of Psychology, Allahabad.
4. Prayag Mehta's Group Intelligence Test (Hindi) published by Mansayan, Delhi.
5. General Mental Abilities Test prepared by Dr. P. S. Hundal of Punjab University (Punjabi).
6. Group Verbal intelligence test prepared by Dr. P. Gopala Pillai of the Kerala University (Malayalam).
7. Samuhik Budhi Pariksha (Hindi), prepared by Sh. P. L. Shrimali of Vidya Bhavan G.S. Teacher College, Udaipur.
8. Samuhik Budhi Ki Jaanch (Hindi), prepared by Shri S.M. Mohsin, Educational and Vocational Guidance Bureau, Bihar, Patna.

The Group Non-Verbal Intelligence Tests

These tests do not necessitate the use of language and are applicable to the group of individuals at a time. The difference between performance test (used for an individual) and non-verbal tests (used for a group) is of degree as far as their non-verbal nature is concerned. The performance tests require the manipulation of concrete objects or materials, supplied in the test, by the subject. Responses are purely in the form of motor acts and seldom require the use of paper and pencil by the testee (except in a case like Maze test etc.). Where the test material in the non-verbal tests, used for group testing, is provided in booklet and requires the use of pencil by the tests.

Still in these tests material does not contain words or numerical figures. It contains pictures, diagrams and geometrical figures etc. printed in a booklet. The subject is required to do such activities as to fill in some empty spaces, to draw some simple figures, to point out similarities and dissimilarities etc. In this way although the subject uses paper-pencil he does not need to know words or numerical figures. What he has to do is explained clearly by the examiner usually through clear demonstrations so as to make the least possible use of language.

The examples of such types of tests are:

1. *Raven's Progressive Matrices Test:* This test was developed in U.K. It is a very popular non-verbal group test of intelligence. The test has been designed to evaluate the subjects' ability: (a) to see relationship between geometric figures or designs, and (b) to perceive the structure of the design in order to select the appropriate part for completion of each pattern.
2. *C.I.E. Non-verbal Group Test of Intelligence:* Originally prepared by J.W. Jenkins, the test is printed by C.I.E. for adaptation into Hindi medium schools. The test contains such items along with the instructions as given below:

Instructions: *Below there are three figures lying on the left that are similar in nature. On the right side there are five figures in which one matches most to the figures on the left. Underline it.*

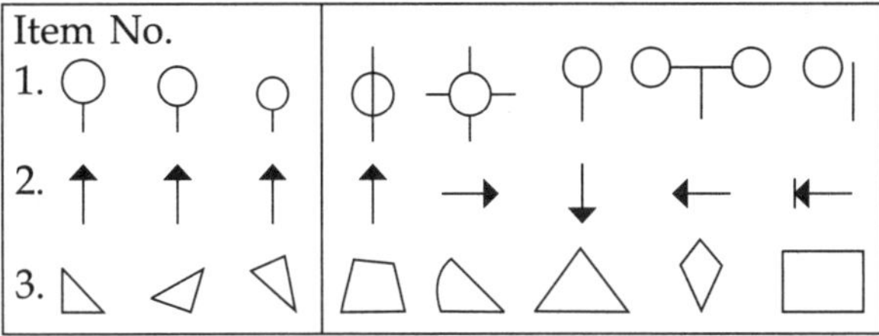

Fig. 2.4: An Item from C.I.E. Non-Verbal Group Test of Intelligence

To Sum Up

For the measurement or assessment of intelligence of the individuals we make use of one or the other types of well developed standardized intelligence tests categorized as individual and group tests involving the use of verbal and non-verbal test material. In individual tests, we test one individual at a time but in group tests a group of individuals can be tested at a given time. In all these individual as well as group tests, we either try to make use of the verbal material, i.e., language, or non-verbal material for testing the intellectual level of our students. Performance tests are a typical example of such non-verbal (language-free) tests where we try to test the intelligence of a student on the basis of his performance in some intellectual tasks.

Concept of Culture-Fare or Culture-Biased Tests

Many of the intelligence tests constructed and used for the measurement of intelligence are loaded with the items that are associated with the cultures and experiences of the individuals who are tested with the help of such tests. Consequently, they show considerable bias and favour to those who belong to those cultures while penalizing others who are ignorant to the language used or contents coloured with the cultures of the region. In this way, where they may be used well for the assessment of intellectual potential of the people belonging to a particular region or culture, they fail to assess the potential of others belonging to other regions or cultures. The verbal intelligence tests provide the good examples of such biased tests. These tests while belonging and serving the interest of testing the people of the particular region, contains the material which has a direct relationship with the language or culture of that region or country.

In contrast, the term culture fare or culture-free tests true to its naming is employed for the development and use of the tests which are loaded with the items or material which can be equally fare in terms of their getting understood and responded on the part of the people who are tested with their use, irrespective of the regions or cultures they belong. Many of the non-verbal and performance tests used for this purpose may be cited as good examples of such culture fare or free tests. They are more or less language and culture free, and hence can be used well for the assessment of the intellectual potentials of the people irrespective of their belongingness to the language and culture of one or the other regions. That is why, when we want to have some type of cross cultural and linguistic study of intelligence, we make use of these culture fare or culture-free tests.

Culture-Fare or Culture-Free Tests: The tests loaded with the items or material proving equally fare to all those being tested irrespective of the regions or cultures they belong.

Concept of Mental Age and Intelligence Quotient

As we have used the term mental age and I.Q. in the interpretation of intelligence test results above, it is worth-while to know something about them.

Mental age: The term mental age was used first by Binet. The idea behind this concept can be clarified through the following example:

Suppose there is a test which has 100 questions (like Jalota's test) and suppose the majority of the subjects whose age is 13 years 6 months, answer successfully 48 questions, then any individual who earns a score of 48, regardless of his chronological age, will be said to have a mental age of 13 years 6 months.

Intelligence Quotient (I.Q.): This term was initiated by the German Psychologist William Stern and put into wide practice by Terman. It appeared to Stern that if a child was 6 years old (chronologically), but could do what an 8 year old normally does he $\frac{M.A.}{C.A.}$ would be 8/6 or 1.33 as bright as the average. And in this way, he made the ratio, measure of the rate of mental development of an individual. The ratio was given the name of Intelligence Quotient (I.Q.). To do away with the decimal point the ratio was again multiplied by 100 and thus the formula to calculate I.Q. was known as

$$\text{I.Q.} = \frac{\text{Mental Age (M.A.)}}{\text{Chronological Age (C.A)}} \times 100$$

(as used in Stanford Binet Scales).

$$\text{or I.Q.} = \frac{\text{Attained or actual score}}{\text{Expected mean score for age}} \times 100$$

(as used by Wechsler).

Mental Age: The term used to indicate the mental level of a child against the level which is normal for the majority of children of his age.

Intelligent Quotient (IQ): The term used for indicating the level of one's intelligence measured through the intelligence tests and computed with the use of the formula I.Q. = Mental age/ Chronological age multiplied by 100.

Classification of Individuals on the Basis of their I.Qs

By making use of the formula of I.Q. given by Stern, Terman tried to classify the individuals into certain specific categories on the basis of the data collected through the administration of his intelligence tests for terming them average, below average and above average as given below:

I.Q.	*Level of Intelligence*
140 and above	Gifted or Genius
120–140	Very Superior
110–120	Superior
90–110	Normal or Average
75–90	Border Line and Dull

50–75	Morons
25–50	Imbecile
Below 25	Idiot

However, as far as, the classification based on the intelligence tests suitable to the Indian conditions, is concerned the, following one presented by professor Udai Shanker may work well.

I.Q.	*Level of Intelligence*
140 and above	Genius
120–140	Very Superior
110–120	Superior
90–110	Average
75–90	Border Line and Dull
50–75	Morons or Feeble minded
25–50	Imbecile
Below 25	Idiots

Limitations and Abuses of Intelligence Tests

Intelligence tests have given birth to so many problems due to their limitations and shortcomings. We can list them as follows:

1. **Intelligence tests and students:** Intelligence tests label some students as superior and the others as inferior. This type of knowledge creates so many problems. Children who are slightly dull are still brilliant enough to realise through the results of intelligence tests that they are slow to learn. It makes them disappointed and causes inferiority feelings and ultimately mars their future. On the other hand, the students with a slight more I.Q. may create over-confidence in them. There is every possibility that these students may not give serious attention to their work. Also, the consciousness of their superiority may result in misbehaviour on their part and can turn them into problematic children.
2. **Intelligence test and teachers:** Teachers, after knowing the I.Q. of the child, make a permanent idea of the child's potentialities and abilities. They try to see him through his I.Q. They leave no attempt to discourage or to create over-confidence in the students according to the level of their intelligence announced by these tests. Moreover, the knowledge of the intelligence of the pupils for a teacher may result in slackness on his part. He may put the entire responsibility of a pupil's failure on his inferior intelligence and for a bright pupil he can think that he would be able to do himself. In this way, the knowledge of intelligence supplied by these tests may bring disastrous results to the teacher.
3. **Given birth to segregation and conflicts:** Intelligence test results have been misused to uphold the theory of royal blood, segregation and sectarian outlook. In the U.S.A. it has led to a conflict between the Black-Americans and the White populations. The conflict, in actual sense, is the result of misconception about the predictive value of these tests and their correlation with hereditary factors. In defence we can put the following points:

   (*a*) No intelligence tests, including most refined performance tests, can be claimed as completely free of practice or coaching effects and independent of cultural, social, racial and other environmental factors. Hence, they cannot be claimed as a measure of initial mental abilities and capacities of the individual. Therefore, it is quite unjust to deny or uphold the right of admissions or job opportunities to the people on the basis of these tests. Now the contemporary researches in this direction have proved that the results of intelligence tests always show favour towards healthy environmental conditions like improved sanitation, family atmosphere, education of parents, cultural background, socio-economic conditions, better educational opportunities, etc.

   (*b*) In fact, intelligence test helps know very little about the total make-up of the child's potentialities. Only cognitive (mental functions) domain can be said to be touched by these tests. They leave untouched many important aspects like interests, attitudes, motives, etc. Hence, they cannot be relied as the predictor of the future success of an individual.

   (*c*) *"The results of all such tests," as Crow and Crow put it, "may be effected by many factors inherent in the testing conditions, the child's background of experience and other favourable or unfavourable elements. Hence, no administrator, teacher or student of education should accept test results as the only measure of an individual's ability to learn." (1973, p. 160).*

In this way it is not proper to give undue weightage to intelligence tests. They should not be accepted as the only measure of an individual's degree of ability to learn. They should not be made an instrument of creating complexes among the students and miss-understanding among teachers. In a nut-shell, the results of these tests must be interpreted and used intelligently. They should be taken as the means, and not the end in themselves.

To Sum Up

The terms are culture-fare or culture-free tests true to their naming are employed for the development and use of the tests which are loaded with the items or material which can be equally fare in terms of their getting understood and responded on the part of the people who are tested with their use irrespective of the regions or cultures they belong.

The concept of mental age and I.Q. is put into use for interpreting the raw scores earned on an intelligence test. The term 'mental age' coined by Binet stands for the mental level of a child against the level which is normal for the majority of children of his age. For the computation of I.Q., we make use of the formula I.Q. = Mental age / Chronological age multiplied by 100.

The data collected after administration of the intelligence tests have helped the psychologists to classify individuals into certain specific categories of average, below average and above average intelligence. It has helped us in the diagnosis and identification of gifted, backward and mentally sub-normal children among a particular group or population.

Intelligence tests have their advantages as well as drawbacks. Regarding their drawbacks we may name their abuse by the students in perpetuating a number of complexes (inferiority or superiority), fears and disappointment etc. They may also colour the viewpoints of the teachers towards their students and give birth to one or the other types of segregations and conflicts in the society.

ASSESSMENT QUESTIONS

Section I: Essay Type Questions

1. Define the term intelligence and throw light on its nature highlighting its main characteristics or established facts along with the misconceptions prevalent in the society about it.
2. Name the important theories of intelligence classified as factor theories of intelligence and discuss any two of them in detail.
3. What is Anarchic or Multifactor theory of intelligence? How does it differ from the unitary and Spearman's two factors theory? Discuss.
4. Discuss and examine Thurston's group-factor theory of intelligence.
5. Discuss the intelligence theory propagated by Guilford in the light of his model of intellect.
6. Name the important theories of intelligence classified as cognitive theories of intelligence and discuss any two of them in detail.
7. What is Cattell and Horn's theory of intelligence? Critically examine how does it help in our understanding about one's intelligence.
8. Critically examine the Sternberg's Information Processing Theory of Intelligence.
9. What is Howard Gardner's Theory of Multiple Intelligence? Name and discuss the seven types of intelligences mentioned in this theory.
10. Discuss the nature and use of a modern theory projected through a model named as Planning Attention-Arousal and Simultaneous-Successive (PASS) Model of Intelligence.
11. Throw light on the nature and use of various types of intelligence tests for the measurement of intelligence named as (i) Individual Verbal Intelligence Tests, (ii) Individual Performance Intelligence Tests, (iii) The Group Verbal Intelligence Tests, and (iv) The Group Non-Verbal Intelligence Tests.
12. Mention some of the verbal/non-verbal tests used in India for measuring intelligence and discuss any one of them in detail.
13. What is intelligence? How will you measure the intelligence of a group of students? Name, the tests that you may use for the purpose.
14. Distinguish between various types of intelligence tests—individual, group, verbal, non-verbal and performance tests—by citing examples of each.
15. What do you understand by the concepts of Culture-Fare and Culture-Biased Tests used for the measurement of intelligence? Discuss.
16. What do you understand by Intelligence Quotient? How is it determined?
17. What is the significance of classifying individuals on the basis of their IQs? Mention about the classification provided by Terman as well as Udai Shankar for this purpose.

18. Explain and discuss about the concept of Mental Age and Intelligence Quotient (IQ).
19. The results of Intelligence tests may be found to have limitations and draw backs in terms of their misuse. Point out and discuss about these abuses.

Section II: Short Answer Type Questions

1. Provide a suitable definition of the term intelligence.
2. Mention any two established facts about intelligence.
3. What are the misconceptions about intelligence? Mention any two of them.
4. What are the factor and cognitive theories of intelligence? In what respects these differ from each other?
5. Name two theories each belonging to the categories of factor and cognitive theories of intelligence.
6. Name the two factors mentioned in the Spearman's two-factor theory of intelligence.
7. Point out all the nine factors belonging to Thurston's Group factor theory of intelligence.
8. Name the three dimensions used by Guilford in the description of his three dimensional model of intellect.
9. Name the two types of intelligence mentioned by Cattell and Horn in his theory of intelligence.
10. Discuss in brief the Analytical intelligence/Experiential intelligence/Practical intelligence mentioned in the Sternberg's Information Processing theory of intelligence.
11. Name the four steps mentioned for the task of information processing in the theory of intelligence represented through the PASS model of intelligence.
12. Name the seven intelligences mentioned by Gardner in his theory of multiple intelligence.
13. Tell in brief about the Group verbal/Group non-verbal/Individual verbal/performance test used for the measurement of intelligence.
14. Name one test each named as individual verbal, group verbal, Group non-verbal and performance test used in India for measuring intelligence of the individuals.
15. Write in brief about the concept of IQ/Culture fare tests/concept of mental age.
16. Name the three misuses of the results of the intelligence tests.
17. Find I.Q.s with the following data
    (*i*) M.A. 10 and C.A. 8
    (*ii*) M.A. 8 and C.A. 10

Section III: Objective Type Questions

1. Tell which one of the following is not true about intelligence?
    (a) The distribution of intelligence in the population follows the properties of the normal distribution
    (b) It is a joint product of heredity and environment
    (c) Differences in sex, race or culture do create differences in intelligence
    (d) Intelligence is no guarantee against delinquency and crime
2. Which one of the following is not a factor mentioned in Thurstone's Group factor theory.
    (a) Verbal factor (V)
    (b) Perceptual factor (P)
    (c) Word Fluency Factor (W)
    (d) Creative Imagination Factor (C)
3. How many types of intelligences have been mentioned by the Gardner in his theory of multiple intelligences?
    (a) 9 (b) 8
    (c) 7 (d) 6
4. Who is credited for propagating "the theory of multiple intelligences"?
    (a) Thurston
    (b) Gardner, Howard
    (c) Gardner, Murphy
    (d) Guilford
5. Compute I.Q. of a child with the following data M.A. 10 and C.A. 8.
    (a) 125 (b) 120
    (c) 80 (d) None of these

Answers

1 (c) 2 (d) 3 (c)
4 (b) 5 (a)

Emotional Intelligence–Concept, Measurement and Development

Learning Objectives

After going through this chapter, you will be able to:

- Define the term emotional intelligence and tell its meaning
- Describe and discuss the significance and importance of knowing about one's emotional intelligence
- Know about the concept of Emotional Quotient (EQ)
- Throw light on the methods and techniques of measuring one's emotional intelligence
- Discuss about the role of teachers/ trainers in promoting emotional intelligence among the students.

Emotional Intelligence—Meaning and Definition

Emotional intelligence, like general intelligence, is the product of one's heredity and its interaction with his environmental forces. Until recently, we have been led to believe that a person's general intelligence measured as I.Q. or intelligence quotient is the greatest predictor of his or her success in any walks of life—academic, social, vocational or professional. Consequently, the I.Q. scores are often used for selection, classification and promotion of individuals in various programmes, courses and job placements etc. However, researches and experiments conducted since the 90s have tried to challenge such over-dominance of the intelligence and its measure intelligent quotient (I.Q.), by replacing it with the concept of emotional intelligence and its measure, emotional quotient (E.Q.). These have revealed that a person's emotional intelligence measured through his E.Q. may be a greater predictor of success than his or her I.Q.

Historically speaking, the term emotional intelligence was introduced in 1990 by two American University professors Dr.John Mayer and Dr. Peter Salovey in their attempt to develop a scientific measure for knowing the differences in people's ability in the areas of emotions. However, the credit for popularizing the concept of emotional intelligence goes to another American psychologist Daniel Goleman (1995).

Let us now consider the views and definitions of the term emotional intelligence given by eminent psychologists and researchers in the field of emotional intelligence.

1. Although the term emotional intelligence has been defined in many best sellers including Dr. Daniel Goleman's 1995 book "Emotional Intelligence" in a number of ways, comprising many personality traits such as empathy, motivation, persistence, warmth and social skills, the most accepted and scientific explanation of the term emotional intelligence may be found in the following definition given by John D. Mayer and Peter Salovey (1995).

Emotional intelligence may be defined as the capacity to reason with emotion in four areas: to perceive emotion, to integrate it in thought, to understand it and to manage it.

According to this definition, every one of us may be found to have varying capacities and abilities in respect to one's dealing with emotions. Depending upon the nature of this ability, he or she may be more emotionally intelligent or lesser, in comparison to others in the group.

Accordingly, a person will be termed emotionally intelligent in proportion if he is able to

(a) identify and perceive various types of emotions in others (through face reading, body language and voice tone etc.);

(b) sense his own feelings and emotions;

(c) incorporate the perceived emotions in his thought (such as using his emotions feelings in analysing, problem solving, decision making etc.);

(d) have proper understanding of the nature, intensity and outcomes of his emotions;

(e) exercise proper control and regulation over the expression and use of emotions in dealing with his self and others so as to promote harmony, prosperity and peace;

2. For further clarification and explanation of the terms emotional intelligence and emotionally intelligent person, we would like to quote the viewpoint of Mr. Yetta Lautenschlager (1997), a NIP teaching fellow of Hamden, Connecticut, U.S.A. He writes:

> To be emotionally intelligent, I submit that you must become proficient in the Four A's of emotional intelligence i.e., Awareness, Acceptance, Attitude and Action. Awareness means knowing what you are feeling when you are feeling it. Acceptance means believing that emotions are a biological process taking place in the body and the brain and that is not always rational. It means being able to feel an emotion without judging it. Attitudes are beliefs that are attached to emotion. These are times when the emotion follows an attitude, or is coloured by an attitude. Unless the attitude is challenged, the emotion will continue to be felt in the same direction. Action is the behaviour you take based on emotion and attitude.

The above viewpoint of Yetta Lautenschlager clearly emphasizes that, for developing as an emotionally intelligent individual, one must develop the ability of (i) emotional awareness (knowing the feelings of the self and the others), (ii) cognitive realization that emotional expression may be irrational or unhealthy and hence one should be cautious in utilising his emotions for action, (iii) have a fresh look or acquire a desired attitude for the proper utilisation of emotional feelings, (iv) resulting ultimately into proper behaviour for the progress of the self, in proper tune with others.

Emotional Intelligence: An intelligence (other than that being measured in terms of IQ) helpful in knowing and managing the emotions of self and others for behaving well in the interest of the self and others.

Based on these, *we may understand one's emotional intelligence as a unitary ability (related to, but independent of standard intelligence) helpful in knowing, feeling and judging emotions in close cooperation with one's thinking process to behave in a proper way, for the ultimate realization of the happiness and welfare of the self in tune with others.*

Significance and Importance of knowing about one's Emotional Intelligence

Knowing about one's emotional intelligence in terms of an emotional quotient has wide educational and social implications for the welfare of the individual and the society. This fact has now been recognized and given practical shape and implications all around the globe. The credit of giving due publicity and acquainting the world-wide population about the importance and significance of emotional intelligence goes to the famous American psychologist Dr. Daniel Goleman through his best-selling books like *Emotional Intelligence – Why it can matter more than I.Q.* and *Working with Emotional Intelligence,* has stressed the following factors while showing the importance of emotional intelligence:

1. Emotional intelligence is as powerful, and at times more powerful than I.Q. While I.Q. contributes only about 20% of success in life, the other forces contribute the rest. We can infer that emotional intelligence, luck and social class are among those other factors.
2. Unlike I.Q., emotional intelligence may be the best predictor of success in life. Emotionally intelligent people are more likely to succeed in everything they undertake in their life.
3. Unlike what is claimed of I.Q., we can teach and improve in children and in any individual, some crucial emotional competencies, paving the way for increasing their emotional intelligence and thus making their life more healthy, enjoyable and successful in the coming days.
4. The concept of emotional intelligence is to be applauded not because it is totally new but because it captures the essence of what our children or all of us need to know for being productive and happy.
5. I.Q. and even Standard Achievement Test (SAT) scores do not predict any person's success in life. Even success in academics can be predicted more by emotional and social measures (e.g. being self-assured and interested, following directions, turning to teachers for help, and expressing needs while getting along with other colleagues) than by academic ability.
6. In working situations too, emotional intelligence helps more than one's intellectual potential in terms of one's I.Q. or even professional skills and competencies. A professionally competent person having poor emotional intelligence may suffer on account of his inability to deal with his self or getting along properly with others.

7. A person's emotional intelligence helps him in all spheres of life through its various constituents or components namely knowledge of his emotions (self-awareness), managing the emotions motivating oneself, recognizing emotions in others (empathy), and handling relationships. The achievement of the end results in terms of better handling of mutual relationships is quite essential and significant in his life. It can only be possible through his potential of emotional intelligence and its proper development.

The viewpoints and ideas propagated by Daniel Goleman have brought a revolution in the field of child care, home, school and work place management. It has also provided sufficient support to guidance and counselling services including physical and mental health programmes. Although there may seem a bit of exaggeration in the tall claim that emotional intelligence is a sure guarantee for unqualified advantage in life, there is no denying the fact that one's emotional make up counts quite substantially towards one's ability to live, progress and adjust to others. In all sense, emotional intelligence essentially reflects our ability to deal successfully with other people and with our own feelings. Since these qualities count significantly towards a person's success in his area of achievement, it may induce him likewise to achieve the required success. Most of the problems in our life, whether childhood problems, adolescent problems, home and family problems, work situation problems or political, regional or international problems are the results of misinterpretation of the involved sentiments, feelings and emotions of the concerned individuals, group of individuals, society and the nations. If proper efforts are made for training the emotions and developing proper emotional intelligence potential among the people right from their childhood, then it will surely help in bringing mutual emotional understanding, empathy, accompanied with right actions and behaviour on the part of the individuals and groups, to lead a better life in peace and cooperation. To progress and let others progress and to live and let others live are thus the ultimate goals of any education or training provided for developing one's potential of emotional intelligence.

Emotional Quotient (E.Q.)

Emotional Quotient represents the relative measure of a person's emotional intelligence similar to intelligence quotient (I.Q.).We know that one's intelligence is an innate as well as acquired intellectual potential. Every child is born with some intellectual potential which grows and develops with the help of maturity and experiences. Similarly, one is also born with some innate emotional intelligence in terms of one's level of emotional sensitivity, emotional memory, emotional processing and emotional learning ability. This potential (unlike intelligence) is liable to be developed or damaged as a result of one's experiences. The difference here is between the development pattern of innate emotional intelligence and general intelligence as a result of maturity and experiences.

Emotional Quotient (EQ): A relative measure of one's emotional intelligence possessed by him at a particular period of his life, measurable and computable in the same way with the help of standardized emotional intelligence tests as done in the case of measuring and computing one's IQ through the intelligence tests.

Where general intelligence is generally not subjected to decline or damage with life experiences (it always picks up the rising trend), the emotional intelligence can be either developed or destroyed depending upon the type of environmental experiences one gets in one's future life. More specifically, if a child starts with a certain level of innate mathematical abilities, he has generally almost no chance of getting his potential lowered through training or experiences since no teacher, parent or television programme teach him that 2 + 2 = 5 or 3. However, here are enough chances that unhealthy environmental influences or lessons taught by the parents, teachers and other models may lead to the declining or damaging of one's innate or previously held level of emotional intelligence. In this way, whatever a person's emotional intelligence at a particular time in life it is that level of his emotional intelligence which is with him at that time as a result of the ongoing emotional lessons or life experiences.

This level or potential of one's emotional intelligence is relatively measured through some tests of situations in life, resulting in one's emotional quotient (E.Q.), a relative measure of one's emotional intelligence or potential. Consequently, *the term emotional quotient (E.Q.) may be defined as a relative measure of one's emotional intelligence possessed by him at a particular period of his life.*

The Measurement of Emotional Intelligence

For the measurement of one's intelligence we make use of one or the other intelligence test (verbal or non- verbal). Similarly for the measurement of one's emotional intelligence we can make use of such measures called emotional intelligence tests or scales. These tests and measures are not available easily or in a sufficient quantity. A few references of such well-known measures of emotional intelligence may be cited:

1. Mayer Emotional Intelligence Scale (MEIS) constructed and standardized by Dr. John Mayer of the University of New Hampshire, U.S.A.
2. Mayer, Salovey and Caruso Emotional Intelligence Test (MSCEIT) constructed and standardized by Dr. John Mayer, Dr. Peter Salovey and Dr. David Caruso of U.S.A.
3. Baron Emotional Quotient Inventory (EQ–i) constructed and standardized by Dr. Reuven Baron and published by Multi-Health Systems, U.S.A. for the first time in 1996. This test covers five areas: intrapersonal, interpersonal, adaptability, stress management and general mood.

In addition to such well standardized measures, we may also come across some emotional intelligence measures which have a limited value or somewhat meant for just a fun or amusement. However, these may provide vital clue to what is expected from an emotionally intelligent person in an arbitrarily assumed emotional situation. The sample items of such tests are reproduced here to give an idea.

Test items of a scale type measure

1. I find myself using my feelings to help make big decisions in my life.

   Always Usually Sometimes Rarely Never

2. People do not have to tell me what they feel ______ I can sense it.

   Always Usually Sometimes Rarely Never

3. I have trouble handling conflicts and emotional upsets in relationships.

   Always Usually Sometimes Rarely Never

Test item of a multiple choice type measure

Item No. 1

Situation: You are hanging out with a group of friends when one of your friends starts to make negative comments about a friend who is not there.

Your response:

- You add a few negative comments about the friend who is not there.
- You say nothing at the moment and later you privately talk about your feelings to your friend who made the comment.
- You tell your friend that you do not feel comfortable talking about people who are not there, and change the subject.
- You keep quiet and beat yourself up for not saying anything to stop it.

Item No. 2

Situation: Your best friend has recently broken up with someone and is taking it hard.

Your response:

- You take him or her out for a wild night on the town to get his or her mind off the breakup.
- You start to worry about your own relationship and if you might get dumped.
- You bash your friend's mate and tell your friend that he or she is better left alone.
- You ask your friend what you can do to help him or her get through this.

To Sum up

A new concept, 'emotional intelligence' with its significance even more than one's general intelligence has emerged in our social and professional life. It may be defined as one's unitary ability (related to independence of standard intelligence) to know, feel and judge emotions in cooperation with a person's thinking process for behaving in a proper way, with the ultimate realization of happiness in himself and in others.

In view of its wide significance from the individual as well as social angles, it becomes quite imperative that serious efforts should be made for its proper development, right from early childhood among human beings. We must be made to acquaint with the degree of its potential named as E.Q. (Emotional Quotient), present in an individual in the same way as we remain interested in knowing about a person's I.Q. (Intelligence Quotient). E.Q. can be computed on the basis of the results of standardized Emotional Intelligence tests to arrive at a judgement of a person's level of emotional intelligence in the same way as we use the intelligence test for knowing his I.Q.

Role of Teachers/trainers in Promoting Emotional Intelligence among Students

The following measures adopted by teachers/ trainers may prove helpful in this direction.

1. Try to help yourself and the trainees develop the ability to understand feelings in the right manners both in one self and others.
2. Do not give away to misgivings and misinterpretations of feelings in others. It leads to a hostility and bias. Remember that love always begets love, while suspicion, hate and aggressions are rewarded with similar emotions.
3. In all situations, self-awareness of the feelings and emotions are important. Try to teach the trainees to know what they are feeling at a particular time.
4. For understanding others and their feelings develop the trait of a good listener. People who have a high E.Q. (emotional quotient) also have a high score on empathy and empathy occurs through effective listening.
5. Try to do away with the wrong notion that thought is most appropriate when not clouded by emotions. Try to get them to learn the integration of thoughts and emotions, heart and mind for appropriate behaviour at the right time. Therefore, they should not try to suppress emotions (as every feeling has its value and significance); instead strike a balance between rational thought and emotions.
6. Teach the trainees that all emotions are healthy (because emotions unite the heart, mind and the body). Anger, fear, sadness, the recalled negative emotions are as healthy as peace, courage and joy. Try to convince the trainees that the important thing is to learn the art of expressing one's feelings or emotions in a desirable way at the desirable time in a desirable amount. In this connection, the remark of the Great Greek Philosopher Aristotle can be referred to as a guideline:

   Anyone can become angry – that is easy. But to be angry with the right person, to the right degree, at the right time, for the right purpose, and in the right way – that is not easy.

7. Try to practice and teach the trainees the art of managing the feelings and emotions as adequately as possible. This is especially important for the distressing emotions of fear, pain and anger.
8. They should not allow the emotions and feelings become obstacles in their path. Make them use their emotions as a motivating agent or a force for achieving their goals.
9. Teach trainees the lessons of empathy, i.e., developing a sense of what someone else is feeling.
10. Make them learn the methods of proper development of social skills for better communication and inter-personal relationship with others. They should try to express their feelings with an equal sense of attending and listening to other's feelings for the better management of relationships.
11. Try to devote more time and take efforts to develop not only the cognitive professional skills among the trainees but also the affective skills for the development of emotional intelligence.
12. Last, but not the least, is to present your behaviour and personality as a model or a companion for maintaining proper emotional bonds. If you have developed yourself as an emotionally intelligent individual, you may inspire or lead others to become so. However, it is not essential to be perfect or complete or guide others as parents, teachers, trainers or bosses. You just need to see what others need, and be there to meet their needs.

To Sum up

In the development of an adequate level of emotional intelligence among students, teachers can play quite a significant role. For this purpose, they should first try to equip themselves with a proper degree of emotional intelligence in order to work as a model for helping their students to imitate and work for getting imbibed with the needed emotional intelligence in understanding and managing their emotions in a proper way for behaving and getting adjusted to their self and others.

ASSESSMENT QUESTIONS

Section I: Essay Type Questions

1. What is emotional intelligence? How does it differ from the general intelligence measured in terms of one's IQ? Explain.
2. Define the term intelligence and throw light on its meaning and nature.
3. What is emotional intelligence? Why is it regarded more important and useful for a person than general intelligence for his welfare and progress? Discuss.
4. What is emotional quotient (EQ)? How is it determined?
5. Define the term emotional intelligence and throw light on the ways and means used for measuring one's emotional intelligence.
6. Discuss about the role of teachers/ trainers in promoting emotional intelligence among the students.

Section II: Short Answer Type Questions

1. Provide a suitable definition of the term emotional intelligence.
2. What is EQ?
3. What is measured through one's emotional intelligence?
4. Say two things in support of the importance and significance of emotional intelligence.
5. Name any two tests used for measuring one's emotional intelligence.
6. Mention any two measures for the promotion of emotional intelligence among the children.

Section III: Objective Type Questions

1. Who is credited for introducing the concept of emotional intelligence?
   (a) Daniel Goleman
   (b) Daniel Goleman and John Mayer
   (c) Daniel Goleman and Peter Salovey
   (d) John Mayer and Peter Salovey
2. Which one of the following statement is not true?
   (a) One's intelligence is an innate as well as acquired intellectual potential
   (b) Emotional intelligence is not innate it is an absolutely acquired phenomenon
   (c) Emotional Quotient represents the relative measure of a person's emotional intelligence
   (d) EQ can be determined through the use of emotional intelligence tests
3. Who is the author of the book "Emotional Intelligence: Why it can matter more than IQ"?
   (a) Bar-On, R
   (b) Daniel Goleman
   (c) John Mayor
   (d) Stein & Book

Answers

1 (d) 2 (b) 3 (b)

4

Creativity-Concept and Measurement

Learning Objectives

After going through this chapter, you will be able to:

- Define the term creativity
- Throw light on the meaning and nature of creativity
- Differentiate creativity from the term intelligence
- Discuss about the identification of creativity among individuals
- Tell about the use of creativity tests for the measurement of one's creativity
- Point out the use of various non-testing devices used for the measurement of one's creativity
- Name and discuss a number of testing and non-testing devices used for the measurement of creativity.

Introduction

The Almighty God, the creator of the universe, is the supreme mind who possesses the finest creative abilities. He has created all of us and all that is revealed in nature. We are elevated to be called His creation. According to our Indian philosophy, we all are constituents of the supreme power as the rays of the sun are the constituents of their creator—sun. Therefore, every one of us ought to possess creative abilities. But every one of us is a unique creation, and thus the degree of possession of creative ability is not uniform. Some of us are found to possess high creative talents and these are the people who move the world ahead by their discoveries and inventions in the fields of art, literature, science, business, teaching and other fields of human accomplishments. They are responsible for coming up with new ideas and bringing about social and cultural changes.

Gandhi, Lincoln, Bhabha, Newton, Shakespeare, Bertrand Russel, Leonardo da Vinci were such creative individuals who left their mark in their respective fields. Certainly, they were endowed with creative abilities but the role of environment in terms of education, training and opportunities cannot be ignored. Good education, proper care and provision of opportunities for creative expressions inspire, stimulate and sharpen the creative mind and herein the parents, society and teachers come into the picture. They are required to help the children in nourishing and utilizing their creative abilities to the maximum degree. Therefore, educational process—formal or informal—should be aimed at developing creative abilities among children. It needs to acquaint the teachers and parents with the actual meaning of creativity, the knowledge of the creative process, and ways and means of developing creativity. In the following pages, we shall try to know something about these aspects.

Concept of Creativity

The real nature and concept of creativity may be properly explained by emphasizing on its following aspects.

- Its meaning (including attempts of its defining)
- Its nature and characteristics.
- Its distinction from general intelligence

Meaning and Definition of Creativity

The term 'creativity' or 'creative process' has been defined by some eminent scholars in the following different ways:

Stagner and Karwoski: Creativity implies the production of a 'totally or partially' novel identity. (1973, p. 314)

Drevdahl: Creativity is the capacity of a person to produce compositions, products or ideas which are essentially new or novel and previously unknown to the producer. (1956, p. 22)

> **Creativity:** One's ability or capacity to create, discover or produce a new idea or object including the re-arrangement or reshaping of what is already known to him.

Wilson, Guilford and Christensen (1953): The creative process is any process by which something new is produced—an idea or an object including a new form or arrangement of old elements. The new creation must contribute to the solution of some problem.

Skinner: Creative thinking means that the predictions and/or inferences for the individual are new, original, ingenious, or unusual. The creative thinker is one who explores new areas and makes new observations, new predictions, and new inferences. (1968, p. 529)

If we try to analyze the above definitions we would find that the creation or discovery of something new is the central element in all these definitions. Therefore, we can easily conclude that *creativity is the capacity or ability of an individual to create, discover or produce a new idea or object including the re-arrangement or reshaping of what is already known to him.*

Nature and Characteristics of Creativity

On the basis of the above-mentioned definitions as well as the findings of various other scholars, the nature and characteristics of creativity or creative expression can be summarized as follows:

- Creativity is universal. Every one of us possesses creative capacity to some degree.
- Although creative abilities are natural endowments, they are capable of being nourished and nurtured by training or education.
- Through creative expression, something new or novel is produced. But novelty or newness does not necessarily imply to produce a totally new idea or an object which has never been experienced or produced earlier. To make the fresh and noble combination for the given separate elements or to reshape or rearrange the already known facts or principles or to bring a slight reform and modification in the previously known techniques, are as much the acts of creative expression as the discovery of a new element in chemistry or a new formula in mathematics. The only precaution for naming an expression as creative is that it should not be a mere repetition or reproduction of what has already been experienced or learned by an individual.
- Any creative expression is the source of joy and satisfaction for the creator. The creator says what he sees or feels in his own way. There is perfect individuality in one's creative expression. He expresses himself, to a great extent, through his creation. It is his own way of looking at things; persons or events and therefore, it is not essential that a creative work may arouse the same feeling or give same satisfaction as experienced by the creator himself.
- The creator is the person who is able to make ego-involved statements like, "It is my creation', 'I have solved this problem.' 'It is my ideas,' etc. In creative expressions there is complete ego involvement.
- Creative thinking cannot be a closed thinking. It must have complete freedom for the multiplicity of responses, choices and lines of action. By traveling on the routine, beaten track, one cannot be able to create but can only reproduce or repeat.
- The field of creative expression is very wide. It covers all the aspects of human accomplishments like scientific inventions and discoveries, composition of poems, writing of stories and drama and good performance in the fields of dance, music, painting, sculpture, political and social leadership, business, teaching and other professions. Our day-to-day life activities also need creativity. Therefore, in a nutshell, life as a whole, presents enormous opportunities for creative expression.
- The question as to what different cognitive factors constitute creativity has been a subject of excessive experiment, action and research. J.P. Guilford, Torrance, Drevadahl and others have tried to identify the important components of creativity. As a result, ideational fluency, originality, flexibility, divergent thinking, persistence, self-confidence, sensitiveness, ability to see relationships and make associations are some of the factors that are found favourable for creative output.

Difference between Creativity and Intelligence

Intelligence and creativity should not be considered as one and the same process. Differences between the two can be summarized as follows:

(i) It has been established that convergent thinking is the basis of intelligence whereas divergent thinking forms the basis of creativity. In convergent thinking, an individual has the tendency to find out the one most appropriate idea or response whereas divergent thinking allows as many responses as possible. Therefore, while in intelligence tests (usually requiring one correct response) convergent thinking is being tested, creativity emphasizes more on testing divergent thinking.

(ii) It has been observed that highly creative persons usually possess intelligence to a high degree but it is not essential for an intelligent person to be creative. One may possess high intelligence without having creative abilities. On the other hand, an adequate level of intelligence is a necessary condition for being creative. A mentally retarded person cannot be expected to be creative.

(iii) In intelligence testing, the speed and accuracy of the cognitive behaviour is emphasized while in creative tests novelty, flexibility and originality are given more weightage.

To Sum Up

Creativity of an individual reflects one of his unique cognitive abilities or the capacity of his mind to create, discover or produce a new idea or object including the re-arrangement or reshaping of what is already known to him. It is both innate as well as acquired and a process as well as a product. It is also known for many of its specific features like open-mindedness, ego involvement etc on the part-of the creative person, the breadth of the field of creative expression and inner joy and satisfaction reached as a result of such expression. As a result of these characteristics it has been found that creativity and intelligence cannot travel side by side.

Identification or Measurement of Creativity

The term 'creativity' cannot be used synonymously with giftedness. Therefore, we should not make a mistake of considering every gifted child as a creative child. Creativity in its all shapes and forms is the highest expression of giftedness that may or may not be found in a particular gifted child. The problem then lies in the identification of the creative children.

Creative behaviour and expression, like other behaviour patterns, possesses its basic components in the form of cognitive, conative and affective behaviour. Consequently, we can label a child creative to the extent to which he is able to demonstrate creative aspect in his thinking, feeling and doing behaviour. For such labeling, we may employ two different approaches:

(i) making use of tests of creativity, and (ii) making use of non-testing devices like observation, interview, rating scale, personality inventory, check-list etc.

Let us discuss these approaches one by one.

Using Creativity Tests

Just as we make use of intelligence tests to label a child as intelligent, so we have the use of creativity tests for labeling a child as creative. There are so many tests available in India and abroad for this purpose. We are mentioning a few of these tests below.

- **Tests Standardized Abroad**
  1. Minnesota tests of creative thinking
  2. Guilford's Divergent Thinking Instrument
  3. Remote Associate Test
  4. Wallach and Kogan Creativity Instrument
  5. A.C. Tests of Creative Ability
  6. Torrance Tests of Creative Thinking
- **Tests Standardized in India**
  1. Baquer Mehdi's Tests of Creative Thinking—Hindi and English.
  2. Passi's Tests of Creativity.
  3. Sharma's Divergent Production Abilities Test.
  4. Saxena's Tests of Creativity.

As pointed out earlier, creativity is a complex blend of a number of abilities and traits. Therefore, in all the creative tests, attempts are always made for the assessment of these abilities and traits with the help of verbal and non-verbal test items. The factors or dimensions commonly measured through these tests are fluency, flexibility, originality, divergent thinking and elaboration.

For having illustration of the nature of the material used in creative testing and the procedure of administrating such tests readers are advised to look into the description provided on this account in the last chapter of this text named as "Psychology Practical Work".

Use of Non-testing Devices

We can also have the assessment of the creative aspect of a child with the use of some non-testing devices like Natural observation method, Situational techniques, Rating scale, Check list, Interview, Personality inventories, Interest inventories, Attitude scales, Aptitude test, Value schedules, and Projective techniques, and so on. These devices help in the revelation of those personality traits and behavioural characteristics that are supposed to be present in a creative child. Some of these traits or characteristics, as identified by the research workers in the field of creativity, are mentioned below.

Personality and Behavioural Characteristics of a Creative Person

1. Demonstrates originality in ideas and actions.
2. Is more adaptable as well as adventurous.
3. Possesses good memory and broad knowledge background.
4. Possesses a high degree of keenness, attentiveness, alertness and power of concentration.
5. Is very curious about nature.
6. Possesses little tolerance for boredom but greater for ambiguity and discomfort.
7. Possesses foresightedness in abundance.

The Abilities or Characteristics possessed by the Creative Persons

- Ideational fluency
- Originality
- Flexibility
- Divergent thinking
- Persistence
- Self-confidence
- Sensitivity
- Ability to see relationships and make associations

8. Has the capacity to take independent decisions.
9. Shows interest in vague and ambiguous ideas.
10. Enjoys a reputation of having strange and silly ideas.
11. Shows preferences to complexity, incompleteness, asymmetry and open-mindedness.
12. Possesses a high degree of sensitivity towards problems.
13. Can express his ideas as fluently as possible.
14. Shows flexibility in his thinking, feeling and doing behaviour.
15. Demonstrates the ability to transfer learning or training from one situation to another.
16. Demonstrates very rich imagination characterized as 'creative imagination'.
17. Is divergent and diversified in his thinking that is convergent and stereotyped.
18. Possesses ability to elaborate, i.e., to work out the details of a plan, idea or outline.
19. Is not frightened by the unknown, the mysterious and the puzzling and on the contrary is often attracted towards it.
20. Welcomes novelty of designs or new solution to a problem, gets enthused and suggests other ideas.
21. Demonstrates the ability to experience self as creative and the originator of one's act and takes pride in one's own creation.
22. Has more of him available for use and employment in creative purposes rather than wasting his time and energy protecting him against his self.
23. Possesses high aesthetic values and good aesthetic judgement.
24. Possesses a high degree of the feeling of self-respect and is self-disciplined, sensitive and intolerant towards injustice. On account of these qualities, is often misunderstood and evaluated disobedient, rebellious and mischief monger.
25. Demonstrates human playfulness, lack of rigidity and relaxation in his behaviour and products.
26. Is always alive to his obligations.
27. Possesses the ability to accept tentativeness and ability to tolerate and integrate the opposites.
28. Has a richer fantasy life and greater involvement in daydreaming.
29. Shows different brain patterns than the less creative, especially during creative activity.
30. Pays respect to others' opinions and welcomes disagreement to his suggestions.
31. Is always found to be more spontaneous and expressive.

To Sum Up

For the identification of creativity, we may employ two different approaches (i) making use of creativity tests like Torrance tests of creative thinking, Passi's test of creativity etc., and (ii) making use of non-testing devices like observation, interview, rating scale, personality inventory, check list etc. The items of most of the creative tests (verbal as well as non-verbal) are highly loaded with the type of activities which are helpful in the assessment of the qualities like originality, fluency, flexibility, divergent thinking, and elaboration etc. In making use of non-testing devices for the identification of creative children the help is generally taken from some well known distinguished characteristics found in the creative behaviour of children.

ASSESSMENT QUESTIONS

Section I: Essay Type Questions

1. What is creativity? Throw light on its meaning and nature.
2. What do you understand by the term creativity? Discuss briefly the characteristics of creative expression or creative thinking.
3. Differentiate clearly between the terms creativity and intelligence.
4. "High intelligence is no guarantee for creativity." In the light of the above statement discuss the relationship between intelligence and creativity.
5. What is creativity? How is the task of identifying creativity among children carried out? Discuss in detail.
6. If you are given responsibility of identifying creativity of one or the other group of children what types of different measures can be adopted by you for the fulfilment of your responsibility?
7. Discuss the use and applications of creativity tests and other non-testing devices for the measurement of one's creativity.
8. How can you test creative potential with the help of a creative test? Illustrate with the help of any creativity test.

Section II: Short Answer Type Questions

1. Give a suitable definition of the term creativity.
2. Write four personality/behavioural characteristics of a creative individual.
3. Name the three creativity tests each developed in India and abroad for the identification of creativity among children.
4. Name three non-testing devices used for measuring creativity.
5. Provide two items mentioned in Torrance test of creativity/ Baquer Mehdi's test of creativity used by you as a part of the psychological practical work in your school for testing the creativity of your own classmates.

Section III: Objective Type Questions

1. What is not true about creativity?
   (a) Creativity is universal. Every one of us possesses creative capacity to some degree
   (b) Creative abilities are natural endowments and there is no scope of nourishing and nurturing them by training or education
   (c) Any creative expression is the source of joy and satisfaction for the creator
   (d) Through creative expression, something new or novel is produced
2. What is not true about a creative person?
   (a) His thinking is convergent rather than being divergent
   (b) He enjoys a reputation of having strange and silly ideas
   (c) He possesses ability to elaborate
   (d) He has a richer fantasy life and greater involvement in daydreaming
3. Which one of the following is not the constituent of one's creativity?
   (a) Originality (b) Non-Flexibility
   (c) Elaboration (d) Sensitivity

Answers

1 (b) 2 (a) 3 (b)

5

Aptitudes–Concept and Measurement

Learning Objectives

After going through this chapter, you will be able to:

- Define the term aptitude
- Tell about the meaning and nature of aptitudes
- Explain how aptitude differs from ability and achievement
- Elucidate difference between aptitude and interests
- Throw light on the classification of aptitudes
- Mention about the means and ways of measuring aptitudes
- Point out and discuss about the utility of aptitude tests

Meaning and Definition of Aptitudes

It is an observable fact that people differ from one another and within themselves in their performance in one or the other field of human activity such as leadership, music, art, mechanical work, teaching etc. Ramesh goes to a commercial institute in order to learn graphic designing. He progresses rapidly with his learning and gets a diploma in due course. Later, when he is offered a job he carries it out satisfactorily. Suresh, although not in any way inferior to the former in general intelligence takes admission to this institute but progresses very slowly and even after getting diploma proves an inefficient designer. Similarly, Radha gains from musical training while Sunita despite similar training makes little or no progress.

So, in many spheres of everyday life, we come across individuals who under similar circumstances outperform others in acquiring certain knowledge or skills and prove more suitable and efficient in certain jobs. Such persons are said to possess certain specific abilities other than intelligence, which help them in achieving success in some specific occupations or activities. Therefore in a simple way, aptitude may be considered a special ability or a specific capacity besides the general intellectual ability which helps an individual to acquire a required degree of proficiency or achievement in a specific field. However, for having a clear understanding of the term 'aptitude', let us consider the following definitions given by different scholars:

Bingham (1937:21): Aptitude refers to those qualities characterizing person's ways of behaviour which serve to indicate how well he can learn to meet and solve certain specific kinds of problems.

Traxler (1957: 49): Aptitude is a condition, a quality or a set of qualities in an individual which is indicative of the probable extent to which he will be able to acquire under suitable training, some knowledge, skill or composite of knowledge, understanding and skill, such as ability to contribute to art or music, mechanical ability, mathematical ability or to read and speak a foreign language.

Freeman (1971:431): An aptitude is a combination of characteristics indicative of an individual's capacity to acquire (with training) some specific knowledge, skill, or set of organized responses, such as the ability to speak a language, to become a musician, to do mechanical work.

Aptitude: A characteristic involving specific capacities or abilities of an individual helping us to predict his future success in a particular area under appropriate conditions.

All these definitions reveal the predictive nature of aptitudes. When we say that Ram or Radha has an aptitude for teaching, we mean that he or she has the capacity or ability to acquire proficiency in teaching under appropriate conditions.

Similarly, when we say Mohan has an aptitude for music we mean that his present condition or ability reveals that if he is to learn music, he will succeed in this line. In this way the knowledge of aptitude helps us in predicting the future success of an individual, under suitable training or experience, in a particular area of activity.

Nature of Aptitudes

Are aptitudes inherited or acquired? Like so many other personality traits or characteristics, it is difficult to say that aptitude is an absolute product of heredity or environment. Certain aspects of many aptitudes may be inborn. For example, a person showing musical aptitude may have a musical throat and a person showing aptitude for typing or watch repairing may have long and dexterous hands. But this is one side of the picture. It is also equally possible that the person's aptitude for music is the result of his living in the company of good musicians or his aptitude for research may be due to his father or mother who happens to be a scientist.

Therefore, it is safer to conclude that the aptitude of an individual at a particular moment is in all probability dependent upon both heredity and environment.

How Aptitude Differs from Ability and Achievement?

Aptitude and present ability do not mean the same thing. You may have no present ability to drive a car but you may have a high aptitude for driving which means that your chances of becoming a successful driver are good provided you receive proper training. So, while aptitude has future reference and tries to predict the degree of attainment or success of an individual in an area or activity after adequate training; ability concerns itself only with the present condition, the potentiality or capability which one possesses at the present moment irrespective of his past and does not try to make any estimate of one's future success or failure.

> **Ability:** The potential of an individual to do a thing at present and thus is present oriented in its nature.
> **Achievement:** A measure of what has been acquired by an individual in the past and thus is past-oriented in its nature.
> **Aptitude** is future oriented in the sense that it helps to predict the future success of the individual in a particular field on the basis of his present ability.

Contrary to the forward-looking nature of aptitude and present-oriented characteristic of ability, achievement is past-oriented. It looks at the past and indicates what an individual has learned or acquired in a particular field.

But by this differentiation it should not be concluded that we can measure an individual's future accomplishment in any area of activity with the help of aptitude measurements. Aptitude tests, in all their forms, measure only the present ability or capacity of an individual which can be exploited for making prediction about his future attainments.

Difference Between Intelligence and Aptitudes

Intelligence tests as they exist usually test the general mental ability of an individual but aptitudes, as we have discussed, are concerned with specific abilities. Therefore, while with the knowledge of intelligence of an individual we can predict his success in a number of situations involving mental function or activity, the knowledge of aptitudes, acquaints us with those specific abilities and capacities of an individual which give an indication of his ability or capacity to succeed in a special field or activity. Therefore, in predicting achievement in some particular job, training, course or specialized instruction we need to know more about one's aptitudes (specific abilities) rather than of his intelligence or general ability.

Difference Between Aptitudes and Interest

To get desirable success in a given activity, a person must have both an aptitude for activity and an interest in it. Therefore, interest and aptitude usually go hand in hand. But by this co-ordination, we should never mean that interests and aptitudes are one and the same thing. A person may be interested in a particular activity, job or training but may or may not have aptitude for that. In such cases, the interest shown in a particular occupation or course of study is often the result of some other temptation or persuasion like ambition of the parents, probability of getting a job, provision of stipend or financial help, the prestige associated with the work rather than the personal aptitude. Similarly, a person may have long and dexterous fingers and can show a good performance on a mechanical aptitude test. Yet he may show little or no interest in becoming a watch maker. Therefore, a guidance or selection programme must give due weightage to the measurement of aptitude as well as of interest. Both are essential for the prediction of the success of an individual in a given activity—job or course of instruction.

To Sum Up

An aptitude related to a particular area or activity refers to certain combination of specific capacities or abilities of an individual which may help us in predicting his future success in that area or activity under appropriate conditions. For example, if Mohan has a teaching aptitude, it will mean that he has the potential or capacity to acquire proficiency in teaching under appropriate conditions.

Regarding the nature and characteristics of aptitude we can say that one's aptitude at a particular moment is always a function of his heredity as well as that of his environment. We can't equate one's aptitude with one's ability and achievement. The ability concerns itself only with the present condition (what one possesses at present in terms of potential for doing a thing). The achievement looks at the past and indicates what an individual has learned or acquired in a particular field. Aptitude, contrary to the present-oriented nature of the ability and past-oriented nature of the achievement is future-oriented (carrying strength for predicting one's success in a field).

Intelligence tests measure the intellectual or cognitive potential of an individual but are hardly appropriate in predicting success of an individual in some particular job, training or specialized instruction: the tasks that can be properly performed through aptitude tests.

Although both interest and aptitude are essential for getting desirable success in a field, yet these are not one and the same things. Both can function independently, which means that presence of one is not at all essential for the perpetuation of the other.

Classification of Aptitudes

Any manifestation of life is activity. We can manifest ourselves in too many ways and forms. Therefore, there is no end for our manifestation and as a result, the list of the activities which may be undertaken by the human beings is limitless. One may have aptitude for one activity and the other may demonstrate an aptitude in something else. Since the activities undertaken by humans are limitless, the number of aptitudes in the same proportion must also be limit less. In this sense, it is quite impossible to have a fixed classification of human aptitudes. However, for the sake of their measurement and application in the field of education, professions and other related fields of life, we may attempt to classify them as under:

Sensory Aptitudes

In this category, we can include all those aptitudes that are related to the sensory capacities and abilities of children. One may have aptitude in the tasks involving the use of his sense of hearing, while others may have aptitude in the tasks requiring the use of the sight, smell, taste or touch. Here depending upon their present ability regarding a particular sensory capacity, we can have an idea of their future success in the area of professions where the use of such sensory ability or capacity is most demanded. Thus, in this category of sensory aptitudes, we can include the aptitudes related to the sensory abilities of the children.

Mechanical Aptitudes

Some persons have a specific bent of mind for the tasks related to the use of mechanical abilities and thus demonstrate aptitudes for all tasks and jobs that require the use of mechanical abilities. When we test their present abilities we can easily infer that a particular individual will be successful as a carpenter (provided he is given due opportunities, training etc.). In other case, we find that one can be a good mechanic looking after the repair of vehicles, engines and machines etc. Someone may have aptitude for the use and innovations in instrumentisation and other sophisticated appliances etc. In this way, human beings can have different mechanical aptitudes varying in their nature and sophistication. All such aptitudes are grouped in the category of mechanical aptitude. The range of such mechanical aptitude may extend from the manipulation and use of needles to the know how of repairing and flying an aeroplane.

Artistic Aptitudes

All the aptitudes related to the expression of artistic abilities and capacities are included in this category. These activities are mostly related to the effective domain of human behaviour. The aesthetic sense is exhibited in such activities. All that is beautiful and the things that are to be appreciated belong to the demonstration of such aptitude. Generally the following types of aptitudes are kept in this category of artistic aptitude.

1. Musical aptitude
2. Aptitude for dance
3. Aptitude for graphic art
4. Aptitude for photography
5. Poetic aptitude

6. Aptitude for acting
7. Debating aptitude
8. Writing aptitude
9. Aptitude for designing, etc.

Professional Aptitudes

The aptitudes related to the activities of various professions and occupations are included in the category. These aptitudes are able to help in predicting the future success of an individual in the field or profession related to these aptitudes. For example, if one has the aptitude for teaching, we can say that he or she will be a successful teacher provided he or she gets appropriate opportunities and training for doing so. The examples of the aptitudes included in this category are as under:

1. Clerical Aptitude
2. Legal Aptitude
3. Teaching Aptitude
4. Pilot Aptitude
5. Navigation Aptitude
6. Banking Aptitude
7. Military Aptitude

Scholastic Aptitudes

The aptitudes of the scholastic and academic nature are included in this category. These aptitudes demonstrate and predict the future success of an individual in the learning of a particular subject or course in the capacity of a student. The examples of such aptitudes are as under:

1. Scientific Aptitude
2. Engineering Aptitude
3. Medical Aptitude
4. Commercial Aptitude
5. Sports Aptitude
6. Linguistic Aptitude

Classifying Aptitudes into Broader Types

- Sensory Aptitudes
- Mechanical Aptitudes
- Artistic Aptitudes
- Professional Aptitudes
- Scholastic Aptitudes

Measurement of Aptitudes

Like intelligence tests, various aptitude tests have been devised to measure aptitudes of the individuals in various specific fields or activities. Generally, these tests can be classified into the following types according to the specific nature of the aptitude tested by them:

1. Mechanical Aptitude tests.
2. Musical Aptitude tests.
3. Art judgement test.
4. Professional Aptitudes tests, i.e., tests to measure the aptitudes for professions like teaching, clerical, medical, legal, engineering, salesmanship, research work, etc.
5. Scholastic aptitude tests, i.e., tests to measure the aptitudes for different courses of instruction.

How the available aptitude tests are administered for the measurement of one or the other types of aptitudes of the procedure on this account can be learned through the illustration provided for this purpose in the last chapter of this text. However, for acquainting you with the nature of the material provided and the type of activities required from the subjects in the aptitude tests we are hereby providing a few examples.

Illustrative items for the testing of the Mechanical Aptitude

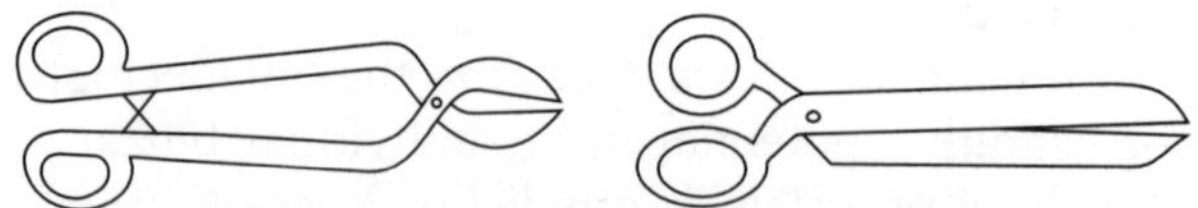

Fig. 5.1: Which would be the better shears for cutting metal?

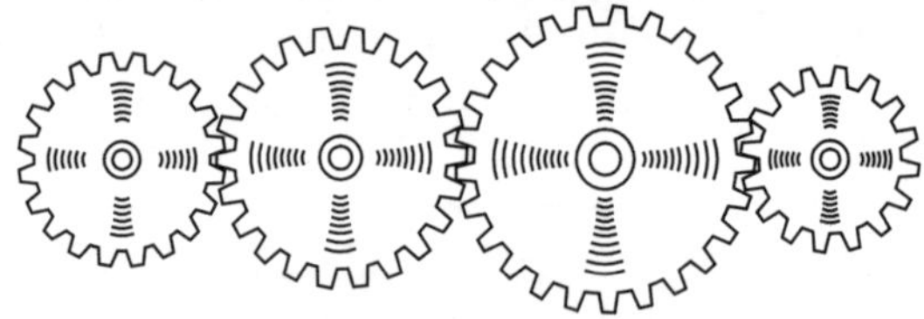

Fig. 5.2: Which gear will make the most turns in a minute?

Specimen item for the measurement of clerical aptitude

Samples of correctly matched pairs of numbers.

79542	79542
5794367	5794367

Samples of correctly matched pairs of names.

John C. Linder	John C. Linder
Investor's Syndicate	Investor's Syndicate

Now try the samples below and mark accordingly

(i)	66273894	....	66273284
	527384578	....	527384578

(ii) New York World . . . New York World.
Cargil Grain Co. . . . Cargal Grain Co.

This is a test for speed and accuracy. Work as fast as you can without making mistakes. Do not turn the page until you are told to begin.

(Reproduced from General Psychology by H.E. Garrett, 1968, p. 477)

Specimen Item for the measurement of Aptitude for graphic art

Select the original and aesthetically superior work on the basis of the shapes of the pots.

Utility of Aptitude Tests

Aptitude tests have a wide area of application. Firstly, they are the backbone of the guidance services. The results of these tests enable us to locate, with a reasonable degree of certainty, the fields of activity in which an individual is most or least likely to be successful. Therefore, these tests are found to be very useful in guiding the youngsters in the selection of special courses of instruction, fields of activities and vocations.

Secondly, they can be safely used for the purpose of educational and vocational selection. They help us in making scientific selection of the candidates for the various educational and professional courses as well as for the specialized jobs as Munn puts it, *"The chief value of aptitude testing is, in fact, that it enables us to pick out from those who do not yet have the ability to perform certain skills, those who, with a reasonable amount of training, will be most likely to acquire the skills in question and acquire them to desirable level of proficiency."*(1967, p. 117).

Therefore, aptitude tests properly anticipate the future potentialities or capacities of an individual (irrespective of the fact whether he possesses those future capacities before the training or not) and thereby, help us in making selection of those individuals who are best fitted for a particular profession and course of instruction or those who are likely to be more benefited by pre-professional training or experiences.

In this way any reasonable guidance and counselling programme or the entrance examination to specialized, academic and professional courses or the selection procedure for specialized jobs is required to give a proper weightage to Aptitude testing. Aptitude testing, when combined with the other information received through Interest Inventory, Personality tests, Intelligence tests and cumulative record etc. can greatly help in avoiding the huge wastage of human as well as material resources by placing the individuals to their proper places and lines of work.

To Sum Up

Aptitudes may be broadly classified as sensory, mechanical, artistic, professional and scholastic aptitudes. All these types of aptitudes can be measured with the help of the suitably designed as well as standardised aptitude tests like we measure intelligence through intelligence tests.

Aptitude tests have a wide area of applications for candidates in choosing special courses of instructions, training, fields of activities and vocations according to their ability and potentialities. These are helpful in providing useful guidance and counselling to students/candidates for planning their educational and vocational career as well as equipping the authorities with the instruments of making proper selection and placing the students/candidates at proper places.

ASSESSMENT QUESTIONS

Section I: Essay Type Questions

1. What is aptitude? How does it differ from intelligence, ability and achievement?
2. What do you mean by aptitudes? How can these be classified?
3. Define the term aptitudes. How are they measured? Briefly describe some aptitude tests for measuring specific aptitudes.
4. Describe a test that measures aptitudes for music or graphic art.
5. What are aptitude tests? How are they administered and recorded? Discuss by administering a particular aptitude test.
6. What are aptitude tests? Throw light on their utilities.

Section II: Short Answer Type Questions

1. Give a suitable definition of the term aptitude.
2. Differentiate between aptitudes and interests. Differentiate between aptitude and achievement.
3. Name four kinds or types of aptitudes.
4. What is mechanical aptitude?
5. What is the musical aptitude/graphical attitude/clerical or mechanical attitude?
6. Mention any two utilities of aptitude tests.
7. Name any two tests used for measuring aptitudes in India.

Section III: Objective Type Questions

1. Which one of the following is not true?
   (a) One's achievement is past-oriented
   (b) One's ability to do a thing is the concern of the present
   (c) Aptitude is future-oriented
   (d) Interest and aptitude is one and the same thing

2. Tell which one of the following is true?
   (a) One's aptitude is the absolute function of one's heredity endowment
   (b) It is the training and education that only helps an individual in the acquisition of aptitudes
   (c) One's aptitude is the joint function of his heredity and environment
   (d) Intelligence tests help well in the measurement of aptitudes

Answers

1 (d) 2 (c)

6

Psychology of the Self

Learning Objectives

After going through this chapter, you will be able to:

- Define the term self and throw light on its meaning and concept
- Discuss about the kinds or types of self
- Distinguish between (i) Subjective and Objective self (ii) Personal and Social self
- Provide the meaning of the term self-concept and throw light on its development among the individuals
- Throw light on the relationship of one's self concept and socio-cultural environment
- Provide the meaning of the term self-esteem and throw light on its development among the individuals
- Mention about the characteristics of persons having high self-esteem
- Define the term self-efficacy and throw light on its nature and characteristics
- Discuss the ways and means for the development of efficacy among the children
- Know about the meaning of the terms self-regulation and self-regulated behaviour
- Discuss about the ways and means of developing self-regulation and self-regulated behaviour among children

Introduction

For having proper interaction and relationships with others in your society and community, you need not only to know and understand others in relation to the available social environment, but should also know and understand your own self in a proper way. The knowledge and understanding of the self in this regard is found to involve a number of the associated attributes and aspects such as self-awareness, self-concept, self-esteem, self-efficacy, and self-regulation etc. Let us try to know about them one by one in some essential details. But, first let us concentrate over knowing the meaning of the term "self" itself.

What is Self? Its Meaning and Concept

Self in its common sense understanding as well dictionary meaning is known as the distinct identity and individuality of a person. In their attempts to throw light on its meaning and concept, various thinkers and authors have tried to define it in various ways. Let us take some of these definitions into our consideration.

Ausubel (1952:13): Self is defined as the combination of one's physical appearance, personal memories and sensory images.

Yinger (1971:158): The term self may be defined as the mental images of who I am or what I want to be.

Taylor, Peplau and Sears (2006:131): Self is the collection of beliefs we hold about ourselves. The contents of these beliefs are called self-concept.

Crisp and Turner (2014:135): The self is a fundamental part of every human, a symbolic construct which reflects an awareness of our own identity.

Self: A symbolic construct in the form of mental images and collection of our beliefs about ourselves to get us aware of our own identity.

Analysis of the above-cited definitions may help us in drawing conclusion about the meaning and nature of the term self in the way as below.

Self is not a reality - anything possessed by us in its concrete form but a symbolic construct. It stands in the form of mental images and collection of our beliefs about ourselves that helps us in getting the answers of some of the basic questions such as who am I and for what I stand, and also enabling us to recall and remember our past, assessing our present and projecting our future.

Kinds or Types of Self

The concept of self can also be understood by dividing it in some distinct types such as (i) Subjective and Objective Self, (ii) Personal and Social Self.

Subjective and Objective Self

In the act of describing the self as a subjective or objective self, attempts are made to treat self as subject or object exemplified as below.

When one says that "I am a teacher and teach in a secondary school". In this case we may see that one is describing the self as a *subject* (who is doing something or behaving in some way).

On the other hand when one says that "I am often misunderstood by others for my helping nature", he may be seen to describe the self as an *object* (gets affected or made a subject of action on the part of others).

Personal and Social Self

The concepts of personal and social self differ from each other with respect to their orientation and field of operation that is distinctively personal in the former and social in the latter.

Consequently, when one is primarily concerned with the satisfaction of his personal needs-biological or socio-psychological, he is said to be living and behaving in its closed personal self. For such a person, self (the satisfaction and care of his own) is always supreme with a least concern or care for the needs, interests and welfare of others. Here one may be found to be caring and attempting for getting more and more wealth and achieving one or the other things of his interests or struggling for getting more personal freedom, comfort, reputation, status and recognition, etc.

Subjective self: Describing the self as a subject-doing something or behaving in some way.
Objective self: Describing the self as an object-making a subject of action on the part of others.
Personal self: Confining of one's self to the caring of its own needs with the least care for the others.
Social self: Going of one's self along with the self of others in the form of seeking unity, cooperation, or even making sacrifices for others.

In the beginning years of life, the infants and little children may be found to be attributed with the type of self-described as personal self. Their primary concern is to aspire and live with the satisfaction and caring for their needs and interests. However, later as they grow and develop, the process of socialisation makes them imbibe the type of self known as social self. Accordingly, now they begin to think about living, behaving and aspiring something in relation to others in their social set up. Their self now gets its bigger shape-merging their self with the self of others or at least allowing it to go along with the self of others in the form of seeking unity, affiliation, cooperation, or even making sacrifices for others.

Self-concept and its Development

Meaning of the term Self-Concept

Humans are not only found to form and possess specific concepts about the objects, persons or events related to their environment but also are characterized with the possession of specific concept about the "self". The concepts formed and possessed by the individuals about their "self" are termed as self-concepts. A self-concept formed by an individual may thus represent a mental image, notion, or generalized idea formed by him through his own experiences, learning or training about his self. The self-concept possessed by us in fact, thus, is the mirror of our "self". It reflects or mirrors all what we think in totality about our "self".

In the words of famous psychologist H.J. Eysenck (1947), the totality of attitudes and qualities may thus be referred to one's self-concept. The concept of the self is, thus, found to reflect one's own ideas and picture drawn about his total self-revealing us many of the things such as (i) what we think about our self, (ii) what we are in fact in our eyes, (iii) what are our strengths and weaknesses, (iv) what are our abilities and incapacities, (v) how we are expected to behave in a particular situation, (vi) how we can stand against odds, (vii) and how can we win co-operation, love and confidence of others etc.

Thinking on this line, Baumeister (1995) tried to define the term self-concept as "the total organised body of information that any given person has about him or herself."

Self-concept of an individual, thus, in its all ways of understanding and defining is nothing but a generalized idea or image formed by him about his self. It helps him to assign the required worth and value for his 'self' in his own eyes (the reflection of his own about himself) irrespective of what is judged and said about others.

As a conclusion, thus, the *self-concept of the individuals may be defined as a generalized idea, notion or mental picture drawn by them about their self through their prior experience or learning enabling them to distinguish themselves from other individuals, or objects and to have a proper estimate about their strengths and capacities.*

> **Self-concept:** A generalised idea or image formed by the individuals about their self helping them in assigning the required worth and value for their 'self' in their own eyes.

Development of Self-concept among individuals

The self-concept or any other concept possessed by an individual is not a matter of one's heredity. It is acquired like other traits, characteristics of one's personality or behaviour through experience and learning. What the individuals get after their birth in the form of direct and indirect experiences from their interaction with the physical, social and cultural environment and how they are reared and receive their education, all cast a powerful impact over the formation of their concept about their self.

The process of self-concept formation starts in the baby infants with their attempts to get their voice and face distinguished and recognized as different from their mother and other persons around them. After standing against the mirror now they are able to rub off any substance poured, powder spread over their face, nose etc. and respond well to the questions identifying their body parts. They can recognize them in their family photo and turn their head after being called by their name. It is the stage of the development of their awareness about their 'self'

The next phase of the development of their self-concept is concerned with the development of ideas or notions of the benefits they may derive through the type and nature of their weeping, smiling, and behaving in one way or the other. They may also have an idea about what is there in them that is liked by others and in what way. The task of formation or development of the concept about self is thus concerned with the task of the formation of an image or drawing of a picture by the individuals themselves, their totality of behaviour, personality characteristics, strengths and weaknesses, power and limitations etc. in a composite way. In doing so, they may be seen to form two types of self-images, one termed as physical self-image and the other named as psychological self-image.

Physical self-images are concerned with images formed by the children in their individual capacity about their body structure, colour, shape, weight and height, strength and stamina, physical and motor abilities, intelligence and cognitive functioning etc. The formation of such images helps them in taking evaluative judgments about their physical appearance, strengths, and stamina, physical and mental capacities, and making anticipation about the reaction of others in reference to the possession of these physical attributes by them.

The psychological self-images are concerned with the psychological-self i.e., thinking and feelings. The realm of these is covered thorough the concepts related to the thoughts, emotion, attitudes, interests, aspirations and feelings of the children in their individual capacity and how they see them in relation to the possession of such concepts. Where the task of developing physical self-image is related with the satisfaction of physiological needs and experiences associated with them; the development of psychological self-images is concerned with the experiences associated with the satisfaction of socio-psychological needs. Since, the satisfaction of physiological needs comes well before the satisfaction of psychological needs the individuals may be seen to acquire physical self-image quite earlier than the acquisition of psychological self-image on their part. However, as individual beings cross the period of adolescence both physical and psychological images get immersed into each other resulting in a unifying and integrated picture of one's self-concept. It has also be seen that where in childhood concrete self-concepts get developed in a substantial form rather than the abstract ones, the adolescence witnesses the development of abstract concepts in an increasing way.

There is one more striking feature regarding the development of self-concept among individuals in the early years of their childhood. The opinions and judgments of their parents, members of the family, peers and teachers play a more dominant role than their own opinions in helping them to form concepts about their self. A child identifies and knows himself in the way and manner as identified and told by others. He is naughty, he is coward, he does not fear anybody, he is too adamant, he does not listen to anybody, that girl is black, unholy or unfortunate. Such types of comments addressed to the children persuades them to pick up the same feelings and conceptions about them. They try to pass value judgment about them and mirror them accordingly as judged and declared by others.

However, as they advance towards maturity, the scope and field of their experiences of learning, cognition, and understanding also increases in a substantial manner. Now they become capable of engaging in the task of developing self-concept in an independent way. They no longer mirror themselves in the way as viewed and judged by others. The past experiences as well as their present interaction with the persons and environment guide the process of formation of their self-concept. However, with the gains of maturity on their part do not guarantee the formation of proper and desirable concept about their self. They may not be able to form the correct concept about their self, meaning there by that they may evaluate themselves in a quite low way or estimate themselves too highly in terms of their actual abilities and capacities. Development of such faulty and improper concepts leads them towards mal-adjustment, failure and frustrations. Here it becomes essential to take steps for helping the individuals to protect them from the ill impacts of the developed faulty concepts by helping them to know the reality about themselves.

Socio-cultural Environment and Self-concept

The type of society, social exposure and cultural interaction available to the children in their developmental age is very much responsible for shaping the formation of their self-concept in a particular way. We may witness the differences in the development of self-concept children brought up in one or the other types of socio-cultural environments. For example, the socio-cultural environment available to the children studying in the famed expensive residential public schools may thus be seen to work for the development of a particular type of self-concept among children characterized with egoistic attitude, dominating and ruling nature, superiority complex, an high achievement motivation opposed the confining in the self, inferiority feelings and low achievement motivation coloured self-concept developed in the children of government and economy schools. Similarly, the socio-cultural influences available to the children in the community and the society in which they live and grow possess a strong potential for colouring the development of self-concept among children. Rural and urban community, orthodox and progressive community, civilized and uncivilized community, criminal and non-criminal community, illiterate and educated community, thus, may be found to nurture a quite diverse type of self-concepts among their developing children. The image of a community as the habitat or abode of the pocket pickers, smugglers or criminals may impress upon its developing children to get imbibed with the self-concept of such undesirable behaviour or bad character. They may begin to think or accept their self in such a bad role.

To Sum Up

The task of self-concept development among the individuals is carried out right from their babyhood in a sequence of certain specific stages. The initial stage, in this sequence, is the stage of the development of their awareness about their 'self'. It is characterized with their attempts to get their voice and face distinguished and recognized as different from other persons around them, responding well to the questions identifying their body parts, recognizing them in their family photo.

The next phase of the development of their self-concept is concerned with the task of the formation of an image or drawing of a picture by them about their self. In doing so, they may be seen to form two types of self-images, one termed as physical self-image (concerning with the possession of one or the other physical attributes) and the other named as psychological self-image (concerning with their one or the other psychological attributes).

However, as individuals cross the period of adolescence and attain maturity, both physical and psychological images get immersed into each other resulting in a unifying and integrated picture of one's self-concept. At this final stage, development of both types of concepts-concrete as well as abstract may be witnessed among the developing individuals. Moreover, now they become capable of engaging in the task of developing self-concept in an independent way rather than mirroring their self in the way as viewed and judged by others.

Self-esteem and its Development

What is self-esteem?

Self-concept and self-esteem both of these terms are connected with our self. In their meaning and development both of them differ in a quite considerable way. In a most generalized sense where one's self-concept helps the people in knowing what they are, the developed self-esteem signifies their liking and paying due regard to their self. Differentiating between these two terms, Feldman, Robert (2016:414) writes:

Knowing who you are and liking who you are two different things. Although children, particularly reaching adolescence become increasingly accurate in understanding who they are (their self-concept), this knowledge does not guarantee that they like themselves (their self-esteem) any better. In fact, their increasing accuracy in understanding themselves permits them to see themselves fully-warts and all. It's what they do with these perceptions that, leads them to develop a sense of their self-esteem.

In this way, while the term self-concept as we have known and discussed in this chapter, stands for what we think about the self; self-esteem denotes the liking shown and value, worth, regard or respect we give to our "self" in the light of its positive or negative evaluation. In literature, therefore, the term self-esteem is often used as synonyms or near synonyms of the terms self-worth, self-regard, self-respect, and self-integrity.

Whatever meaning we attach to the term self-esteem, in its roots, basically, it stands for the value judgment passed by the individuals themselves about their worth and capability in terms of facing problems and difficulties, feeling happy and adjusted and getting successes in their personal, academic, social and professional life. What is their attitude towards their self, how they value and respect their self, what they think about their abilities and capabilities, how much they feel satisfied or dissatisfied with their functioning, how much respect, love and affection, regard and respect they receive from others? All such things singly or in combination work towards defining the people's self-esteem.

Much has been explored about the term self-esteem by the scholars. The humanistic psychologists like Karl Rogers and Abraham Maslow have termed self-esteem as a higher order basic needs for the attainment of which every one of us struggles and gets a feeling of inner satisfaction and happiness only after knowing and valuing one's self. Ones' self esteem, besides helping one to pay respect or regard to one's self is also properly linked with one's sense of confidence in one's worth and capability. Reflecting on such nature and form of the term self-esteem, Branden, Nathaniel (1969) has provided an understanding of the term self-esteem in the following words:

Self-esteem is the sum of self-confidence (a feeling of personal capacity) and self-respect (a feeling of personal worth). It exists as a consequence of the implicit judgment that every person has of their ability to face life's challenges, to understand and solve problems, and their right to achieve happiness, and be given respect.

Thus, as conveyed in the above assertion, self-esteem may be found to represent an ability, disposition or trait of our personality that helps us first in making an overall evaluative judgment about our self (incorporating both positive and negative aspects) and then assists us in maintaining a healthy positive attitude towards "self" for valuing and respecting ourselves.

Self-esteem: A unique ability possessed by the individuals enabling them to respect and appreciate their self by accepting and owning it as a whole with its both positive as well as negative aspects.

Looking in this way, *self-esteem may be thought as a unique ability possessed by the individuals enabling them to respect and appreciate their self by accepting and owning it as a whole with its both positive as well as negative aspects.*

The Characteristics of Persons having High Self-esteem

1. An individual equipped with an appropriate amount of self-esteem may be found to feel good about his self and its capabilities despite a number of weaknesses, limitations and negative attributes of his personality and behavioural functioning. In fact, the person having self-esteem may be said to have a blind love for his self. A true lover loves, admires and accepts his beloved with all her positive and negative aspects. The person having self-esteem also in the similar way admires and pays regard to his self by accepting it in its existing form-a mixture of positive and negative attributes. He has an overall good "Impression" and attitude marked with the feeling of "All is well" towards his self. It results in making him feel better and developing a sense of utter satisfaction, love and respect for the self.
2. The people with high self-esteem have no complaint and never blame or curse their self for their inadequacies and failures. Instead of cursing their self and blaming others for their failures and hardships they begin to think of doing away with their limitations and shortcomings by working on them in a desirable way.
3. With a healthy self-esteem, they feel that they have positive characteristics and skills they can offer to other people, and they also feel they are worthy of being loved, admired, and accepted by others. Persons with healthy self-esteem are more likely to be happy, to make and keep positive relationships and friends circle, and to persevere in working through difficult situations that occur in relationships.

4. Self-esteem serves a motivational function by making it more or less likely that people will take care of themselves and explore their full potential. People with high self-esteem are therefore found to demonstrate a natural inclination and favourable motivation for taking care of themselves and to persistently strive towards the fulfillment of personal goals and aspirations.
5. Persons with high esteem are more likely to see challenging situations as opportunities to try something new, even if they're not completely successful. They prove themselves as capable problem solvers. When challenges arise, they can work toward finding solutions and voice discontent without belittling themselves or others. For example, rather than saying, "I'm an idiot," a child with healthy self-esteem says, "I don't understand this."

Characteristics of the Persons having high self-esteem

- Have a sense of utter satisfaction, love and respect for the self
- Never blame or curse their self for their inadequacies and failures
- Remain happy and to make and keep positive relationships and friend's circle
- Highly motivated in exploring their full potential for achieving their personal goals and aspirations
- Proving themselves as problem solvers in the challenging situations;
- Having hopes and optimisms even in the time of difficulties
- Remaining away from the acts downing them in the eyes of their self and others.

6. They remain away from the feelings and thinking of frustration and depression by giving them positive suggestions and engaging in appropriate self-talk and thus remain always surrounded with hopes and optimisms even in the time of difficulties and troubles.
7. Since they value and pay regards to the self, they always try to remain away from the acts and activities that can bring them down in the eyes of others and particularly their own "self".

Development of Self-esteem among the Individuals

Nobody is born with the concept of the self and traits of self-esteem. Both are invariably the product of environmental exposure and organised experiences called learning. The type of experiences (good or bad, positive or negative, pleasant or unpleasant) one gathers from his environment, work for the formation of positive or negative attitudes towards the self. It is the formation of such positive and negative attitude that may result in creating a sense of liking and respect or disliking and disrespect towards the self. However, the best period of habit formation and imbibing of the proper traits is the developmental period. Here also it is quite beneficial to start quite earlier so that the child may pick up the right things at the right time. For this purpose, the growing children may be helped through presenting (i) role model of the self-esteemed behaviour and biographies, and (ii) behaving and treating them in an appropriate way suitable for inculcating among them the trait of self-esteem and characteristics of the persons having high self-esteem.

Self-efficacy

What is self-efficacy?

Why some individuals are eager to learn and willing to tackle new challenges when others seem uninterested or unmotivated in the similar situations? Why do some individuals demonstrate high levels of confidence in their abilities in the learning of one or the other material, while others seem unsure of themselves? Psychologists may reply such questions by saying that the interested and willing ones are endowed with a unique ability known as self-efficacy while the uninterested and unwilling ones may fall short of such necessary ability. But what is then this unique ability known as self-efficacy?

Self-efficacy in its simple meaning stands for a state or quality of efficacy demonstrated on the part of an individual. In dictionaries (Merriam-Webster, Oxford etc.), the term efficacy is defined as (i) the power or capacity to produce a desired result or effect, or (ii) effectiveness.

Consequently, we can understand by the term self-efficacy of an individual, his effectiveness or the confidence demonstrated by him in his capacity to produce a desired result or effect (i.e., doing and performing a task, achieving a target).

The famous psychologist Albert Bandura has also tried to endorse the similar meaning by defining the term self-efficacy in the manner given below:

(i) Self-efficacy refers to an individual's belief in his or her capacity to execute behaviours necessary to produce specific performance attainments (Bandura, 1986)

(ii) Perceived self-efficacy is defined as people's beliefs about their capabilities to produce designated levels of performance that exercise influence over events that affect their lives (Bandura, 1994)

> **Self-efficacy:** The effectiveness or the confidence demonstrated by us in our capacity to perform a particular activity or attain a desired thing or objective.

The term self-efficacy in this way stands for the confidence shown by an individual in his ability or capacity to perform a particular activity or attain a desired thing or objective. It shows or refers to "one's beliefs about one's ability to perform behaviours that should lead to expected outcomes" (Weiten et al. 2012: 198). In short, one's self-efficacy conveys us his/her effectiveness in respect of facing a particular situation as judged by the individual him or herself.

Nature and Characteristics of Self-efficacy

The characteristics like below may help us more in understanding and grasping the meaning and concept of the term self-efficacy in a better way.

1. Self-efficacy is a person's judgment about being able to perform a particular activity. It is an individual's "I can" or "I cannot" belief.
2. Self-efficacy beliefs determine how people feel, think, motivate themselves and behave.
3. Unlike self-esteem, which reflects how one feels about his worth or value, self-efficacy reflects how confident one is about performing one or the other tasks.
4. High self-efficacy in one area may not coincide with high self-efficacy in another area. Just as high confidence in playing cricket may not be matched with high confidence in playing tennis; high self-efficacy in mathematics may not necessarily accompany high self-efficiency in English.
5. Self-efficacy is specific to the task being attempted. However, having high self-efficacy does not necessarily mean that one believes she will be successful. While self-efficacy indicates how strongly one believes she has the skills to do well, she may believe other factors may keep her off from succeeding.
6. A growing body of research however reveals that there is a positive, significant relationship between one's self-efficacy belief and his/her performance in the related task (i.e., student's performance in an academic task)
7. It has been also found that while individuals with low self-efficacy toward a task are more likely to avoid it, those with high self-efficacy are not only more likely to attempt the task, but they also will work harder and persist longer in the face of difficulties.
8. Self-efficacy is also found to exert considerable influence in the matters like below
   (i) What activities people select
   (ii) How much effort they put forth
   (iii) How persistent they are in the face of difficulties, and
   (iv) The difficulty of the goals, they set.

Ways and Means for the Development of Self-efficacy

The self-efficacy possessed by the individuals is an acquired phenomenon. It is learned as a consequence of one's experiences and interactions occurring in one's socio cultural environment. For helping them in this direction, it can be useful for adopting the measures like: providing orientation about the concept and significance of self-efficacy; producing models of exemplary behaviour; providing opportunities for demonstrating self-efficacy; and reinforcing their self-efficacy behaviour.

To Sum Up

The term self-efficacy stands for the confidence shown by the individuals in their ability or capacity to perform a particular activity or attain a desired thing or objective. It conveys to us the effectiveness of an individual in respect of facing a particular situation as judged by the individual himself. Unlike self-esteem, which reflects how people feel about their worth or value, self-efficacy reflects how confident one is about performing one or the other tasks. The sense of self-efficacy possessed by the individuals may be found to help them in setting and pursuing appropriate goals by maintaining proper level of their motivation and aspiration; equipping with a sense of necessary self-confidence, and making useful attempts for pursuing their goals with the necessary capability and persistence. Regarding its development among the individuals we may see that it is an acquired phenomenon. It is learned as a consequence of one's experiences and interactions occurring in one's socio cultural environment.

Self-regulation and its Development

What is self-regulation?

In its word meaning the term self-regulation stands for regulating or controlling our 'self' by the ourselves in terms of our functioning and performing one or the other types of behavioural acts and thus giving birth to a special type of behaviour named as self-regulated behaviour helpful in our adjustment, development and progress in a proper way. In this way, what is called as the self-regulated behaviour of the individuals is said to be described as a type of behaviour that is regulated or controlled by the individual themselves. For knowing more about the meaning and concept of self-regulated behaviour let us take the help of a few available definitions of the term "self-regulating behaviour" and "self-regulated children".

Self-regulation: The process of regulating and exercising restraint or control over one's behaviour for functioning and performing well in one or the other situations.

1. **Ormrod (2009):** Self-regulated behaviour describes a process of taking control of and evaluating one's own behaviour for the good and welfare of the self and others.
2. **Paris and Paris (2001):** Self-regulated behaviour emphasizes autonomy and control by the individual who monitors, directs, and regulates actions toward goals of information acquisition, expanding expertise, and self-improvement.
3. **Winne & Perry (2000):** Self-regulated children/individuals are successful because they control their learning and functioning environment. They exert this control by directing and regulating their own actions toward their learning, performance and developmental goals.

In the light of the above cited definitions of the term self-regulated behaviour and self-regulated people we can conclude about the meaning and nature of the term self-regulation and self-regulated behaviour in the following way.

- Self-regulation stands for the characteristics of one's ability or capacity to regulate and exercise restraint or control over his behaviour (conative, cognitive and affective) through one's own initiative and attempts.
- Self-regulation or self-regulated behaviour is not thrust up on the individuals from outside. It is a wilful act undertaken by the individual themselves for serving their own interests and goals.
- Self-regulation and self-regulated behaviour as a whole is initiated, undertaken and executed to its desired end with the full intention, motivation, attention and involvement of the individual.
- In a self-regulated behaviour, the behaviour gets fully regulated and controlled by the individuals themselves from the beginning till end in terms of the objectives set, strategies planned, and methods used for their functioning in one or the other situation.
- In a self-regulated behaviour, people are found (i) to take responsibility of their behaviour for attaining their immediate and far reaching life goals (ii) to direct and regulate their behavioural acts well by making use of their thought processes (ii) to enjoy full autonomy and control over the processes and products of their functioning (iv) to show the necessary potential of self-efficacy (confidence in their ability to perform an act and attain the desired objectives, (v) to take work or interactions opportunities as a challenge for meeting their developmental goals and (vi) to exercise necessary restraint and control over their working and interactive environment in attaining their desired immediate and life goals.

Development of Self-regulation and self-regulated Behaviour

The ability or capacity to exercise control over one's functioning and behaving is not at all an inherited phenomenon but gets developed and acquired by the children much like the acquisition of other characteristics of one's behaviour and personality traits. It also needs a reasonable level of mental maturity on the part of children for the self-regulation of their behaviour. In the task of getting equipped with such behaviour, the children may also be helped by the parents, teachers and elders with the measures like:

- Playing the role of guide and facilitator in place of dictating and controlling everything about them

- Providing orientation about the self-regulated behaviour
- Working as model and producing exemplary behaviour opportunities before them
- Providing exposure in the form of formal or informal learning or training experiences for catching hold of the idea and practice of regulation and regulated behaviour
- Giving needed freedom to the children for regulating their behaviour and its outcomes
- Reinforcing the self-regulated behaviour of the children by providing them encouraging feedback

To Sum Up

By the term self-regulation or self-regulated behaviour we mean the behaviour of individuals in which they are found to function well by exercising needed restraint or control over one's behaviour and work with the required zeal and enthusiasm for performing well in proper tune of the demand of the situation. Regarding its presence and development among the individuals it may be seen that it is not at all an inherited phenomenon but needs to be developed and acquired from early childhood much like the acquisition of other characteristics of one's behaviour and personality traits with the active cooperation and guidance of the parents, teachers and elders.

ASSESSMENT QUESTIONS

Section I: Essay Type Questions

1. What is "self"? Discuss in detail about its meaning and concept.
2. While defining the term self throw light on its types and kinds classified as (i) subjective and objective self (ii) personal and social self.
3. Define the term self-concept and throw light on its meaning and development among the individuals.
4. What is self concept? Discuss its relationship with one's socio-cultural environment
5. What do you understand by the term self-esteem? Throw light on its development among the individuals.
6. What is self-esteem? Point out the characteristics of persons having high self-esteem.
7. What is self-efficacy? Throw light on its meaning and characteristic features.
8. Define the term self-efficacy and discuss the ways and means for its development.
9. What do you understand by the terms self-regulation and self-regulated behaviour? Discuss about the ways and means of developing self-regulated behaviour among children.

Section II: Short Answer Type Questions

1. Provide a definition of the term 'self'
2. Give an example of the term subjective self.
3. What is objective self?
4. Differentiate between personal and social self
5. Provide a definition of the term self-concept/ self esteem/ self efficacy.
6. Tell two things about the relationship of self concept with one's socio-cultural environment.
7. Mention about two measures for the development of self-concept/ self-esteem/ self-efficacy among children.
8. Point out three characteristics of the persons having high self-esteem.
9. What is self-regulation or self-regulated behaviour?
10. Point out two measures for the development of self-regulated behaviour among the children on the part of the parents and elders.

Section III: Objective Type Questions

1. "I am a teacher and teach in a secondary school" It is an example describing one's
   (a) Personal self (b) Social self
   (c) Subjective self (d) Objective self

2. "A child recognizes him in his family photo and turns his head after being called by the name", it is the stage of the development of his:
   (a) Self-concept
   (b) Self-esteem
   (c) Self-efficacy
   (d) Self-regulated behaviour
3. What is not true about the characteristics of the persons having high self-esteem?
   (a) They have a sense of utter satisfaction, love and respect for the self
   (b) They blame or curse their self for their inadequacies and failures
   (c) They have hopes and optimisms even in the time of difficulties
   (d) They remain away from the acts downing them in the eyes of their self and others
4. What is not true about the measures taken for developing self-regulated behaviour among the children?
   (a) Enforcing rules and regulations for regulating behaviour in a strict way
   (b) Providing orientation about the self-regulated behaviour
   (c) Giving needed freedom to the children for regulating their behaviour and its outcomes
   (d) Reinforcing the self-regulated behaviour of the children by providing them encouraging feedback

Answers

1 (c) 2 (a) 3 (b)
4 (a)

7

Personality-Meaning, Types, Theories and Assessment

Learning Objectives

After going through this chapter, you will be able to:

- Define the term personality and explain its meaning
- Throw light on the characteristics and distinguishing features of personality
- Know about the different approaches adopted for describing one's personality in the name of the theories of personality
- Discuss about the personality types provided by Hippocrates/Kretschmer/ Sheldon/ Jung/ Friedman and Rosenman.
- Discuss Allport's trait theory of personality/ Cattell's trait theory of personality
- Elucidate Eysenck's theory of personality based on Type cum Trait Approach
- Know about the theories adopting Psychodynamic Approach such as (i) Freud's Psychodynamic Theory, (ii)Adler's Individual Approach to Personality, and (iii) Jung's Analytical Approach to Personality
- Discuss about the theories adopting Humanistic Approach such as (i) Self-Actualization Theory of Abraham Maslow, and (ii) Karl Roger's Self Theory
- Throw light on the theories adopting Learning Approach such as (i) Dollard & Miller's Learning Theory of Personality, and (ii) Bandura and Walter's Social Learning Theory of Personality
- Know about the use of techniques like Observation, Situational Tests, Questionnaire, Personality Inventory, Rating Scale and Interview for the assessment of one's personality
- Throw light on the use of Projective techniques like Rorschach Ink Blot Test, TAT, CAT, Word Association Test, and Sentence completion Test for the assessment of personality

Meaning and Definition of Personality

The term "personality" stems from the Latin word *persona*, which was the name given to the masks actors wore and the characters they portrayed. The meaning of the word personality in practice has changed little since classical time, for it is still quite common to hear the comments such as "I do not know what he sees in her; she has a very poor personality", or "look at that young man, what a fine personality he has". Remarks like this make us believe that personality is a thing or quality that is possessed by all of us and we can paste such labels as fine, good or poor on it on the basis of the physical make-up, manner of their walking, talking, dressing and a host of other similar characteristics possessed by individuals. However, what is believed in this way is quite wrong as the psychological concept of personality goes far beyond and deeper than mere appearance or outward behaviour. How it should be given a proper meaning or definition has remained a serious problem from time immemorial before psychologists. It has been defined by them in so many ways according to their own points of view. Some of these well-known attempts at defining personality are presented below:

1. **Watson:** "Personality is the sum of activities that can be discovered by actual observations over a long enough period of time to give reliable information." (1930)

   In this manner, Watson gives emphasis upon the behaviour of an individual and say that personality is nothing but the useful effect one makes upon the person coming into his close contact.

2. **Morton Prince,** accepting the role of both heredity and environment, defines it as—

   "Personality is the sum-total of all the biological innate dispositions, impulses, tendencies, appetites and instincts of the individual and the dispositions and tendencies acquired by experience." (1929, P. 532)

3. **Allport:** After evaluating 49 definitions of personality written by so many eminent persons, Allport summarizes his own concept in the following words:

"Personality is a dynamic organisation within the individual of those psycho-physical systems that determine his unique adjustment to his environment." (1948, p.28)

Although Allport has tried to give a comprehensive definition of the term personality including the words organisation, dynamic, psycho-physical system, unique adjustment, environment, etc. yet he, like other previous ones, only describes it. By emphasizing merely on theoretical aspect and describing it in terms of behavioural or dynamic concepts the true nature of personality cannot be understood. The contemporary psychologists like R.B. Cattell and Eysenck are of such opinion. They feel very strongly that personality should be called philosophy or art, and not personality theory in psychology if it cannot be demonstrated, measured and quantified.

Below we give their ideas in connection with the meaning of the term personality.

4. **R.B. Cattell:** "Personality is that which permits a prediction of what a person will do in a given situation." (1950, p. 2)

5. **Eysenck:** "Personality is the more or less stable and enduring organisation of a person's character, temperament, intellect, and physique, which determine his unique adjustment to the environment." (1971, p.2)

He has tried to make certain terms clear in the following way:

Character denotes a person's more or less stable or enduring system or organisation of conative behaviour ("Will").

Temperament denotes a person's more less stable or enduring organisation of affective behaviour ("Emotions").

Intellect denotes a person's more or less stable or enduring organisation of cognitive behaviour ("intelligence").

> **Personality** of an individual is all that possessed by him in terms of his physique, intellect, and behavioural traits determining his unique adjustment to the self and the environment.

Physique denotes a person's more or less stable or enduring organisation of bodily configuration and neuro-endocrine endowment (glands + nervous system + bodily configuration).

Evaluation of the Definition

(*i*) This definition gives a balanced consideration to heredity and environment in building one's personality.

(*ii*) Eysenck stresses the concept of structure and organisation and criticises just naming of some of the behavioural characteristics like bricks in describing a home.

(*iii*) This definition gives personality a physiological base.

(*iv*) It gives a complete picture of the human behaviour patterns by including cognitive, conative, affective and somatic (constitutional) aspects.

(*v*) This definition aims at making personality somewhat measurable and assessable and thus gives it a scientific base.

The above-mentioned characteristics do not suggest that Eysenck's definition has explained everything about the term personality or it does not have any weak-point. Like other definitions, this also suffers from some limitations and drawbacks, which are given below:

(*i*) Eysenck advocates that personality must have a physiological base, but it is not a case always. Every time we cannot have a physiological base due to the very complex nature of personality.

(*ii*) His definition leads us to form an opinion that personality is fixed and cannot be changed.

This is an extreme approach. It is true that personality should be evaluated on the basis of generality of the behaviour (the behaviour must be consistent in a number of situations) but on the other hand, changes cannot be denied. The person who is an extrovert may turn into an introvert depending upon so many intervening factors.

In this way, for understanding the concept of personality, the evolution of an ideal definition still needs further research. In fact, the concepts like personality are difficult to be explained as they have the identity like sound, electricity, etc. the impact of which can be felt but the real nature of them is always a matter of secrecy. Something about them can be known by their utility or describing some of their characteristics and distinguishing feature known as topography of personality. Let us seek the meaning of the term personality also on similar lines.

Characteristics and Distinguishing Features of Personality

The notable characteristics and distinguished feature of the term personality may be summarised in the manner given below.

1. Firstly, the personality is something unique and specific. Every one of us is a unique pattern in himself. No two individuals, not even the identical twins, behave in precisely the same way over any period of time. Every one of us has specific characteristics for making adjustments.
2. The second main characteristic of personality is self-consciousness. The man is described as a person or to have a personality when the idea of self enters into his consciousness. In this connection, H.R. Bhatia writes, "*We do not attribute personality to a dog and even a child cannot be described as a personality because it has only a vague sense of personal identity.*" (1968, p. 371)
3. Personality includes everything about a person. It is all that a person has about him. It includes all the behavioural patterns, *i.e.,* conative, cognitive and affective, and covers not only the conscious activities but also goes deeper to semi-conscious and unconscious.
4. It is not just a collection of so many traits or characteristics which is known as personality. By counting the bricks only how can we describe the wall of a house? It needs something more and actually personality is more than this. It is an organisation of some psychophysical systems or some behavioural characteristics and functions as a unified whole. Just as to tell what an elephant is, we cannot say that it is like a pillar only by examining its legs. In the same way by looking through one's physique or sociability, we cannot pass judgment over one's personality. It is only when we go carefully in all the aspects—biological as well as social—we can make an idea about his personality.
5. Personality is not static; it is dynamic and ever in process of change and modification. As we have said earlier, personality is all that a person has about him. It gives him all that is needed for his unique adjustment in his environment. The process of making adjustment to environment is continuous. One has to struggle with the environmental as well as the inner forces throughout his life-span. As a result, one has to bring modification and change in one's personality patterns and it makes the nature of personality dynamic instead of static.
6. Every personality is the product of heredity and environment. Both contribute significantly towards the development of the child's personality.
7. Learning and acquisition of experiences contributes towards growth and development of personality. Every personality is the end-product of this process of learning and acquisition.
8. Personality should not be equated with one's character. Character is an ethical concept. It represents a moral estimate of the individual. While personality, as a psychological concept, is a more comprehensive term which encircles in its sphere the character as one of the constituents of one's personality.
9. Personality may further be differentiated from temperament which can be called a system of emotional disposition. This system of emotional disposition represents only the effective side of one's personality, so personality must be taken as much beyond that of one's temperament.
10. Personality should be viewed as different from the ego or the individual self. The word "ego" is generally used for that unified part of one's personality which in ordinary language we call "I". However, as the psychoanalytic view of personality advocated by Freud explains, it is only a small aspect of one's total personality. Personality, therefore, stands for more than what the ego carries.
11. Every person's personality has one more distinguishing feature that is, aiming to an end—towards some specific goals. Adler asserts this view frankly in his book "*Individual Psychology*". He is of the opinion that a man's personality can be judged through a study and interpretation of the goals he has set for himself to achieve and the approaches he makes to the problems of his life.

While going through all that has been said in terms of the definitions and characteristics of personality, we may accept a workable definition of the term personality as under:

Personality is a complex blend of a constantly evolving and changing pattern of one's unique behaviour emerged as a result of one's interaction with his environment, directed towards some specific ends in view.

Theories of Personality

The search for the nature of personality will be rather incomplete if we do not mention some important theories of personality. This helps us in classifying the people into some categories according to their personality characteristics and gives a base for the assessment of their personality. The theories of personality, in general, can be classified into four broad categories according to their modes of approach.

(i) *The theories which adopt Type-approach:* The viewpoint of Hippocrates, Kretschmer, Sheldon and Jung belong to his category. They hold that human personalities can be classified into a few clearly defined types and each person can be put in one or the other types according to his personality traits.

(ii) *The theories which adopt Trait-approach:* Worth mentioning in this category is Cattell's theory of personality. This approach believes in the mathematical analysis and quantification of the personality constituents and helps in the prediction of human behaviour in a particular situation.

(iii) *The theories which adopt Type as well as Trait approach:* Eysenck's theory of personality belongs to this category. He goes a step ahead to the approach adopted by Cattell. He does not only mention the personality traits for assessing one's personality but also tries to give definite personality types.

(iv) *The theories which adopt Psychodynamic or psychoanalytic approach:* These are the theories which try to explain the growth and development of personality by adopting the ideas and approaches propagated by the school of psychoanalysis. The psychodynamic theory of Freud, theory of individual psychology by Adler, and theory of analytical psychology developed by Jung falls into this category.

(v) *The theories which adopt Humanistic approach:* These are the theories which try to explain the development of human behaviour and personality through the ideas and approaches propagated by the school or philosophy of humanism. The theories like the self-actualization theory of Abraham Maslow and Carl Roger's self- theory fall in this category.

(vi) *The theories which adopt Learning approach:* These are the theories which try to explain the development of one's behaviour and personality by advocating that personality in shaped and developed by acquiring social experiences through indirect and direct learning. The theories named as Dollard and Miller's learning theory of personality and Bandura & Walter's social learning theory fall in this category.

Let us summarize the view- points of above mentioned theories.

A. Theories adopting type approach

Psychologists advocating type approach have advocated that human personalities can be classified into a few clearly defined types and each person can be put in one or the other type depending upon his behavioural characteristics, somatic structure, blood types, fluids in the body, or personality traits. Based on such approach, the physicians of ancient India broadly categorized all human beings into three types. This classification was based on the three basic elements of the body, *i.e.* pitt (bile), bate (wind), and kuff (mucus). Almost the same approach was followed by the Greek physicians like Hippocrates, one of the disciples of the great philosopher Aristotle. In the subsequent years, many more scholars and psychologists tried to divide persons into certain types depending upon their own specific criterion. Let us describe a few of such approaches:

1. *Hippocrates' classification:*

He tried to classify all human beings into four characteristic groups according to their temperaments as:

(i) Choleric
(ii) Melancholic
(iii) Phlegmatic
(iv) Sanguinic

The following table explains the classification:

Table 7.1: Hippocrates' Classification Temperamental characteristics and the associated personality types:

Choleric (−+) (Emotionally weak but bodily strong) Active but irritable (easily angered)	Sangunic (+ +) (Bodily strong and emotionally stable) Excessive blood, cheer-ful, energetic and optimistic
Melancholic (− −) No energy & no happiness Pessimistic (Emotionally as well as bodily weak)	Phlegmatic (+ −) (Emotionally strong but bodily weak) Happy but lazy

2. *Kretschmer's classification:*

Kretschmer classified all human beings into certain biological types according to their physical structures and has allotted definite personality characteristics associated with each physical make-up as follows:

Table 7.2: Kretschmer's classification

Types of Personality	Personality Characteristics
I. Pyknic (having fat bodies)	Sociable, jolly, easy-going and good-natured.
II. Athletic (balanced body)	Energetic, optimistic and adjustable.
III. Leptosomatic (lean and thin)	Unsociable, reserved, shy, sensitive and pessimistic.

Fig. 7.1: Kretschmer's Types of Personality

3. *Sheldon's classification:*

He too, like Kretschmer, classified human beings into certain types according to their physical structures and attached certain temperamental characteristics to them as explained in table 7.3.

The approach adopted by the above psychologists to have classification on the basis of seeking correlation between structure of the body and personality characteristics, is only lopsided. It is somewhat misleading. There is no such perfect body-mind or body-heart correlation as the propagators of these approaches have assumed.

Table 7.3: Sheldon's classification

Personality types	Somatic or body structure	Personality characteristics
Name	Description	Description
(i) Endomorphic	Person having highly developed viscera but weak somatic structure (Like Kretschmer's Pyknic type).	Easy-going, sociable and affectionate
(ii) Mesomorphic	Balanced development of viscera and somatic structure. (Like Kretschmer's athletic type).	Craving for muscular activity, self-assertive, loves risk and adventure
(iii) Ectomorphic	Weak somatic structure as well as undeveloped viscera (Like Kretschmer's Lepto-somatic).	Pessimistic, unsociable, and reserved

4. *Jung's classification*

He divided all human beings basically into two distinct types—Introvert and Extrovert—according to their social participation and the interest which they take in social activities. Later on, he further sharpened his two-fold division by giving sub-types. In this process, he took into consideration the four psychological functions—thinking, feeling, sensation and intuition, in relation to his previous extrovert and introvert types. Diagrammatically, we can represent this division, along with main characteristics of each sub-type, as shown in Fig. 7. 2

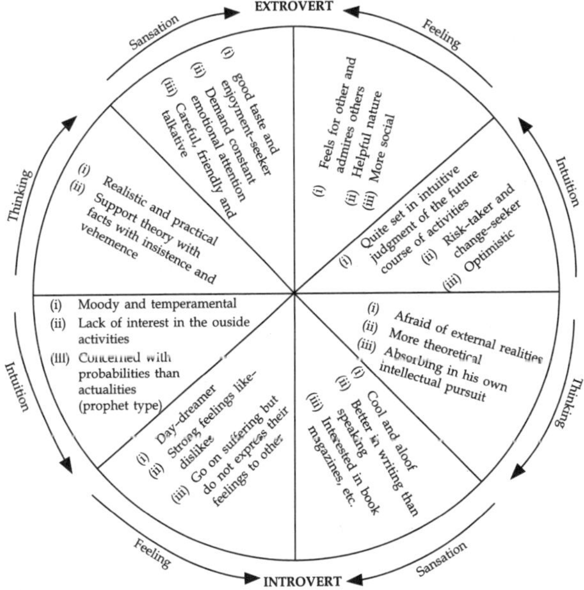

Fig. 7.2: Jung's description of the types of personality

The classification has been criticised on the ground that in general, such different types of classes as suggested by Jung do not exist. Most of us, on the basis of typical characteristics prescribed for extrovert and introvert, may belong to both of the categories. This brings complication and hence, the type approach does not give any clear picture of the classification or description of personality.

5. Friedman's and Rosenman's classification: This classification of personality type is given by Meyer Friedman and Ray Rosenman. It classifies the people into two types of personality, type A and type B on the basis of their personality traits and then points out which types of people are more prone to heart ailments, particularly coronary heart disease. In coronary heart disease, there is malfunctioning of the heart on account of the deficiency in supply and circulation of the blood through blood-carrying arteries and veins. For a long time, it was thought that cholesterol deposits in arteries and veins put obstacles in the free flow of blood through them which, in turn, proves a potent factor for the deficiency in supply and circulation of the blood to the heart. Friedman and Rosenman with the active assistance of some medical men tried to establish through their researches that stress is an important causative factor for the coronary heart disease. They further established that a particular type of people possessing a set of particular personality traits named as type A are more prone to the stress producing behaviour in sharp contrast to the people belonging to type B. They further outlined the typical personality traits associated with these personality types 'A' and 'B' in the way given in table 7.4.

Table 7.4: A & B Type Personalities

A type Personalty	B type Personalty
Emotionally unstable, tense, worried, irritating, competitive, high achieving motive, moody, indifferent, active and restless, aggressive, crazy, perfectionist, idealist, rigid, much worried about punctuality and rules, hasty, jealous, dissatisfied from the self and others, suspicious, sensitive, insecure, believer in action and not in fate and fortune, etc.	Emotionally stable, tension-free, happy and jolly, average achieving motive, insensitive, patient, self-satisfied, calm and quiet, flexible, tolerant, realist, optimist, having faith and trust in one's self and others, adjusted to one's self and others, believer in the philosophy of fate and fortune, sincere but not too serious about the execution and result of the work etc.

To Sum Up

Theories adopting type approach hold that human personalities can be classified into a few clearly defined types and each person can be put in one or the other types according to his personality traits. Accordingly Hippocrates classified peoples into four types according to the humour or fluids—blood, yellow bile, mucus and black bile. Kretschmer and Sheldon described specific biological types based on body structures and attached certain personality characteristics to them. Jung while adopting type approach tried to classify people basically into two distinct types introvert and extrovert. Friedman and Rosenman classified people into two personality types—type A and type B on the basis of their personality traits and then described which types of people are particularly more prone to heart ailments.

B. Theories adopting trait approach

In trait approach, the personality is viewed in terms of traits. In our day-to-day conversation, we label our friends and near ones with traits such as being honest, shy, aggressive, lazy, dull, dependent, etc. In the real sense, traits are defined as relatively permanent and relatively consistent general behaviour patterns exhibited by an individual in many situations. These patterns are said to be the basic units of one's personality that can be discovered through observing one's behaviour in a variety of situations. A person if he behaves honestly in several situations, after having generalization may be labelled as honest and honesty or laziness becomes a behavioural trait of his personality. A number of Psychologists have adopted trait approach for defining the personality of the individuals. We will be focusing on two of the important ones here.

Allport's Trait theory of Personality

G.B. Allport (1897-1967) was the first personality theorist who adopted trait approach in providing a theory of personality. He rejected the notion of a relatively limited number of personality types in favour of the descriptions of highly individual personalities made up of a large number of traits. According to him, an individual develops a unique set of organized tendencies or traits-the basic structure of one's personality. He classified the numerous traits defining the personality of an individual in to three main types named as cardinal, central and surface traits.

Cardinal traits are the most active and dominant traits of one's personality. Although present in a very small number just as one or two, these are enough to colour the personality according to their characteristics. As an example, we can cite sense of humour as a cardinal trait in one's personality. This trait may colour his personality in a specific way as much as that he may be identified or known through his behaviour almost dominated by the sense of humour at all the times and occasions.

Central traits are those traits which are frequently employed for identifying and describing one's personality, e.g., honesty, kindness, timidity, shyness, rigidity, cruelty, etc. Usually seven or eight such central traits are enough for knowing and describing the personality of an individual.

Secondary traits are those traits of an individual's personality which play a secondary or to say quite insignificant role in the identification and description of one's personality. These are in fact not the essential part of one's personality. That is why these are reflected quite rarely in one's behaviour e.g., a person named as miser, selfish, and greedy contributing generously for a common cause.

Depending up on their nature and importance, thus, it is quite common to take in to account mainly the cardinal and central traits present in the behaviour of the people in naming and describing their personality.

Cattell's theory

The most recent advanced theory of personality based on trait approach has been developed by Raymond B. Cattell, a British born American researcher. He has defined trait as a structure of the personality inferred from behaviour in different situations and describes four types of traits:

(*i*) **Common traits:** the traits found widely distributed in general population like honesty, aggression and cooperation.

(*ii*) **Unique traits:** unique to a person as temperamental traits, emotional reactions.

(*iii*) **Surface traits:** able to be recognized by our manifestation of behaviour like curiosity, dependability, tactfulness, etc.

(*iv*) **Source traits:** underlying structures or sources that determine one's behaviour such as dominance, submission, emotionality etc.

The theory propagated by Cattell intends to give certain specific dimensions to personality so that the human behaviour, related to a particular situation, may be predicted. Cattell has adopted factor analysis as a technique for this work. We shall try to understand how he has done it in a non-technical way.

1. Cattell began by attempting to obtain a complete list of all possible human behaviours. In 1946, he formed a list of over 17,000 traits and by eliminating similarities and synonyms reduced them to a list of 171 words (dictionary words) related with personality and called these trait-elements.
2. The next step was to find out how they are related. He found that each trait element correlated high with some and low with others. In this way, he managed to form some specific groups and called them Surface Traits. These surface traits identified were 35 in number.
3. Again, he went on examining these surface traits in terms of their intercorrelations. There was overlapping. The removal of such overlapping gave him the desired basic dimensions which he called Source Traits, *i.e.* the real structural influence underlying personality.
4. After obtaining source traits (which are 15 in number) he tried to use them to predict behaviour employing what is known as specification equation.

$\text{Response} = s_1T_1 + s_2T_2 + s_3T_4 + \ldots \ldots snTn$

In this way, the response or behaviour of an individual is predicted from the degree to which he exhibits each source trait (T) modified by the importance of the trait for that response(s).

Let us clear it by an example.

Suppose that academic performance (AP) is predictable from two source traits called Intelligence (I) and Reading habits (R), then

$AP = s_1I + s_2R$

Now also suppose that Intelligence is more important for this behaviour than Reading habits (in the ratio of 5: 3); then we might have an expression such as

$AP = 5I + 3R$

Thus, in order to predict academic performance (A.P.) for an individual we need to know his intelligence and scores on reading habits.

In addition to this in 1950, Cattell devised the *Sixteen Personality factor questionnaire* in the form of an inventory, these factors, which he claimed, may work as "building blocks" of personality.

These sixteen factors (twelve independent and four partially independent) involved in the personality structure, are produced below:

Table 7.5: The set of opposite traits discovered by Cattell in his sixteen personality factors

	Trait	Opposite Trait
1.	Emotional/easily upset	V/s Calm/stable
2	Intelligent	V/s Unintelligent
3	Reserved/ Unfriendly	V/s Outgoing/friendly
4	Assertive/ dominant	V/s Not assertive/ humble
5	Sobre/Serious	V/s Happy-go-lucky
6	Conscientious	V/s Expedient
7	Shy/timid	V/s Venturesome
8	Tender-minded	V/s Tough-minded
9	Suspicious	V/s Trusting
10	Practical	V/s Imaginative
11	Shrewd	V/s Forthright
12	Self-assured/ placid	V/s Apprehensive
13	Conservative	V/s Experimenting
14	Group-oriented	V/s Self-sufficient
15	Undisciplined	V/s Self-disciplined
16	Relaxed	V/s Tense/driven

Further researches in the field of trait conception of the personality have highlighted the repetition and similarity of the terms used by Cattell for describing human behaviour in terms of sixteen dimensions. For example, there stands much similarity and high correlation between the traits represented by factors 1 and 16 and also by factors 3 and 7. The individual who is calm is automatically relaxed and one who is tense can be described as emotional or easily upset. Similarly, who is shy and timid can be described as reserved or unfriendly and an outgoing friendly personality will be found also venturesome. Therefore, the latest researchers have been able to reduce the number of traits as well as the number of dimensions (factors) for describing the human personality (Pediment, Mccral and Costa, 1991) as below:

Table 7.6: Five dimensions of personality and the related traits

Dimension or Factor	*Traits*
1. Extraversion	Traits like talkative, sociable, and adventurous
2. Agreeableness	Traits like good natured, cooperative and likeable.
3. Conscientiousness	Traits like demonstrating responsibility, neatness and task motivation.
4. Emotional stability	Traits like calmness, poise, and composure.
5. Culture	Traits like intelligence and interest in philosophy and art.

To Sum Up

Theories adopting trait approach try to make use of the personality traits for underlying and describing the personality of an individual. The personality theories put up by Gordon Allport and R.B Cattell belong to this category. Allport identifies three types of traits namely cardinal, central, and secondary, contributing towards the personality make-up of an individual. Cattell used factor analysis to identify surface traits and source traits and ultimately arrived at 16 factors or basic dimensions for describing one's personality. Latest researches have been able to reduce these traits to five namely Extraversion, Agreeability, Consciousness, Emotional Stability and culture.

C. Trait cum type approach

Eysenck's Theory of Personality :

H.J. Eysenck, the famous contemporary psychologist has adopted trait cum type approach for explaining the structure of personality. For this purpose, he actually tried to blend all which could be availed from the previous theories of personality.

While Allport and Cattell, his predecessors, tried to give dimensions to personality by giving traits, Eysenck gave it more specification by grouping traits into definite types. Hence his approach is trait cum type approach.

How the individual behaviour is organised and gets the shape of a definite type can be understood through the figure 7.3 given ahead:

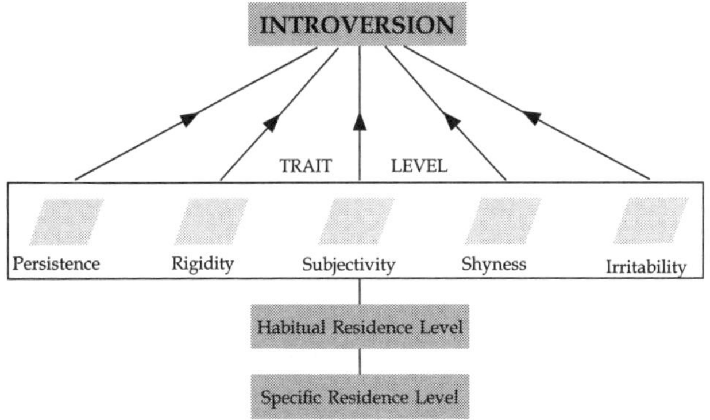

Fig. 7.3: Organisation of individual behaviour

We have four levels of behaviour organisation

(*i*) At the lowest level, we have specific responses. They grow out of particular responses to any single act. For example, 'blushing' is a specific response.

(*ii*) At the second level, we have habitual responses. If the individual reacts in the similar fashion when the same situation reoccurs, we get habitual responses. For example, the responses like

- (*a*) Not easily picking up friendship
- (*b*) Hesitant to talk to strangers, etc. are habitual responses.

(*iii*) At the third level we have organisation of habitual acts into traits. The behavioural acts which have similarities are said to belong to one group called "trait". In the above example the habitual responses no. (a) and (b) etc. give birth to a group or trait called 'Shyness'.

(*iv*) At the fourth level we have organisation of these traits into a general type. A type is defined as group of correlated traits. The traits which are similar give birth to a definite type just as in the Fig. 7.3 the traits like persistence, rigidity, shyness etc. have been grouped into a type which is 'Introversion'.

Now at this final stage, ultimately, we obtain a definite type. A person now can be classified as Introvert if he has traits as described at III level, habits and habit systems as described at level II and responds specifically as described at level I.

Eysenck has given the following distinct types—

(1) Introversion (2) Extroversion
(3) Neuroticism (4) Psychoticism

He has also tried to link different traits and characteristics with each of these types. In this way, Eysenck has tried to put forward trait cum type approach for the explanation of the structure and integration of our personality.

To Sum Up

Theories adopting type-cum-trait approach like Eysenck's theory of personality try to synthesize the viewpoints of both the type and trait approach. They start with the description of trait initially and then end up with some distinct personality types. Eysenck in his theory has given four such distinct personality types namely introversion, extroversion, neuroticism and psychoticism by linking different personality trait with each of these types.

D. Theories adopting Psychodynamic approach

Freud's psychodynamic theory of personality

Freud's theory of personality is built on the premise that the mind is topographical and dynamic: there are provinces or divisions which are always moving and interrelated. The human mind has three main divisions in the form of conscious, semiconscious and unconscious.

These three levels of the human mind continuously clash and compromise to give birth to one or other types of behavioural characteristics leading to a particular type of personality. Besides this human personality may be considered to have a three-storied structure composed of one; Id, Ego super ego. Let us know something about them.

Id: It is the raw, savage and immoral basic stuff of a man's personality. It consists of such ambitions, desires, tendencies and appetites of an individual as are guided by the pleasure-seeking principle. It knows no laws, follows no rules and considers only the satisfaction of its needs and appetites.

Ego: If the raw Id were left to its own devices it would bring disastrous effects. Therefore, there is Ego which acts as a policeman to check the unlawful activities of the Id. It is the executive unit with Veto powers. It follows the principle of reality and acts with intelligence in controlling selecting and deciding what appetites have to be satisfied and in which way they are to be satisfied.

Super ego: The super ego is the ethical moral arm of the personality. It is idealistic and does not care for realities. Perfection is its goal rather than pleasure. It is a decision-making body which decides what is bad or good, virtue or vice according to the standard of society which it accepts.

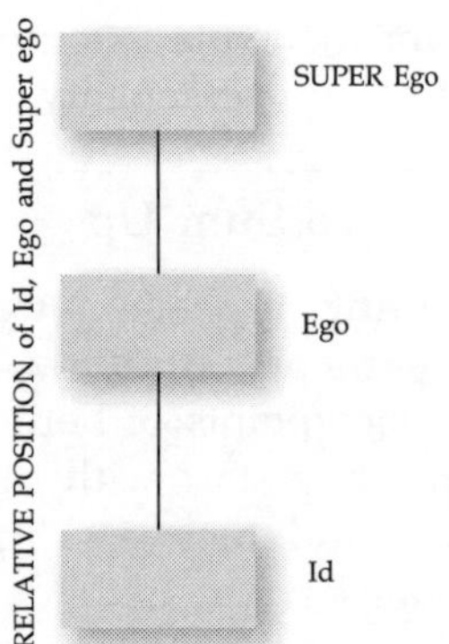

Fig. 7.4: Relative position of Id, Ego and Super Ego

The above-mentioned constituents of personality play a significant role in deciding the personality of an individual. Let us see how.

1. The individuals who have a strong or powerful ego are said to have a strong or balanced personality because in their cases, ego is capable of maintaining proper balance between super ego and Id.
2. In case an individual possesses a weak ego, he is bound to have a maladjusted personality. Here two situations may arise. In one situation, the super ego may be more powerful than ego; it does not provide a desirable outlet for the repressed wishes and impulses. Consequently, it may lead towards the formation of a neurotic personality. In another situation Id may prove more powerful than ego. The person, thus, may engage himself in unlawful or immoral activities leading towards the formation of a delinquent personality.

In addition to the above structure of the personality, built around the concept of the Id, ego and superego, Freud tried to provide an explanation of the development of human personality through his ideas about sex. He held that sex is the life-energy. The sexual needs of the individual are basic needs which have to be satisfied for a balanced growth of the personality. The knowledge of the sex needs of a person and the status of their satisfaction is sufficient to tell us all about a person's personality. He will be an adjusted or maladjusted personality depending on the extent to which his sexual needs are satisfied.

So much was his emphasis on sex, that he linked the whole development of the personality with the sex behaviour by putting his theory of psycho-sexual development. In this theory, he outlined the five various psycho-sexual stages for the development of personality namely, oral, anal, phallic, latency and genital.

Let us have a look into these Stages

1. *The oral stage:* According to Freud, the mouth represents the first sex organ for providing pleasure to the child. The beginning is made with the pleasure received from the mother's nipple or the bottle. Thereafter, the child derives pleasure by putting anything, candy, a stick, his own thumb, etc. into his mouth.
2. *The anal stage:* At this stage, the interest of the child shifts from the mouth as the erogenous zone to the organs of elimination, i.e. the anus or the urethra. He derives pleasure by holding back or letting go of the body's waste material through the anus or the urethra. This stage, generally, ranges from two to three years.
3. *The phallic stage:* This phase starts from the age of four years with the shifting of the child's interest from the eliminating organs to the genitals. At this stage children come to note the biological differences between the sexes and derive pleasure by playing with and manipulating the genital organs. This stage, according to Freud, may give rise to a number of complexes like deprivation and *Electra* complexes in girls and castration and *Oedipus* complexes in boys. The deprivation complex is the result of the feeling generated in the minds of the little girls that they have been deprived of the male organ by their mothers. Castration complex is generated in boys through their fear of being deprived of the male organs certainly as a result of the threat received from elders that the organ would be cut off if they did not give up the habit of playing with it. About the Oedipus and Electra phases, Freud says that they are the result of the sexual attraction or pleasure that children experience in the company of the parent of the opposite sex. In case the parent of the same sex frustrates the desire, expresses his or her resentment and is not friendly to the boy or girl, the child may develop Oedipus or Electra complex by loving the opposite sex parent more and rather hating the like sex parent.
4. *The latency stage:* This period starts from six years in the case of girls and seven to eight years in the case of boys and extends up to the onset of puberty. At this stage, boys and girls prefer to be in the company of their own sex and even neglect or hate members of the opposite sex.
5. *The genital stage:* Puberty is the starting point of the genital stage. The adolescent boy and girl now feel a strange feeling of strong sensation in the genitals and attraction towards the members

of the opposite sex. At this stage they may feel pleasure by self-stimulation of the genitals, may fall in love with their own self by taking interest in beautifying and adorning their bodies and may be drawn quite close to members of the opposite sex even to the extent of indulging in sexual intercourse.

Adler's individual approach to personality

Adler opposed the Freudian's structure of personality. He said that sex is not the life-energy or the centre of human activities. Actually, power motive is the centre urge. Human beings are motivated by the urge to be important or powerful. All of us strive towards superiority but each strives in a different way. He named it as 'style of life'. Therefore, what kind of personality one possesses, can be understood by studying his style of life, *i.e.* the goals of life he has set for himself and the way of striving for achieving these goals.

In this way, he gave birth to the individual approach in the study of a personality pattern and maintained that there are no definite types or classes of personality. Each individual is a unique pattern in his self because everybody has definite goals and his own life style.

Jung's Analytical Approach to Personality

Differing with the views of Freud especially his notion of making sex the centre of explaining and describing all in the behaviour and personality of the people, Jung established a separate school of thought named Analytical psychology for experimenting with and propagating his ideas. Let us have a view of the main things related to his system of psychology.

1. While agreeing with Freud with the existence of the unconscious besides the conscious in the structure of one's psyche, Jung differed a great deal in his concept of unconscious. According to him below the upper layer of the conscious mind (only a fraction of the human mind) there lies one's vast unconscious divided into two parts-the personal unconscious and the collective unconscious.
2. One's personal unconscious is highly individualistic and personal in nature. It contains all the repressed things and private experiences occurring in the life time of the individual.
3. Collective unconscious lying beneath the layer of the personal unconscious is neither personal nor private but is universal to all individuals. It contains the various types of universal ideas or images called archetypes such as our concepts about God, Mother Earth, Saints, Devils, etc. They are available in abundance in old myths, fairy tales, folklores, and enduring literature and art.
4. Thus, according to Jung, we can view the psyche structure of an individual in the form of various archetypes as the roots (resting in the deep inner) stemming out into the personal unconscious and blossoming out in the open as the conscious. In this way, it is one's unconscious that gives birth to consciousness and not otherwise.
5. One's unconscious in the form of the collective unconscious, in view of Jung, thus, is responsible for shaping one's personality and making him behave in one or the other ways in the actual life situations.
6. Since one's psyche is governed and controlled by the archetypes (universal good ideas and actions) available in one's collective unconscious, one has an inherited tendency to strive for self-actualization. In this way, it is not the sex motive (as urged by Freud) or power motive (as urged by Adler) but the motive of self-actualization that works in making one to behave and developing his personality in some specific ways.
7. According to Jung, there lies a great treasure of good and sparking ideas available in the form of various archetypes in one's unconscious mind that makes him to aim and strive for the achievements of higher goals in his life. In this connection, Jung opines that altruism is as innate in man as egoism and religious feelings and morality is also deep seated in the collective unconscious. Similarly, there is an innate creative spark in every individual the basis of which is also lies in the unconscious depths of his mind. These inner well intended aspects of one's mind need some forms of expression and it is what is seen to be attempted by him through his striving for self-actualization. Accordingly, it is not unusual to see people to strive for climbing higher and higher on the ladder of continuous growth and development by getting maximum opportunities for self-expression as well as the development of one's self and ultimately wishing for the union of the self (atma) with the universal self (parmatma, the God).
8. Depending up on the extent to which individuals are able to satisfy their urge of self-actualization (becoming what their self urges them to be), they remain satisfied and their behaviour is termed as normal. Once the equilibrium is

disturbed, they may be seen to fall in the trap of maladjustment turning them into an abnormal or socially deviant personality.

To sum Up

Psycho analytic approach of Freud holds that the anatomy of our personality is built around three unified and inter-relating systems Id, Ego and Super ego. The dominant and submissive role played by one's Id and Super ego in relation to one's ego plays a significant role in deciding the structure of one's personality, like balanced, neurotic or psychotic personality. Freud while providing much importance to sexuality, laid down five stages namely, oral, anal, genital, latency, phallic stage through which a child passes with respect to the psycho sexual development of his personality.

Adler, while opposing Freud's sex-centred approach, held that power motive plays a dominant role in structuring one's personality. In the course of one's struggle for power, one picks up a distinct style of one's life for attaining his life goals. Since everybody has his unique way of striving and has definite goals in his life, he is distinguished with his own individuality (style of his life) and unique personality. The views so expressed by Adler thus gave birth to individual approach and tendencies for the study of human personality.

Jung while advocating the doctrine of analytical psychology and giving more importance to unconscious held that one's unconscious in the form of the collective unconscious is responsible for shaping one's personality and since one's psyche is governed and controlled by the archetypes (universal good ideas and actions) available in one's collective unconscious, one has an inherited tendency to strive for self-actualization. In this way, it is the motive of self-actualization that works in making one to behave and developing his personality in some specific ways.

E. Theories adopting Humanistic approach

This approach to personality came from a group of psychologists subscribing to the humanistic school of psychology. Humanistic psychology, the so-called third force in psychology (the other two being behaviourism and psychoanalysis) reflects a humanistic trend in dealing with and understanding human behaviour. In believes in the goodness of man and reposes optimistic confidence in man's positive nature. Contrary to the unconscious of psychoanalytical psychology here, a person's conscious experience (what he or she feels and thinks) forms the basic structure of his or her personality. Consequently, the approach adopted by the humanists does not assume that personality is governed by biological forces from within or that destructive drives are inherent in human beings but instead points out that every one of us has the potential for self-actualization through spontaneity, creativity and personal growth. A number of theories, such as those of Godlstein, Angyal, Rogers and Maslow subscribe to the approach advocated by humanistic psychology. We shall now discuss the viewpoints of the highly influential humanistic thinkers, Abraham Maslow and Carl Rogers.

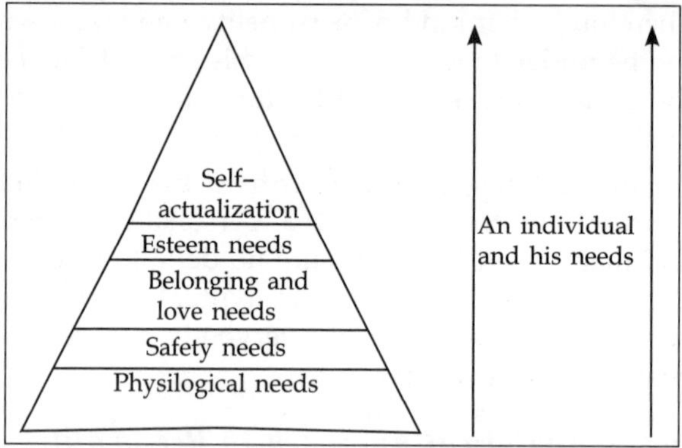

Fig. 7.5: Maslow's Hierarchical Structure of Needs

The self-actualization theory of Abraham Maslow

Abraham H. Maslow, an American psychologist, has been the major theorist adopting the humanistic approach for studying human behaviour and personality. According to his theory, human beings are basically good or neutral rather than evil and there lies in every one an impulse craving towards growth or the fulfilments of one's potentials. The goal is to seek self-actualization. It usually comes from the pursuit of knowledge, the appreciation of beauty, playfulness, self-sufficiency, insight into the truth or other constructive and creative expression. The behaviour or personality of a human being thus depends upon his style of striving towards the ultimate goal of self-realization. However, the path leading towards the ultimate goal may have sub-goals in the form of satisfaction of the lower-order needs. In this way, Maslow's theory of self-actualization suggests a hierarchy of needs (See Fig. 27.6).

Actually, as Maslow suggests pattern of human behaviour is always governed by the satisfaction of our needs from the lower, base level to the upper, top level. We have to satisfy our biological needs for our survival and for our social and psychological needs, we have to strive for the satisfaction in the socio-psychological context. The satisfaction of these needs is, however, not the end of man's pursuit for excellence. His craving for the actualization of his inner potential continues till he reaches his ultimate goal of attaining fine humanistic values.

These values or characteristics of a self-actualized person to which one's efforts are directed in terms of the development of his personality have been enumerated by Maslow through sixteen basic characteristics. These characteristics have been arrived at by him through the study of a selected group of thirty-eight persons. This select group had included the well-known personalities past and present, e.g., Albert Einstein, Abraham Lincoln, Roosevelt, etc., and also his own professors and persons who were known for self-actualization in their respective fields. From this study Maslow concluded that the self-actualized people have the following common characteristics which distinguish them from the average person (Source: Maslow, 1962):

1. Ability to perceive reality accurately.
2. Willingness to accept reality readily.
3. Naturalness and spontaneity.
4. Ability to focus on problems rather than on themselves.
5. Need for privacy.
6. Self-sufficiency and independence.
7. Capacity for fresh, spontaneous, non- stereo typed appreciation of objects, events and people that they encounter.
8. Ability to attain transcendence.
9. Identification with humankind and shared social bonds with other people.
10. They may have few or many friends but have deep relationships with at least some of these friends.
11. A democratic, egalitarian attitude.
12. Strongly held values and a clear distinction between means and ends.
13. A broad, tolerant sense of humour.
14. Inventiveness and creativity with the ability to see things in new ways.
15. Resistance to confirm or succumb to social pressures.
16. Ability to go beyond dichotomies and bring together opposites.

Thus, the goal for personally development according to Maslow's theory is self-actualization, i.e. realization of one's basic human potential to the maximum extent and as effectively as possible. The theory, thus, presents a very bright picture of human behaviour and personality by setting an ultimate motivating goal of self-actualization. However, it is criticised on account of its not being objective and scientific in its approach, especially in view of its subjective criteria for self-actualization.

Carl Roger's Self- theory:

Carl Ransom Rogers, an American psychologist, in 1947 propounded a new theory of personality called the self- theory quite distinct from the earlier theories of personality. He stressed the importance of an individual's self for determining the process of his growth, development, and appropriate adjustment to his environment. There are two basic systems underlying his personality theory — the organism and the self. Rogers considers them as systems operating in one's phenomenological field (a world of subjective experience, the personal and separate reality of each individual). The organism is an individual's entire frame of reference. It represents the totality of his experience — both conscious and unconscious. The second system, the 'self is the accepted, aware part of experience. The self as a system of one's phenomenal field can perhaps be best understood in terms of our concept of "I", "me" or "my- self".

What we recognize as the personality of an individual is the product of interaction between the above-mentioned systems of one's phenomenological field. The acquisition of the concept of self is a long and continuous process. Human beings have inherited the tendency to develop their self in the process of interpersonal and social experiences which they acquire in the environment. In other words, our inner world (in the form of our natural impulses) interacts with our total range of experience to form the concept of our self. For example, if one is told that one is a handsome person, one tends to include in the concept of one's self, the idea that one is handsome. We are in a continuous process of building the concept of our self in this manner. The concepts of self thus developed may differ from person to person as they are based purely on one's own personal experiences. The concept of self is sometimes based more on personal needs than on reality, and at other times as Rogers believes, we develop an ideal self, i.e. the kind of person we would like to be.

Rogers does not advance a set of specific stages in the development of personality as proposed by Freud, rather, he advocates continuity of growth in terms of a continuous evolution of the concept of 'self'. Once a concept of self is formed, the individual strives to maintain it by regulating his behaviour. Whatever is consistent with the concept of his self is readily accepted and maintained at the conscious level while that which threatens that image may be totally ignored or buried deep in the unconscious.

The most unfortunate results in the development of personality occur in cases where an individual develops some false self-image. This false image is sometimes so strong that even indisputable reality is vehemently denied. Inconsistency between one's actual image and a false self-image, may then lead to abnormality in one's behaviour. Similarly, the development of an ideal self, too unreasonable and unattainable or too different from one's real self, may result in maladjustment and serious personality disorder.

An individual's adjustment, happiness, growth and development all depend upon the union and harmony between the image of the self and the organism i.e. the experience or situations he meets in his life. Stressing the psychological personality theory, Rogers emphasizes that a person normally possesses considerable capacity for growth and the realization of his individual potential and thus tries to advance continuously towards the development of his self (i.e. self-actualization) to lead to harmony between the concept of his self and his real- life experiences resulting in feelings of self-integrity, self-fulfilment and a satisfying sense of psychological growth. The development, however, runs into trouble when the self fails for some reason to incorporate, and learns to live with its own new thoughts, feelings or behaviour. The goal of a therapist as Rogers advocates in his therapy, in such cases lies in bringing the individual in a unified way, from what he or she is not, to what he or she really is.

To Sum Up

Among humanistic theories, the self-actualization theory performed by Abraham Maslow believed that individuals are motivated by their needs arranged in a hierarchical order from the lower base level of physiological needs to the upper top level of the need for self-actualization. The personality built up of an individual, therefore, depends upon his striving for the level of his needs and the extent to which he feels that he has been successful in his attempts. The other important humanistic theory, Carl Rogers' self-theory, holds that personality is a function of the interaction between the two systems (the organism and the self) of one's world of subjective experience. He linked the personality with the development and maintenance of the self-concept and the effort to achieve the ideal self.

F. Theories Adopting Learning Approach

The learning theories of personality depict a new developmental approach quite different from psychoanalytic and phenomenological theories of personality in the sense that they emphasize the importance of learning and objectivity to understand personality. The notable psychologists who are known to have developed personality theories are Pavlov, Watson, Guthrie, Thorndike, Skinner, Dollard & Miller; Bandura & Walters, etc. Here for the purpose of illustration, we are briefly describing the learning theory of personality put forward by Dollard &Millerand Bandura &Walters.

Dollard & Miller's Learning Theory of Personality

By combining the psychology of learning with aspects of psychoanalytic theory, John Dollard and Neil Miller (1950) in the institute of human relations at Yale University put forward their theory of personality. In this theory they tried to substitute Freud's concept of a pleasure principle with the principle of reinforcement, the concept of ego with the concept of learned drive and learned skills, the concept of conflict with competing reinforcers etc.

The theory of Dollard and Miller tries to describe the development of personality from simple drives to a complex function from a learning theory angle. It emphasizes that what we consider as personality is learned. The child at birth is equipped with two types of basic faculties: *reflexes and innate hierarchies of responses and a set of primary drives,* which are internal stimuli of great strength and are linked with known physiological processes which impel him to action. Thus, impelled by drives (both conditioned and unconditioned) one acquires responses to the extent that they reduce the drives. Drive reduction results in reinforcements or rewards which in turn may give birth to many other drives or motives and impel the individual to learn new responses and new behaviour patterns. Since our social environment is a major source of reinforcement, it plays a key role in creating new drives and motives, our learning new responses and consequently developing our personality. Dollard and Miller's theory stressed the development of a personality on the basis of the responses and behaviour learnt through the process of motivation and reward. Dollard and Miller's theory of personality did not really ascribe any static structure to personality, and emphasized, instead, habit formation through learning as a key factor in the development of personality. Habits are formed by S.R. connections through learning. As one's fund of learning grows on the basis of experiences and interaction with one's environment, one's habits are reorganised, new habits are learned and consequently one's personality is modified and developed in terms of learning new behaviour and picking up new threads or styles of life.

Bandura & Walters' Social Learning Theory

Albert Bandura and Richard Walters (1963) came out with an innovative approach to personality in the form of their social learning theory. They advanced the view that what the individual presents to the world at large as his personality is acquired through a continuous process of structuring and restructuring of experiences, gathered by means of social learning and later imitated in corresponding situations. Social learning may involve real as well as symbolic models. Children, for example, pick up etiquette and attitudes by watching their parents and elders; viewers garner traits and mannerisms from popular actors and models seen by them on television or in films. The imitation of the model's behaviour is further reinforced in the viewer's mind by the recognition or reward the model receives as a result of his actions. An individual thus acquires numerous traits and modes of behaviour from many sources, and all these together contribute to the formation and development of his unique, distinctive personality.

To Sum Up

Dollard and Miller in their learning theory of personality attempted to combine the learning theory with the psychoanalytic theory and viewed personality as a function of drive reduction. On the other hand, Bandura and Walters in their theory of social learning emphasized that people acquire personality characteristics by observing and imitating real life as well as symbolic models.

Assessment of Personality

The methods used for the assessment of personality are often classified as (i) Subjective methods (ii) Objective methods (iii) Projective methods. But this classification suffers from so many drawbacks. It is difficult to draw a straight line between subjectivity and objectivity; even projective techniques cannot be saved from the subjectivity and self-projection of the examiner. Actually speaking, there is nothing like absolute objectivity in these methods. Objectivity (if at all we can have it) is nothing but subjectivity pooled together. Therefore, it is proper to seek other ways of classifying the methods of personality assessment.

We can classify these techniques in the following five categories:

First, there are techniques, where we can see how an individual behaves in actual life situations. The main techniques in this category are:

(a) Observation technique, (b) Situation tests

Second, there are techniques by which we can find what an individual says about himself. The main techniques in this category are:

(a) Autobiography (b) Questionnaire and Personality Inventory (c) Interview

Third, there are techniques by which we can find what others say about the individual whose personality is under assessment. The main techniques in this class are:

(a) Biographies (b) Case-history method (c) Rating Scales (d) Sociometric techniques

Fourth, there are techniques by which we can find how an individual reacts to an imaginative situation involving fantasy. All kinds of projective techniques are included in this class.

Fifth, there are techniques by which we can indirectly determine some personality variables in terms of physiological responses by machines and technical instruments.

Description of Some Important Techniques

Observation

Observation is a popular method to study the behavioural pattern of an individual in actual life situation. What personality traits or characteristics the observer needs to know, are first decided by him and then he observes relevant activities of the subject in real life situations. The observation can be done in two ways. In one, the observer does not hide his presence. He rather becomes more or less a part of the group under observation. While in the other, he takes a position at a place where his presence is least disturbing to the group but from where he can observe in detail the behaviour of an individual under observation. For having a clear idea, the observer can make use of tape-recorder, photographic cameras, telescope, etc. To ascertain whether the observer can rely on the observed results, he can repeat observations in the same situation a number of times, or the subject may be observed by a number of observers and the results may be pooled together.

Situational tests

Here the situation is artificially created in which an individual is expected to perform acts related to the personality traits under testing. For example, to test the honesty of an individual, some situations can be created and his reaction can be evaluated in terms of honesty or dishonesty. Does he feel temptation of copying? Does he try to pick up the ten-rupee note in a given situation? All such instances can lead towards the assessment of the trait of honesty in the individual.

Questionnaire

What is a questionnaire can be understood by the following description given by Goode and Hatt:

"In general, the word questionnaire refers to a device for securing answers to questions by using a form which the respondent fills in himself." (1952, p. 33)

This definition makes it clear that in collecting information from the subject himself about his personality characteristics, a form consisting of a series of printed or written questions, is used. The subject responds to these questions in the space provided in the form under the columns yes, no or cannot say (?), etc. These answers are then evaluated and used for personality assessment. Items, like the following, are included in the questionnaires:

Do you enjoy being alone?	Yes,	no,	?
Do you enjoy seeing others successful?	Yes,	no,	?
Do you laugh at a joke on you?	Yes,	no,	?
Do you get along well with your relatives?	Yes,	no,	?

It is the most popular method and is quite useful in collecting quantitative as well as qualitative information.

Personality Inventory

It resembles questionnaires in so many aspects like administration, scoring, interpretation etc. The difference can be seen in two ways.

Firstly, the questionnaire is the general device and can be used for collecting all kinds of information (not only connected with personality traits or behaviour of an individual). Personality Inventory is specially designed to seek answers about the person and his personality.

Secondly, the questions, set in the Questionnaire, are generally addressable to the second person. They are such as:

Do you often feel lonely? Yes, no, ?

While in the Personality Inventory, they are usually addressed to the first person such as:

I often feel lonely Yes, no, ?

The best-known Personality Inventory is the Minnesota Multi-phasic Personality Inventory (MMPI). The questions included in this inventory are such that their answers are known to indicate certain specific personality traits. It consists of 550 items. Some of these items are presented below for illustration:

I sweat very easily even on cool days.

There is something wrong with my sexual organs.

I have never been in love with any one.

I like to talk about sex.

Each item is printed on a separate card. The subject reads the questions and then, according to the category of his response—yes, no or doubtful—puts them at three places. With the help of these responses, evaluation in terms of the important personality traits can be obtained.

The Questionnaire and Personality Inventory suffer from the following drawbacks:

(*i*) It is difficult to get the responses to all the questions.

(*ii*) The subject may give selected responses rather than the genuine ones (hide his weaknesses, etc.).

(*iii*) He may be ignorant of certain traits or qualities which he may possess.

7	6	5	4	3	2	1
Excellent	Very Good	Good	Average	Below average	Poor	Very poor

Rating Scale

Rating scale is used to know from others where an individual is in terms of some personality traits. Usually with the help of this technique, we try to have some specific idea about some of the personality traits of an individual (whom we do not know well), from the person, who knows him very well. It reflects the impression the subject has made upon the person who rates him. The three basic things involved in this technique are:

(*i*) The specific trait or traits to be rated

(*ii*) The scale by which degree of possession or absence of the trait has to be shown

(*iii*) The appropriate persons or judges for rating

First of all, the traits or characteristics, which have to be evaluated by the judges are to be stated and defined clearly. Then a scale for rating work is to be constructed. How it is done can be understood through the following example.

Suppose we wish to have rating on the 'Quality of Leadership' of the students of a class. We can have divisions of this quality into degrees such as very good, good, average, poor, very poor, etc. Now the arrangement of these divisions along a line, at equal intervals, from high to low or otherwise will be named as Rating Scale for assessing the quality of leadership. Usually, the degrees are indicated by numbers, 1 to 3, 1 to 5 or 1 to 7, comprising three points, five point or seven points scale. The seven-point scale is of the following type:

Now the raters, who are in a position to rate the individuals properly, can be asked to rate them and give them scores, ranging from 1 to 7, according to the degree of leadership they possess.

Rating techniques suffer from some drawbacks like subjective bias, halo effect, etc. In the former, the rater may have his own likes and dislikes and this may go to colour his estimates about the individuals under rating; where under the halo effect, he may rate an individual (on the basis of general impression) to be more honest or likeable than his actual potentialities.

To bring some reliability, it has been suggested that instead of having rating by only one judge, we can assign the rating work to a number of judges—for example to different teachers, classmates, parents, etc.—who can pool in their judgements or ratings.

Interview

Interview is a technique of getting information, directly from the subject about his personality in face-to-face contacts. It gives an opportunity for mutual exchange of ideas and information between the subject and the psychologists. For this purpose, the psychologist tries to fix a face-to-face appointment with the person or persons under assessment. He makes sure of the personality traits or behaviour he has to assess and then he plans accordingly. Usually, a list of questions, to be put, is prepared for this purpose and after taking the subject into confidence, the psychologist tries to seek answers to his pre-planned questions. He does not only care for the content of the responses but the tone, behaviour and other similar factors, are also kept in mind for the proper evaluation of the desired personality pattern of the individuals.

The limitation of this technique is that it needs a well-trained competent interviewer. It is costly in terms of labour, time and money. It also suffers from the subjective bias of the interviewer. Here also like Questionnaire and Personality Inventory, we cannot have any safeguard to stop the subject to hide his feelings or to respond in terms of selective answers. On the credit side, cent per cent answers to the questions put to the subject, are obtained through interview. There is very little danger of not getting answers to the questions. Moreover, we can get most confidential information from the subject which otherwise, he hesitates to reveal through writing. In fact, interview is relatively a more flexible tool. It permits explanation, adjustment and variations according to the situation and thus proves one of the essential and important tools for the personality assessment.

Projective Techniques

So far we have discussed only those techniques which usually evaluate the overt or conscious behaviour of an individual. The covert or unconscious behaviour, by all means, is not so insignificant; rather it is more significant than the former, as Freud believes that our conscious behaviour is only one-tenth of the total behaviour. Therefore, there should be some other techniques which not only emphasize on the observable part of the human personality but also can reveal his inner or private world and go deeper in the unconscious behaviour of an individual to dig out the repressed feelings, wishes, desires, fears, hopes and ambitions, etc.

Projective techniques are devised to accept the challenge. They try to assess the total personality of an individual and not in fragments. Let us see what these techniques are.

What are the projective techniques ?

These techniques are based on the phenomenon of projection. In these techniques relatively indefinite and unstructured stimuli (like vague pictures, ink-blots, incomplete sentences, etc.) are provided to the subject and he is asked to structure them in any way he likes. In doing so, he unconsciously projects his own desires, hopes, fears, repressed wishes, etc, and thus not only reveals his inner or private world but also gives a proper clue to estimate his total personality.

The common Projective Techniques are:

The Rorschach Ink-blot Test

This technique has been developed by the Swiss psychologist, son of an art teacher Mr. Harmans Rorschach. Material of the test consists of 10 cards on which we have ink-blots. Five of them are in black and white and five are multi-coloured. These ink-blots are completely unstructured—the shapes of the blots do not have any specific meaning.

Administration of the test

(*i*) The cards are presented one at a time in a specified order. When the subject takes his seat, the examiner gives him the first card with necessary instructions. He is asked to say what he sees in it, what does it look like, etc.

(*ii*) The subject is allowed as much time as he wants for a given card and is permitted to give as many responses to it as he wishes. He is also allowed to turn the card around and look at it from any angle to find things in it.

(*iii*) Besides keeping a record of the responses of the subject concerning these ink-blots on different pieces of paper, the examiner notes the time taken for each response, position in which cards are being held, emotional expression and other incidental behaviour of the subject during the test period etc.

(*iv*) After all the cards have been presented, the second phase of inquiry follows. It is intended to seek clarification or addition to original responses.

Fig. 7.6: An inkblot similar to that used in Rorschach test

Scoring, analysis and interpretation of the test: For the purpose of scoring, the responses are given specific symbols which are entered in 4 columns.

These scoring categories are named as:

(*i*) Location, (*ii*) Contents, (*iii*) Originality and (*iv*) Determinants

Location (The first column): Location refers to the part of the blot with which the subject associates each response. The symbol W, D, d and s are used for scoring the location responses. The symbols stand for the things given ahead:

(W) for that response which shows that the subject is seeing the card as a whole

(D) indicates large details

(d) indicates small details

(s) indicates the subject's response to the white spaces within the main outlines

Contents (2nd column): This column concerns itself with the contents of the responses. It simply takes note of what is seen by the subject and not the manner of its perception. Below we are writing some of the symbols used for scoring the content of the responses:

Scoring symbol	*Content of the response*
H	Subject sees human forms.
A	Subject sees human forms.
A_d or H_d	Subject sees animal detail or human detail
N	Subject sees natural objects like rivers, mountains, green fields etc.
O	Subject sees inanimate objects like lamp shade, pot, etc.

In this way for details of the contents, the symbols are used and entered into the 2nd column.

Originality (3rd column): For each of 10 cards, certain responses are scored as popular, by symbol P, because of their common occurrence with some others in which something new is given, and thus they indicate some type of originality in them, are scored as original and depicted by the symbol O.

Determinants (4th column): This column takes note of the manner of perception, *i.e.* the particular characteristics which have helped the subject determine the blot of deciding his manner of perception. The main determinants are:

(*i*) the form (F) of the blot, (*ii*) its colour (C), (*iii*) movement (M) and (*iv*) shading (K).

For example, if the subject responds to a blot as butterfly, then, we can say that it is the "form" which led to this way of seeing it and then we score the response as F. On the other hand, if the subject sees something like fire, blood, etc., then the determinant is certainly the "colour" and we enter C in the fourth column.

The subject's responses on account of "shading" e.g., perception of rough or smooth surfaces, smoke, cloud, etc. are scored as K, whereas if the subject responds in terms of "movements"—movement of human beings (like boy running, dancing, etc.), animal being (like dog barking) or inanimate objects (water flowing, cloth moving, etc.); the symbols. M, F_m or m are entered. It is not the case always that the responses are evaluated in terms of C, F, K, M, etc. We can have the cases where we note them by mixed symbols as (CF), (FK) etc.

Interpretation: Now, in all the four columns the different symbols are counted. It gives an idea of the relative frequencies of different kinds of responses. The entry of the scores (in symbols) in different columns can be now made in the following way:

	III Columun: Location					II Columun: Contents						III Columun Originality		IV Columun: Determinants			
Symbols	W	D	d			H	A	Ad	Hd	N	O	P	O	F	K	M	Mixed Category
Frequency																	

The relative frequencies of the different symbols within the scoring categories and among the several categories help the interpreter to decide personality characteristics of the subject.

For example, if

(*i*) the number of Ws are greater than *d* or D, then the person is said to be mature, intelligent and is expected to possess the ability to synthesize.

(*ii*) More frequency on the side of the colour at the expense of human movement indicates an extrovert nature while the domination of M over colour an introvert.

(*iii*) Dominance of shading responses expresses anxiety, depressed attitudes and feeling of inferiority and

(*iv*) Relatively more emphasis on movement indicates richness of one's imaginative life.

It is not only the relative importance or occurrence of certain kinds of responses which help in interpretation, but also the various other factors like time factor, the behaviour of the subject at the time of reactions, etc. have their meanings.

Therefore, it is only through various kinds of relationships, observations, records and integration of results from various parts that a final global picture about a subject's personality can be drawn. The test demands a lot of training and skill in scoring an interpretation on the part of the examiner and therefore, the work should be considered as serious and should only be done by an experienced and trained Psychologist.

T.A.T. or Thematic Apperception Test

The test consisting of the perception of certain pictures in a thematic manner (revealing imaginative themes) is called T.A.T. or Thematic Apperception Test. This test was developed by Murray and Morgan.

Test Material and Administration: It consists of 30 pictures which portray human beings in a variety of actual life situations. 10 of these cards are meant for males, 10 for females and 10 for both. In this way the maximum number of pictures used with any subject is 20. The test is usually administered in two sessions, using 10 pictures in each session.

The pictures are presented one at a time. They are vague and indefinite. The subject is told clearly that this is a test of creative imagination and that there is no right and wrong response. He has to make up a story for each of the pictures presented to him within a fixed time period. He has to take care of the following aspects while knitting the story:

(*i*) What is going on in the picture?

(*ii*) What has led to this scene?

(*iii*) What would likely happen in such a situation?

In making up the stories the subject unconsciously projects so many characteristics of his personality. There is no time to think. Therefore, the stories express his own life—natural desires, likes and dislikes, ambitions, emotions, sentiments, etc. Its special value resides in its power to explore the underlying hidden drives, complexes and conflicts of the personality. An expert examiner can know much about the personality of his subject by carefully interpreting the given responses.

Scoring and interpretation : Originally, Murray analyzed the contents of the stories according to need and pressures (the need of the hero and the environmental forces to which he is exposed). Today this way of interpretation is not generally followed. Nowadays system of scoring and interpretation takes account of the things given ahead:

(*i*) Hero of the story. What type of personality he has?

(*ii*) Theme of the story. What is the nature of themes of plot used in making story?

(*iii*) The style of the story. Length of the story, language used, direct or indirect expression, forced or poor expression, organisation of the contents, originality, creativity, etc.

(*iv*) The content of the story. What interests, sentiments, attitudes they depict? In which manner (reality or fantasy) the behaviour has been expressed? What inner state of the mind, the story reveals?

(*v*) **Test situation as a whole.** The subject's reaction to be listed as a whole.

(*vi*) **Particular emphasis or omissions.** The omission, addition, distortion and attention to particular details.

(*vii*) **Subject's attitude towards authority and sex.**

(*viii*) **Outcome.** Conclusion of the story—happy, unhappy, comedy, etc.

Fig. 7.7: A picture used in TAT

As a whole, the recurring themes and features contribute more than single response towards interpretation. Moreover, the global view of one's personality should be based upon the responses of all the 20 pictures shown to the subject. There are so many chances of misinterpreting the contents of the story by an immature examiner. Therefore, the future of T.A.T. hangs on the possibility of perfecting the interpreter more than in perfecting the material. He should be given full opportunity for acquiring essential knowledge and training for this purpose.

C. A. T. (Children Apperception Test)

T.A.T. test works well with adults and adolescents but for children it is not suitable. For children between 3 to 10 years, C.A.T. was developed by Dr. Leopold Bellak.

Description of the test : It consists of 10 cards. The cards have pictures of animals instead of human characters since it was thought that children could identify themselves with animal figures more readily than with persons. These animals are shown in various life, situations. For both sexes, all the 10 cards are needed. The pictures are designed to evoke fantasies relating to the child's own experiences, reactions and feelings. Whatever story the child makes, he projects himself. It is a colour-free test but it demands some alterations according to the child's local conditions.

Administration of the test : All the 10 cards are presented one by one and the subject is asked to make up stories out of these. The child should be brought in confidence and he should take the story making a pleasant game to play with.

Interpretation. The interpretation of the stories is centred round the following eleven variables:

(*i*) **Hero.** The personality traits of the hero as revealed by the story.

(*ii*) **Theme of the story.** What particular theme has he selected for the story building?

(*iii*) **The end of the story.** Happy ending or unhappy, wishful, realistic or unrealistic.

(*iv*) **Attitude towards parental figures.** Hatred, respectful, devoted, grateful, dependent, aggressive, fearful, etc.

(*v*) **Family role.** With whom in the family the child identified himself.

(*vi*) **Other outside figures introduced.** Objects or external elements introduced in the story but not shown in the pictures.

(*vii*) **Omitted or ignored figures.** Which figures are omitted or ignored should be noted as they may depict the wish of the subject that the figures or objects were not there.

(*viii*) **Nature of the anxieties.** Harassment, loss of love, afraid of being left alone, etc. should also be noted.

(*ix*) **Punishment for crime.** The relationship between a crime committed in the story and severity of punishment given for it.

(*x*) **Defence and confidence.** The type of defences, fight, aggression, passivity, regression, etc. the child takes, nature of compliance or dependence, involvement in pleasure and achievement, sex desire, etc.

(*xi*) **Other supplementary knowledge.** The language, the overall structure of the stories, time taken for completing them and the reactions of the subject at the time of making the story, etc.

With all this knowledge an expert interpreter can take judgement on the various aspects of the child's personality.

Word Association Test

In this technique, there are a number of selected words. The subject is told that:

(*i*) the examiner will speak a series of words, one at a time.

(*ii*) after each word the subject is to reply as quickly as possible with the first word that comes to his mind, and

(*iii*) there is no right or wrong response.

The examiner then records the reply to each word spoken by him; the reaction time and any unusual speech or behaviour manifestations accompanying a given response. The contents of the responses along with the other recorded things give clues for evaluating the human personality and thus help a psychologist in his work.

Sentence-Completion Tests

These tests include a list of incomplete sentences, generally open at the end, which require completion by the sentence in one or more words. The subject is asked to go through the list and answer as quickly as possible (without giving a second thought to his answers). For example, we can have the following sentences:

I am worried over......

My hope is......

I feel proud when......

My hero is......

The sentence completion tests are regarded as superior to Word Association because the subject may respond with more than one words. Also, there it is possible to have a greater flexibility and variety of responses and more area of personality and experience may be tapped.

In addition to the projective techniques mentioned above, there are some others which may prove useful in so many situations. These are play technique, drawing and painting tests, etc. Both of these techniques are very useful in case of small children. In the former, the examiner observes the spontaneous behaviour of the children while playing or constructing something with the help of given material. In the latter, the natural free-hand drawing and paintings of the children are the matter of the study. Both of these techniques offer a good opportunity for the careful analysis of a child's personality.

To Sum Up

The task of actual measurement in the case of personality is not possible. We can only estimate and assess it by a variety of techniques like observation, situational tests, questionnaire, personality inventory, rating scale, interview and projective techniques.

In adopting observation technique, observer tries to observe the relevant activities concerning one or the other personality traits of the subject in real life situations. In the situational tests, situations are artificially created for the observation of one's behaviour related to the personality traits under testing. Questionnaires as a technique of personality assessment refers to a form consisting of some questions related to the personality characteristics requiring responses on the part of the subject for the assessment of his personality. Personality inventory resembles questionnaire in many aspects like administration, scoring, interpretations etc. However, it differs from questionnaires in the sense that it is specially designed for seeking information about the personality traits or behaviour of an individual rather than collecting all kinds of information like questionnaire. Rating scale refers to a technique of rating (telling where an individual stands in terms of some personality traits) on three, five or seven point scale for getting idea about some of the personality traits of an individual whom we don't know well from someone who knows him very well. Interview refers to a technique of getting information directly from the subject about his personality in face-to-face interactions.

Projective techniques are based on the phenomenon of projection. In these techniques relatively indefinites and unstructured stimuli like vague pictures, ink blots, incompletes sentences, etc. are provided to the subject and he is asked to structure them in any way he likes. In doing so, he unconsciously projects his own desires, hopes, fears and repressed wishes etc., and then not only reveal his inner or private world but gives a proper clue for the assessment of his total personality. The various techniques involved in this category may be named as Rorschach Ink Blot Test, Thematic Apperception Test (TAT), Children Apperception Test (CAT), Word Association Test and Sentence Completion Test etc.

ASSESSMENT QUESTIONS

Section I Essay Type Questions

1. What is personality? Discuss the wrong notions carried out in general with the concept of personality.
2. Describe the concept of personality by explaining its meaning and defining it in various ways.
3. What is personality? Discuss In detail the things associated with the nature and characteristics of the term personality.
4. Tell about different approaches for classifying the various theories of personality. Discuss any one theory of personality in detail.
5. What are types of personality? Discuss various approaches adopted for classifying personality into certain distinctive types.
6. What is the type approach towards personality? Throw light on the classification suggested by Hippocrates, Kretschmer and Sheldon
7. What are personality traits? Discuss some of their important features.
8. What is the trait approach towards the description of personality? Discuss about Allport's and Cattell's theories of personality based on the trait approach.
9. What is the Eysenck's approach towards personality termed as trait cum type approach? Discuss it in detail.
10. Discuss in detail Freud's psychoanalytic/ psychodynamic approach towards personality.
11. Throw light on the ((i) Adler's Individual Approach to Personality and (ii) Jung's Analytical Approach to Personality
12. Discuss about any one of the theories adopting Humanistic Approach
    (i) Self-Actualization Theory of Abraham Maslow, and
    (ii) Karl Roger's Self Theory
13. What are learning theories of personality? Discuss, any one of them in detail
14. Explain in detail Bandura and Walter's social learning theory of personality.
15. State different methods and techniques used for assessing one's personality and explain any one of them in detail.
16. Discuss the following methods and techniques used in the measurement of personality.
    (a) Rating scale (b) Personality Inventory
    (c) Interview (d) Observation
    (e) Questionnaire
17. What are the projective methods of assessing personality? Discuss any of these methods in detail.
18. Discuss about the Rorschach Ink Blot Test as a projective technique for the assessment of one's personality.
19. What is C.A.T.? How can it be used for the assessment of the personality of children?
20. What is Thematic Apperception Test (TAT)? How will you make its use for the assessment of one's personality?
21. Discuss about the use of projective techniques like Word Association Test, and Sentence Completion Test for the assessment of one's personality

Section II Short Answer Type Questions

1. Give a suitable definition of the term personality.
2. Provide any three characteristics or features of one's personality.
3. Name different approaches used to provide theories of personality
4. Name any six important theories helpful in understanding the structure of personality.
5. Name and explain the various types of personality given by Sheldon or Kretschmer/ Jung/Friedman's and Rosenman.
6. What do you understand by personality traits?
7. In how many main types has Allport divided the personality traits?
8. Mention the differences between Jung's introverts and extroverts on the basis of their personality traits.
9. How many factors or dimensions of personality have been mentioned in Cattell's personality inventory?
10. Write five characteristics each of the A type and B type personalities.
11. Write in brief about the concept of Id, Ego and Super ego mentioned in Freud's analytical theory of personality.

12. Write in brief about Adler's approach to personality or Carl Rogers' self-theory of personality.
13. Write in brief about Dollard and Miller's theory of personality or Bandura and Walter's social learning theory.
14. What is Rating Scale? How is it used for measuring personality?
15. Discuss interview as a technique of assessing personality.
16. Discuss the use of personality inventory.
17. What are projective techniques of assessing personality?
18. Describe briefly any projective test of personality.
19. What is word association test? How is it used for assessing personality?
20. Write the use of sentence completion test for assessing one's personality.

Section III: Objective Type Questions

1. What is not true about the characteristic features of the term personality?
   (a) Personality includes everything about a person.
   (b) Personality is not static; it is dynamic and ever in process of change and modification.
   (c) Every personality is the product of heredity and environment.
   (d) Personality may be well equated with one's character.
2. Which one of the following is not included in the category of projective technique or method of assessing personality?
   (a) Thematic Apperception Test
   (b) Word Association Test
   (c) Personal Interview
   (d) Dramatic or play way activities
3. Eysenck's theory of personality is claimed to adopt
   (a) Type approach
   (b) Type cum trait approach
   (c) Learning approach
   (d) Trait approach
4. Self actualization theory of personality has been propagated by
   (a) Carl Rogers (b) Abraham Maslow
   (c) Albert Bandura (d) R.B. Cattell
5. How many cards are used for assessing the personality of children in the Children Apperception Test (CAT)?
   (a) 8 (b) 10
   (c) 20 (d) 30

Answers

1 (d) 2 (c) 3 (b)
4 (b) 5 (b)

8

Attitudes–Concept, Formation and Measurement

Learning Objectives

After going through this chapter , you will be able to:

- Define the term attitude and throw light on its meaning and nature
- Mention about the characteristic features of attitudes
- State about the components of attitudes
- Throw light on the formation of attitudes with a necessary detail of how they get developed and maintained in the individuals
- Name and discuss the factors influencing the formation or development of attitudes
- Establish a link between attitudes and behaviour
- State what is attitudinal change
- Throw light on the ways of bringing change in the attitudes of people
- Discuss how attitudes can be measured

Introduction

The study of Psychology is mainly concerned with the study of the behaviour of the human beings. The Behaviour is composed of many important attributes. One of these important attributes is attitude. One's behaviour, therefore, to a great extent depends upon one's attitude towards the things—idea, person, or object—in one's environment. Their entire personality makeup and working is very much affected and influenced by the type of attitudes imbibed by them in their social behaviour. What are these attitudes; how are these formed and developed; how do they affect and influence one's behaviour; are these fixed or liable to be changed somehow; how are these measured? Let us, find answers for all these questions in this chapter.

What are attitudes?

As a concept and attributes of one's behaviour, the term attitude has been defined variously by authors and psychologists. Let us reproduce a few of these definitions for understanding the meaning of attitude.

Travers (1973:337): *An attitude is a readiness to respond in such a way that behaviour is given a certain direction.*

Mckeachie and Doyle (1966: 560): *We define an attitude as an organization of concepts, beliefs, habits and motives associated with a particular object.*

Sorenson (1977: 349): *An attitude is a particular feeling about something. It, therefore, involves a tendency to behave in a certain way in situations which involve that something, whether person, idea or object. It is partially rational and partially emotional and is acquired, not inherent, in an individual.*

Whittaker (1970: 591): *An attitude is a predisposition or readiness to respond in a pre-determined manner to relevant stimuli.*

According to the first definition, attitude is responsible for behaving in a particular and definite way. If one keeps a positive and favourable attitude towards an object, he will be attracted towards it; he will admire it and try to achieve it. On the other hand, if one has a negative or unfavourable attitude, one will try to avoid it and even feel hostile towards it. For example, a person having a positive attitude towards democracy will respond positively to democratic practices and institutions and negatively to authoritarian procedures. His behaviour will speak about his attitude.

The second definition takes into account all the concepts, beliefs, habits and motives associated with the object. The concepts and beliefs associated with an attitude are often referred to as the cognitive component of attitude, the habit as the action component, and the motives as the affective component. In this way, all that one thinks, feels and the way one reacts expresses one's attitude towards an object. For example, the formation of favourable or unfavourable attitude towards a political party is the result of his thinking and feeling towards that party and it would be exhibited overtly through some ace tendencies like heated discussion with associates or strangers, casting a vote in favour of the party candidate or doing active party-work during the election campaign.

The third definition explains why an individual behaves in a certain way when he is needed to respond to a particular object for which he has developed a positive or negative attitude. He has an almost definite set of feelings, likes or dislikes for that object and they partly stand on rational and partly on emotional footing. But in all the cases, they are acquired and learnt through varying experiences. One's attitude towards one's religion is an acquired tendency or disposition. He is not born with enthusiasm or apathy towards a particular religion. He has developed a sort of attachment or favourable feeling towards his religion due to his own experiences since his early childhood. His feeling is partly rational and partly emotional. He may be able to give very good reasons for advocating and appreciating his religion but his basis is partly beneath conscious reasoning.

The last definition accepts attitude as a predisposition or tendency to behave in a particular and definite way to a particular situation. One's attitude decides one's response to a particular stimulus. For example, in responding to all stimuli related with a particular political party one has a predisposition or tendency to act in a certain way if one has developed an attitude towards that party.

In this way, attitudes are, to a great extent, responsible for a particular behaviour of a person towards an object, idea or a person. But by this, it should not be concluded that one's behaviour is an absolute function of one's attitude. Behaviour by all means is a function of both characteristics of the behaving person and the situations in which he behaves. Hence a person may hold strong attitude and yet under certain circumstances, may behave in quite contradiction to those attitudes.

In this way, one's behaviour towards an object related to a particular attitude cannot be safely predicted through that attitude but it can be safely said that it makes the individual respond in a particular way to a particular stimulus.

Therefore, we may understand attitude *as a determining acquired tendency which prepares a person to behave in a certain way towards a specific object or a class of objects subject to the conditions prevailing in the environment.*

> **Attitude:** An acquired tendency propelling an individual to behave in a certain way towards a specific object or a class of objects, subject to the conditions prevailing in the environment.

Nature or Characteristics of Attitudes

We defined attitudes as predispositions or determining tendencies to respond in a specified manner. Now the question arises: should all the predispositions like habits, interests, traits and physiological motives be classified as attitudes? The answer is no. For a clear distinction, an attitude should meet the following six criteria:

Attitudes have a Subject-Object Relationship

Attitudes always involve the relation of an individual with specific objects, persons, groups, institutions and values or norms related to his environment.

Attitudes are learnt

Attitudes, as pointed out earlier, are learnt and acquired dispositions. They are not innate and inherent in an individual. Consequently, they may be differentiated from physiological motives. Hunger, for example, is an unlearnt physiological motive, while preference for a particular food, an acquired tendency, is classified as an attitude. Again, while almost any suitable member of the opposite sex may satisfy a man's sexual need, when the need becomes attached to a particular person, the attachment (acquired) becomes an attitude.

Attitudes are relatively Enduring States of Readiness

Attitudes represent the state of readiness to respond to a certain stimulus. Physiological motives also do the same. But in their case like hunger and sexual tension, the states of readiness disappear for a period when they are gratified. Attitudes, on the other hand, are relatively enduring states of readiness. Consequently, a wife may hold affective attraction to her husband even after the sexual tension has been resolved.

Attitudes have Motivational-affective Characteristics

Attitudes have definite motivational characteristics. Other dispositions like habit of writing with right hand do not have any motivational or affective quality; but attitudes towards one's family, nation, religion or other sacred and hallowed institutions have definite motivational affective characteristics.

Attitudes are as numerous and varied as the Stimuli to which they respond

We may have a number of attitudes depending upon the number of stimuli to which we respond. Attitude is an implicit response. Therefore, it stands to be varied with the number and variety of the responses which the individual makes. The change in environment and the situations further bring variety in the expression of these attitudes. Therefore, it is correct to say that attitudes are as numerous as the object towards which they are directed and the situations in which they are expressed.

Attitudes Range from Strongly Positive to Strongly Negative

Attitudes involve direction as well as magnitude. When a person shows some tendency to approach an object, he is said to have a positive attitude towards it but when he shows tendency to avoid the object, his attitude is described as negative. These positive or negative attitudes may involve intense feelings and vary from the large negative values to increasingly positive ones.

To Sum Up

Our attitudes are those predispositions or determining tendencies that propel us to respond to one or the other objects related to our environment in a specified manner. In order to make them distinguishable from other dispositions like interests, traits and motives, our attitudes are said to be carrying some specific features like (i) they have a subject-object relationship for reacting to the environmental objects in a specific way, (ii) they are learned or acquired, (iii) they represent relatively enduring state of our readiness to respond to a certain stimulus, (iii) they are attributed with definite motivational affective characteristics, (iv) they are as numerous and varied as the stimuli to which they respond, and (v) they range from strongly positive to strongly negative.

The Components of Attitudes

All what we think, feel and the way we react, expresses our attitude towards an object. Accordingly, our attitude towards an attitude objects (persons, things, ideas and issues etc.) is composed of its three components-cognitive, affective and conative or behavioural. Let us, know about them.

The Cognitive Component of Attitudes

Our thinking and thought processes associated with the attitude object represent the cognitive component of our attitude towards that particular attitude object. Our thought processes, in this connection, may include all sorts of cognition such as facts, knowledge and understanding, ideas and opinions, assumptions and beliefs regarding that object irrespective of their nature- true/untrue, simple/complex or favourable/unfavourable etc. Regarding the presence of cognitive components in one's attitude we may argue in the manner as below.

- In a number of cases, our attitudes might be based primarily upon a consideration of the positive and negative attributes about the attitude objects. For example, when we go for purchasing a washing machine for our domestic use, we pay a lot of attention to the factors associated with the appropriateness of the washing machine such as the popularity of the brand and model, effectiveness of washing provided by it, consumption of water and electricity, price and guarantee period, risk of its damage and repair requirements, availability of after sale services etc. In this example, we may also see that we already have or acquire on the spot (after our survey of the market) a certain type of attitude towards a particular model and brand of the washing machines on the basis of the cognizance taken about their positive and negative characteristics. In this way, what we call as the cognitive element of an attitude, it is concerned with the use of the available information or opportunity for the needed cognition on our part for forming an opinion, whether favourable or unfavourable, about the attitude object.
- Our thought processes and cognitive exercises play a quite important role as well as cast a quite sizable impact on the formation and functions of our attitudes concerning our social life. One's attitude towards smoking has a quite stronger cognitive component visible in his arguments highlighting the health hazard of smoking. Similarly, the presence of a quite influential cognitive component in the people's attitudes (favourable or un-favourable) about the legalization of abortion or same sex marriages may be witnessed quite properly in the cognitively drawn arguments in favour of their opinion.
- We know that the most of our attitudes-positive or negative are formed out of our beliefs (particular type of considerations) centred round the particular attitude objects. What we believe is the result of a quite thoughtful consideration or cognitive exercise performed on our part for the formation of such a belief. The involvement of the cognition in the formation of our beliefs provides a good testimony that attitudes are

derived from more elementary cognitions about the attitude object.

- The favourable or unfavourable opinion formed about an attitude object gets stored in our memory for its timely revival in the future. Memorization and recall, as we know, are the cognitive processes and their bonding in such a way with our attitudes, provides a valid testimony about the presence of cognitive component in our attitude. The negative attitude regarding alcohol consumption formed on account of experiencing or witnessing its negative and damaging consequences gets stored in one's memory for becoming a quite enduring component of one's negative attitude towards alcohol consumption.

The Affective Component of Attitude

While cognitive component of an attitude is associated with our thinking and cognitive processes, the affective component of this attitude is concerned with what one experiences in terms of his emotions and feelings attached to that very attitude object. What we term as an affective component of our expressed attitude towards an attitude object, is judged and known through the intensity of our feeling and emotions associated with that attitude object.

Regarding the presence of affective components in one's attitude we may argue in the manner as below.

- Where, cognitive part of one's attitude plays its role and functions in the background in a passive way, the affective component in term of its outlet in emotions and feelings remain vocal and expressive in nature. One can read the intensity of feelings and emotions while observing and judging the type of attitude shown by an individual towards a particular attitude object.
- Affective responses influence attitudes in a number of ways. A primary way in which feelings affect attitudes is due to affective reactions that are aroused in the individual after exposure to the attitude object. For instance, many people indicate that lizards/ spiders/ cockroaches make them feel scared. These negative affective responses are likely to produce a negative attitude towards lizards/ spiders/cockroaches. On the other hand, some special kind of fragrance, voices of birds, meeting with some special groups of people, celebrations of some occasions may arouse positive affective responses (i.e., pleasant feelings, attraction, happiness etc.) producing positive and favourable attitudes towards these attitude objects.
- The intensity of emotions and feeling associated with positive or negative attitudes towards the various stimuli (attitude objects) may vary a lot in the individuals depending on their own personality characteristics and experiences associated with the development and expression of these attitudes. Accordingly, where people may be found to have a strong favourable feelings and positive emotions about environmental protection, they may possess a causal or a quite weak emotional feelings or reactions for the freedom of speech or road safety.

The Behavioural Component of Attitudes

What we think and feel about an attitude object and imbibed by us as the components of that attitude is translated into action through the behavioural component of this attitude.

Regarding the presence of affective components in one's attitude we may argue in the manner as below

- Behavioural component of people's attitude towards an attitude object (person, place, thing, idea or issue) is visible to us through their actions and behaviours. The favourable and positive attitude about an attitude object supported through its cognitive and affective components is reflected through the positive actions and behaviour demonstrated by them in their social behaviour. The reverse is also true for the unfavourable and negative attitude possessed by the individuals towards an attitude object.
- The behavioural component of attitudes refers to the actions performed and behaviour demonstrated with respect to an attitude object. For instance, people who have favourable and positive attitude towards same sex marriage or gay rights may be found to demonstrate the likewise actions and behaviours in support of their attitude in the manner such as: (i) presenting their arguments before others in conversation, panel discussions, or through print and on line media, (ii) holding demonstrations and putting banners, (iii) highlighting and honoring of the same sex marriages or attempts made for providing equal rights to the gay community in one or the field of the social life. Similarly, in the individuals who have a negative attitude towards the

members of other races or religions, the presence of the behavioural component related to this attitude will be reflected through the actions and behaviours such as (i) demonstrating their negativity towards them through their comments, and opinions expressed about them in the conversation with their own community, (ii) showing disrespect, apathy, and unsociability while interacting with them, (iii) writing and expressing negative views about them in the print and online media, (iv) maintaining a quite sizable distance from them in the social interaction and social behaviour, and (v) indulging in insulting and aggressive activities against them.

To Sum Up

Our attitude towards an attitude objects (persons, things, ideas and issues etc.) is composed of its three components-cognitive, affective and conative or behavioural.

The cognitive component of our attitude towards an object is represented through our thinking and thought processes involving all sorts of cognition such as facts, knowledge and understanding, ideas and opinions, assumptions and beliefs regarding that object.

The affective component of our attitude towards an object is concerned with what we experience in terms of our emotions and feelings attached to that very attitude object. It is judged and known through the intensity of our feeling and emotions associated with that attitude object.

The behavioural component of our attitude towards an object refers to the actions performed and behaviour demonstrated by us in reacting and responding to that object. Actually, what we think and feel about an attitude object and imbibed by us as the components of that attitude is translated into action through the behavioural component of this attitude.

Formation of Attitudes - How do we learn or acquire attitudes?

Experience-direct or indirect is said to be the greatest teacher in making us learn one or the other things in our life. It equally applies for the learning and acquiring of attitudes on our part. The favourable or unfavourable attitudes developed for eating or not eating the particular type of food stuff, bearing or not bearing the particular type of dress material or using of the cosmetics etc. on the part of individuals are mostly the result of the generalization of their experiences occurring in their past. Not only the direct but the indirect experiences occurring in one's life, through the reading of literature, listening from others, watching from the electronic devices also after getting generalized, take the shape of the deeply rooted positive or negative attitudes towards the one or the other attitude objects. How does the process of imbibing one or the other attitudes through one or the other experiences goes on in one's life? It can be explained through the explanations provided by a number of learning theories developed by the psychologists for this purpose. Let us have a brief look at the role played by some of these learning theories in the task of attitude formation and development among the individuals.

- The theory of classical conditioning: A number of our interests, attitudes, habits, likings and dis-likings, fears and phobias are said to be the product of our conditioning occurred in our past through the available social experiences. For example, let us take into consideration the formation of the attitude towards the idols of the God. A child in his early childhood sees his mother to pay respect to the idols of the Gods by joining hands and performing other formalities of worshiping every time when she pays visit to a temple. While accompanying her mothers the child initially has little or no mentionable reaction in the form of regard and respect to the idols of the Gods. However, after witnessing repeated pairing of her mother's paying regard to the idols of Gods, he himself begin to respond in the same way showing respect and worshiping the idols of the Gods irrespective of the presence or absence of his mother.
- Theory of operant or instrumental conditioning: In accordance to the principles of operant conditioning, we learn though the consequences of our own actions. The positive or negative attitudes towards an attitude object, according to instrumental conditioning, thus are formed as well as maintained by the type of rewards or punishment we get in consequences of our responding or reacting to the object. A child who is appreciated and praised for taking part in a particular sports or cultural activity may be found to develop a quite favourable attitude towards that sports or cultural activity. On the other hand, the individuals who have a quite bad experience at the time of their first puff of the cigarette, or first day of their alcohol

intake might learn to remain away from the consumption of these stuffs and also develop an aversion or negative attitude towards smoking and alcohol consumption.

- Theory of social or observational learning: The most of our social learning including the formation and maintenance of our positive and negative attitudes, according to the social or observational learning theory propounded by Albert Bandura, takes place by observing and imitating the behaviours of others especially the elders and our role models. Our attitudes towards one or the other things good or bad in our life are the outcomes of what we observe in their behaviours in our real life or on silver screen. As consequences of such observational learning, individuals are found to have positive and favourable attitudes towards standing firm for the rights of women, and legalizing of abortion and negative attitudes towards drugs consumption, child abuse and rampant corruption in the society.

To Sum Up

Regarding the development or formation of our attitudes, it is to be remembered that these are not inherited, but are learned and acquired through our conscious efforts. We imbibe our attitudes-positive and negative through the generalization of experiences-indirect as well indirect occurring in our past. The act of such imbibing of our attitudes can be described through the explanations provided by a number of learning theories such as classical conditioning, operant conditioning, and social or observation learning.

The theory of classical conditioning in this concern tries to tell us the way we imbibe a number of positive and negative attitudes as a result of our conditioning occurred in our past through the available social experiences.

According to theory of operant or instrumental conditioning, our positive or negative attitudes towards an attitude object are formed as well as maintained by the type of rewards or punishment we get in consequences of our responding or reacting to the object.

According to the theory of social or observational learning, most of our social learning including the formation and maintenance of our positive and negative attitudes takes place by observing and imitating the behaviours of others especially the elders and our role models.

Factors Influencing the Formation or Development of Attitudes

Attitude is unquestionably an acquired disposition and therefore, conditioned by learning or acquisition of experiences. Heredity factor does not play any role in the formation or development of attitudes. Environmental force helps an individual to form and develop various attitudes. An attitude at any stage is essentially a product of the interaction of one's self with one's environment. Therefore, the factors influencing the formation and development of attitudes can be divided into two parts as follows:

A. Factors within the individual himself

B. Factors within the individual's environment

Factors within the individual

All individuals do not respond similarly to the same situations. The effect of environmental stimuli in acquiring some predispositions is very much conditioned by the growth and development pattern of an individual child. Let us try to emphasize these developmental factors.

1. **Physical Growth and Development:** In the development of attitude, physical growth and development plays a significant role. Poor physical health, low vitality and undeveloped somatic structure are responsible for poor emotional and social adjustment, and poor social adjustment inevitably exercises an important effect on the formation of attitudes in many different directions. A crippled and undersized girl of fifteen years is unlikely to form the same attitudes as those formed by another girl of fifteen who is tall, well proportioned and charming for her age. Even the colour of the skin, weight of the body or bio-chemical changes in the body tissues and fluids, for example, sex hormones, have a vital effect on the development of attitudes through their connection with social adjustment.
2. **Intellectual Development:** Development of attitudes is conditioned by the growth of intelligence. The components of intelligence like memory, understanding, thinking and reasoning play a significant part in attitude formation as they help gain perceptual experience. Due to his limited intellectual capacities, a young child is incapable of forming attitudes about remote or complex abstract things. His attitudes are always of a particular kind that are related to his own immediate problems and experiences. With the growth of intellectual capacities, an intelligent

adult is capable of having more abstract and generalized attitudes.

3. **Emotional Development:** Emotional development also affects the formation of attitudes. Emotions play a dominant role in overt or covert behaviour manifestation and behaviour is related to attitudes. As the child develops with age and growth, the capacity for varied emotional experiences and attitudes is gradually developed. Emotional maturity helps in social adjustment and seeking social approval. In turn it makes an individual to develop numerous attitudes through his direct or indirect experiences.
4. **Social Development:** Attitudes are rarely individual affairs. Social interaction and group processes are the key to attitude formation at any stage of human development. Children having poor social adjustment are more likely to have antisocial attitudes and are less likely to be influenced by groups while forming attitudes. Children with healthy social adjustment easily pick up social attitudes from their respective groups.
5. **Ethical and Moral Development:** Each individual develops certain ideals, values and concept of the self in which he takes pride. For enhancing his feelings of self-esteem, one tries to develop those attitudes that suit his values and ideals. A student who values historical events or objects will have a favourable attitude towards the subject of history. A man who thinks that God is one will not have unfavourable attitude towards the persons belonging to the religion other than his own.

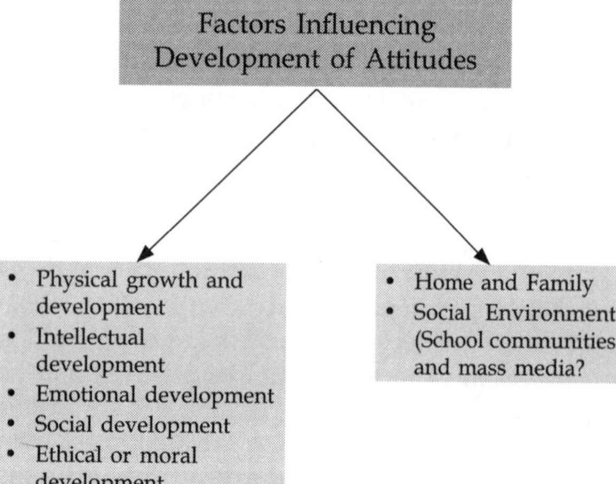

Fig. 8.1: Factors Influencing Development of Attitude

Factors within the individual's environment

Besides the individual variations shown by their various personality characteristics on account of the pattern of their growth and development, attitudes are largely borrowed from the groups within one's environment to which one owes one's stronger allegiance. It has now been firmly established that environmental forces, in the shape of the social groups, institutions and community, cast a strong influence on shaping the beliefs and attitudes of an individual. Let us try to understand a few important environmental factors.

1. **Home and family:** In attitude formation, home and family environment plays a leading role. A child by identifying himself with his parents and other members of the family picks up their attitudes. The family more or less defines for the child the expected roles which he must play in various situations and thus initiates the formation of specific attitudes. A healthy family environment and positive attitudes of the parents and other members of the family bring desirable impact on children in picking up desirable attitudes while negative parental attitudes, for example, of hostility and rejection, lead them to imbibe ascendant and aggressive attitudes. Similarly, many antisocial attitudes are said to be the product of the faulty upbringing and uncongenial environment at home and in the family.
2. **Social environment:** While the family and home environment plays its role in the formation of early attitude, contact with the people in neighbourhood, school, community and society and norms and traditions of the community, to which one belongs, cast strong influence in reshaping early attitudes and acquisitions of many more new attitudes. As a child grows older and has wider social contacts, he is influenced by many social institutions and groups. As a result, he tries to pick up the attitudes of those groups for which he has stronger allegiance or that suits his own nature and motives. In schools, factors like teachers and their behaviour, classmates or schoolmates and their behaviour, the teaching methods, curriculum, general tone and discipline of the institution all contribute towards attitude formation.

The religious groups, social clubs or constitution where one learns or earns has a definite set of emotional and intellectual environment as a result of which members of the group pick up characteristic attitudes of the group. In this way, social groups play a leading role in attitude formation. Besides this, mass media in the form of newspapers, radio and television, moving pictures, propaganda literature and advertisement also play a key role in shaping and reshaping attitudes. Individuals tend to identify themselves with the views expressed through these agencies. Thereby, heroes and heroines on screens and in radio programmes, attractive figures shown in the advertisements and slogans of a popular leader prove potent sources for the formation of attitudes.

> **To Sum Up**
>
> The factors influencing the formation and development of our attitudes can be divided into two distinctive categories, namely, Factors lying within our self, and Factors lying within our environment.
>
> In the former category, we may include one or the other developmental factors such as Physical growth and Development, Intellectual Development, Emotional Development, Social Development and Ethical and Moral Development.
>
> In the latter category, the environmental factors related to the prevailing environment in one's home and family, and the factors lying outside home and family in one's social environment such as: neighborhood, school, community and society, the religious groups, social club and institutions, mass media, and mores and traditions of the community to which one belongs, etc. are found to occupy their unique place.

Behaviour and Attitudes

By definition our attitudes, favourable or unfavourable, represent our predispositions to react or respond to certain stimuli (e.g. situations, persons or objects) in a fairly consistent manner which has been learnt by us through our direct or indirect experiences. In this sense, it becomes quite imperative that our responses or reactions to the stimuli observable in one or the other type of our conative behaviour are the product or outcome of our attitude towards those objects, persons or situations. Behaviour and attitude thus may be found to travel together to the extent of a popular claim that 'as the attitude so the behaviour'. The findings related to the observed behaviour in our day-to-day life may provide sufficient testimony to establish a direct relationship between one's behaviour and attitude (positive or negative) towards a thing, person or situation. Let us view the instances like below for this purpose :

- In case one has a negative attitude towards a religion or followers of that religion, it will colour his thinking, feeling and actions towards them in a negative way. He may be seen to be joking about their ways of worshipping, condemning their idols and worship places, eating, dressing, cultural tradition, etc. all associated with them and their religion.
- A person having a positive attitude towards a political party will be appreciating the functioning, ideology and governance of that party. He may be seen engaged in hot discussions with the persons found criticizing the ideology and working of the leaders of this party and at the time of election he may be seen to ask the people to vote for this party besides voting himself in its favour.
- The positive or negative attitude towards social evils and issues like untouchability, dowry system, child marriage, remarriages of widow, population control, environmental protection may be seen fully reflected accordingly in the behaviour of the persons. They think, feel and act in the ways and direction provided by their favourable or unfavourable attitudes towards these issues.
- Not only in social life, but also in the world of work and profession we may witness a close link between one's attitude (positive or negative) and his behaviour.

Attitudinal Changes

Attitudes are by no means fixed and unchanging predispositions. They can change. The task of attitudinal changes is related to their formation. As discussed earlier, attitudes are formed through experiences—direct or indirect. Consequently, they may be changed through the acquisition of new experiences as Sorenson remarks. "*Such factors as social, experiences, propaganda, education and personal experience with different attitudes do make for modifications and shifts in people's predispositions towards objects, persons, ideas and situations in their environment.*" (1977, p. 187)

What can be done for bringing change in attitudes?

In the light of what has been said above by Sorenson, the ways and means of modifying attitudes may be summarized as below:

1. **Providing proper education:** One of the popular ways for bringing desirable changes in one's attitude is to provide appropriate education

aimed to induce such changes in his behaviour. It can be done through both the curricular and co-curricular and formal and informal means. For example, the removal of all those things that causes communal disharmony, regionalism, disparity and inequality among the citizens and introduction of those texts or activities that helps acquire positive, desirable attitudes towards other's religion, caste, colour, region and language may prove a best educative attempt in this direction.

The organization of co-curricular activities may also provide a forceful medium in arranging needed education for the purpose of desired attitudinal changes in the educational institution and other places of formal and non-formal education for the varying groups and masses.

2. **Making use of propaganda machinery:** The most popular way utilized nowadays for bringing attitudinal change among the particular group of the people or masses is to make use of the propaganda mechanism. The government and non-government organizations all know well the power of propaganda machinery for influencing the thinking and feelings of the recipients by the persuasive message inherent in their propaganda material.

There has been considerable success in changing and moulding the attitudes of the people regarding many social, cultural, ethical, national and international issues of great importance such as family planning, energy saving, pollution, cleanliness and sanitation, road safety, pulse polio day, etc.

3. **Using fear-inducing mechanism:** Threats, punitive measures, strict disciplinary rules and legal laws are many times employed in bringing attitudinal changes among individuals. The laws against social evils like dowry, killing of the girl child in the womb of the mother, public smoking, urinating, child marriage, polygamy, sex abuses, trafficking, drug addiction trading, etc may provide sufficient ground in bringing attitudinal changes among people. However, the use of the mechanism of fear responses for bringing attitudinal changes should be made with a little caution and care as it may sometimes provide contrary results. Commenting on this aspect, Gross and Kinnison (2007:188) write:-

The practice does not work satisfactorily, simply on the ground that you can frighten people into attending to a message, comprehending it, yielding to it and retaining it, but not necessarily acting upon it. Indeed, fear may be so great that action is inhibited rather than facilitated. However, if the audience is told how to avoid undesirable consequences and believes that the preventive action is realistic and will be effective, then even high levels of fear in the message can produce changes in attitude and related behaviour.

In this way, success in using fear responses can only be reached in case the people take actual cognizance of the danger involved in sticking with an undesirable attitude, *i.e.* favourable attitude towards smoking or chewing *paan paraag* or sticking to alcoholism, drug addiction, etc. For the necessary awakening and desired awareness a high level of fear is then generated through a planned educative and propaganda machinery, posters, advertisements, radio talks, television programs, films and other audio-visual materials for bringing attitudinal changes. The demonstrations like blackening of all the lungs and inner parts on account of smoking, a skeleton type dead body left on account of using alcohol, etc may be cited as examples of high fear-generating mechanisms for bringing desired attitudinal changes among the masses.

However, in realizing its objective by arousing fear, it is not enough that a health risk has serious consequences: the individual must also feel personally at risk (*i.e.* vulnerable). If the person feels vulnerable to a threat-having cancer by chewing paan paraag, he will begin to show a high degree of concern for getting pushed into attitudinal and behavioural changes. Fear appeals are also most likely to be effective for individuals who are unfamiliar with a given health risk. For example, the information related to the danger involved in unprotected intercourse with strangers, has been responsible for bringing the desired attitudinal changes in the masses for using condoms.

4. **Use of modelling technique:** The mechanism of modelling as suggested by the social psychologists like Bandura (1977) and Rogers (1983) may provide greater help in shaping and moulding the attitudes of the people in a desirable way. The people are easily attracted to the model behaviour of their role models for bringing changes in their own attitudes and behaviour. They can learn and exercise favourable attitudes towards the good practices and unfavourable attitudes towards the evil practices by observing and imitating the behaviour of the heroes and heroines of the novels, television serials, filmy world and real social and political horizons of their own

social living. Sometimes a group of people, a community, institution or organization, district, region or country may work as a role model for infusing lights in the heart of other people and groups to bring desired changes in their attitudes and behaviour. They can give up their orthodox-ridden primitive attitudes for giving space to progressive and changed outlooks and attitudes.

Attitudinal Changes -Ways and Means

- Providing proper education
- Making use of the propaganda machinery
- Using fear-inducing mechanism
- Using modelling technique
- Direct personal experience
- Using cognitive dissonance mechanism
- Bringing desired changes in beliefs and values

5. **Direct personal experiences:** The most enduring changes in the behaviour of the people are introduced through their own direct personal experiences. When person at the time of intense communal riots, gets his survival through the active help and generosity of the people belonging to the other community, his personal experience automatically directs him to bring the desired change in the previously held attitude towards the members of that community or religion. The person who has invited diabetes or heart problems for him on account of his negative attitude towards healthy practice of eating and exercising may be spontaneously dragged to have the desired changes in his attitude after experiencing the effects of healthy diet and regular exercises by himself. Similarly, the personal experiences related to other aspects and events in one's life may help one to bring sufficient changes in the previously held attitude—social, emotional and professional by testing and comparing the outcomes of the old and changed attitudes.
6. **Making use of the cognitive dissonance mechanism:** In view of the mechanism or phenomenon of cognitive dissonance, there may exist simultaneously two different cognitions of a particular thing, event or phenomena in the minds of an individual that are psychologically inconsistent or contradictory e.g. the cognition 'I smoke' is psychologically inconsistent with the cognition 'smoking is dangerous to health'. In such a situation, it is but natural for the individual to experience a state of 'psychological discomfort or tension' named as the state of dissonance. One can get rid of one's state of dissonance if he brings desired change in his attitude and behaviour.

In the present case, one has to replace a positive attitude towards smoking with a negative attitude. For bringing such attitudinal change, one has to seek ways and means to reduce dissonance by resorting to the most effective (and certainly the healthiest) way, *i.e.* stop smoking. However, instead of it many people may work on the other cognition for example, they might rationalize their smoking behaviour or favourable attitude towards smoking by:

- Belittling the evidence about smoking and cancer (e.g. "the human data are only correlational")
- Associating with other smokers (e.g. "if so-and-so smokes, then it can't be very dangerous)
- Smoking low-tar cigarettes
- Convincing themselves that smoking is an important and highly pleasurable activity

However, as may be seen that all such above alternatives to stop smoking are nothing but to rationalize one's present attitude towards smoking. In such a situation, attempts should be made to make one's cognition associated with his rational thinking instead of rationalizing his otherwise wrong thinking or attitude towards smoking.

7. **Bringing desired changes in beliefs and values:** An attitude can be thought of as a blend or integration of beliefs and values. The negative or erroneous attitudes held by an individual thus may offer the results of the erroneous beliefs and negative values held by the person. Therefore, in case we want to bring desirable changes in the attitudes of a person, we have to rectify the erroneous beliefs and replace the negative values with the positive values. The person who has a negative or undesirable attitude towards girl child, widow, lower caste people and other religions on account of his sheer ignorance, false beliefs and superstitions, may then be properly informed and guided for doing away with his false beliefs so that he may be helped in replacing his undesirable attitudes with the desirable ones. Similarly, a person who values a thing, person or situation in an unfavourable, unpleasant or negative way may be seen to have an unfavourable or negative attitude towards it. Therefore, alterations in his value system is needed for bringing required

changes in the attitudes associated with that particular value system. This is why we must have a proper value orientation program for individuals who need to have desirable changes in the attitudes held at present on their part.

Psychometric Assessment of Attitudes

We have defined attitudes as implicit responses or predispositions to objects, persons, ideas, values or situations in the social surroundings. Thereby they are essentially covert tendencies. If we want to have their psychometric assessment, there must be some means to draw them out or make them manifested in the form of overt behaviours. This can be done in the following two ways:

1. **Direct Method.** Measuring the verbal report of the attitude
2. **Indirect Method.** Interpretation of the attitude from the unsaturated or indirect responses

Let us discuss these methods.

Direct Method for Measurement of Attitude

In this method, the opinion of an individual about a particular subject in the form of a verbal report is collected, and based on this his attitude towards the subject is estimated. Generally, the following devices are used for the purpose:

(*i*) Asking the individual directly how he feels about a subject (questioning and interview techniques)

(*ii*) Asking to mark those statements from a list with which he is in agreement. (Check list, etc.)

(*iii*) To indicate his degree of agreement or disagreement with a series of statements dealing with the same subject (Attitude scales)

The last-mentioned devices known as attitude scales are most widely used for the measurement of attitudes. Generally, the following two types of scales are popular.

Thurstone's attitude scales

These are also known as equal-appearing intervals scales. In constructing such scales, a large number of statements representing a variety of opinions on a subject are collected. These statements are then given to a number of judges who are asked to sort the statements in two categories—say from "very favourable" to "very unfavourable". Whenever the judges disagree significantly over an item, it is rejected. The finished scale then consists of the remaining statements or items that represent clearly defined opinions on the subject. Each of these final statements is then assigned a scale value based on the median scale position given by the judges. If half the judges, for example, had assigned a particular statement to position 4 or lower and half had assigned it to position 5 or higher, the scale value assigned to the statement could be 4.5. Some of the statements from the Thurston's scale for measuring attitude towards the church with the scale value of each statement is shown below:

Item	Scale value
I believe the church is the greatest institution in America today	0.2
I believe church membership is almost essential to living life at its best	1.5
I believe in what the church teaches, but with mental reservations	4.5
I believe in religion but I seldom go to church	5.4
I do not receive any benefit from attending church service but I think it helps some people	5.7
I think the church is a parasite on society	1.0

In administering the scale, individuals are asked to check all the statements with which they agree. For each individual, then a scale position is computed as the average of the scale values of all the items he has checked.

Likert attitude scale

This scale is more popular than Thurstone's scale. It employs a larger number of items than Thurston's scale and discards the methods of scaling by several judges. In constructing such a scale, a number of statements or items concerning a particular subject are collected. These items, each of which clearly represents either a favourable or an unfavourable attitude, are then tested for internal consistency, *i.e.* to see all the statements or items are actually concerned with the same subject. The tested items constitute attitude scale. The individual is asked to indicate the degree of his agreement or disagreement with each item on a five-point scale. Thus, for assessing attitude towards internationalism, the sample items such as follows are presented:

Encircle one of the symbols preceding each of the following statements. 'A' stands for "Agree", S.A. stands for "Strongly Agree", D for "Disagree", S.D. for "Strongly Disagree" and I for "Undecided."

Response	Items
S.A., A, I, D, S.D.	We should be willing to fight for our country whether it is in the right or in the wrong.
S.A., A, I, D, S.D.	Our country should never declare war again under any circumstances.

For scoring the items, a value of 5 may be given to the responses indicating strong agreement, 4 for simple agreement, 3 for undecided, 2 for simple disagreement and 1 for strong disagreement. Thus, each individual can be assigned a single quantitative score for the measurement of his attitude.

Indirect Method for Measurement of Attitudes

The process of inferring attitude directly from the verbal report or expressed opinion has many limitations. One may conceal one's real attitudes and may not really know what one feels and be unable to know one's attitude about a situation in the abstract. Even overt behaviour is not always a true indication of one's attitude. When politicians cuddle babies, their behaviour may not be a true expression of their attitude towards children.

To avoid this problem, it has been tried to make use of the measurement methods that are indirect or disguised in nature. In these methods, the subjects are given opportunities to structure their own responses without letting them know the real purpose of the task. The projective techniques used for the assessment of personality are the good examples of these indirect methods. These techniques have been discussed in detail in the chapter elaborating on the measurement of personality. The essence of these techniques is that the subject expresses his covert tendencies while responding to unstructured stimuli. An intelligent interpretation of his responses may show his attitude towards a particular object or issue.

Now the question arises as to which of these two techniques—direct or indirect—should be used for measuring attitudes. Both of these are very good instruments and have their own values and limitations. Perhaps in our opinion, the best method or the procedure adopted for the measurement of attitudes is the one that combines the verbal report and the interpretative techniques. It will surely help us get an extensive and intensive measurement of attitudes covering their covert tendency and overt manifestation.

To Sum Up

For the measurement of people's attitude towards an attitude object, two types of measures classified as direct or indirect methods may be employed.

In making use of the Direct method for the measurement of attitudes, opinions of the individuals about a particular subject in the form of a verbal report are collected and then on their basis, their attitude towards the subject is estimated. The devices we make use for this purpose may be named as questionnaires and interview techniques, check lists and rating scales, and constructed attitude scales such as Thurstone attitude scale and Likert attitude scale.

In the use of the Indirect method for the measurement of attitudes, attempts are made to infer attitudes of the people with the help of projective techniques such as Rorschach Ink Blot Test, Thematic Apperception Test (TAT), Children Apperception Test (CAT), Word Association Tests, Sentence Completion Tests, Play Way Techniques etc.

ASSESSMENT QUESTIONS

Section I: Essay Type Questions

1. What are attitudes? Throw light on their nature and characteristics.
2. Name and discuss all the three components of one's attitude.
3. Throw light on the development or formation of attitudes among individuals.
4. Discuss various factors affecting the development of attitudes among individuals.
5. Discuss the relationship between one's attitudes and his behaviour.
6. "Attitudes, although quite stable, are liable to change." Comment on the statement and throw light on the ways and means of bringing changes in one's attitudes.
7. What do you mean by the term attitudinal change? Discuss the measures for introducing attitudinal changes in one's behaviour.
8. How can the task of psychometric assessment or measurement of attitudes be carried out? Discuss the type of direct and indirect measures involved in this regard.

Section II: Short Answer Type Questions

1. Provide a suitable definition of the term attitude.
2. Name any two features or characteristics of attitudes.
3. Name the internal factors (lying in the environment) influencing the formation or development of attitudes.
4. Name the external factors (lying in the environment) influencing the formation or development of attitudes.
5. How does home and family environment influence the formation of attitudes?
6. How do beliefs held by the individual influence formation of his attitudes?
7. Give three examples to explain how one's attitudes influence his behaviour.
8. Define the term attitudinal change.
9. Tell, how does propaganda help in the change of attitude?
10. Give two examples of the role of fear-inducing mechanism in attitudinal change.
11. Mention about the role of belief and values in attitudinal change.
12. Tell about the use of modelling technique in attitudinal change.
13. What is cognitive dissonance? Give one example for illustrating its role in attitudinal change.
14. Tell in brief about one of the following:
    (i) Direct method of attitude measurement
    (ii) Indirect method of attitude measurement
    (iii) Thurstone's attitude scale
    (iv) Likert's attitude scale

Section III: Objective Type Questions

1. What is not true about the nature and characteristics of attitudes?
   (a) Attitudes represent an innate as well as acquired phenomenon
   (b) Attitudes are relatively enduring states of readiness
   (c) Attitudes have motivational-affective characteristics
   (d) Attitudes range from strongly positive to strongly negative
2. Which one of the following does not fall in the category of external factors affecting one's attitudes?
   (a) Family and home
   (b) Social development
   (c) Neighbourhood
   (d) Mass media
3. Which one of the following does not contribute to introducing attitudinal change among children?
   (a) Educating and warning their parents
   (b) Making use of propaganda machinery
   (c) Using modelling technique
   (d) Using cognitive dissonance mechanism

Answers

1 (a) 2 (b) 3 (a)

9

Stereotyping, Prejudices and Discrimination

Learning Objectives

After going through this chapter, you will be able to:

- Know about the meaning and concept of stereotyping
- Tell about the types or forms of stereotyping behaviour
- Elucidate the relationship of stereotyping with prejudices and discrimination
- Define the term prejudices
- Know about the meaning and nature of prejudices
- Discuss about the sources of prejudices
- Throw light on the evil impact of prejudices on the interpersonal relationships
- State about the meaning and nature of discrimination
- Discuss about the consequences or impacts of discrimination
- Throw light on the various techniques used for countering the ill effects of stereotyping, prejudices and discrimination

Introduction

We live in a diverse society, where we may find that people differ from each other in so many aspects-physical, mental, emotional, social and behavioural in a variety of ways. For the understanding of such diversity among the individuals and their groups we try to classify and categorize them in some social classes and categories on certain social differentiations such as religion, caste, colour, creed, gender, socio-economic status, marital position, profession and means of livelihood, language spoken, locality, and nationality etc. With our experiences-direct and indirect about the individuals belonging to these social groups we have developed certain types of specific attitudes towards these social groups or categories reflected usually through some particular type of thinking, feeling and acting behaviours on our part known by the terms stereotyping, prejudices and discriminations. In the pages to follow, here, we would be focusing on knowing the essentials about the nature and application of these important concepts.

Stereotyping

Meaning and Concept

As its etymological derivation, the term stereotype has been derived from a combination of two Greek words-"stereos" (meaning firm or solid) and "typos" (meaning impression or opinion). In its literal sense, thus, the term stereotype stands for a type of plate that works as a mould. We can prepare or manufacture many articles of an identical nature with the help of a mould. In a similar way persons, places and objects of a particular category may appear identical to us by getting colour through stereotypes. The stereotypes in this way, may be termed as a sort of some ideational or emotional patterns or moulds set up in our mind that may give birth to our over-generalized beliefs and the concepts about the persons, places and objects etc. such as: Hilly people are hard working; The bald are rich and prosperous; Women can't keep a secret; Afro-Americans are violence-prone; The people wearing spectacles are studious; Green fruits are always sour and red are sweet.

As a matter of definition, the terms stereotype and stereotyping have been variedly defined in the available dictionaries and writings of scholars. Let us try to have a glimpse of these definitions.

1. **The American Heritage New Dictionary of Cultural Literacy (2005):** It defines the term stereotype in the following two ways:
   (*i*) A too-simple and therefore distorted image of a group, such as "Football players are stupid" or "The English are cold and unfriendly people."

(ii) A generalization usually exaggerated or oversimplified and often offensive, that is used to describe or distinguish a group.

2. **Webster's Seventh New Collegiate Dictionary (1970: 860):** Stereotype is "a standardized mental picture held in common by members of a group and representing an over simplified opinion, affective attitude or uncritical judgement as of a person, a race, an issue, or an event"
3. **Judd, C.M. and Park, B. (1993):** The thoughts and beliefs maintained about the people or issues. These thoughts or beliefs may or may not accurately reflect reality.
4. **Sears et al. (1991):** Stereotypes are beliefs about the typical characteristics of group members.
5. **Kimble Young (1953):** Stereotype is best defined as a false classificatory concept to which as a rule, strong emotional feeling, tone of like or dislike, approval or disapproval is attached.
6. **Secord and Backman (1964):** Stereotyping is an exaggerated form of typification that has three characteristics, namely,
   (i) people identify a category of person according to certain attributes,
   (ii) people agree in attributing sets of traits or characteristics to the category of persons, and
   (iii) people attribute the characteristics to any person belonging to that category.
7. **Fisher (1982):** Stereotypes involve gross generalizations that are acquired through misinformation and that ignore individual differences and are resistant to change even in the light of new evidences
8. **Aronson, et al (2014):** Stereotypes can be defined as a generalization about a group of people, in which certain traits are assigned to virtually all members of the group, regardless of actual variation among the members.

Stereotyping: Our thoughts and beliefs in the form of over simplified generalizations about a group of people, objects or issues.

The definitions given above may help us in drawing following conclusions about the meaning and nature of the term stereotyping:

- Stereotyping reflects the oversimplified attitudes and feelings of the people in general towards specific types of individuals, groups and communities.
- It is the result of incomplete or distorted information accepted as fact without questions or putting into verification and critical judgement.
- The stereotypes are best known for influencing our perception and social judgements we have about the other group, they influence how much we like or dislike a person or a given group.
- Most of the time stereotypes are found to make us feel superior in some way to the person or group stereotyped.
- Stereotyping is responsible for breeding an antagonistic attitude, ill feelings and prejudices against the persons who are subjected to stereotyping.
- It is not necessary for the stereotypes or stereotyping to be always negative in its nature resulting into negative consequences. Sometimes, we may have positive over-generalizations or stereotypes like: Hilly people are hard working; Asians are good students and employees; Black men are good at basketball, etc.
- Under the negative influence of stereotyping, the victims (individuals or groups) may be found to suffer from *(i)* the prejudices, isolation, discrimination, or marginalization on a group/ community level and *(ii)* anxiety of failure, inferiority complex and lack of confidence in terms of their adjustment and progress at the personal level.
- Stereotypes ignore the uniqueness of individuals by painting all members of a social category or group with the same brush. However, as we know, each individual is unique, and, therefore, it should not be assumed that the actual traits, characteristics or behaviours of the person being stereotyped will concur with those that are suggested by the stereotype (Luthans, 2010).
- It is true that most of the time stereotyping can lead to inaccurate perceptions and inappropriate behaviour towards people. But it does not mean, however, that all stereotypes are incorrect. Many of them may be filled up with a lot of truthfulness/possess a kernel of truth (Whitley & Kite, 2006).
- Stereotypes are also difficult to contradict once they are formed, mainly because as stereotypes are used, they determine the type of information that is remembered by us. And information that is not consistent with the stereotype is not remembered. (Taylor, 1984)

Types or Forms of Stereotyping behaviour

A stereotype is simply a widely held belief that an individual is a member of a certain group based on its characteristics. Due to the process of overgeneralization within social perception, stereotyping leads to a great deal of inaccuracy in social perception. Sex, race, age, sexual orientation, religion and physical ability are various categories which exist in stereotyping.

Let us discuss common types of stereotypes existing in our society

A. *Sexual or gender stereotypes*

- Girls like to remain dependent, protected, and looked after than the boys.
- Parents hold an opinion that their daughters need nurturing of passivity and dependency and their sons to be aggressive and independent. (Therefore, they punish independence in daughters and passivity in sons.)
- Females are more conforming and more concerned about displaying socially desirable behaviour than males are.
- "Boys don't cry" and "Girls don't fight".
- Girls and females are most fit for doing household job and the boys and males for the outdoor work.
- Girls and females are talkative and are not fit for serious and responsible assignments.
- Girls are not supposed to study mathematics, sciences, computer, commerce and technical subjects. They are suitable for the study of humanity and languages.
- In work-outputs girls and females are quite inferior and often lag behind their male counterparts.
- Girls are not supposed to take part in games and play activities involving adventure, muscle power and stamina like wrestling, boxing-shooting, paragliding and trooping, rock climbing, weight-lifting etc.
- Girls always surpass boys in the demonstration of communication and social skills, musical and dancing abilities, aesthetic sense and artistic abilities.

B. *Social class or racial stereotypes*

- People belonging to lower castes possess inferior cognitive, social and emotional intelligence than those belonging to higher castes.
- People belonging to low socio-class and communities and Blacks (in relation to western countries) are better in athletes, games particularly in boxing, wrestling and the activities requiring toughness, physical stamina and adventurism.
- People from urban backgrounds and urban culture are superior in intelligence but lag behind rural children in the performances in sports.
- Children belonging to lower castes, low socio class, rural backgrounds and backward areas lag behind in their studies, create problems in class and school, and have more chances of becoming delinquents.

C. *Poverty related Stereotypes*

- People belonging to poor families have quite a low level of aspiration and achievement motivation.
- The poverty-ridden individuals easily fall victim to the problematic and delinquent behaviour.
- The poverty-ridden people usually suffer from maladjustment, as well as problems related to poor physical and mental health.
- The poverty-ridden children are poor in their school attendance, find little time and face difficulties in doing their home assignments and project activities.

Relationship of Stereotypes with Prejudices and Discrimination

Stereotypes, although having their separate identity and existence as the firm beliefs and attitudes of a person, are firmly attached with the other concepts like prejudices and discrimination. Stereotypes are regarded as the most cognitive component and often occur without conscious awareness, whereas prejudice is the affective component of stereotyping and discrimination is the behavioural component of prejudicial reactions. Thus, in this tripartite view of intergroup attitudes:

(*i*) Stereotypes reflect expectations and beliefs about the characteristics of members of groups perceived as different from one's own, (cognitive behaviour exhibited by the person having stereotype)

(*ii*) Prejudice represents the emotional response exhibited by the person possessing the stereotype (affected behaviour exhibited by the person having stereotype)

(*iii*) Discrimination or marginalization refers to actions (conative behaviour exhibited by the person having stereotype)

In this way, a stereotype (unfounded beliefs, expectations, opinions or attitude maintained about members of groups perceived as different from one's own) is first responsible for generating the prejudiced feelings and emotions against the group members and then acting in a prejudiced way showing a lot of discrimination and marginalization. As a result,

- A teacher who is under the influence of the gender stereotype, "girls are talkative, and non-serious" and the related prejudiced feelings will always be found automatically appointing boys as "group leader" and girls as "secretary" for the project or association activities.
- The members of a selection committee under the influence of gender, religion, or caste stereotyping may be found to have prejudiced feelings and discriminatory attitudes in selecting the candidates for the various posts by setting aside the merit and suitability criterion for the purpose.

To Sum Up

Our stereotyping formed about a group of people, community, race, certain kinds of objects and issues represent our rigid attitude, firm belief and thinking towards them. Most of the time, these prove as a false representative of the reality on account of our oversimplified and misjudged interpretation reached about the stereotyping objects.

In general, a number of stereotypes may be seen to be prevalent in almost all the societies and communities all over the globe. These stereotypes may be broadly classified as sexual or gender stereotypes, social class or racial stereotypes, and poverty-related stereotypes, etc.

Regarding the relationship of stereotypes existing with the prejudices and discrimination it may be properly witnessed that where our stereotypes are considered the cognitive component of our attitudes towards the social groups or issues, prejudices and discrimination represent their affective and behavioural component respectively. Consequently, a stereotype is first responsible for generating the prejudiced feelings and emotions against the group members and then acting in a prejudiced way showing a lot of discrimination towards them.

Prejudices

In our social perception and behavioural sequence of stereotyping, prejudice and discrimination, a prejudice evolves from or follows a stereotype. In their mutual relationship and dependence on each other where, stereotypes as a cognitive component are associated with our thinking about the object or people, and prejudices as the affective component with our feelings and emotions towards these objects or people, discriminations then as the behavioural component find their expressions in the prejudicial reactions of the stereotypes stored in our minds. Our thinking makes us feel and behave with a person and react to a social situation in a particular way. The stereotype we have formed about the social group or class to which a person belongs, works as a base or root for germinating and perpetuating prejudice against him or her. Negative stereotyping thus may be found to lead us in negatively prejudiced feelings. In this way, based on our stereotypes if we start forming hostile or negative opinions of others or when we begin to dislike someone belonging to out-group for no good reason before even getting to know him, it is termed as prejudice. Let us know more about the meaning, nature, and impact of prejudices in our social life.

Meaning and Nature of Prejudices

Etymologically, the word *prejudice* has been derived from the Latin word *praejudicum* meaning before judgement or pre-judgement in the English language (Taylor,1984). In this sense, the term prejudice may mean arriving at a judgement without hearing or going through the proceeding of a case, making own opinion without listening and attending others, reaching at conclusion without getting acquainted with the facts, etc. In or day to day life, we can illustrate the term prejudice along with its situational meanings through the following instances.

(i) One may be prejudiced against beautiful women for arriving at a pre-judgement that they do not prove a good marital partner.
(ii) On the basis of prejudice, one may form an opinion that the girls performing on the stage as actresses or singers are loose characters.
(iii) One as an individual or a group of people belonging to the upper caste may hold prejudices against people belonging to scheduled castes by considering them untouchable, unintelligent or unbelievable.
(iv) Urban people may be prejudiced against the village people by arguing that they are uncivilized, uncultured and unintelligent.
(v) One may show prejudice in declaring that the girls belonging to rural and tribal areas are good in playing and athletic activities.

In this way, people may get prejudiced in one way or the other favourably or unfavourably by having a pre-established judgement or opinion about the preferences for educated v/s uneducated, working women v/s housewives, upper caste v/s lower castes, members of one's village and province v/s others, black colour v/s fair colour, fatty v/s thin body structure, etc. However, once, they get prejudiced in favour or against an object, individual or a group, their whole behaviour pattern gets moulded and colour in the spirit of the set prejudices. They now think, feel and act in the way guided and directed through their established prejudices.

To know more about the meaning, nature and characteristics of prejudices, let us now consider the views expressed by some well- known authors and social psychologists in this concern.

1. **Krech and Crutchfield (1948):** Prejudice is an unfavourable attitude toward an object which tends to be highly stereotyped, emotionally charged and not easily changed by contrary information.
2. **Asch, S.C. (1952):** Prejudice is a negative attitude toward a socially defined group and toward any person perceived to be a member of that group.
3. **Allport (1954):** A prejudice is an antipathy based on faulty and inflexible generalization directed towards a group as a whole or towards an individual because he is a member of that group. It may be felt or expressed.
4. **Secord and Backman (1964):** Prejudice is an attitude that predisposes a person to think, perceive, feel and act in favourable or unfavourable ways towards a group or its individual members.
5. **Aronson, et al. (2014):** Prejudice is defined as a hostile or negative attitude towards people in a distinguishable group, based solely on their membership in that group.

In case we have proper analysis of all the above definitions of the term prejudice, it may lead us to conclude about its meaning, nature and characteristics in the following ways.

- Prejudices are based on as well as affected by a lot of stereotypes tendencies and rigidity inherent in the people's behaviours.
- A prejudice represents a special type of biased attitude formed about the objects, individuals or groups. Its cognitive component is the stereotype; the affective component is a feeling of liking or disliking; the behavioural component is the various types of discriminatory actions.
- Prejudices tend to arouse intensive emotional current in the individual compelling or drifting him along the current of the prejudiced thinking.
- Prejudices are strong enough to control and direct the interaction and social behaviour of people with other individuals or groups without giving them any time or opportunity for thinking and making decisions. Here the mode of behaving or reacting to a situation is already set in the mind of the individuals on the basis of a biased attitude held against the person or the group to which they belong.
- The prejudiced behaviour is not based upon the reactions or responses at the present situation but is specifically dependent upon the pre-conceived notions and attitude formed towards the persons or the groups to which they belong. For example, if the boss of a company is prejudiced against a particular caste or religion he will try to behave quite negatively towards every employee of that caste or religion irrespective of their good performance and talents.
- The prejudices may involve both positive and negative attitudes and, in this way prejudiced behaviour may provide undue favour to somebody along with harming others in the same situation. The teachers or administrators who have a strong prejudice in favour and against the people of their own caste and others may show such favouritism while dealing with their students or subordinates.
- Prejudices with the involvement of a totally biased and partisan attitude may prove a potent cause for the deterioration and impairment in the interpersonal relationships. It may give birth to the feelings of segregation, casteism, regionalism, communalism, and class conflicts. The negatively affected individuals may be found to be drifting towards aggressiveness, anti-social behaviour, delinquency and crimes.
- Prejudices are not inborn or inherited. These represent the learned or acquired behaviour resulted through one's interaction with one's social environment.

> **Prejudices:** Our prejudgement, opinion and attitudes formed on false premises persuading and compelling us to think, feel and act with the individuals and social groups in a quite biased or partial way.

Taking clue from the above-mentioned characteristics of prejudices we may be tempted to define the term prejudices as following.

The term prejudices stand for all our prejudgement, opinion and attitudes formed on the false premises persuading and compelling us to think, feel and act with the individuals and social groups in a quite biased or partial ways.

Sources of Prejudices

Prejudices are learned and acquired behaviour patterns. The factors and sources responsible for their birth in the individuals may be classified and discussed as below.

1. **The process of socialization:** The individuals at the time of their birth are free from any type of prejudices and ill feeling towards others. It goes well for a quite long time to them in their early childhood. However, as they come into contact with the stereotypes and prejudices prevalent in their social surroundings, their mind gets vitiated and influenced by one way or the other. They may thus catch up the infection of behaving in a biased manner from the prejudices prevalent in the present socio-cultural environment. The parents, family members, neighborhood, peer groups, school, and the impact of other societal factors may thus teach the growing individuals lessons of factionalism, casteism, regionalism, linguistic separation, and so many other things related to the learned behaviour of so many prejudices. Their own experiences related with suffering from prejudices shown towards them may add fuel to their already agitating and partitioned minds. As a result, they may begin to demonstrate the prejudiced behaviour by showering favour or disfavour to individuals and groups leading to the impairment of interpersonal relationships.
2. **Personality structure and characteristics:** We know that many of us who are physically and psychologically weak may easily fall prey to a number of diseases in comparison to those who possess the strength for fighting with the diseases spreading viruses and conditions. Thinking on the same lines, various research studies have concluded that the persons possessing personality make up, and behavioural traits are most susceptible to the acquisition of prejudices. A few such traits and characteristics may be named as below.
   - Superstitious, intolerant and impatient behaviour;
   - Admiration for power and toughness;
   - Too much obedience and loyalty;
   - Emotional instability;
   - Feeling of insecurity, anxiety and frustration;
   - Too much aggressiveness and hostility;
   - Lonely and unsocial;
   - Rigid adherence to conventional values;
   - Intolerance of ambiguity, indiscipline and disorganization, etc.
3. **Intergroup rivalries and conflicts:** prejudices are more often the results of intergroup rivalries and conflicts. It is quite natural for an individual as a member of some social group to be loyal and possessing 'We' feelings towards it. On the other hand, it is also quite natural for him to treat the 'Out' groups and their activities as a matter of competition and rivalry. As an employee of a business organization you may feel elevated on the success and progress of the establishment in the form of its economic growth and getting recognition in the national and international market. However, there may arise situations for giving birth to unhealthy competition and bitter rivalries among the establishments and employee of an establishment. Imagine here a scene, where there are deficiencies, shortage and limitations in terms of the availability of opportunities or resources. As a result, everybody in the group (here in this case a business establishment) wants to gain, achieve and snatch the things or benefits only to himself and his organization. This may result in showing undue favour to the members of one's own social group, caste, religion, province and region on one hand and disfavour and denial of facilities/opportunities to the others. It may lead to the growth of separatist tendencies and birth of slogans like Assam is for Assamese; hills are for the hill people etc. The people belonging to minorities then try to develop a sense of fear and insecurity forcing them to develop negative attitudes and prejudices against the majority community and people. They may also think all about them as good and positive resulting in the formation of positive attitude and prejudices in favour of their own community and members. In this way intergroup rivalries and conflicts may be held responsible for giving birth to the likewise prejudices for and against their own group and others.

The Evil impact of Prejudices on the Interpersonal Relationships

The prejudices, the learned pattern of specific favourable or unfavourable attitudes and behaviour towards the individuals, groups or community as a whole prove the germinating seed for a number of unhealthy group rivalries, tensions, conflicts and so many other ills and disharmonies in our society. Infected with prejudices, we tend to work against the interest of one or the other members of the groups belonging to other religions, political parties, castes or regions, resulting in the chains of over reactions towards them. In such an atmosphere of mutual distrust, panic and anxiety, how can we expect the continuity of cordial and harmonious interpersonal relationships among the affected individuals or groups? Prejudices are bound to create biases in the form of positive and negative attitudes and this in turn may germinate the seed of doubt, fear, panic reactions and distrust segregating one individual, group and community from the other. It may colour our vision and obstruct the whole process of logical and rational thinking. We then view the situations and persons through the eyes and ears provided by the built up prejudices and as a result the interpersonal relationships get deteriorated and spoiled. A distressful personal experience then may further give the valid grounds for furthering the amount of tensions, conflicts and torn up relations-leading to group and class infighting as well as regional and global world war.

To Sum Up

The term prejudices stand for all our prejudgement, opinion and attitudes formed on the false premises persuading and compelling us to think, feel and act with the individuals and social groups in a quite biased or partial way.

Our prejudices are learned and acquired us much like our other personality traits and behaviour patterns. The factors and sources responsible for their birth in the individuals may be named as (i) catching up the infection of behaving in a biased manner from the prejudices prevalent in their socio-cultural environment, **(ii)** possession of weak and negative personality make up, and behavioural traits and (iii) intergroup rivalries and conflicts.

Regarding the ill impact of prejudices it can be well observed that our prejudices are responsible for creating an atmosphere of mutual distrust, panic and anxiety, which in turn casts a quite damaging effect on our interpersonal relationships and spreads evils and disharmonies in the society.

Discrimination

Meaning and Nature of Discrimination

In this very chapter we have already discussed that there exists a chain like interrelationship among the three-stereotypes, prejudice and discrimination. Where the stereotypes are regarded as the cognitive component of the special type of attitude termed as prejudice possessed by us about the members of a social group or the group as a whole, the expression of the feelings and emotions attached with our prejudice takes place in the form and shape of discriminating behaviour shown towards the target of our prejudice. In this way, what we think (though stereotypes) and feel (through the prejudice formed) finds its expression in a quite biased and partial behaviour known as the discriminatory behaviour shown by us towards the members of a social group or the group as a whole.

Discrimination: Behavioural manifestation of the prejudices possessed by us about members of a social group or the group as a whole.

Discrimination is, thus, may be safely termed as prejudice in action or the behavioural manifestation of prejudice. It stands for the negative and harmful reactions and behavioural acts directed towards persons or groups who are the targets of our prejudice. In the execution of such discrimination, we usually treat the members of a social group or the group as a whole in a quite unfavourable, discriminatory and marginalized way exemplified as below.

- The boss of a company may be seen to demonstrate discriminatory behaviour against the candidates of a particular community/ religion/ gender/ state or country for whom he or she has the fixed form of stereotyping and prejudices by not selecting them for certain employment positions even when they are meritorious and deserving.
- A girl child belonging to the same family may fall victim of the indiscrimination on account of her gender at the hands of her parents and family members. She may get less attention, love and affection, incentives and encouragement, opportunity of education, development and progress in comparison to her male siblings or cousins.
- The disabled children may feel discriminated and marginalized when they are not allowed to make use of the educational facilities available in their neighborhood. They are debarred from taking parts in the social functions of the family and community.
- The people belonging to a socially untouchable, scheduled caste or tribe may face the hardships of discriminatory behaviour demonstrated by

the members of upper castes in various forms such as denial of water from a well (the only source of drinking water in the village), or the right of worship by not getting entry in the temples.

- The rural community may experience the blunt of acute discrimination by getting deprived of many such facilities that are easily available to the urban people. Similarly a minority community may get victimized at the hands of majority and consequently may feel quite uncomfortable and unsafe even in their living and enjoying civic rights (*e.g.*, Kashmiri Hindu population in the disturbed Kashmir regions).
- Many of the districts or regions of a particular state or nation may also suffer from acute discrimination and marginalization by denying opportunities and facilities available to other citizens on account of the negative attitude and prejudiced feelings shown by the ruling party or government. The people of Bangladesh remained victims of acute discrimination and exploitation in the hands of the mighty Pakistan, then rulers who showered undue favour to the progress of western Pakistan at the cost of the present Bangladesh.

The Consequences or Impacts of Discrimination

The discriminatory behaviour shown towards the individuals or social groups at one or the other times by the majority community or people, who holds power for making and marring their future carries a quite notable damaging impact and negative consequences for the development, progress and welfare of these so affected victims. Depending on the nature of stereotypes held and prejudiced attitude formed about them (in the individual capacity or as a group or community as a whole) they may be denied opportunities for participating fully in the economic, social, and political life of the society in which they live. They often become victims of acute apathy, hate and discrimination carried out towards them on one or the other discriminatory grounds such as gender, race, caste, colour, creed, sect, religion, language, locality or nationality etc. The ills of the discriminatory behaviour shown towards the individuals may be found to show their profound impact on their development and welfare right from their early childhood and schooling in the manner as described below.

1. *Discrimination suffered at home and family:* It is quite possible for the children to suffer from a lot of discrimination at the hands of their own parents, step-mother and father, care taker and family members in a number of ways. The apathy and antagonistic attitude of the family members towards, the girl child, widow child, or children losing their mother/father or both, disabled etc. in our society is well known. In such discriminatory and deprived physical and socio-psychological environment of the family the children fail to get needed love and affection, attention and care, rearing and nourishing supplements, healthy interactions and timely guidance, incentives and reinforcement for their good behaviour and progress. As a result, there arises a big gap in the physical and socio-psychological needs and their satisfaction. It leads them nowhere, other than the path of painful maladjustment and failure in terms of achieving age-related milestones of their wholesome development and progress.
2. *Discrimination suffered in schools and educational institutions:* The environment available to the growing individuals in schools and educational institutions where they get their schooling and higher education may be quite defective, improper and discriminatory. Accordingly, they may be found to face acute discrimination and marginalization in the school on one or the other grounds like belonging to a particular gender, caste, colour, creed, religion, social status, region, language group and nationality, suffering from one or the other types of disabilities and incapacities, or may face the wrath of the personal disliking, negative attitude, jealousy and envy developed towards them on the part of their teachers and authorities. In consequence, they may be excluded and prevented from taking part in the regular activities of the school/educational institute, ridiculed or treated badly in front of others, face injustice in evaluating their performance and achievements and thus getting harmed psychologically and educationally in a way as to put a lot of barriers in their adequate adjustment, development and progress. Such discriminated and marginalized individuals then with no fault of them may be seen to be drifting towards backwardness, failure, unemployment, truancy, delinquency, drug addiction, and other types of antisocial and morally deviant behaviours.
3. *Discrimination faced in community living at the hands of the society:* Members of the majority community and the environment also try

to display a lot of marginalization and discrimination towards the individuals by not allowing them to take part in the activities, festivals, rituals, worships and functions organized in the community venues from time to time. The discrimination and prohibition may be on any ground (such as being a women/girl, widow, disabled, lower caste or untouchable, poor, villager, following other sects, faiths or religion, black colour or disliked nationality) but in all its way it casts a quite negative and damaging influence on the adjustment, and progress of the individuals by snatching the valuable opportunities of social interaction, community and social learning and outward self-expression.

4. *Discrimination faced in the employment market or professions:* It is no secret that people have to face a lot of discrimination in seeking job opportunities in the employment market both in the private and public sectors on account of the stereotypes and prejudices held about them as an individual or members of a certain specific social group or category. One may be denied selection on a particular post, his or her promotion may be withheld or he/she may have to face a lot of hurdles in going with his/her occupation or profession well on account of his or her belongingness to a particular gender, race, caste, religion, locality or nation. Such cruel jokes played with them through the well-planned discriminatory behaviour on the part of the prejudiced employers, bosses, customers and others for depriving them with for all that they actually deserve in their professional life, occupation and business career may prove quite costly to these victims in terms of their physical, psychological, social and economical well-being.
5. *Ill consequences of discriminating a group or community as a whole:* It is also quite common in the world societies and regions to show a lot of discriminatory behaviour to a particular community or social group on one or the other grounds such as caste, religion, colour, race, gender etc. Frequent clashes in our country and abroad between the followers of different sects or religions (e.g., Hindu-Muslim riots in India, Sunni-Shia conflicts in The Muslim-dominated regions and countries etc.); caste wars resulting in the atrocities on Dalits in our country and racial conflicts occurring in Europe and USA are the clear testimony of the role of stereotypes, prejudices and discrimination played by one social group against the other.

To Sum Up

What we think (though stereotypes) and feel (through the prejudices formed) finds its expression in a quite biased and partial behaviour known as the discriminatory behaviours shown by us towards the members of a social group or the group as a whole. While engaging in such discriminatory behaviours, we usually treat the members of a social group or the group as a whole in a quite unfavourable and discriminatory way.

In its consequences, the discriminatory behaviour shown towards the individuals or social groups carries a quite notable damaging impact and negative consequences for the development, progress and welfare of these so affected victims. They may be denied opportunities for participating fully in the economic, social, and political life of the society in which they live. They often become victims of acute apathy, hate and discrimination carried out towards them on one or the other discriminatory grounds such as gender, race, caste, colour, creed, sect, religion, language, locality or nationality etc.

Techniques for Countering the Ill effects of Stereotyping, Prejudices and Discrimination

Stereotyping, prejudice and discrimination all of these three as we have seen are quite notorious in playing a quite damaging and negative role for bringing damaging consequences for the development and well-being of the victimized individuals and affected social groups. The question here may arise, that are there any ways and means that can be applied for countering their evil impact and damaging consequences? The socio-psychologists and thinkers on this aspect have suggested making use of one or the other techniques and ways discussed ahead.

1. Providing opportunities for direct interaction or contact with the out-groups

In most of the situations and times we are spending time and working with the members of the in-group and accordingly have enough time to know and understand the individuals comprising this group. However, it does not happen in the case of our dealings with the members of the Out-group. The lack of contacts with the individual members of the out-group compel us to form opinion and behave with them in the light of stereotypes developed and prejudiced attitudes formed about them on the part of our own group. Such negativity in our thinking, feeling and behaving with the members of out-groups can be checked and restrained in a satisfactory way if efforts are made for having direct interaction and contact with the members of the out-groups.

The availing of one or the other well meaning opportunities of direct contact has been found to help much in restraining the spread of negativity resulting through stereotyping, prejudices and discrimination. Commenting over this aspect Baron and Byrne (2001:217) write:

Direct intergroup contact can be an effective tool for combating cross- group prejudice. When people get to know one another, it seems, many of the anxieties, stereotypes, and false perceptions that have previously kept them apart can melt in the face of new information and warmth of new friendships.

2. Re-categorization: redrawing the boundary between 'us and them':

In the sports tournaments or science fairs organized in your district or state, it is quite natural for you to view your school team as "us'(in-group) and the teams of other schools as "them" (out-group). You along with your school students cheer your team and aspire for its win over the rivals. It is also quite natural for the rival teams getting one or the other types of rifts, annoyance and prejudices against each other. However, at the time of witnessing the inter-district tournament, you are there to cheer the same rival teams belonging to your district that were the main targets of your hooting and prejudices. Why? For the simple reason that now they are accepted by you as us (in-group). Your whole sympathy and cheering then lies with them.

In this way, as soon as the people or groups treated as "they" (out-groups) are accepted as "we" (in-group) by us, our disliking, hate and prejudice toward them disappears at once. Reminding people that they are part of a large group-for instance, that they are all Tamils, Indians, Americans, or even human beings-can help much in achieving this kind of re-categorization which may prove a potent weapon against the narrow mindedness and prejudiced feelings about the out-groups.

3. Undermining and restricting the role of stereotyping:

Stereotypes prevalent about the members of one or the other social groups are responsible for the formation of prejudiced attitudes and discriminating behaviour towards them. Under the influence of stereotypes such as women are not good managers, women executive may be denied promotion otherwise deserved well on her part. For saying halt to such negative consequences of the stereotypes, there must be earnest attempt for undermining and restricting their role in our day-to-day and professional behaviour. Let us see how it can be done.

It is almost an established fact that most often the acts of our prejudiced and discriminatory behaviour towards the people belonging to specific social groups are based on the assumption and unfounded belief that all people belonging to that group are all alike-they share the same characteristics. These misconceptions need essentially to get weakened by resorting to one or the other suitable techniques such as below.

- People should be encouraged to think about others as individuals not simply as members of social groups. Here thus they need to think carefully about others by paying due attention to their own unique individual traits and characteristics instead of assuming that these people and their characteristics will be the same as stereotyped about the group to which they belong. In this way, people should be encouraged and advised to take object judgement about knowing and judging other people instead of getting driven by the misconceived stereotypes.
- Attempts should also be made to organize useful affirmative action programs and activities in schools and colleges, community gatherings and social set up that may provide proper platforms for down grading/undermining the stereotypes prevalent in the society.
- Stereotypes are very much associated with one's thinking directed through one's own cognition. In case a suitable cognitive intervention is erected in the minds of the people against the stereotypes, then it can help much in restricting their impact. If one repeatedly says "no" to the existing stereotypes about the specific social group it may help in combating prejudices against the individuals belonging to that group.

4. Formation of super-ordinate goals:

To provide a challenge for the realization of a particular type of goal named as super-ordinate goals may also prove a good technique for reducing prejudices and conflicts among the members of the rival groups. We may know the sub-ordinate goals as the goals which can be observed through the cooperative efforts of the groups involved in a particular social situation. The realization of these goals, in this way, demands or in a way compels and persuades the members of different groups to come closer for the purpose. The socio-psychologist Sheriff (1966) was the first to emphasize the significance of the setting of super-ordinate goals for reducing tension and conflicts among the members of the out-groups. For deriving his conclusions in this connection, he conducted a series of experiments with groups of children of different schools attending a summer camp during vacation at some place in USA. During their stay, certain type of conflicts and clashes arose among these groups of children. For dealing with the situation, he invented an idea of creating some emergencies before these conflict-ridden groups in the shape of stage managing the disruption of water supply and breakdown of the camp lorry. It compelled the groups of the conflict-ridden children to come closer, be friendly and work jointly for dealing with the emergency resulting in the reduction of their intergroup conflicts and prejudices in a quite mentionable amount.

5. Becoming the good role models for the growing children:

What we have with us in the form of acquiring and imbibing good and bad things, it comes to us right from our childhood through social learning by observing and imitating behaviour of our elders and other role models. It is equally true for acquiring and imbibing of stereotyping, prejudices, and discrimination against the out-groups. The reverse can also happen well if parents at home and teachers in school, and role model available in the society provide a good example of acceptance, tolerance and large mindedness (instead of rejection, intolerance and narrow mindedness) along with the feelings of due respect for the opinions, culture and status of out groups. If tried honestly, this step may play wonders in checking the growth and curbing the evil influence of stereotyping, prejudices, and discrimination prevalent in our society against the members of the out groups.

6. Role of Mass media:

Despite its negative role as emphasized earlier, media can play a substantial role in getting rid of the evils of stereotyping, prejudices and discrimination in our society in the ways and means summarized below:

- Instead of reporting, viewing and glorifying the things concerning stereotyping, prejudice and discrimination, it can adopt a positive approach of addressing these issues in a constructive of way. In adopting this role, basically the media should try to say and exhibit all of them as the evils and vices and thus need to be side-lined or abolished. It should provide the news and stories, write ups and experience videos, serials and films that can contradict the notions and beliefs prevalent in our society in the form of gender, race, caste, religion and social class based stereotypes, prejudices and discriminations
- Media through its various platforms may try to portray the negative outcomes and devastating effects of prejudices and discriminatory behaviour shown towards the individuals and the specific social groups. The sufferings and difficulties felt on the part of targeted individuals or groups on this account should be brought into the notice of the media users and viewers in such a way as to make them realize the necessity of stopping the evil practices of prejudices and discrimination.
- Media should try to portray the positive image altogether contradicting the traditionally held stereotyped negative images of the individuals and groups. For example, it should report that girls are doing wonders in excelling in various areas and sphere of human life disproving and rejecting various stereotypes. Similarly, the other types of stereotypes, prejudices and discriminations related to caste, races, religion, poverty, and social class should also be properly addressed at the hands of media reporting. It should report well that how a particular individual or group is excelling or contributing towards the welfare of the society, nation and humanity irrespective of the negative stereotype held by the public about it. How a person, belonging to a particular religion, caste race or extremist section has saved the lives of others by aborting a terrorist act and how it is unfair on our part to brand all the people belonging to a particular community race or cast as villains, bad guys or terrorists. Such things and events then should be properly highlighted and glorified by the media through its untiring efforts.

To Sum Up

Stereotypes, prejudices and discrimination all of these three are quite notorious in casting their damaging impacts over for the development and well-being of the victimized individuals and affected social groups. It needs to be checked by adopting appropriate techniques and means such as: Providing opportunities for direct interaction or contact with the out-groups-the target of our stereotyping , prejudices and discrimination, Re-categorization: redrawing the boundary between 'us and them', Undermining and restricting the role of stereotyping, Formation of super-ordinate goals needing the cooperation of all in the society for their realization, Becoming the good role models for the growing children, and desirable role of mass media.

ASSESSMENT QUESTIONS

Section I: Essay Type Questions

1. What do you understand by the term stereotyping? Throw light on its meaning and concept.
2. What is stereotyping behaviour? Tell about its various forms or types.
3. Discuss about the relationship of stereotypes with prejudices and discrimination.
4. What are stereotypes? From where do they emerge?
5. Define the term stereotyping and discuss the impact of stereotyping on the progress and well-being of the individuals and the societies.
6. What are prejudices? Throw light on their meaning and nature.
7. Define the term prejudices and throw light on their sources.
8. Discuss in detail about the evil impact of prejudices on the interpersonal relationships and well-being of the society.
9. What do you understand by the term discrimination? Explain by throwing light on its meaning and nature.
10. What is discrimination? Discuss about its consequences or impact over the development and welfare of the victims.
11. What are the various techniques that may be employed for countering the ill effects of stereotyping, prejudices and discrimination? Discuss them in detail.

Section II: Short Answer Type Questions

1. Give a suitable definition of the term stereotypes/prejudices/discrimination.
2. Throw light on the meaning and nature of stereotypes/ prejudices /discrimination.
3. Provide one example each of stereotyping behaviour falling in the category of:
   (i) Sex and gender stereotypes, (ii) Social class or racial stereotypes and (iii) poverty related stereotypes.
4. What is the relationship of stereotypes with prejudices and discrimination?
5. How do one's stereotypes, prejudices and discrimination shown on his part work as cognitive, affective and behavioural component of his behaviour? Explain through one example.
6. Name the different sources of one's prejudices.
7. Give two examples of the evil impacts of one's prejudices on his interpersonal relationships.
8. Tell two things about the consequences or impacts of discrimination.
9. Name four techniques of countering the ill effects of stereotypes, prejudices and discrimination.

Section III: Objective Type Questions

1. Which one of the following is not true?
   (a) Stereotyping works as a cognitive component of one's behaviour
   (b) Stereotyping occurs with full conscious awareness
   (c) Prejudice is the affective component of stereotyping
   (d) Discrimination is the behavioural component of one's prejudices
2. When we begin to dislike someone belonging to out-group for no good reason before even getting to know him, it is termed as:
   (a) Prejudice
   (b) Stereotyping
   (c) Discrimination
   (d) None of these

3. Which one of the following does not work as a source of our prejudices?
   (a) Regionalism
   (b) Inter-group rivalry
   (c) Emotional stability
   (d) Superstitious and impatient behaviour
4. Which one of the following does not prove as a good technique for countering the ill effects of stereotyping, prejudices and discrimination?
   (a) Avoiding opportunities for direct interaction or contact with the out-groups
   (b) Redrawing the boundary between 'us and them'
   (c) Becoming good role models for growing children
   (d) Desirable role of mass media

Answers

1 (b) 2 (a) 3 (c)
4 (a)

10

Social Cognition

Learning Objectives

After going through this chapter, you will be able to:

- Define the term social cognition
- Throw light on the meaning and concept of social cognition
- Tell, what happens in the process of our social cognition
- Explain the roles of schemas in our social cognition
- Define the term attribution and explain its meaning
- Explain the role of attribution in assigning causes for others' behaviour
- Tell about the various theories of attribution
- Point out and throw light on the various types of attribution biases or errors
- State about the meaning of the term impression formation
- Explain how the task of impression formation is carried out
- Tell about the meaning of the term impression management
- Throw light on the methods and techniques used for impression management
- Elucidate the phenomenon "Performance of individuals in the presence of others"
- State and discuss about the phenomenon of Social Facilitation and Inhibition
- Know about the various theories explaining the phenomenon of Social Facilitation and Social Inhibition such as (i) Drive Theory, (ii) Theory of Evaluation Apprehension, and (iii) Theory of Distraction Conflict
- Tell about the phenomenon of Social loafing.
- Explain why does social loafing occur?
- Discuss about the ways and measures for reducing Social loafing
- Define the term pro-social behaviour and throw light on its characteristic features
- Know about the explanation given for the people's pro-social behaviour in various theories of Pro-Social Behaviour
- Tell about the characteristics of those being helped
- Mention how people feel in receiving help from others at the time of need

Social Cognition–Meaning and Concept

The word meaning of the term social cognition is the cognition of the social. The term cognition according to *Oxford Advanced American Dictionary available online* refers to the process by which knowledge and understanding is developed in the mind. Social cognition is, thus, nothing but an act of mental processing on our part for helping us in knowing and understanding the information available regarding social (the social environment or social behaviour of others in one or the other context). For getting acquainted with the meaning and concept of the term social cognition in a more useful way, let us try to concentrate over some of the following definitions provided by eminent authors and thinkers.

1. ***Higgins (2000):*** Social cognition is the study of how people make sense of other people and themselves, that is, learning about what matters in the social world.
2. ***Moskowitz (2005):*** Social cognition is concerned with the study of the thought processes both implicit and explicit, through which humans attain understanding of self, others, and their environment.
3. ***Baron, Byrne and Branscombe (2008):*** Social cognition can be defined as a process by which we interpret, analyse, remember and use information about the social world.

Let us look at the above-cited definitions one by one.

- The first definition given by Higgins, considers social cognition as the field of study helping people in learning about the ways and means of getting adjusted in their social world. For this adjustment it is quite natural for them to have proper interaction and relationship with each other which further needs knowing, understanding and taking judgement about their self and others on their part. In its totality, thus, the study of social cognition helps us to know and learn what is essential for us to lead our social life in a proper way in the environment in which we live and behave.
- The second definition, given by Moskowitz, considers social cognition as a field of study that provides knowledge to the people about their mental or thought processes that can prove helpful to them in knowing and understanding their self, others, and their environment involved in their social behaviour at one or the other times. These mental or thought processes, the application of which is so essential to our social behaviour, may be implicit (unconscious and automatic) and explicit (conscious and deliberate) in their nature. You may have studied them well in the course of your General Psychology or Cognitive Psychology in the name of sensation, perception, attention, memory, thinking, reasoning and inferences drawing etc.
- The third definition considers the task of social cognition, equivalent to the task of information processing, where the information related to the social world of the individuals in the form of sensory input is received as well as processed through their brain by employing the useful cognitive tools/mental or thought processes (such as attention, sensation, perception, previous experiences or learning, remembering, thinking, reasoning and inferences drawing etc.) for resulting into an output in terms of derived conclusion for behaving in one or the other ways in one or the other social situations.

What has been conveyed and analyzed through the above-cited definitions of the term social cognition may help us to derive some of the following conclusions about the meaning and concept of the term social cognition.

- Social cognition helps us to take cognizance of various social signals helpful in knowing and understanding the social world around us.
- Social cognition is the cognition in which we perceive, think about, interpret, categorize and judge our own social behaviour and those of others in one or the other social situations.
- Social cognition, while getting equated with the term information processing, refers to the ways in which we try to handle and process the information about our social world (the self, others and the environment) for deriving our own interpretation and analysis and then remember and use the result in our own ways.
- In the task of information processing of our sensory output about our social world we make use of a number of psychological/mental processes named as sensation, perception, previous experiences and learning in terms of their memory, thinking, reasoning, inferences drawing, and decision making etc. All these cognitive processes are important in social interaction and the study of information processing in a social setting is referred to as social cognition. The output available through our social cognition (information processing) can then be successfully used for carrying out our interactions at a group or individual level.
- Social cognition, in this way, is concerned with the mental processes that sub-serve/promote people's understanding of their self, other individuals and the associated social environment.
- The efforts made by us in our social cognition stand for providing us the mechanistic, process-oriented explanations of the complex social phenomena involving human social interactions.

Social cognition: A type of cognition helping us in knowing and understanding our social world (the self, others and environment) in one or the other social situation through the application of our thought or mental processes.

The discussion carried out above, for understanding the meaning and concept of the term social cognition, may now help us for adopting a workable definition of this term in the words as given below.

Social cognition refers to the type of cognition (act of knowing and understanding) helping the people in knowing and understanding their social world (the self, others and environment) in one or the other social situation through the application of their thought or mental processes.

What happens in the process of our Social Cognition?

Social cognition, as discussed above, stands for getting us to know and understand others well for carrying out the process of our social interaction and maintenance of relationship with them in one or the other social situations. The question arises how can we know and understand others involved in our social interaction? Surely, the clues for their knowing and understanding are to be supplied by these other persons themselves in the form of what they say and do as well as express themselves through their non-verbal behaviour involving facial expression, gestures, and eye movements, etc. These clues or signals available in their social behaviour at the time of our interaction with them are to be properly handled for deriving needed meaning for understanding and knowing them well in furthering the process of social interaction and it is that which is helped through the process of our social cognition. The data available in the form of verbal and non-verbal behaviour is put under close scrutiny and analysis for deriving one or the other interpretations and conclusions about the social behaviour and the personality characteristics of the people involved in the interaction. It is nothing but the task of information processing, the term used in cognitive psychology and computer science for the processing of information or available data for deriving useful conclusions in the form of final output for the needed use on the part of users. Therefore, what happens during our social cognition can be well equated with the task of information processing i.e., processing of information or data available in the form of verbal and non-verbal behaviour of the persons engaged in the social behaviour at one time or the other.

In our social cognition i.e., the processing of information or input available in the form of verbal and non-verbal behaviour of the persons engaged in social behaviour, is carried out through the execution of a number of properly sequenced cognitive or mental processes such as attention, sensation, perception, thinking, reasoning and inference drawing, memorization or remembering for its application and use in the ongoing or future social behaviour. Let us have a look in this sequential happening.

- The work starts through the process of *attention and sensation*. We attend to what is conveyed by others through their verbal and non-verbal behaviour with the help of our sense organs-eyes, ears, nose, touch, smell etc. It works as input for processing what is received by us through our sense organs.
- The act of *perception* (meaning derived from the sensory output) is carried out by the brain on the basis of prior knowledge, experience and learning as well as current context.
- The meaning derived through the act of perception, is then subjected to further analysis, interpretation, *drawing inferences for arriving at decisions* to respond and act in a particular way demonstrable well in our behaviour at the time of interacting with others.
- In responding to the social behaviour demonstrated by others in the ongoing social interaction, in such a particular way, our behaviour is also influenced and guided through our perception and *understanding about our self.* Besides this, it also gets influenced and directed by the type of *social situations and environment* available at the time of the ongoing social interaction.

To Sum Up

Our social cognition helps us in knowing and understanding others well for carrying out the process of our social interaction and maintenance of relationship with them in one or the other social situations. This task of our social cognition is carried out through a phenomenon of information processing-the processing of the input (information available in the form of verbal and non-verbal behaviour of the persons engaged in social behaviour). In the reception of this input and its subsequent processing for deriving necessary meaning, we are helped by a number of cognitive or mental processes such as attention, sensation, perception, thinking, reasoning and inference drawing, memorization etc. carried out by us in a properly sequenced way.

Cognitive Strategies involved in our Social Cognition

The task of our social cognition involving processing of information about our social world is found to employ some useful cognitive strategies such as the use of Schemas. Let us know about it.

Schemas employed in our thought process for taking cognizance of the social world in a social situation represents those already existing cognitive or mental structures/frameworks of our mind (built through earlier experiences or exposure in the similar social situations) that comes to help us in a quite ready-made fashion for the organization and interpretation of the social information available to us at present on the lines and models inherent in the built up of the one or the other relevant schema.

Schemas: The already existing mental frameworks built through earlier experiences in the similar social situations helpful to us in a quite ready-made fashion at present in the similar social situations for the organization and interpretation of the available social information.

Let us illustrate the use of schemas in facing the new situations related to social behaviour.

- You visit the place of one of your acquaintances and find that a cake is being cut.
- You try to talk to a person in the party, but he continues to look around somewhere and does not attend to your conversation.
- You meet a person, gent or lady, first time, dressed and behaving in a particular way and now need to have interaction with him/her.

In all such cases, you certainly did not take long to arrive at the conclusion about the things going around in that very social situation. In the first case, you may conclude that there is a birthday or marriage day celebration party. In the second, you immediately take note of getting ignored as the person you are speaking is not interested in you and needs to avoid you. In the third case, you try to conclude about the expectations from his/her role by concluding about one or other things concerning his/her personality and profession etc.

What makes you reach such a rapidly fast conclusion or interpretation of the observed event, behaviour of a person, or personality traits visible in them? It seems that there is something already lying in you to help you in processing the input provided by your sense organs in that very social situation in a quite rapid, automatic or mechanical way in the attempt of your information processing or social cognition task. Definitely, here it is so. You are being helped by the particular types of cognitive or mental tools or structures available for your social cognition (information processing) task being performed by you in dealing with the faced situation. It is that which is named as schemas (specific mental frameworks or structures).These schemas of ours are built around one or the other specific themes/concepts associated with our social world involving self, others and the environment. This built up is resulted through our previous experiences gained in the similar faced social situations. Their built up is also affected though a number of other factors such as social norms, traditions, superstitions, stereotypes, attitudes and prejudices etc. prevailing during the processing of their establishment.

To Sum Up

We often make use of an important cognitive strategy named as schemas in the task of our social cognition. The term 'schemas' here stands for the types of mental framework possessed by us about the people, things or events built up through our past experiences about them in the similar situation. They are found helpful to us at present in the task of our social cognition in the similar situations.

In respect of the role played by schemas in our social cognition, we may definitely say that all of our schemas exiting in its various types and forms provide a quite valuable prompt service in helping a number of cognitive processes such as attending, encoding and retrieval of the related information each of which is found to play a key role in the task of our social cognition.

Attribution

Meaning and Definition of the term Attribution

Attribution in its word meaning stands for an act or process of attributing something. In *Cambridge English Dictionary available online*, the term attribution in its generalized way has been defined as "the act of saying or thinking that something is the result or work of a particular person or thing". When we say that the Taj Mahal is the result of the efforts of Mughal Emperor Shahjahan; 'Ram Charit Manas' is the creation of Tulsidas; or this railway accident is the outcome of the carelessness of the engine driver or signal man, we are making attribution, identifying the person or thing responsible for the creation or happening of a thing or event. However, in the field of psychology when we talk about social cognition, the use of the term attribution is strictly confined to attribute reasons or causes for one or the other types of behaviour demonstrated by others in a particular social situation. It is in this reference that the term attribution has been defined by the authors and researchers in the following way.

1. ***Delamater and Myers (2009):*** The term attribution refers to the process through which the observer infers the causes of another's behaviour.

2. ***Baron & Byrne, (2001):*** Attribution refers to our efforts to understand the causes behind others' behaviour and, on some occasions, the causes behind our behaviours, too.

These two definitions are hereby clearly pointing out about the objective or goal of the task of attribution carried out on our part in any process of our social interaction. We have a natural curiosity of establishing cause and effect relationship in the happening of an event or observed phenomenon. Accordingly, when anybody is found to behave in a particular way or demonstrate a particular type of social behaviour, we begin to assign attribution i.e., thinking about the possible causes or reasons underlying this behaviour. Let us try to make it clear through examples.

> **Attribution:** Our attempts to assign possible causes or reasons behind the type of behaviour demonstrated by others as well as ourselves in one or the other social situations.

Imagine yourself sitting in an arm chair and all of a sudden, a child, while screaming, thrusts herself into your arms. It is natural for your thought process now to be engaged in the task of attribution–assigning one or the other reasons for the behaviour of the child such as (i) she is scared on some account, (ii) somebody is chasing her during the child play, (iii) she is just kidding, (iv) she is missing you, or (v) she is demonstrating love and feelings of attachment towards you.

It is only after the close scrutiny of all these possibilities that you try to respond in the most suitable way for carrying out your social obligation and interaction in this situation.

Theories of Attribution

Attribution as we have seen above stands for the explanation you provide or causes you assign for the happening of an event, or demonstration of a certain type of behaviour on the part of others or by yourself in the ongoing social interaction. What guides or dictate us in carrying out such attribution tasks? How the process of attribution, in general, is carried out by us in our day-to-day social interaction and social perception (taking cognizance of the traits and social behaviour of others)? The questions like these may be answered on the basis of the views expressed in different theories of attributions put forward by the renowned socio-psychologists and thinkers from time to time. Let us here try to present the viewpoints of two renowned theories–Heider's Naïve Psychology Attribution theory and The Weiner's attribution theory in this regard.

Heider's Naïve Psychology Attribution Theory put forward by Fritz Heider emphasizes that the people in general, as a naïve psychologist are found to adopt a quite simple approach in attributing causes for the one or the other types of behaviour of others. They either hold responsible the person himself for his behaviour or search for the causation of this behaviour in his environment.

> **Heider's Naïve Psychology Attribution Theory**
>
> A theory of attribution providing a workable account of the manner and ways in which we, as an ordinary or common people (termed as naïve psychologist), explain the causes of the events concerning with the social behaviour of the individuals by holding the individuals or the things lying in their environment responsible for the display of such behaviour.

Accordingly, the factors responsible for a particular type of behaviour of the people in one or the other social situations may be divided into two major categories as explained below.

- **Internal causes or attributions:** Internal causes as the name suggests are internal in nature. They lie within the individual rather than outside in the environment. While attributing internal causes for the behaviour of the individuals we look for the things lying within the individuals such as their personality characteristics, health condition–physical and mental, nature of the mood, feelings and emotions felt, and abilities, capacities, motivations, aspirations, competencies etc. possessed on their part. Our attributions like *"He is angry and fighting with others because he is bad tempered and quarrelsome"* belong to the category of internal attributions.
- **External causes or attributions:** External causes as the name suggests are external in nature. They lie outside the individuals in their environment rather than within the individuals themselves. These causes are also referred to as situational implying that occurrence of the behaviour in individual has been resulted through the creation of a situation or happening of something bad or negative in the environment of individual. In this regard, our attributions like *"He is angry and fighting with others because they have uttered abuses against him and his family"* belong to the category of external attributions.

The Weiner's attribution theory put forward by Bernard Weiner is focused on attributing causes for the success or failure of the people in a task.

For this purpose, it talks about blaming one of the four factors namely people's ability to do the task, their efforts for performing the task, the difficulty level of the task or more a chance or luck causing their success or failure in the task. In deciding about which one of these four factors is responsible for the success or failure in the assigned task, it further talks about categorizing and weighing each of them on the three dimensions provided in the model in the name of internal-external, stable-unstable, and controllable-uncontrollable in the manner as provided below in the table 10.1. Here by the terms stable and unstable he means the factors that do not change or get changed with time. Similarly, the terms controllable and uncontrollable here stand for the factors (things and situations) that are in the control or beyond the control of the people.

Table 10.1: Weiner's Attribution Model: Displaying the Task of Attribution on Success and Failure falling in each of the three dimensions.

	Internal		**External**	
	Stable	**Unstable**	**Stable**	**Unstable**
Controllable	Personality Traits/ Temperament Typical Effort	Unusual Effort	Help from Parents, Friends, and Teachers.	Help from Unknown
Uncontrollable	Ability	Physical and Mental Health, Mood, Interest.	Task Difficulty	Luck/chance

Attribution Biases or Errors

Quite often, when we engage in the task of attribution, we begin to evaluate the people and their behaviour on the basis of incomplete information/evidences, or apply short cuts for drawing inferences and making judgements about them. It may result in one or the other types of errors and biases referred to as attribution error or biases in our understanding of others. We may broadly classify them as:

- *Fundamental attribution bias or corresponding attribution bias* (the type of bias creeping on account of our tendency to overvalue the role of internal factors and undervaluing the role of external factors.
- *Actor-observer bias* (the type of bias in which people involved in an action as actors view things differently from people behaving as observers),
- *The Self-serving attribution bias* (the type of bias creeping on account of the tendency to attribute one's own success to internal causes and one's failures to external causes for serving the interest of one's ego self).

Impression Formation

The term impression formation is used for the processes involved in the formation of impression about others on the basis of available information about them. It begins in the form of the first impression one makes on others. However, whatever simplicity and ease may be reflected in making first impression about others, in practice, it needs the adoption of an elaborate cognitive process for its execution. Actually, for this purpose, what is available to us for knowing and understanding the person in a particular social situation or social encounter (i.e., his appearance, dress, way of talking, walking, expressing his opinion and behaving one or the other ways etc.) is organized into a gestalt whole on our part for making a unified impression of the person concerned. Thus, it is this process of organizing diverse information into a unified and gestalt impression of the other person, that is referred to as impression formation (Delamater and Myers, 2009).

How the available information about others is used for the formation of first impression about them in our first social encounter, the explanation about this came at the first time from the famous socio-psychologist, Solomon Asch through the use of *configuration model* (perception of information about the person in the gestalt form) developed by him on the basis of a few experimental studies conducted by him in the year 1946. On the basis of his studies, he tried to conclude that the task of the formation of first impression about the strangers at the time of our first encounter with them is performed by us by organizing all pieces of information regarding their personality traits (central and peripheral) into a synthesized whole.

Impression management

As a matter of definition, we can define the term impression management as the efforts made and methods applied by us for presenting ourselves in a way to creating a favourable impression of ours on others. The task of impression management is a quite skilled and carefully organized venture. It needs the application of the quite well thought and planned methods and techniques of impression management. These methods and techniques used by us for the task of impression management may be broadly categorized as (i) Self-enhancement techniques and (ii) Other- enhancement techniques.

While, in the former category we may include all the efforts and provisions made on our part to boost our own self-image, the other enhancement techniques are meant for enhancing the self of others and thus may include all such efforts and provisions made on our part to enhance the self image of others.

In the use of both these types of techniques, we should however be quite careful in making judicious and proportionate use of them so that the efforts for enhancing the ego of the self or the ego of others may seek a proper balance with the overall interests and welfare of the self and others.

Behaviour or performance of Individuals in the Presence of Others

It is commonly observed that the behavioural functioning or performance of the individuals is significantly affected in the presence of others. In general, it may lead to the enhancement or reduction in the performance level of the individuals in one or the other tasks giving birth to the foreplay of the phenomenon of social facilitation, social inhibition, and social loafing. Let us know about them.

The Phenomenon of Social Facilitation

Social facilitation refers to a social process or phenomenon in which the presence of others facilitates the enhancement in the performance level of the working individuals in a task being performed by them at that time. This phenomenon was first reported by Norman Triplett (1897) in his observation of the cyclists. He noted that the cyclists rode faster when they were racing along with other fellow cyclists than when they raced alone. In our observation in day-to-day routine life we may find that the workers perform better when they work in a group, women spin yarn more in the company of other fellow spinners, children study more and perform better in the competition along with the fellow children.

Social facilitation: A social process or phenomenon in which the presence of others facilitates the enhancement in the performance level of the working individuals in a task being performed by them at that time.

The Phenomenon of Social Inhibition

Quite contrary to social facilitation, the phenomenon of social inhibition refers to a social process or phenomenon in which the presence of others may work to interfere with or inhibit/reduce the performance of the working individuals in a task being performed by them at that time. As a day-to-day example of this phenomenon we can quote the case when a student dancer providing a commendable performance during her training, fails badly in providing her performance at the University youth festival before a sizable audience.

Social Inhibition: A social process or phenomenon in which the presence of others may work to interfere with or inhibit/reduce the performance of the working individuals in a task being performed by them at that time.

This phenomenon became apparent when the socio-psychologists testing the validity of the claim of the phenomenon of social facilitation found that the presence of others while helping in a variety of cases obstructs or inhibits the performance of the individuals so many other times (Aiello and Douthitt, 2001). Particularly, it was noted by them (Travis, 1925; Pessin, 1933; Bond and Titus,1983) that while the phenomenon of social facilitation stands true in the performance of the simple tasks or the tasks being perfectly skilled or practiced, it does not work well or even otherwise work in opposite for giving birth to the phenomenon of inhibition in performing the difficult and complex tasks or the task not well experienced or properly practiced before.

Now the question arises that why and how it happens that the presence of others sometimes helps and at other times inhibits the performance of the individuals in the tasks. The socio-psychologists have worked out some theories like Drive theory, Theory of evaluation apprehension and Theory of distraction conflict for providing explanation for the same.

1. According to *Drive theory,* brought out by Robert Zajonc, an individual's behaviour is driven to social facilitation or inhibition depending on whether or not the dominate response evoked by physical arousal caused through a mere presence of others in the working situation

suits well to his performance or not. If it suits it results in increasing our performance in the presence of others and if not, it results in a decrease of our performance.

2. *Theory of Evaluation Apprehension brought out by* Cottrell, et. al. (1968) and Cottrell (1972), emphasizes that it is not the mere presence of others but the apprehension of being evaluated by others that is responsible for improving or impairing the performance of the individuals. A blind folding or deep sleeping audience cannot produce evaluation apprehension among the performing individuals, but, it is the fear of being judged by a well conscious or say more knowledgeable audience that creates evaluation apprehension among the performers for influencing or affecting their performance in a better or worse way.
3. According to the *Theory of Distraction Conflict, brought out by* Barron, More, & Sanders, (1978), it is nether mere presence nor evaluation apprehension that cause the psychological arousal that leads to facilitation or inhibition effects, but it is the conflict experienced between the task at hand and attending to others in the immediate surroundings, that work for the same. Here, on one hand is the individual's intention of performing the task as properly as possible and on the other hand lies the audience and co-actors generating conflict in the shape of increased physiological arousal. Such increased arousal, in turn, enhances the tendency to perform dominant responses. If these are correct in a given situation, performance is enhanced, but, if they are incorrect, performance is impaired (Baron and Byrne, 2004:444).

In this way, the theories cited above try to put explanation for the occurrence of social facilitation and social inhibition associated with the enhancement or impairment of the performance of the individuals in the presence of others in their own ways. A happy synthesis of the viewpoints expressed by these theories may help in arriving at a proper explanation of such behaviour.

To Sum Up

In general, the performance of the individuals in one or the other tasks seems to be significantly affected in the presence of others giving birth to the foreplay of the phenomenon of social facilitation, social inhibition, and social loafing.

Social facilitation refers to a social process or phenomenon in which the presence of others facilitates the enhancement in the performance level of the working individuals in a task being performed by them at that time. This phenomenon was first reported in the year 1897 by Norman Triplett in his observation that the cyclists rode faster when they were racing along with other fellow cyclists than when they raced alone. Later on, in the year 1920, Floyd Allport, conducted a lot of experimental work for describing the tendency of people to perform better in the presence of others and coined the term *social facilitation* for describing this phenomenon.

Instead of getting an increase in the performance, the presence of others may cause decrease in the performance of the individuals in the task. The socio-psychologists have named this phenomenon as social inhibition. As a matter of definition, thus, social inhibition stands for a social phenomenon in which the presence of others may work to interfere with or inhibit/reduce the performance of the working individuals in a task being performed by them at that time.

For explaining the presence of others sometimes helping and other times inhibiting the performance of the individuals in the tasks, the socio-psychologists have worked out some theories like Drive theory, Theory of evaluation apprehension and Theory of distraction conflict.

According to *Drive theory,* brought out by Robert Zajonc, an individual's behaviour is driven to social facilitation or inhibition depending on whether or not the dominate response evoked by physical arousal caused through a mere presence of others in the working situation suits well to his performance or not.

Theory of Evaluation Apprehension brought out by Cottrell, et. al. (1968) and Cottrell (1972), emphasizes that it is not the mere presence of others but the apprehension of being evaluated by others that is responsible for improving or impairing the performance of the individuals.

According to the *Theory of Distraction Conflict, brought out by* Barron, More, & Sanders, (1978), it is nether mere presence nor evaluation apprehension that cause the psychological arousal that leads to facilitation or inhibition effects, but it is the conflict experienced between the task at hand and attending to others in the immediate surroundings, that work for the same.

The Phenomenon of Social Loafing

There may be occasions in the working of the individuals in the group, when the performance of the group as a whole also gets adversely affected besides the reduction and impairment in the quality of the performance behaviour of one or the other members as per expectation by the group for achieving its common goal. It happens at the times when contribution of each member in the group is not put under evaluation on individual basis. The members have no apprehension of getting detected for not contributing towards the attainment of group goal in a desired way. They find a golden opportunity of escaping from giving their own contribution in the expected way and letting others do the work in group tasks by taking a free ride for themselves. Let us make this situation clear by citing some examples from social life.

1. In the case of a group of people getting involved in shifting a heavy load from one place to another one or the other members of the group may not be putting their best but only pretending to do so.
2. In the case of working on the completion of a group project by the students of a class, there may be some students playing hide and seek by not contributing their best for the proper execution of the project.
3. There is a strange story depicting the behaviour of the people letting others contribute as per expectation from the group members for the success of the group task. In this story people of a particular religious group were supposed to put a certain quantity of milk in a container covered by a lid one by one with a possibility of not being seen by others while putting their share of the milk in the container. The people put the water in place of milk by assuming that a small quantity of water in a big container, supposed to be filled up with the milk contributed by others in the group, carries no significance. Afterwards, when all contributed to their share of milk, the container was opened by the priests to find to their surprise that it was totally filled up with water.

What happens in the examples cited above is referred to as an outcome of a social phenomenon called as social loafing on the part of sociopsychologists. It is characterized with the reduction in motivation and effort when individuals work collectively in a group compared to when they work individually or as independent co-actors (Karau & William, 1993).

Social Loafing: A social phenomenon in which people, while working in a group not put under evaluation on the individual basis, are found to escape from providing their own contribution in the expected way and letting others do the work by taking a free ride for themselves.

This phenomenon of social loafing occurring in a group work (not put under evaluation on the individual basis) is quite universal. It has been found to take place across genders, age spans, cultures, social situations as well as tasks (simple or complex; cognitive or physical). Truly speaking, social loafing appears to be a basic fact of our social life. However, in all its forms or ways it is quite harmful in any process of group working. It cannot be taken too lightly. We have to think about the ways and measures of reducing its possibilities.

Ways and Measures for Reducing Social Loafing

Based on the causes inherent and the possibilities arising in the occurrence of social loafing, socio-psychologists have suggested the use of various measures and techniques measures (in their combination or alone) for its reduction and controlling. We can summarize them as under.

1. There is a need of proper identification, and evaluation of the efforts of the individual members in the group task preferably throughout the execution of the group activities.
2. The work done and responsibilities shared on the part of the individual members should not only be identified but also dully rewarded through the adoption of certain specific rules and norms for this purpose.
3. The task done and responsibilities shared on the part of group members in this concern should be made more meaningful, interesting, specific and challenging for leaving little chances of social loafing.
4. It is also a good thing to provide the opportunity for the group members to choose the task they want to execute and responsibility they want to share in the group project. It gives them fewer excuses for their social loafing and work more for the team success.
5. Efforts should be earnestly made for increasing the commitment of the group members to successful task performance (Brickner et.al., 1986).
6. Necessary efforts should be made for increasing the apparent importance or value of the task being executed by the group (Karau & Williams, 1993).
7. Efforts should be made to the people working in a group to provide some kind of standard of performance such as how much others are doing or their own past performance (Williams et.al, 1981).

8. Social loafing can be reduced when the group members view their contribution to the group task as unique rather than merely redundant with those of others (Weldon & Mustari, 1988).
9. And last but not the least, efforts should be made to bring an environment of co-operation and cohesiveness in the group for reducing the chances of social loafing in the work execution (Baron & Byrne, 2004).

To Sum Up

In the working situations, at the times, when contribution of each member in the group is not put under evaluation on individual basis, the members have no apprehension of getting detected for not contributing towards the attainment of group goal in a desired way. Here, they find a golden opportunity of escaping from giving their own contribution in the expected way and letting others do the work in group tasks by taking a free ride for themselves. Such behaviour, is referred to as an outcome of a social phenomenon called social loafing on the part of socio-psychologists. It is characterized with the reduction in motivation and effort when individuals work collectively in a group compared to when they work individually or as independent co-actors.

The factors or things responsible for the occurrence of social loafing have been identified as: Lack of Motivation (finding that no purpose served by their hard work); No assigning of specific responsibilities and their evaluation on an individual level; and feeling on their part that whether they work or not work does not matter for the success of the group.

For avoiding the loss affected through the occurrence of social loafing in a group work, it is always advisable to adopt meaningful measures for reducing social loafing. The cure lies in the prevention of its occurrence, i.e., taking proper care of the things which may be considered a contributor for the occurrence of such behaviour among the group members.

Pro-social behaviour

Meaning and Definition

We know that there are people who stand by the sufferers and needy at the time of their distress and need, on a voluntary basis. Such behaviour of helping others at the time of their need is termed as helping behaviour. It may range from simple act of picking the dropped stick, of a disabled/ aged, providing food to a hungry person, giving donations to a charitable trust, to provide legal help to the needy poor or risk one's own life in saving a victim of flood, fire or any nature/man created disaster or painful incidence. We name all such types of helping behaviour of the human beings as pro-social behaviour in the field of social psychology as they serve the social cause of serving humanity by providing the required help to the needy in the human society. It is a simple self-explanatory explanation of the term pro-social behaviour. For understanding more about it, let us look into some formal definitions provided by the social psychologists.

Staub (1978): Pro-social behaviour is defined as behaviour that benefits another person or has positive social consequences.

Eisenberg and Miller (1987:92): Pro-social behaviour is the "social glue" that enables people of different ages to live together peacefully and productively. Specifically, pro-social behaviour has been defined as voluntary intentional behaviour that results in benefits for another person.

Eisenberg and Mussen (1989:3): Pro-social behaviour refers to voluntary actions that are intended to benefit another individual or group of individuals.

Sears et al (1991:367): Pro-social behaviour is defined as any act that helps or is designed to help others, regardless of the helper's motives.

Batson (1998): Pro-social behaviour is a much broader category. It is defined as any helpful action that benefits other people without necessarily providing any direct benefit to the helper and it may even involve risk for the helper.

Crisp and Turner (2014:250):Pro-social behaviour in the form of helping behaviour refers to acts where people voluntarily and intentionally behave in a way that they believe will benefit others, although at the same time the behaviour may benefit them as well.

Barrett, (2017): Pro-social behaviour as a concept includes varied behaviours including volunteering, cooperation, conformity with social norms and even being polite.

Pro-social behaviour: A form of helping behaviour being performed intentionally on a voluntary basis regardless of the helper motives-selfish or self-less resulting in benefits to another individual or group of individuals.

The definitions cited above may help in revealing the following characteristic features of the term pro-social behaviour.

(i) Pro-social behaviour is a specific form of helping behaviour that is intended to benefit others.

(ii) Individuals in their personal capacity or as members of the group are helped through the pro-social behaviour of the helpers.

(iii) Besides proving beneficial to the individuals or group of individuals at the time of their need, it aims to bring harmony, peace, as well as welfare and progress of the society.

(iv) The people as helpers get engaged in the pro-social behaviour at their own intentionally and purposefully for benefitting others.

(v) The voluntary and intentional nature of the pro-social behaviour gets it separated from other behaviours incidental or forced that may result in benefitting others.

(vi) Pro-social behaviour in the form of a helping behaviour is much a quite broad category or concept involving or including the features like:

- Pro-social behaviour helps others regardless of the helper motives-selfish or self-less.
- It may or may not provide any direct or indirect benefit to the helper.
- It may or may not involve risk for the helper.
- It is a quite broader concept in the sense that a number of varied activities/behaviours termed as serious or low cost as well as serious and high cost may be performed by people for benefitting others (Bierhoff, 2001).
- A quite varied number of acts or behaviours may be performed by the people as a part of their pro-social behaviour in the form of assisting, cooperating, encouraging, comforting, sharing, listening and attending others in a decent way.

(vii) The most distinguishing feature of the pro-social behaviour is its capacity to benefit others in the domain of social welfare and progress irrespective of the helper's motive-self or self-less.

(viii) The behaviours known as altruistic behaviours-providing voluntary help to others with no selfish motive or expectation of reward in any form is a sub-part or constituent of the broader term pro-social behaviour.

Theories of Pro-Social Behaviour

Socio-psychologists have provided some theories to give necessary explanation for the pro-social behaviour of the people, named as Empathy-Altruism Theory, Negative State Relief Theory, Empathic Theory, Competition Altruism Theory, and Kin Selection Theory

According to *Empathy - Altruism theory,* brought out by Batson, Duncan, Ackerman, Buckley and Birch (1981), people engage in pro-social behaviour on account of the emotional arousal resulted through the empathy (understanding the situation from other's perspective) felt for the victim in distress.

According to *Negative State relief theory,* brought out by Cialdini, Baumann & Kenrick (1981), we help the victim in distress because our doing so makes us provide a sense of relief or upright our spoiled mood by reducing our own negative feelings aroused for one or the other reasons.

According to *Empathic Joy theory,* brought out by Smith, Kealing & Stotland (1989), empathy alone cannot make a helper respond and help a victim it should be accompanied by an inherent joy or a purpose that is well visualized by him to get served as a result of his helping the victim. In other words, according to this theory a helper engages in a pro-social act not because of empathy but because he wants to accomplish something and doing so is rewarding for him.

According to *Competitive Altruism theory,* brought out by Hardy and Van Vugt (2006); and Flynn et.al (2006), people help others because in doing so they foresee the possibility of the enhancement of their status and reputation in the society as well as in the eyes of the person being helped. In competing with others in this case, they try to demonstrate themselves as more and more altruistic.

According to *Kin Selection theory,* brought out by Burnstein, Crandall and Kitayama (1994), people generally do not provide help to anybody anywhere indiscriminately. For engaging in the pro-social behaviour, they certainly seem to be quite choosy and help only those who are somewhat known to them and in this respect also particularly prefer their kith and kin who are biologically related to them.

Characteristics of those being helped

Regarding the characteristics of those being helped by the pro-social persons at the time of emergency we may see them to be attributed by the characteristic features like:

- Adjudged as not at all responsible for the creation of the problems that they are suffering from
- Possessing a favourable sense of appeal for seeking help from others
- Demonstrating characteristics of being perceived as a deserving one for getting priority in help

How one feels in receiving help from others at the time of need

It may be seen that people may demonstrate a mixed type of positive and negative responses. While in majority of cases they feel obliged and respond by expressing thanks, there are possibilities where the people receiving help experience discomfort and even feel resentful towards a person who is providing help to them. In all such cases, it happens because they feel hurt on account of the lowering of their self-esteem and as a reactionary measure develop the feeling of disliking and resentment towards the helper.

To Sum Up

Prosocial behaviour is a type of behaviour in which one is found to provide voluntary help to the needy with a self-less motive. In view of the various prosocial behaviour theories people engage in such type of behaviour on account of:

- The emotional arousal resulted through the felt for the victim in distress.
- Experiencing a sense of relief or to upright their spoiled mood.
- Getting an inherent joy along with feeling empathy for the victim.
- Seeing the possibility of the enhancement of their status and reputation in the society as well as in the eyes of the person being helped.
- Feeling the need of helping those who are somewhat known to them and in this respect also particularly preferring their kith and kin.

In this concern, it has also been found that those who are helped by the pro-social persons at the time of emergency are, in general, those people who possess a favourable sense of appeal for seeking help from others. It has also been seen that after getting help from other at the time of need people may demonstrate a mixed type of positive and negative responses in the shape of feeling obliged or showing resentment towards the helper.

ASSIGNMENT QUESTIONS

Section I: Essay Type Questions

1. What is social cognition? Discuss its meaning and concept in detail.
2. Define the term social cognition and tell actually what happens in the process of social cognition.
3. What are schemas? What role is played by them as a cognitive strategy in our social cognition? Explain
4. "The performance of individuals in the presence of others is said to be affected in a considerable way". Evaluate the truth of this statement in the light of the views expressed and research work done by the socio-psychologists.
5. State and describe the phenomenon of social facilitation and inhibition.
6. Name the various theories explaining the phenomenon of social facilitation and social inhibition and discuss any one of them in detail
7. Throw light on the following theories explaining the phenomenon of Social facilitation
   (i) Drive Theory
   (ii) Theory of Evaluation Apprehension, and
   (iii) Theory of Distraction Conflict
8. What is social loafing? Explain why does it occur and discuss about the ways and measures for its reduction.
9. What is pro-social behaviour? Throw light on its main characteristics and features.
10. Throw light on the following aspects of social behaviour.

(i) Possible explanations for the pro-social behaviour in various theories propagated on this account.
(ii) The characteristics of those being helped during the pro-social behaviour acts.
(iii) The reactions or responses of the people who get help through pro-social behaviour.

Section II: Short Answer Type Questions

1. Provide a suitable definition of the term social cognition
2. Tell two things about the meaning and concept of social cognition.
3. Name the cognitive strategies involved in our social cognition.
4. Tell in brief about one's schemas as a cognitive strategy helping in the task of social cognition.
5. What is attribution?
6. Name two important theories of attribution
7. What are the attributions biases or errors?
8. Name any three attributions biases or errors arising in one's social cognition
9. What is Fundamental or Corresponding attribution bias/ Actor observer bias/ Self-serving attribution bias?

10. What is impression formation?
11. What is impression management?
12. Name the three phenomena representing the behaviour or performance of individual in the presence of others.
13. What is social facilitation/ social inhibition/ social loafing?
14. Name any two theories explaining the phenomenon of social inhibition.
15. Provide a suitable definition of the term pro-social behaviour.
16. Name the different ways and measures for the reduction of social loafing.
17. Name two theories explaining people's pro-social behaviour.
18. Tell two characteristics of the people being helped in their need by the pro-social behaviour
19. Tell in brief how people may react or feel after getting help in emergency from the pro-social people.

Section III: Objective Type Questions

1. Which one of the following is not correct?
   (a) Social cognition is a term used for the process of knowing and understanding about the true self of the person.
   (b) Attribution refers to our efforts to understand the causes behind other's behaviour.
   (c) Weiner has provided a useful theory related with the phenomenon of attribution
   (d) Social facilitation is a phenomenon representing the behaviour of the people in the presence of others.
2. Haider's Naïve Psychology is a theory propagated for explaining the phenomenon of
   (a) Attribution
   (b) Social facilitation
   (c) Social inhibition
   (d) None of these
3. Who is credited to bring the phenomenon of social facilitation in our notice at the first time?
   (a) Bernard Weiner
   (b) Fritz Haider
   (c) Norman Triplett
   (d) None of these
4. What is not true about people's social behaviour?
   (a) The people get engaged in the pro-social behaviour at their own intentionally and purposefully for benefitting others.
   (b) All types of helping behaviour are termed as the pro-social behaviour
   (c) Pro-social behaviour is a specific form of helping behaviour that is intended to benefit others.
   (d) The behaviours known as altruistic behaviours is a sub-part or constituent of the broader term pro-social behaviour.

Answers

1 (a)	2 (a)	3 (c)
4 (b)		

11

Psychology of the Group

Learning Objectives

After going through this chapter, you will be able to:

- Define the term group and know about the meaning and characteristics of groups
- Tell about the types or kinds of groups
- Differentiate between group and crowd
- Tell about the difference between the terms group and team
- Explain, how groups are formed and developed
- Discuss what makes us join one or the other groups.
- Discuss, how does a group function
- Throw light on the phenomenon of cohesiveness in the groups.
- Explain how the task of decision-making is performed in groups.
- Throw light on the potential dangers and pitfalls in group-decision making
- Know about the phenomenon of group polarization, the causes of its occurrence and its effect on group decision-making.
- Define the term group think and throw light on its meaning and concept.
- Discuss about the causes inherent in the development of groupthink
- Tell about the measures for preventing the occurrence of groupthink.

Introduction

It has been commonly observed and also established through various experimental studies that there are differences in the behaviour of individuals when they are alone and when they are together with other individuals. An individual, as a member of a group, behaves quite differently than what he would otherwise do. As a member of the group, he exhibits group behaviour. Group behaviour is not a mere sum-total of the behaviour of the individuals who constitute that group. Under the influence of group behaviour, even the most disciplined and obedient students have been found indulging in the most irresponsible and undesirable behaviour. On the other hand, the most cowardly, unsocial or irresponsible ones are found contributing significantly when observed to work in a group. Therefore, it should be clearly understood that in a group, the behaviour of the individual rests on a different psychic level and, thus, psychology of the group should be considerably different from the psychology of the individuals. It is therefore quite essential to have proper knowledge and understanding about the psychology of the groups and their functioning with regard to their composition, formation and group processes. For this purpose, let us begin by understanding the meaning of the term group.

Meaning and Definitions of the term 'Group'

In an ordinary sense, a group is said to be a collection or aggregate of two or more objects or persons. But from the socio-psychological angle, mere collection or aggregate of people does not form a group. A psychological group in the opinion of Kretch, Crutchfield and Ballachey (1950: 283) may be defined "as two or more persons who meet the following conditions:

(i) The relations among the members are interdependent—each member's behaviour influences the behaviour of each of the others, and

(ii) The members 'share an ideology'—a set of beliefs, values and norms which regulate their mutual conduct."

In this sense, the members of a psychological group are said to be interdependent to some significant degree. They share common interests and aims and observe agreed rules of conduct and behaviour. In more clear terms, the members of a psychological group must have a common psychology, *i.e.* they must feel, think and act together. *A group, therefore, may be defined as the collection or aggregate of two or more interdependent individuals who usually feel, think and act together.*

Defined in this manner, a number of children playing independently their respective games in a public park, cannot be regarded as the members of one group. Similarly, a number of people passing through a street each going his or her own way or passengers unrelated and unfamiliar to one another in a railway carriage cannot be said to form a group. They are merely in the togetherness situation at a particular place at a particular moment. Unless they feel and act together and thus share experience of each other, they cannot be said to form a psychological group.

Group: Collection of two or more inter-dependent individuals who usually feel, think and act together.

In a situation when the fellow passengers of a railway carriage take note of and accommodate one another, resist a newcomer trying to enter their compartment and, thus, begin to think, feel and act together, their simple togetherness turns into a psychological group. Similarly, the people passing at a particular moment through the street may be found to form a psychological group when they are faced with a common danger. The children playing in the park are said to form such a group when they engage themselves in a common game.

Moreover, a sort of belongingness or we feeling is essential for the formation of a psychological group. When the people say, 'we teachers', 'we Rajasthanis', 'we labourers', etc. it means that they are the members of a psychological group. Under such feelings, they can feel, act and think together and, therefore, can be called the members of a psychological group.

Characteristics of a Group

On the basis of the analysis of the definitions given above, we can summarize the characteristics of a group in the following way:

1. **Existence of two or more than two members:** A single individual can't form any group. There must be at least two or more individuals for the formation of a group.
2. **Interdependence in relationship:** A mere collection or gathering of two or more individuals does not constitute a group. The essential thing for the formation of a group is the existence of some type of relationship or interdependence among the group members on one account or the other. How much different their functions and activities may be in the group, there must be some type of inter-relationships and interdependence in the exercise of their duties, actions and behaviour as members of the group.
3. **Common goal:** The group for its proper existence and functioning must have a common goal or purpose to be achieved by the members of the group. With such same target to be reached the members may thus try for its satisfactory achievement even when having different approaches and styles of functioning.
4. **Group loyalty:** The members of the group are always loaded with the feelings of loyalty towards the ideals and purposes of their group. In the perfect harmony, they even merge their individuality with the image and goals of the group. It helps them to side down their own interests for saving and achieving the larger interest of the group.
5. **Definite set of values or norms:** Every group possesses a set of values or norms of its own to regulate the behaviour of its members to seek the common goal or purposes.
6. **Demonstration of group behaviour:** The individual behaviour of the members does not remain individualistic and self-centred while working in the group. It takes the shape of a collective and group behaviour meaning thereby all the members of the group are forced or impelled to feel, think and act together at least to a particular moment at a particular place.

Group and Crowd

The collection or assembly of two or more persons exhibiting some definite characteristics and showing group behaviour, as you have known till now in this chapter, is known by the term 'group'. However, every collection or assembly of the persons at some place on one occasion or the other is not necessarily designated as group. We often name it as crowd. You must have come across with such an assembly of a large number of persons at the roadside enjoying the amusing, entertaining and strange behavioural activities of the street dancers, and trick players. A spontaneous gathering of such a type may also be seen at the site of an accident or mis-happening. Examining the nature of such assembly or collection of the people you may very well realize that such collection does not possess many of the distinctive characteristics of a group and group behaviour and that is why it is being designated by a different term 'crowd' instead of the usual term 'group'. Let us try to see what distinguishes the term group from the term crowd.

(i) The assembly of even two persons may be named as group. However, this does not happen in case of a crowd which requires the assembly of a relatively larger number of people.

(ii) Groups are relatively permanent in nature in comparison to a crowd which is quite transitory, spontaneous and temporary.

(iii) In comparison to group behaviour, crowd behaviour is quite irrational in nature and does not involve a well-thought-out plan of action.

(iv) In group behaviour, the activities and behaviours of the individuals to a great extent is properly organised, controlled and disciplined. On the other hand, crowd behaviour does not follow any rule. It is known for its rudeness, indiscipline and miss management

(v) In a group, the members exhibit interdependence and interrelations based on the common purpose. They have group loyalty and follow the prescribed rules and ideals. On the other side, the individuals forming a crowd do not show any of such group behavioural characteristics.

Group and team

We make use of these two terms group and team in our day to life quite frequently including the world of sports. In their meaning and application both have a lot of similarities such as (i) the members of both may like and be attracted to other members,(ii) they may have a close interaction with each other including their dependency on one another (iii) they may share some common goals (e.g., a group of a fitness centre and team members of a sport activity may concentrate on losing weight and tone muscles).

With such similarities and commonness in them however, these are not one and the same. They differ a lot from each other in their meaning, nature, and application. The term team stands for a special type of group. It is why, where all teams may also be designated as groups, not all groups can be considered teams. As pointed out by Weinberg & Gould, (2007:161), for a group being designated as a team it should be loaded with the following additional key characteristics not essentially present in the term group:

- Collective sense of identity- "we-ness" rather than "I-ness"
- Distinctive roles-all members know their job
- Structured modes of communication- lines of communication
- Norms-social rules that guide members to do and not to do.

Types of Groups

Every one of us is a member of some group that exists in society. Various attempts have been made to classify these groups on one ground or the other. Some of these classifications are discussed ahead:

1. **Sumner's classification:** W.G. Sumner (1960, p. 92) classifies the group into two main categories:
   (i) In-group or we-group.
   (ii) Out-group or others-group.

In-group or we-group is the group with which we identify ourselves. The out-group or others-group is the group, the members of which are considered as outsiders by us. Therefore, there are only two categories 'we' and 'they' and an individual might belong to either in-group or out- group. Those who are not the members of the 'we-group' are of the 'they- group'. Antagonistic feelings are often common between these groups. We do not try to understand the members belonging to out-group and show an attitude of indifference or scorn or even hate. For example, to the white American child a Black-American child belongs to the out-group and, therefore, he hates him. In schools where segregation is observed, the girls or boys form two opposite groups. For the girls, the boys are the members of the out-group. Similarly, boys consider girls to be belonging to out-group.

2. **Cooley's classification:** The classification suggested by Cooley (1960, p. 94) is based on the degree of intimacy which the individual feels with other persons or groups or a sort of we-feeling found among them. On this basis, groups may be classified as primary, secondary or tertiary.

In primary groups, there is an intimate face-to-face relationship and cooperation. We-feelings are found to a maximum degree among the members of such groups. Also, they are bound with a mutual bond of interest. The family, play-group of children and village community are some of the examples of primary groups.

In secondary groups, the relationships are more or less casual. Here the relationships are usually marked by a single bond of interest. Examples of this type of groups are Trade Unions, Professional Associations, social organisations and associations, Lodges and Clubs.

In Tertiary groups, the degree of intimacy or relationship is quite marginal and transient in character. The group of the audience in a cinema hall and passengers in a railway carriage etc. are the examples of such groups.

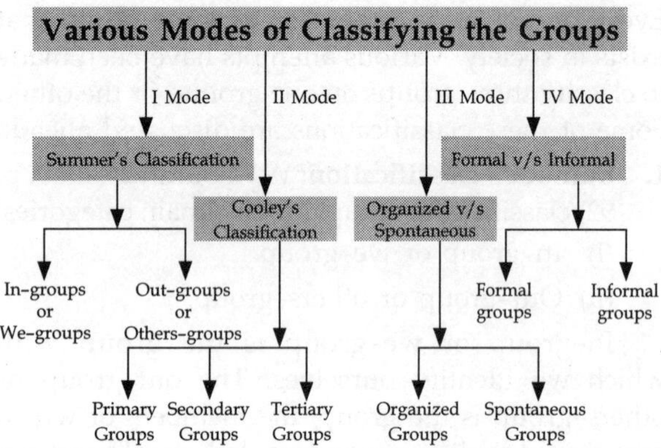

Fig. 11.1: Various Modes of Classifying the Groups

3. **Organised v/s Spontaneous groups:** Groups may be classified as organised groups and spontaneous groups. In a spontaneous group, the individuals belonging to it come together naturally without any previous planning or specific purpose. But organised groups exist for some specific purposes and are formed as a result of careful pre-planning. The family, the army, the school, etc. are the examples of such organised groups.
4. **Formal v/s Informal groups:** Psychological groups, according to another mode of classification, can be classified as Formal and Informal groups.

In formal groups, the members of the group observe formalities and are bound by some specific rigid rules, values and norms; on the other hand in informal groups, members are not bound by specific rigid rules. They may enjoy liberty of thought and freedom of action, and are very informal in their relationships and behaviour.

Semi-formal groups fall in between these two categories. The group of the students in a class-room is an example of a formal group. Various kinds of work organisations also belong to this category. In informal groups, we can include family, play or peer group, hobby and recreational groups, etc. Under semi-formal groups, lodges, temples, social clubs can be considered.

By this sort of above classification it should not be concluded that an individual is a member of only one group and he cannot belong to more than one group. An individual may belong to many groups and can be a member of many groups at a particular time. He may be the member of his family group, class or school group, play group, club and association and other so many primary, secondary or tertiary groups, formal or informal groups, spontaneous or organised groups, in-groups or out-groups etc. Similarly, it should not also be considered that the classification of groups suggested above is rigid or static. The groups, whatever their structure or composition may be, are always quite dynamic in nature. For example, a formal group like participants in a seminar may turn into an informal group while taking tea or lunch. Similarly, a spontaneous group that has been formed, incidentally, may take the shape of an organised group and a secondary group like lodge or hostel may perform the function of a primary group.

Group Formation

Groups whether formal or informal, formed spontaneously or deliberately have some or the other intended purposes. Their formation depends or is facilitated through the presence of certain conditions or factors. Let us see what are such conditions or factors that pave the way of group formation.

1. **Physical proximity or closeness:** There is a need for the assembly of at least two or more persons for the formation of a group. This is possible only if the persons comprising a group get opportunity of meeting one another. The distance between them should be reduced and they should be drawn nearer and nearer for the formation of a substantial group. When the persons travel in a bus or train, they get an opportunity for coming closer to one another. The physical proximity provides the opportunity for them to share the opinion and ideas. The more time they will spend in such proximity, the more cohesiveness will emerge in their group behaviour. As a result a group of tourists travelling in the same bus or railway compartment for a number of days form a more meaningful and stable group than the co-passengers travelling for a limited time in a bus or a train. Similarly, the inhabitants of a new born Muhalla, Sector, Colony or Village may turn into a group as soon as they get an opportunity in terms of physical proximity or closeness to one another. The

people who spend their nights on a platform, in a night shelter or under any shelter may also be found to form a group on account of such physical proximity.

2. **Interaction among individuals:** Mere physical proximity or closeness is not enough for the formation of a group. It is only the starting point and the base. People may sit, stay or travel together, but if there is no interaction between them, we can't expect any type of group formation comprising them. That is why while the inhabitants of an ordinary residential colony may soon engage in the formation of a group, those living in the posh colonies and multi-storey buildings in the big cities fail to do so. The success in the quality group formation, then again depends upon the quality and impact of such an interaction. In case the consequences of the interaction are not satisfying, there will either be no group formation or, if formed, it will have a very short life.
3. **Similarity in attitudes:** Those who have similar bent of mind and attitudes towards certain things, persons or ideas are naturally drawn nearer to one another. Very soon they develop closeness and begin to travel on the path of the group formation. For example, people having similar attitude towards a political, social or religious ideology, may easily become a member of the organisation loaded with that ideology.
4. **Similarity in interest:** The persons having the same likes and dislikes, interests and disinterests, feel pleasure in coming closer as well as working and living together. It opens the path of group formation. The similarity of the tastes and interests makes them feel, think and act together. For example, those who are interested in a morning walk or are lovers of nature may soon find themselves as the members of a morning walk or nature lover group. The formation of various religious, social, entertainment or hobbies clubs may be cited as examples of such group formation process based on similarities in interests.
5. **Similarity of purpose:** The bond of the common target or purpose being served by our behavioural actions may become a potent factor for the group formation. For example, we come across organised groups in the form of labour unions, employees' federations, students' unions in our surroundings. Such groups are formed on account of the similarity of purpose, the common goal or targets to be achieved by the members of the group.
6. **Group attraction:** The organisational structure of a small group may influence and attract the people towards its activities. They may soon come closer and bring to enroll themselves as members. In this way, a mere togetherness of a few people on account of the impact of their name and fame, personality, behavioural actions and group activities may soon become a substantial cause for the formation of a well-organised and properly structured group. Many of the political parties, vichar manchs, social clubs and religious organisations have risen to their present status by starting merely with a very few people.

Factors Associated with the Formation of Groups

- Physical proximity or closeness
- Interaction among individuals
- Similarity in attitudes
- Similarity in interests
- Similarity of purposes
- Group attraction
- Serving specific purposes
- Similarity in occupation or means of livelihood
- Distress or stressful situations
- Security

7. **Serving specific purposes:** Some people may join a group or are found to take initiative in the formation of a group simply because of serving their narrow and specific interests. One may try to form a group of rural students or employees belonging to rural areas or specific castes and religions simply because he wants to exploit their sentiments for becoming their leader and then fulfilling his specific aims and narrow interests. In the same way, a businessman or an insurance agent may be found to become the member of Rotary or Lion Clubs not because of the urge of social service but on account of an opportunity to get new customers and business contacts.
8. **Similarity in occupations or means of livelihood:** In the formation of the group, the similarities in terms of adopting the same profession or means of livelihood may also count significantly. The partners working on a railway station or bus station, the labourers working in a factory, the employees working in a private or government organisation all may be found to work and live in their own professional or occupational groups. It gives them a sense of security and safety on the economic, social

and psychological grounds and also serves their specific occupational and professional interests. The telegraph workers' union, bank union, teachers' unions, traders' organisations all are examples of the groups formed on the basis of similarities in occupations or means of livelihood or organisation simply because we feel that it will help us provide the needed physical, social or psychological security.

9. **Distress or stressful situations:** The distress or stressful situations, mis-happenings or accidents, natural or man-made calamities may provide opportunities and necessities for thinking, feeling and acting together, and they may prove a very potent factor for the formation of a group. The people affected due to the natural calamities like drought, excessive rain, earthquakes may be forced to form a group for their existence and survival. A similar group may also be formed by the residents of a locality after being attacked by a mob of religious or regional fanatics or a group of dacoits. The attack by an enemy army may also provide an opportunity for the citizens of the invaded nation to stand and fight together by forming a meaningful large group. In such emergencies, where the individuals who are affected and sufferers may be found to form their own groups, the other type of groups, then and there are also formed comprising of those people who come forward to help and defend the sufferers.
10. **Security:** Individuals may also be forced or persuaded to come closer and form a group on account of specific security reasons. All the members of a family may then be found to have a sense of security on account of being the part of a formal and organised group and sharing the same means or ways of living together. Since every one of us needs security and protection on physical, psychological and social grounds, the fulfillment of this need may compel, attract or persuade us to become a member of one or more groups. We may join a fanatic minority or caste-based body.

In this way, we can conclude that the process of the formation of the group is guided by various types of factors serving individual and social needs of the individual joining these groups as a member. The effectiveness, cohesiveness and strength of a group or organisation, thus is essentially linked with the general and specific interests of its members being served through the name, fame and functioning of this organisation.

What makes us join one or the other groups?

As a rational being all our actions are aimed to serve some purposes. This is also true for our decision to join a group. In the opinion of Baron & Byrne (2004: 435) people are found to join a group for serving specific purposes like below.

1. *Satisfying a number of social and psychological needs:* The satisfaction of our so many socio-psychological needs is quite vital for our wellbeing and survival. We have a craving for love and affection (to love and be loved by others), want to have a social company, urge to give and take in social transaction, affiliation with some social organization etc. Such, socio-psychological needs of ours can be met with our becoming the members of one or the other social groups.
2. *Achieving what could not be achieved as individuals:* The joining of a group may help an individual to do a task or achieve a target that is quite strenuous or almost impossible for them to achieve single handed by on an individual basis.
3. *Getting and sharing a lot of knowledge and information:* In the group we have a lot of opportunity and ease to receive a lot of information and knowledge from the sources available in the group environment that could not otherwise be possible for us.
4 *Meeting the need of safety, and security:* The joining of a group helps us in meeting our needs of safety and security. We feel safe and secure, not only as a member of the primary groups such as family, and community but the membership of the secondary groups such as a professional organization, union, and club also provides us the needed safety and security in our social life.
5. *Establishing a positive self-identity:* The membership of one or the other groups helps us in the establishment of our identity on a positive note. Our self-concept is well enhanced by considering ourselves as a member of one or the other social groups. We, an individual, may be found to have a lot of increase in our self-perception by getting us accepted as a member of some prestigious club or organization.

The Process of Group Formation or Development

The groups have to evolve and struggle for reaching a state of well-meaning functioning. For this purpose, a rising group has to pass through certain stages of evolution and development. We can call them the stage of group formation or evolutionary development. The socio-psychologist Bruce Tuckman (1965), in this concern, has identified four stages that characterize the formation or development of groups. He has named them as stage of forming, storming, norming and performing. Let us know about them.

1. **Stage of Forming:** This is the initial and starting phase or stage of group formation. In the case of some social groups the beginning in this direction is made when some like-minded individuals come closer and decide about starting a group for serving some cause. In the case of others, the individuals have to work along with others in a group for carrying out some professional business such as completing a project or doing some specific job as members of a sport team or professional workers. Whatever, form or motive may be for the start-up it is the stage when members of the group come together, begin to develop their relationship with one another and learn what is expected from them. This stage is said to be complete when the members of the group start well to assume themselves as part of the group.
2. **Stage of Storming:** After passing of the first stage of group formation, this second stage creeps up in the evolution or development of a group. It is characterized with the initiation of interpersonal and intra-group conflicts and differences of opinion. These may be related to the goals of the group functioning, the division of responsibilities in the group, selection of leader, and the behaviour of the members towards each other or complaint about the favouritism exhibited by the group leader. At this stage, therefore it becomes important to work through the dissensions and conflicts growing in the group by resorting to the desirable measures such as establishment of clear common group goals, having necessary open discussion on the issues of dissensions and provide opportunity for everybody in the group to be listened. Gradually, with the adoption of suitable measures, the conflicts and differences in the group start settling and members begin to respect majority opinion and leadership hierarchy of the group for working together in the group.
3. **Stage of Norming:** At this third stage of group development everything seems to be normal and in a good working condition among the members of the group as their dissensions and differences get almost settled. Expectations of one another are clearly articulated and assimilated in their routine by members of the group. They pick up the needed patterns, norms and rules of working united and fulfilling their responsibilities towards the achievement of common goals. They feel adjusted in the group and also seem to be fully satisfied with the group goals and distribution of roles and responsibilities to individual members. In this way, as a whole, members of the group come to understand how the group as a whole operates and what as individual and group members they have to do for its proper working.
4. **Stage of Performing:** As the name suggests, this final stage of group development is of action and performance. The group is now focused on its task. Therefore, now, each and every member tries to concentrate fully on giving his or her best for the fully functioning and maximum output of the group towards the achievement of group goals. The understanding about each other and the spirit of working cooperatively is seen among the group members at its most at this stage of intensive performing. The members, here, now also try to learn new skills and adopt creative ideas for taking the group accomplishments at the new heights of celebrating its glories. In this way, at this stage, the group is aimed to reach the top of its functioning and accomplishments.

However, as it happens to everybody, nothing remains on a set position for ever. The stage of performing-functioning full and performing at the top also does not last long. There may be a rise and fall in the functioning of the group. It may get disintegrated or cease to be in its existence due to one or the other reasons. The old members may leave and new join and it may necessitate to get engaged in a new process of forming, storming, and norming for coming to a full stage of functioning and performing on the part of the group. Moreover, midway during the performing stage, the possibility of arising conflicts and growing of dissensions among the members cannot be ruled out on account of so many internal and external factors. The leadership and the group as a whole should be prepared for facing such eventualities. There should be a healthy democratic environment for having a constructive discussion on the matter of mutual discord and differences so that all may go well in the group regarding its proper functioning and continuance.

To Sum Up

Formation of groups in any social set up depends up on the people's intention of becoming members of one or the other groups. In general, they are attracted and motivated to join a group for serving the specific purposes like: satisfying a number of social and psychological needs; achieving what could not be achieved as individuals; getting and sharing a lot of knowledge and information; meeting the need of safety and security; and Establishing a positive self-identity.

The process of group formation or development is found to involve certain specific stages such as the stage of forming, storming, norming and performing.

Stage of forming is the initial and starting phase or stage of group formation where members of the group come together, begin to develop their relationship with one another, learn what is expected of them and start to develop necessary trust among them. This stage is said to be complete when the members of the group start well to assume themselves as part of the group.

The next one, the *Stage of storming* is characterized with the initiation of interpersonal and intra-group conflicts and differences of opinion arising on one or the other accounts. However, gradually, with the adoption of suitable measures, the conflicts and differences in the group start settling and members begin to respect majority opinion and leadership hierarchy of the group for working together in the group.

At the third stage, the *Stage of norming,* everything seems to be normal and in a good working condition among the members of the group as their dissensions and differences get almost settled. At this stage of group development, as a whole, members of the group come to understand how the group as a whole operates and what as individual and group members they have to do for its proper working.

Stage of performing, the final stage of group development, is the stage of action and performance. The group is now focused on its task and tries to achieve its maximum and rise to its peak in its performance and fame.

How Do Groups Function?

The day to day working and functioning of a group depends upon some basic elements inherent in its structure and working such as the role and status of the members comprising the group; the norms of the group to regulate the behaviour of the members; and cohesiveness–the glue that binds members to function as a team.

Let us discuss about these elements one by one.

The Roles of the Members in the Group: In the functioning of a group each and every member belonging to the group is expected to play a definite role for contributing its share in the accomplishment of the common group goals. Many times, these roles are received by the members on account of their position in the organization and other times these may be assigned to them on account of their abilities and capacities or may be willingly taken by them on account of their interest and desire to do so. However, in whatever manner, the roles are there for the members comprising a group, the differentiation in terms of the specification of these roles is expected to make the functioning of the group reasonably smooth and productive by allowing the members to work according to their interests and capabilities. However, for ensuring that the group functions in a proper way, the leader of the group and the members of the group themselves should try to maintain a proper coordination and accord among their role performance.

The Status of the Members within the Group: The status of the members within the group is concerned with the position and rank of the individual members in the group. Members of a group or organization are expected as well to play their role according to their status in the functioning of the group. In fact, the members belonging to a group or organization are quite conscious of their status or position and contribute always in the functioning of the groups in proportion of what is expected from them in terms of their status in the group. The awarding of higher status or position in the structure and working of a group carries a thing of significant importance on the part of the group members and this is why conferring or withholding of the status in the group to a member may work as a great morale boosting or reprimanding for his actions or behaviours in the group. One rises to the higher status in the group as a fair award for his contribution in the group's functioning and rise. However, everybody in the group expects a fair treatment to him by the members of the group according to his status or position in the group. The satisfaction and dissatisfaction of the members on this account may result in influencing the functioning of the group in a quite favourable and adverse way. The leader and the members as a whole should be quite careful about this important issue concerning the status of the members for the effective functioning of the group.

The Norms of the Group: Any group or organization for its survival and proper functioning needs the establishment of certain norms–rules and principles (implicit or explicit) and their strict adherence on the part of its members. Certainly, these norms represent the rules of the game–the behaviour to be exhibited towards each other and the manner in which responsibilities are to be exercised by the members of the group. In this way, the norms of the group, by pointing out to the members what to do and not to do, work as an effective means for regulating the behaviour of the members, which in turn results in the improvement of the functioning of the group in a needed way.

The Cohesiveness in the Group: The fourth basic element associated with the proper composition and functioning of a group is its cohesiveness. Etymologically, the term cohesion is derived from the Latin word *cohaesus,* which means "adhering or sticking together". Taking clue from such etymological meaning of the word cohesion, the term cohesion or cohesiveness existing in a group has been defined by Carron, (1988: 341) as *a "dynamic process that is reflected in the group's tendency to stick together while pursuing its goals and objectives".*

Cohesiveness: The glue like tendency or characteristic of the group to keep members together as a team for achieving the common group goals.

In this way, cohesiveness or cohesion reflects a tendency or magnet like characteristic of a group that helps in attracting as well as keeping members together in the form of a solid working group or team. It helps the group in team building, to have the joint collaborate efforts of each and every member, and the spirit of sink and float together for achieving the targets of the groups.

To Sum Up

Regarding the functioning of the groups, we may observe that their day-to-day functioning depends upon some basic elements inherent in their structure and functioning such as:

- The role and status of the members in the group (what position is given in the group and what is expected from them accordingly for the accomplishment of common group goals)
- The norms of the group–in the form of what to do and not to do, for regulating the behaviour of the members, and
- Cohesiveness–the glue that binds the members to function as a team.

Decision Making in Groups

Every group informal or formal, small or large, institutional or organizational has to pass through the decision-making process at one or the other times for carrying out its one or the other functions. The task of decision making in the group may be performed by resorting to the means and ways as briefed below.

Consensus: The group members try to reach a consensus–a solution or work plan agreed and acceptable to all through mutual discussion.

Compromise: When no consensus is arrived at a particular plan or proposal, then attempts are made to seek compromise sought out of the differing opinions expressed in the discussed proposals.

Majority Vote: When two of the above methods do not work, then, attempts are made to abide by the majority decision for putting a particular proposal to vote.

Decision by Leader: In this mode of decision making the group members take a safest mode for leaving the entire matter of taking final decision to their group leader.

Seeking Arbitration: At the time when the group leaders may also feel hesitation in taking full and final decision at their own then efforts may be made to approach an external body or person to take decision on behalf of the group as an arbitrator

Potential Dangers and Pitfalls Faced in Group-Decision Making

Whatever mode or method such as consensus, compromise, majority vote, leaving on the leader or arbitrator may be employed for the decision making in group, there remain possibilities for the turning of the group decisions as highly damaging, painful and disastrous in their after effects. In history of civilization and countries we may have a number of examples of such bad group decisions and their ill consequences. Remember, the grave consequences of the bad decisions like attacking Pearl Harbour by Japan and invading Russia by the Nazi Germany dragging both America and Russia in the war and thus unnecessarily inviting their doom in World War Second. Question arises why it happens? What is responsible for arriving at such faulty decisions on the part of groups? The answer to such queries may be available in the discussion about the potential dangers and pitfalls inherent either in the process of decision making or in the minds of the decision makers. In this connection, socio-psychologists and researchers have pointed about certain things more responsible for this mess such as (i) The phenomenon of Group Polarization, and (ii) The phenomenon of Groupthink. Let us understand them.

The Phenomenon of Group Polarization

According to Baron & Byrne (2004), "the tendency of group members to shift towards more extreme positions than those initially held as a result of group discussion" is referred to as polarization.

In this way, we may consider polarization as a phenomenon visible during the group decision making in the form of a general tendency that is exhibited on the part of the group members in the form of shifting their viewpoints towards a position that is similar to but more extreme than the viewpoints held by them before group discussion. Actually here under the influence of the phenomenon of polarization, the groups are more likely to take extreme decisions than individuals alone.

> **Group Polarization:** A general tendency exhibited on the part of the group members to shift their viewpoints towards a position that is similar to but more extreme than the viewpoints held by them before group discussion.

Let us try to understand what is conveyed through the above-cited definition and explanation through an example.

A group of committee formed for taking decision about the action taken for an act of indiscipline committed by a student in general is supposed to take such disciplinary action according to the punishment prescribed under the rules and code of conduct of the institution or the practices being adopted for this purpose in earlier cases. However, in the influence of the phenomenon of polarization the committee may be seen here to adopt the quite extremely viewed position in its final decision-to get the student go scot-free or expel him from the school depending up on the nature of the decision initially held by the group before having a detailed discussion on this issue stand taken by the members at the beginning before having a detailed discussion on this issue. Suppose, in this initial stage, there was an environment of taking action on a tougher basis than adopting a soft or lenient stand. It gets strengthened and becomes hardened picking up the extreme end (the polar position on the tougher side) resulting in expelling the student from the school.

Similarly, in the case of taking decision for dealing with the management of a factory, the labour union may be found to move from the average linear stand maintained at the initial stage in the form of resorting to a few days token strike to a higher degree of risky position (e.g., going for indefinite hunger strike or becoming violent for teaching the management a good lesson) after the group deliberations. In these deliberations, the discussion may turn hotter and hotter and individual members may be found to shift their stand in tune with the current flowing in the majority of the members.

Why such Polarization occurs?

Why such polarization occurs during the group-decision making, has been searched out by the socio-psychologists with some of the plausible causes as under:

1. A more common explanation for the occurrence of group polarization may come through the mechanism of *social comparison*. It is a natural craving on the part of us, to get ourselves compared with others especially with those belonging to our own group and, then, try to show that we are not ordinary but extraordinary. It is this tendency of showing themselves quite unique and distinctive from others that make some members or whole of the group get polarized and adopt an extreme approach or stand on an issue while reaching a final stage of the decision making.
2. Another good explanation for the occurrence of group polarization may be available from the view point emphasized in the *persuasive-information perspective*. According to it, it is the persuasion effect of the strong views and opinions expressed by a majority of the group members during group discussion and a type of new information contained in them, that makes many of the individual members convinced that it is the *right* view and shift towards it with increased strength resulting in the emergence of group polarization (Vinokur & Burnstein, 1974).
3. The third explanation for the occurrence of the phenomenon of group polarization may stem from the perspective known as self-categorization in which a group member is seen to put himself in a defined category of the member of his own group and thereby identify him well with the group. Accordingly, he may not only try to show his agreement with the opinion and views expressed by the majority of the group members during group discussion but even adopt an extreme approach for furthering a majority opinion to become a group decision

and thus proving his solidarity and cohesion with the group.

However, whatever causes and factors may work in generating group polarization, the drift of the group toward polarization is a serious problem. In all its forms, it certainly interferes with the groups' ability to think in the right ways. It leads the groups to adopt positions that are increasingly extreme, and thereby make the groups to take extremely one-sided disastrous decisions (Baron & Byrne, 2004) and thereby every precaution needs to be adopted by the groups while making decisions for settling an issue.

The Phenomenon of Groupthink

Concept and Meaning

Another quite significant phenomenon that interferes with the ability of groups to proceed on the right-thinking path for taking appropriate group decision is known by the term groupthink. It was first used by Irving Janis in 1972 and was later explained in one of his publications in the manner as below.

Groupthink as a term may be considered as "a strong tendency for decision-making groups to close ranks, cognitively, around a decision, assuming that the group can't be wrong, that all members must support the decision strongly, and that any information contrary to it should be rejected (Janis, 1982).

In this way, the phenomenon of groupthink, once functioning, gives birth to a collective state of mind among the group members. There is now no individual thinking and acting on the part of individual members. In its place, the intention of going with the group decision prevails among the members for maintaining cohesiveness in the group.

> **Groupthink:** A strong tendency or a type of collective thinking developed among the decision- making groups forcing the members to believe that their group can never make a mistake in arriving at some decision, resulting in siding with the group with no second thought on their part.

In general, problems created and negative effects produced through the operation of groupthink in the group decision making may be briefed as below.

- Groupthink forces the group members to think and believe that their group can never make a wrong decision or mistake in arriving at some decision, resulting in siding with the group with no second thought on their part.
- They are found to be the victim of a phenomenon known as collective rationalization, in which all the members together try to rationalize and go by the group decision by setting aside any information that goes against the group's point of view.
- Under the influence of the phenomenon of groupthink, the group is found to insulate itself from the dissenting views thus, creating all possibilities for generating an improper and defective decision proving harmful and disastrous to the group.

The Causes inherent in the Development of Groupthink

The phenomenon of groupthink is found to take its root in the decision-making process of the groups on account of some of the reasons highlighted by the socio-psychologists in the manner named and briefed below.

- *The prevalence of a high level of cohesion* among the group members. Such environment of the group leads the group members to develop a collective group mind resisting the individual members to think beyond the decision taken by the group in any situation on an issue.
- The *strict observance of some or the other types of group norms* for the conduct of the group members may seal off any voice of dissent arising within the group and thus pushing the members not to think of anything beyond what is thought and done by the group.
- In many of the cases, the *role of the group leaders* particularly their authoritative and dictatorial role provides a quite favourable environment for germinating and perpetuating the seeds of the groupthink among the groups.
- Groupthink is particularly said to be *a product of the environment* in which:
  - ♦ Group suppresses ideas that are critical or not in direct support of the direction in which the group is moving.
  - ♦ Group is denied information or lack the confidence or ability to challenge the dominant views of the group.
  - ♦ Group members are found to live in a belief that their group is superior and infallible. It cannot err and therefore it is always wise to go along with its decision.

- ♦ There is no systematic procedure to evaluate the alternatives coming for decision making in the group.
- ♦ The group feels high stress on external threats coupled with the sign of no hope for finding its early proper solution and thus to seek safety in numbers.
- ♦ The groups are found to make use of a system of self-censorship refraining members to comment against the group decision and taking action against the members who dare to do so.

Measures for preventing the occurrence of Groupthink

Groupthink carries a quite damaging effect on the decision-making ability of the groups. There should be something to be done essentially for restraining and preventing the occurrence by following the measures like below.

- The group should try to promote democratic principles in arriving at some decision for the group.
- The leaders of the groups should always promote and encourage the ideas suggested by the individuals or section of members for brining alteration and modification in the proposal or viewpoints earlier considered for arriving at some group decision.
- To prevent the occurrence of groupthink, it is also better to think about the solution of a felt problem by different sub-groups.
- A technique known as Devil's advocate technique may also work well in the prevention of the occurrence of groupthink phenomenon. In the use of this technique, one member is assigned to play the role of devil's advocate. He dares to criticize the perspective or decision of the group members by giving his own arguments. It may open a chain of open discussion, accept or reject the earlier arrived group decision or modify and replace it by some improved one.

To Sum Up

The work of taking decision by the group on an issue is carried out by allowing its democratic discussion and employing one or the other mode such as consensus, compromise, and majority vote, leaving matter to the leader or arbitrator for arriving at the final decision in this regard..

In such decision making in group, there always remain possibilities for arriving at such group decisions that may prove highly damaging, painful and disastrous in their after effects. Socio-psychologists and researchers have mentioned certain things responsible for this mess such as: The effect of the phenomenon of Group polarization; and Groupthink. The term *Group polarization* may be defined as a general tendency exhibited on the part of the group members to shift their viewpoints towards a position that is similar to but more extreme than the viewpoints held by them before group discussion. In view of socio-psychologists, it happens on account of the phenomenon of social comparison, and perspectives like the persuasive-information perspective and self-categorization perspective.

Another phenomenon, known as *groupthink* also affects the group decision making in a quite substantial way. As a term it may be defined as a strong tendency or a type of collective thinking developed among the decision-making groups forcing the members to believe that their group can never make a mistake in arriving at some decision, resulting in siding with the group with no second thought on their part. In view of socio-psychologists it happens on account of the prevalence of a high level of cohesion among the group members; emergence of some types of group norms for the conduct of the group members; authoritative and dictatorial role of the group leaders; and the environment conducive for the emergence of the phenomenon of group think

There is a need of restraining and preventing the occurrence of the phenomenon of group think by taking suitable measures like: Promotion of democratic principles in arriving at some group decision, the need of playing proper role on the part of group leaders, and providing an opportunity for the review of the previously arrived decision on the part of group through the sub-groups formed for this purpose.

ASSESSMENT QUESTIONS

Section I: Essay Type Questions

1. What do you understand by the term 'Psychological Group'? Describe the characteristics and essential features of such a group.
2. What is a group? Discuss the various modes of classifying the groups.
3. Throw light on the following modes available for classifying the groups.
   (i) Sumner's classification
   (ii) Cooley's classification
   (iii) Organized v/s Spontaneous groups
   (iv) Formal v/s Informal groups
4. Distinguish between a crowd and a group in detail.
5. What is a team? In what way it is similar and dissimilar to the term group?
6. What are groups? Discuss the factors operating in the formation of groups.
7. What makes us join one or the other group? Discuss.
8. How do groups function? Discuss in detail.
9. Discuss the role of the following in the day-to-day functioning of a group
   (i) The role and status of the members of the group
   (ii) The Norms of the groups
   (iii) Cohesiveness of a group
10. Discuss in detail the process of group formation or development.
11. How the task of decision making is carried out in the groups? Discuss in detail.
12. What do you understand by the potential dangers or pitfalls in group decision making? Discuss in brief the effects of group polarization and groupthink in taking wrong decisions by the group.
13. What is group polarization? Why does such polarization occur and how does it affect the decision-making process in the group?
14. What do you understand by the phenomenon of groupthink affecting adversely the group-decision making? Why does it occur and how can it be prevented? Discuss.

Section II: Short Answer Type Questions

1. Provide a suitable definition of the term group
2. Name three characteristics of a group.
3. Tell about the classification of groups provided by the sociologists Sumner or Cooley.
4. What are formal or Informal groups?
5. Mention the names of any two informal groups.
6. Differentiate between organized and spontaneous groups by an example.
7. Name three differences between a group and a crowd.
8. Mention two things differentiating the term team from the term group.
9. Name three conditions or factors paving the way for group formation.
10. Name four reasons that make one join one or the other groups.
11. Discuss the role of any one of the following in the functioning of groups.
    (i) The specific role to be played in the group
    (ii) The status in the group
    (iii) Norms of the group
    (iv) Cohesiveness of a group
12. What is cohesiveness of a group?
13. Name the four stages associated with the process of group formation or development.
14. Name the different ways and means adopted by a group for decision making.
15. What is group polarization?
16. Name three factors or causes inherent in the occurrence of the phenomenon of group polarization/ groupthink.
17. Tell in brief about the phenomenon of groupthink.
18. Tell about the ill effect of group polarization/ groupthink in the decision making of the groups.

Section III: Objective Type Questions

1. Tell what is not true about the characteristics of a group?

(a) Existence of two or more than two individuals
(b) Absence of interdependence among them
(c) Common goal
(d) Group loyalty

2. The group of audience in a cinema hall is an example of
(a) Primary group
(b) Secondary group
(c) Tertiary group
(d) None of these

3. Which one the following is not an example of informal group?
(a) The group of students in a class-room
(b) Family
(c) Peer group
(d) Hobby or recreational group.

4. Which one of the following is not a factor paving the way for the formation of groups?
(a) Distress or stressful situations
(b) Group attraction
(c) Absence of interaction among individuals
(d) Similarity of purposes

5. Consider the following as the different explanations for the occurrence of group polarization in the group decision making.
(i) Mechanism of Social comparison
(ii) Persuasive-information perspective
(iii) Self-categorization
(a) Only (i) is true
(b) Only (i) and (iii) are true
(c) Only (i) and (ii) are true
(d) All are true

Answers

1 (b)	2 (c)	3 (a)
4 (c)	5 (d)	

12

Group Processes–Cooperation, Competition and Conflicts

Learning Objectives

After going through this chapter, you will be able to:

- Throw light on the concept and meaning of the term cooperation
- Tell about the different characteristics or features of cooperation
- Name and discuss the various forms or types of cooperation
- Elucidate the needs and significance of cooperation in our social life
- Explain the concept and meaning of the term competition
- Throw light on the characteristic features of the process of competition
- Name and discuss the various forms or types of competition
- Discuss the role and functions of competition in our social life
- Explain the concept and meaning of the term conflict
- Elucidate the characteristic features of the conflict process
- Name and discuss the various causes of conflict
- Name and discuss the various forms or types of conflicts
- Throw light on the role and functions of conflicts in our social life
- Discuss the different techniques used for the resolution of the conflict

Introduction

You have already read about what we mean by the term group, its structure, and functioning in our social life. While working in groups, for achieving a common target, the members of a group are in general found to have a proper degree of cohesiveness for remaining united and demonstrate a lot of cooperation in the functioning of their group. Such cooperation is also visible among the different groups working in a set up, locality, or region on a national or global basis. However, besides showing the spirit of cooperation in their functioning, groups may also be found to get engaged in the process of competition and inflicted from a number of internal or external conflicts, mutual rivalries proving harmful in many ways. In the present chapter we would like to know about these three important group processes- cooperation, competition and conflicts in some essential details.

Cooperation

Concept and Meaning

The term 'cooperation' has been derived from two Latin words – 'Co' meaning 'together' and 'Operary' meaning 'to work'. Hence, cooperation means working together for the achievement of a common goal or goals. In this way, when two or more persons work together to gain common goal, it is called cooperation. There is hardly any field or sector of human life and society where individuals are not found to demonstrate togetherness and cooperation in their peaceful living, harmoniously adjusting to each other's need and jointly working for the achievement of common goals. Family members cooperate in running the household matters, students share their time and efforts for completing a project, players and teams work jointly for achieving their common targets, and similarly, the workers in production, professionals in business, public officials in police, army and other public service outputs work day and night in an endless variety of beneficial activities in a jointly united way that make possible for all of us an integrated and social life worth living.

Actually, as we may find, cooperation may be termed as one of the fundamental processes of our social life. It is a form of social process in which two or more individuals or groups work together jointly to achieve common goals for the benefits of all participants. It is in this reference, that the term cooperation has been formally defined by Fairchild (1944) as "a process by which the individuals or groups combine their effort in a more or less organized way for the attainment of common objective".

Cooperation: A social process or behaviour characterized with some specific type of social interaction in which two or more individuals or groups are found to work together to achieve certain common ends or goal.

The characteristic features of the process of cooperation

The following things can be said about the characteristic features of the process of cooperation.

- Cooperation involves two elements: (i) Common end or goal and (ii) Organized effort. When different persons or groups have the same goals and also realize that individually on their own, they cannot achieve these goals, they work jointly for the fulfillment of these goals.
- Cooperation is an associative process of social interaction which takes place between two or more individuals or groups.
- Cooperation is a conscious process in which individuals or groups have to work consciously and willingly to attain what they aim to achieve in a particular social situation.
- Cooperation is a personal process in which individuals and groups personally meet and work together for a common objective.
- Cooperation is a continuous and common endeavor of two or more persons involving the elements of proper interaction and continuity throughout its beginning till end.
- Cooperation is a universal process in the sense that it is found in all groups, communities, societies and nations.
- Common ends or goals in one or the other social situations can be better achieved by cooperative efforts of the people and it is necessary for the progress of individuals as well as society.
- Cooperation also results from necessity. It is not possible to run many of our tasks, projects, businesses and even household affairs without the proper cooperation of others.

In this way, it is evident from the above discussion that we may term co-operation as one of the forms or types of social processes or behaviours characterized with some specific type of social interaction in which two or more individuals or groups are found to combine their motivations and efforts to achieve certain commons ends and purposes.

Needs and Significance of Cooperation

Why do people need to cooperate with each other in one or the other social situations at one or the other time? What role is played by cooperation in the life of the individuals and progress of the society? The things like below can be said in response to these queries.

1. **Helping in the satisfaction of individual's needs and goals:** Cooperation as one of the important means of social exchange process helps individuals living in a community or society to meet each other's physiological, and socio-psychological needs. We can fulfill our so many basic and fundamental needs such as food, clothing, shelter, sex, and other day-to-day comfort-giving needs through a process of give and take or mutual exchange associated with the phenomenon of cooperation. The same also applies to the satisfaction of our psychological needs (e.g., to love and to be loved, giving and getting recognition, showing sympathy and getting sympathy from others etc.) through the mechanism of cooperation. In addition to the satisfaction of our basic needs, cooperation also plays wonders in helping us in the realization of our life goals, motivations and aspirations by taking and giving help to each other at the time of need at one or the other time. Take any sector or field of your social life and think a while, would it be possible for you single handed to reach your destination or respective goals without the active co-operation of other members in society?
2. **Helpful in the existence and survival of human beings:** We all owe our existence in this world through the courtesy of the cooperation mechanism. It is the cooperation between male and female in the society that has made possible the continuity of human race through the reproduction and upbringing of the children. Cooperation is the most elementary form of social process without which society cannot function or even exist. The security and protection that is available for us for our living and working have been made possible through the cooperative efforts of all of us paving way for the establishment of the system of governance and formation of laws, rules and

regulations for this purpose. At the time of any crisis–natural or man–made, it is not unusual for us to stand united and work jointly for coming out of the problem. Similarly, a unique type of cooperation is visible from all the corners of a country among its citizens having too much diversity in their opinions and behaviour for providing their contribution for the defense of the country and survival of their own.

Cooperation helps in the task of
- Satisfying our needs and goals,
- The existence and survival of human beings,
- Making the human being social,
- Maintenance of the social fabric, and
- Development and progress of the society.

3. **Helping in making the human being social and maintenance of the social fabric**: It is the spirit of cooperation that makes human beings the social being by crossing over their narrow self–interests. They begin to think about the collective gains and happiness for all. How to get on the path of the individual progress while maintaining the needed social structure and fabric of the society can be well learned and practiced on their part with the help of the spirit of cooperation demonstrated by them in their working and behaving.
4. **Helping in the development and progress of the society:** Cooperation in the form of an integrative and associative phenomenon always works for the constructive, creative and developmental activities and goals. It is why a variety of individuals and social development and progress may be seen to be engineered and monitored through the cooperative efforts of the people of a community or nation. The saying, "united we stand and divided we fall" tells us how cooperation contributes in a big way towards our progress and development and non–cooperation results in stagnation and downfall. Today, what we see as tremendous progress and development in the field of science and technology, agriculture and industry, transport and communication, space science and missions, would not have been possible without the active cooperation. In fact, all the progress that mankind has made in the various fields from time to time is credited well to the cooperating spirit belonging to all people over the globe.

To Sum Up

The term co-operation stands for one of the forms or types of social exchange processes characterized with some specific type of social interaction in which two or more individuals or groups are found to combine their motivations and efforts to achieve certain commons ends and purposes.

Cooperation is found to play a significant role in our social life by helping us in the satisfaction of individual's needs and goals; in the existence and survival of human beings; in making the human being social and maintenance of the social fabric; and in the development and progress of the society.

Competition

Concept and Meaning

Much like cooperation, competition is that form of group process that is considered quite essential for providing needed motivation and hitting target for striving and achieving excellence and success on the part of the involved parties. However here, there are no such united efforts for achieving a common target as visible in cooperation. It happens chiefly for the reason that where the rewards in cooperative situations are group rewards, these turn into individual rewards in competitive situations. Thereby, all individuals/groups taking part in a competitive event or racing for a prized or scarce thing, struggle in their own ways for achieving it somehow with the least consideration of the interests of others. There are countless examples in our social life such as struggling hard for getting gold in the athletic event, standing first in class, getting promotion by excelling over others, etc. that we may encounter in our participation and interaction in the groups. Not only individuals there is a race for getting one or the other things–material or symbolic such as position or status, name and fame on the part of social and professional groups, business establishments and nations as a whole to engage in the game of cut–throat competitions by pushing the rivals on a side. In this way, as a matter of some formal definition, the term competition may be referred to "a type of impersonal, universal, continuous and unconscious social processes in which the people are found to strive or struggle for achieving the desired scarce things or the targeted goal by surpassing their rivals."

Competition: A group process in which people are found to strive or struggle with others for achieving the targeted goal by surpassing all rivals.

The Characteristic Features of the Process of Competition

The process of competition in its unique form and type of the social processes is known to be attributed with some of the specific characteristic features detailed below.

1. *Competition springs up due to the scarcity or limitation of the things:* As a generalized rule, people compete with each other in a most pronounced form whenever there is an insufficient supply of anything that they desire most. It is insufficient in the sense that here demand outturns supply and all cannot have as much of it as they wish. Many times, there is only one prized item, position or status that two or more persons want to achieve. In this case, there is tough competition for its attainment that can be possible to only one out of the several.
2. *Competition is both dissociative and associative in its nature and consequences:* In comparison to other social processes like cooperation and conflict, competition lies in between these two in terms of its nature and consequences in the sense that it has a capability of proving dissociative as well as associative. It is associative or integrative in the sense that no other social process can match it in terms of providing the needed motivation to the individuals or groups for working wholeheartedly for achieving the set target in a competitive event. How the candidates work and struggle for obtaining the desired rank or position, the motivation of doing all this is brought out through the competition organized for this purpose. It remains constructive till the competitors struggle for excelling each other without obstructing or harming the efforts of others, however, once the norms set for the competition are broken, it turns into unruly conflicts and clashes making it highly dissociative and disintegrative in its nature and consequences.
3. *Competition is Universal:* Competition may be termed as the most universal social processes in the sense that it is found in all societies, whether civilized or uncivilized, rural or urban, traditional or modern, in all periods of history and among all classes of people all over the globe. It happens on account of a simple reason that there is no end to the wishes and needs of individuals living on this earth, but the material or psychological resources available for their satisfaction is quite scarce and limited. There, thus, arises a universal struggle for existence and survival in the form of competing with each other for attaining what all need or wish to achieve.
4. *Competition is Impersonal:* Take any competitive event in its true form. In this event, individuals may be found to take part in competing with each other for getting something they desire in terms of some object, reward, position or status. They struggle and strive for achieving or attaining a common objective. In this way, here, clearly, the competitors do not compete with each other on a personal level. The attention of all the competitors is fixed on the goal or the reward they aim at. Moreover, at a number of times at different occasions in different field of life, the competitors while competing with each other do not know one another at all. These are the reasons for calling and considering the competition act as an impersonal affair.
5. *Competition is an Unconscious Activity:* Competition takes place on the unconscious level in the sense, that competitors in most of the cases hardly know each other. Take the case of any competition–competitive examination or test/ interview organized for securing the highest marks in the final–examination or getting selected for a course of job, the competitors here may be found to be reasonably conscious of what they are doing, what they want to achieve, and how should they struggle for achieving their target but on the other hand, they are not at all conscious of the presence of other competitors. They bother for doing their efforts with a least consideration of who their competitors are and what will they do. Hence competition is said to take place mostly on an unconscious level.
6. *It is a Continuous Process:* In a general way, people compete with each other for the satisfaction of their needs or fulfilling their wishes. The sphere and dimensions of these needs and wants always remain in the chain of their continuity. One's needs or desire in terms of getting wealth, name, glory, power and status when satisfied may give birth to another need or desire for competing with others. It is why the process of competition never comes to an end. It goes continuously throughout one's life span.

7. *Competition is always governed by norms:* Take the case of any competing event in the fields or spheres of our life. It is always organized and governed through the set rules and norms. All the competitors are required to follow these rules and norms. In the examination hall, all examinees have to follow the norms of appearing in the examination and surrender their answer sheets to the invigilators at the fixed time. Similarly, at the sport complex, all the players and teams while competing with each other have to abide by the rules and norms of the respective games being played there at that time. In any way, whenever the rules and norms are violated, it results into conflicts and clashes between the players and teams.

Role and Functions of Competition

Competition, as mentioned earlier in this chapter, is a social process that may be characterized as integrative as well as disintegrative in its nature and consequences. Accordingly, it can play both positive as well as negative roles in exercising its functions in our social life. Let us try to discuss them.

Positive Role and Functions of Competition

Positive Role and Functions of Competition in our social life can be summarized as below.

1. *Helping the individuals in meeting their needs and desires:* In our social world, there are things which are quite scarce but are more needed on the part of the people for the satisfaction of their physiological and socio-psychological needs and wants. Demand is scaling the supply in many areas. Accordingly, it is quite natural to have shortage of employment or positions in one or the other private or public sectors. The competition opportunities available for the individuals in this regard make them hopeful for the fulfillment of their wishes in a properly fair way by doing their best in struggling and striving for the purpose. Many of the individuals, thus, are helped by the phenomenon of competition in the realization of their needs and wants. Moreover, by utilizing competition as a mode and means, we may protect the individuals from direct conflicts and clashes for achieving the scarce things and thus may secure a solution to the problem of limited supply and unlimited demand of goods in a peaceful way.
2. *Allotment of right individual to proper place in a right way:* Individuals differ from each other in relation to the possession of abilities and capacities of performing the task related to one or the other social and professional areas. With the help of means and measures employed for providing opportunities to compete for places and positions in the respective social or professional fields it becomes quite easy to place the right person judiciously to the proper places. Competition helps in distinguishing and determining who can do better in the respective fields and who can do justice for being selected for a particular job, status or position in the society. Thus fitting the round pegs in the round holes and square pegs in the square holes can properly be possible with the help of the phenomenon of competition.
3. *Proving a good source of motivation to go ahead in life:* You have the ability and strength to do a job or do the needed hard work for earning wealth or status in a particular area, the pushing needed and opportunities provided for this purpose can be properly possible in a society where there lies a democratic system to compete and excel in the desired fields. Actually, competition opportunities always prove a constant source of motivation to the peoples of all cadre and social status to excel or to obtain recognition or to win an award in one or the other social and professional areas. The practice of organizing contests and awarding prizes and scholarships to those who occupy the few top positions on the merit is specially meant not only for providing the needed reinforcement to them but also to work as a good motivational source for others to come forward for striving for excellence.
4. *Helpful in the development and progress of the society:* The phenomenon of competition, has a great potential to throw a challenge for the individuals, societies and nations to increase their strengths and capabilities for keeping them in the race of economic, social, industrial, scientific and technological progress at the regional and international level. The progress and development visible on this account all around the globe owes much of its glory to the practice of competition. The type of advances and progress going on in the space science, artificial intelligence and robot technology in different countries at present may be cited a good example of the outcome of the phenomenon of competition. Moreover, in a generalized way, in our common day-to-day life, social sectors and work areas, competition has helped us in allotting right persons to the different assignments. It has naturally resulted in making use of the best human resources and

talents available for the purpose of the required progress and development of the society and nation. The continuation of competition, after entering the field further pushes the talented and capable people to remain conscious of providing their best in their respective work domains, thus making the wheel of progress and development of society move on with the required speed.

Negative Role and Functions of Competition

Competition has both positive as well as negative sides for affecting the welfare of the individual and the society. We can expect good positive outcomes discussed above through the courtesy of the competition phenomenon. However, all of such advantages and benefits derived for competition can only be possible if the process of competition remains within its limits and is carried out in all its fairness and positive spirit. However, when derailed, it can drift heavily on the negative side giving birth to a number of negative outcomes briefed below.

1. *Resulting in the sheer wastage and stagnation of resources:* Unfair and unreasonable use of competition may result into a high degree of wastage and stagnation of the resources in the society. In a joint family we may see that the family members buy things they don't need and consume more in competition to other members causing a great deal of wastage of the material and economic resources. Similarly, in competing with others people are found to spend more on their pomp and show resulting in a lot of economic wastage. In addition, an unreasonable competition among the individuals or groups may also result in stagnation, as no one is ready to cooperate with others and leave one's wrong course of actions.
2. *Causing great inequalities and injustice in the society*: Unlimited and unrestricted competition in society may provide too much power and supremacy to a few ones at the cost of others. They may monopolize the resources while leaving others to remain dependent on them for the satisfaction of their needs and aspirations. In the blind race of unfair competition, the powerful and status holders become more and more wealthier and powerful leaving others quite behind in this race to the extent of getting them starved or deprived of their basic needs. In fact, most of what is visible in our society or world community in the form of too much inequality and injustice may be termed as the outcome of the unrestricted cut throat competitions of one or the other kinds prevalent among them.
3. *Creating psychological and emotional problems*: Unhealthy and unfair competition is responsible for creating one or the other types of psychological and emotional problems to the participant individuals or groups. Due to some or the other bitterness creeping during the competition, competitors may develop unfriendly and unfavourable attitude towards one another. The failure and the experience of losing face in the public may make them fearful, anxious and frustrated. In some cases, it may lead to neurosis and competition phobia. On the other hand, it may also have a possibility of turning some competitors as a rebel and rules-breaking personalities. They pick up the habit of not following any rules and norms while competing with others in the social life or business field causing serious harms to the integrated fabric of the society.
4. *Competition may lead to conflicts and clashes:* The unfairness, partiality and rules breaking in a competition may develop a quite unhealthy bitterness among competitors. It may result in drawing a deep gulf of a wide variety of differences between them. They begin to suspect and doubt every step of their competitors and thus always remain in the state of conflict and clashes with one another. They begin to employ quite underhand methods for pulling and harming each other. Business rivals, for example may try to ruin and destroy the business of each other and professionals may think about downgrading the image of their competitor colleagues before the seniors or public in general. On the big screen, the conflicts and clashes among the competitors, many times may take the shape of group fighting, communal clashes and spoiling of relationship between the nations on the international scenarios.

Therefore, we must try to learn the lesson from the bitterness and harm caused by the unfairness and unhealthy competition. Where on one hand, competitions should always be encouraged for harnessing the various individual and social advantages available from it, it should be kept under proper control by following the needed rules and norms and concentrating fully on the attainment of a target on our part by increasing our competency rather than planning for creating obstacles in the path of the other competitors.

To Sum Up

Competition is that form of group processes in which people are found to strive or struggle with others for achieving the desired scarce things or the targeted goal by surpassing their rivals.

Competition is attributed with some specific characteristic features such as: Springing up due to the scarcity or limitation of the things; Proving dissociative and associative in its nature and consequences; Demonstrating its universality, impersonality, unconsciousness and continuity in its functioning; and Governed always by norms.

Competitions can play both positive as well as negative roles in exercising its functions in our social life. Here, in terms of playing its positive roles, competitions may be found to exercise the functions like: Helping the individuals in meeting their needs and desires, allotment of right individual to proper place in a right way, proving a good source of motivation to go ahead in life, and helpful in the development and progress of the society.

Regarding its negative roles competition can be found to exercise the functions such as: Resulting in the sheer wastage and stagnation of resources, causing great inequalities and injustice in the society, creating psychological and emotional problems, and leading to conflicts and clashes.

Conflict

Concept and Meaning

When cooperation turns into non-cooperation, obstructing others rather than helping them in their tasks and competition turn into apprehension in the minds and bitterness in the hearts of the competitors for one another, then the social process and social interaction between the individuals and groups is said to take the form and shape of a socio-psychological phenomenon named as conflict. In its forms and shapes the social process or behaviour named as conflict is essentially a dissociative or disintegrative social process in the sense that it always leads to disintegration proving harmful to the individuals and groups under conflict. For understanding the meaning and nature of the term conflict in a more appropriate way, let us take into consideration the characteristic features of the process of conflict arising among individuals or groups.

Conflict: A type of group process or behaviour in which people, after feeling pressure from their opponents, deliberately resort to some emotionally charged negative behaviour for inflicting harm or to weaken the opponents with a sole motive of achieving their desired ends in any way.

The Characteristic Features of the Conflict Process

Socio-psychologists and researchers have tried to conclude things like below about the characteristic features of the process of conflict.

1. *It is a universal process:* Conflict much like the cooperation and competition is an ever-present process. It exists at all places and all times in all sectors of our social life throughout the globe. In the interaction and social exchanges between the individuals and groups, there arise situations and circumstances before them to have clashes in their interests at one or the other points and particularly while contesting and contending for some scarce things or common objective. These situations and circumstances are also universal, they may occur in the life of the individuals or groups all over the globe at all times. Conflicts in our societies have therefore been present from time immemorial and would be having their presence in all the incoming times.
2. *Unlike competition, conflict is specifically personal:* Competitions when and wherever are held under the rules and norms these remain peaceful allowing all the competitors to struggle for the realization of the common objective according to their own ability and capacity. However, when these become personalized, centreing only on one's personal interests with no care of norms and other's welfare, these are turned into conflicts. Here, instead of putting the attention and energy in the realization of the goal, it is shifted to harm or even eliminate the opposite party from the scene of the competition. Since, the conflicting parties personally know each other, the process becomes quite personal and as a result, both the parties, locked in conflict, get engaged in harming each other instead of concentrating over the realization of their goal or objective.
3. *It is a conscious and deliberate act:* In getting engaged in the social behaviour named conflict the involved parties are quite conscious of their conflicting behaviour. Here one individual or group makes a deliberate attempt for opposing

and resisting the will or causing harm and injury to another. While in conflict, attention of each is fixed on the rival quite consciously for teaching him a lesson rather than minding their own business of attaining the goal. In this way, every conflict on the social scene represents a conscious and deliberate attempt on the part of the involved parties to harm or cause loss to another in some or the other ways.

4. *Unlike cooperation and competition, it is an intermittent process*: In contradiction to cooperation and competition processes, the process of conflict lacks the continuity. It is occasional and intermittent. Two parties cooperating and competing well with each other may be found to get indulged in the conflicting behaviour all of a sudden. Most often, the conflict between parties also subsides soon in the manner it erupts. If the conflict becomes continuous, no society can sustain itself. Therefore, its intermittent nature also proves a boon to the individuals and the society as a whole.
5. *It is highly emotional and violence-ridden act:* The highly surcharged atmosphere loaded with a number of negative emotions of intensive speed is a quite known birth place of the conflicts arising in the interaction and competitions among human beings. Quite suddenly, the minor and ordinary-looking conflicts are found to take the shape of a quite violent behaviour on the part of the involved parties. Such uprising of violence in the behaviour of involved parties not only proves quite detrimental to the interests of both the parties but also proves quite harmful to the growth and wellbeing of the society.
6. *It is loaded with a lot of disintegrative or dissociative functions:* As a process, conflict in its nature and consequences may be termed as a highly disintegrative and dissociative process. In its functioning it is the anti-thesis of cooperation. Here instead of providing assistance to others for achieving their ends, all sorts of hindrance or obstacles are placed in their path by resorting to violent means. Conflict as a disintegrative process persuades the competitors to make use of all sorts of fair and foul means at their disposal including elimination or weakening of their rival competitors in the pursuit of the common goal. Here competitors may be found to engage in a deliberate attempt to oppose, resist or coerce the will of their opponents as well intentionally harm them through a lot of violence shown towards them.

8. *On its positive side, it can work as an instrument of social change and reconstruction*:

Besides a lot of things, lying on the debit side of the process of conflicts, held responsible for causing loss and harm to the interests and welfare of the competitors and society as a whole, there are some things that may be quoted to fall on its credit side. The mentionable ones are (i) stiffening the morale and promoting the cohesion and solidarity of the group (ii) raising the status and position of the dominant individual or group, (iii) bringing change in the ideology, value systems and social structure and (iv) persuading the members of the society to think about the ways and means for reducing conflicts and clashes between competitors.

On the basis of what has been conveyed by the above cited characteristic features, *we can understand conflict as a type of social process in which individuals or groups, after feeling that others are heavily coming in their way, consciously and deliberately resort to some emotional charged negative activity such as violence or direct attempt to harm or weaken the opponents with a sole motive of achieving their desired ends in any way.*

Causes of Conflict

Conflict is a quite conscious and deliberate process. It may happen at any time in all societies and social sectors around the globe. Although it is a universal process, its causes vary from individual to individual, group to group and from time to time. Accordingly, it is regarded to be caused on account of the interaction of a number of biological and socio-psychological causes or factors as discussed below.

Biological Causes

In the category of biological causes, we may place the factors like below responsible for the eruption of conflicts among the individuals and groups working in the society.

1. *Inborn and innate aggressive tendency:* According to some thinkers like Freud and other physiological psychologists, some people are born with aggressive and hostile tendencies making them engage in conflicts in their later social behaviour.
2. *The need to struggle for existence and survival*: There are limitations and scarcity of material objects and physical facilities in our social world in comparison to the needs and wants of the people for their attainment. When demands outplay supply, it is but natural for the needy ones to get into struggle and conflicts with other aspirants. They think it quite essential for their survival and existence.

3. *Individual differences:* No two individuals are exactly alike. They differ from each other not only in relation to their somatic structure and physiological conditions but also with respect to their attitudes, aspirations, ideologies, values and interests. Such differences in individuals may create a wide gulf between their ways of thinking, feeling and doing one or the other things causing a lot of maladjustment and possibilities of confrontation and clashes with one another.

Socio-psychological Causes

In the category of Socio-psychological causes responsible for creating conflicts among individuals and groups we may place the factors or attributes like below.

1. *Socio-cultural differences:* One of the major causes for the eruption of conflicts among the individuals and groups in our society is linked with a lot of differences lying between the social living and cultural traditions of the people. Our communities and societies all over the world remain disintegrated and strained in their relationships at their bitterest on account of belonging to different castes or ethnic groups, following different religions and believing in one or the other faiths or philosophies of life. The separation tendencies and conflicts may also be clearly visible among the people and groups on account of the boundary lines drawn between them on the basis of urban-rural division, public and private establishments, local v/s immigrants, speaking of language etc.
2. *Social changes:* In our societies nothing is permanent. It remains changing with the change in time. Individuals and society as a whole, need to adapt themselves to these rapid changes in order to keep pace with them for the individual and social progress. When some individuals or a particular segment of the society does not change along with ongoing changes in the society, it may create a serious cultural lag leading to mutual confrontation between those who welcome or resist these changes. The conflicts visible in the ideology of the old and new generation may be cited as one of the good examples of the role of social changes in the creation of conflict.
3. *Wide gap in demand and supply*: When there becomes an unreasonable gap between the demand and supply of certain commodities at one or the other times in society, then everybody wants to compete for or to say obtain the scarce by hook and crook. The desire or competition for obtaining undersupplied or scarce things in the society, after taking a quite bit more fierce form, is found to be converted into conflicts between competitors.
4. *Economic disparity:* The distribution of economy in a reasonable way among the individuals and groups is essential for their proper and harmonious living in society. There erupts a lot of tension and conflict in societies where there becomes too much disparity between the economic earnings, and socio-economic status of the individuals or groups living in those societies. It may take the form of class struggle between poor and rich or haves and have nots of those belonging to these societies.
5. *Clashes of mutual interests:* A very big cause of the mutual rivalries and conflicts between individuals and groups in society is the clashes of their mutual interests. The hoarders always want to monopolize the purchase and sale of commodities in the market and it can make them engage in conflict with the producers and consumers of these commodities. Similarly, we can observe the conflicts and clashes between the labor class and the owners of the factories as both parties are locked in the struggle of serving their own interests.

Techniques Used for the Resolution of the Conflict

Conflict, how necessary they may appear for the reorganization and restructuring of the social systems, actually prove quite unhealthy and damaging for the wellbeing of individuals and society. These should be resolved as early as possible by taking suitable measures and adopting proper techniques. These measures and techniques are applied with the proper consonance of reasons or causes responsible for creating them as well as the need of the situation prevailing at the time of their application in the manner and ways as mentioned below.

1. *Introduction of Humour:* Humour is a great medicine and a sure shot for extinguishing the fire ignited through an emotionally charged environment of the conflict. It can also prove a great medicine for relieving the involved parties from the tension and stress created through the struggle and clashes experienced in the conflict. Therefore, some attempts should always be initiated by someone present on the scene for the introduction of humour for diverting attention of the conflicting parties to something else than reacting and responding to the verbal and motor duel.

2. *Introducing variety and change in the existing situation:* Conflicts, many times, are the consequential product of momentary or situational-based reactions and responses of the involved parties. If somehow a change is brought out in the existing situation, then conflicting parties may be helped in coming out of the vicious conflicting scene. When two parties have a duel over an issue, then the change of topic may save them from the aggravation of the conflict.
3. *Resorting to social distance or avoidance*: For the management of conflict arising between two parties, it remains quite beneficial on their part to suspend for the time being their interaction and social exchange, maintain necessary social distance and avoid conversation and actions, particularly associated with the thorny issues loaded with the possibility of mutual conflicts. The initiative for taking such steps may come from any one of the two parties or both may simultaneously go for it. One of the individuals out of the two in conflict may take a decision to withdraw from the conflicting scene and it may help in putting a brake in their mutual conflict.
4. *Introducing super–ordinate goals:* You must have seen the conflicts and clashes between two groups of the same class or schools for the regular winning of one or the other competition or earning the top position. However, in case we put a target before them to win a position in the inter–school tournament, than the introduction of such super–ordinate common goal may help a lot in saying goodbye to their mutual conflict and beginning a chapter of mutual cooperation for the attainment of common goal.
5. *Bringing Attitudinal change:* There are conflicts in the segments of the social fabric that arise on account of the stereotypes, prejudices, and negative attitudes prevailing in the minds of the people for the people belonging to the other sex, caste, region or religion. By adopting suitable measures for bringing the needed proper attitudinal changes through one or the other means such as education, media, enactment and enforcement of laws a lot can be done for the prevention of such conflicts.
6. *Dealing with discrimination and disparity:* In many society or regions, the discontent growing among one or the other sections of the society due to disadvantages suffered by them on account of one or the other types of discrimination shown towards them by the majority or ruling section is found to work as the major cause of class struggles or conflicts in the society. For the prevention of such an occurrence, there is a great need of adopting an measures for doing away of such discrimination or disparity prevalent in the society or regions of the country by following the principles of equity, equality and common brotherhood.
7. *Adopting the means of negotiation and compromise*: In the conflict resolution, the adoption of the strategy of seeking negotiation or compromise between the involved parties is considered the most viable, useful and applicable strategy. It calls for sitting on the table and seeking a compromise by searching for a midway and coming to a win–win position for the parties involved in a conflict. For seeking such a compromise, one of the parties may come forward to take necessary initiative for breaking ice with the party in conflict and start useful dialogue with it for coming to a position of compromise. However, in some situations a third party or person may prove quite useful in playing the role of a negotiator. How he should play his role, let us think over it.
   (i) He should first try to know and understand the true nature of the conflict between the two parties in its full aspect and consequences by giving a patient hearing to both. After hearing both separately at their respective places, he should, then, propose and persuade them for seeking negotiation with each other.
   (ii) He should then take their views about what they actually want to seek from such negotiation. They may be asked to prepare a list or set agenda for the things to be needed on their part priority–wise through this negotiation.
   (iii) He should then try to convince and take them in confidence for providing their willing cooperation for the success of the negotiation. They should be made to realize that in negotiation one should show a reasonable flexibility for giving something to attain other things present in his list.
   (iv) He should then take initiative for breaking the ice between the parties in conflict by appropriately planning and organizing their meeting at a suitable place accidently or purposely. The lists from both the parties containing what they want through negotiation should then be made the subject

of negotiation between them. The task may, then, be further carried out as below.

- The top priority should be given to the things in their lists which can be negotiated quite easily. Usually, such items are centred around the differences in their thinking and perspective. These conflicts exist mainly in the minds of the people. They should be helped here to resolve such conflicts by putting themselves into other's shoes so that they can understand each other's point of view and narrow down the list of their differences in their negotiation agenda.
- After then attempts should be made to allow the involved parties to identify and openly discuss differences in perceptions. Here the negotiator should be careful not to allow discussion to become an opportunity to place blame on each other but to make them understand the other side's emotions and interests.
- Both parties should now be asked to fix their attention on the remaining ones left unresolved out of the two lists and attempt further to engage in negotiation on a give and take basis for the mutual satisfaction of one another.
- For the difficult ones, if left still unresolved, lottery or draw system may be adopted or attempts may be made for getting them agreed that for the first half of the period one party will be enjoying a certain benefit and for the second half the other in turn.
- Once all is negotiated, it should take a formal form of written agreement.

To Sum Up

As a term conflict may be understood as a type of group process in which individuals or groups, after feeling that others are heavily coming in their way, consciously and deliberately resort to some emotionally charged negative activity such as violence or direct attempt to harm or weaken the opponents with a sole motive of achieving their desired ends in any way.

Regarding the characteristic features of the process of conflict we may say that it is a universal, specifically personal, and intermittent process and is termed as a highly emotional and violence-ridden act loaded with a lot of disintegrative or dissociative functions. On its positive side, however, it can work as an instrument of social change and reconstruction.

Regarding the causes or factors responsible for creating conflict we may safely conclude that it is caused on account of the interaction of a number of biological and socio-psychological causes or factors.

Conflict, arising between two parties needs to be resolved as early as possible by making use of one or the other useful techniques such as: introduction of humour, introduction of variety and change in the existing situation, resorting to social distance or avoidance, introducing super-ordinate goal, bringing attitudinal change, dealing with discrimination and disparity, and adopting suitable means of negotiation and compromise.

ASSESSMENT QUESTIONS

Section I: Essay Type Questions

1. What is cooperation? Throw light on the concept and meaning of the term cooperation as a form or type of group processes.
2. Discuss in detail about the needs and significance of cooperation in our social life
3. What is competition? Throw light on its concept and meaning as a form or type of social exchange.
4. While defining the term competition, throw light on the characteristic features of the process of competition.
5. What is competition? Throw light on its various forms or types.
6. Discuss in detail about the role and functions of competition in our social life.
7. What are conflicts? Explain their concept and meaning in a proper way and point out the characteristic features of the conflict process.
8. Discuss in detail about the various causes and factors responsible for the creation of conflicts
9. Discuss in detail about the different techniques used for the resolution of the conflicts arising between two parties in one or the other social situations.

Section II: Short Answer Type Questions

1. State in brief the meaning of the term cooperation as one of the group processes.
2. Point out three characteristic features of the process of cooperation.
3. Tell two things about the needs and significance of cooperation in our social life
4. State in brief the meaning of the term competition as one of the group processes.
5. Point out three characteristic features of the process of cooperation.
6. Tell two things each about the positive and negative outcomes of the process of competition in our social life.
7. State in brief the meaning of the term conflict as one of the group processes.
8. Point out three characteristic features of the conflict process.
9. Name three factors each designated as biological and socio-psychological creating conflict in the groups/society.
10. Point out two techniques used for the resolution of conflicts among individuals or groups.

Section III: Objective Type Questions

1. What is not true about the process of cooperation?
   (a) Cooperation is a specific individualized inherited phenomenon
   (b) Cooperation helps in the satisfaction of our needs and goals
   (c) It helps in the maintenance of social fabric.
   (d) It helps in the existence and survival of human beings.
2. What is not true about the process of competition?
   (a) It is a universal process
   (b) It demonstrates continuity in its functioning
   (c) It springs up due to the availability of things or opportunity in abundance.
   (d) Here one tries to surpass his rivals for achieving the targeted goal.
3. What is not true about the process of conflict?
   (a) In the process of conflict people attempt to harm or weaken the opponents.
   (b) It has no positive role and beneficial functions at its disposal in the interest of the society.
   (c) It is a universal phenomenon.
   (d) A number of biological factors also work as a cause of its creation.
4. Which one of the following is not a way or means used for conflict resolution?
   (a) Leaving people to settle their score for their pent up extra emotional energy.
   (b) Introduction of humour in the conflicting situation.
   (c) Resorting to social distance or avoidance
   (d) Bringing attitudinal change

Answers

1 (a) 2 (c) 3 (b)
4 (a)

13

Social Influence

Learning Objectives

After going through this chapter, you will be able to:

- Explain what is Social Influence
- Tell about the forms and ways of social influence
- Elucidate the concept and meaning of conformity
- Mention about the types or forms of conformity
- Distinguish between private and public conformity
- Throw light on the factors affecting conformity
- Throw light on the Sheriff's classical experiments on private conformity and Asch's classical experiments on public conformity
- Elucidate the concept and meaning of compliance
- Throw light on the various principles or factors governing one's compliance
- Discuss about the various techniques of compliance-making people comply
- Know about the application and use of various techniques of compliance such as (i) The Foot in the Door technique, (ii) Law Ball technique, (iii) Door-in-the-face technique, (iv) The Foot in the Mouth technique, (iv) That's not all technique, and (v) Dead line technique.
- Elucidate the concept and meaning of obedience
- Tell about the various forms of obedience
- Throw light on the Stanley Milgram's Study on obedience
- Describe the mechanism of exercising restraint or control over destructive obedience

What is Social Influence?

In its word meaning, the term social influence means the type of influence that is social in nature. It, thus, stands for an influence exercised on the part of an individual/ group to make the desired change in the behaviour of others. Under the impact of social influence, people tend to behave differently other than what they would have if left entirely to them. Sociologists and socio-psychologists both take this phenomenon of social influence as quite essential and significant for the adjustment of the individuals in their social set up and also running of the social set up itself in a desired way. For understanding the meaning and concept of the term social influence let us now think over some of its well-known definitions provided by scholars and thinkers in this field.

1. **Baron & Byrne (2001:318):** Social influence may be defined as "efforts by one or more individuals to change the attitudes, beliefs, perceptions, or behaviours of one or more others."
2. **Avermaet (2004:404):** Social influence is the change in the judgments, opinions and attitude of an individual as a result of being exposed to the views of others.
3. **Crisp & Turner (2014:85):** Social influence is an umbrella term. It refers to any effect that another person or group has on your attitudes and behaviours.
4. **Barrett (2017:190):** Social influence is an internal or external change in a person caused by the real or imagined pressure from others.

The analysis of the above definitions may reveal the following things about the meaning and nature of the term social influence.

- Having basically, a social nature and feeling the need to remain attached to his social group/ society the individuals are prone to yield under social influence-introduce changes in the ways of their thinking, feeling and behaving as asked and desired by others who are considered recognizable and valuable by them for this purpose.
- Social influence has a great potential to bring changes in the behaviour of a person or group of

persons. These changes are internal (introduced in their ways of thinking and feeling) as well as external (reflected in their acts and actions performed by them in their social encounters).

- As a result of these changes, the affected individuals try to behave somewhat in a quite different way demonstrable in their changed beliefs, opinions, attitudes, perception of the things and ideas, ways of doing and performing in the real-life including interaction and responding to others.
- These changes are brought out in their behaviour through the pressures (indirect as well as indirect) exerted on them by other people or group of people in the form of providing direction, setting norms and ideals, emphasizing majority opinion, providing incentives or motivation of some sort or imposing their authority of one or the other kind.
- It is not essential for an influencing exerting agency to remain present in person, the norms, rules and regulations, traditions and modes of living and behaving established by the society, or authority in a social and work situation may work by themselves as a pressure exerting agent in influencing the thinking, feeling and behaviour of the people for making them behave in a set or desired form. Here, in this change of behaviour of the people through social impression, their anticipation of some negative consequences for not conforming to the group or individual (termed as symbolic social influence) may prove quite enough as equivalent to the direct presence or instructions from others.

Social Influence: A type of influence, essentially social in nature, exerted on an individual or group by another individual / group for bringing changes in their social behaviour.

On the basis of what is conveyed through the above-cited definitions about the meaning and nature of the term social influence we may understand it as a *type of influence essentially social in nature that is exerted on an individual or group directly or indirectly by another individual/group for bringing changes in the behaviour of the former in areas like opinions, perceptions, beliefs, attitudes, doing work and performing skills, and ways of interacting and behaving with others in one or the other social situation.*

The Forms and Ways of Social influence

Under the phenomenon or mechanism of social influence, the efforts made by an individual or group of individuals/society are found to influence the social behaviour of the influenced or affected individual/ group for behaving on their part in one or the other ways as named and described as below.

The Forms and Ways of Social Influence

- Conformity (Yielding to majority opinion)
- Compliance (Complying with the request or suggestion)
- Obedience (Obeying the orders)

Conformity

Concept and Meaning

There might have been so many things in our social life that we have not liked to do but did simply for gong along with the majority opinion or set norms or ways of behaving prevalent in the society. Accordingly, one may get engaged in a stereotyping and prejudiced behaviour towards a minority neighbor for going along with the majority of neighbors of his residential locality despite his broad mindedness on this account. The other may engage in a violence-ridden strike against the school authorities simply for conforming to the majority decision of his schoolmates despite his unwillingness and known standing against such acts as a matter of principle.

Such socially influenced behaviour committed by individuals is termed as conformity in the language of social psychology. It is in this sense that Baron and Byron (2006) have termed conformity "as pressures to go along with other people around you, to behave in the same manner as other persons in one's group or society".

Conformity: A form or mode of social impression putting pressure on the individuals to bring changes in their behaviour in tune with the existing social norms.

In this way, as emphasized above the term conformity stands for a form or mode of social impression putting pressure on the individuals to bring changes in their thinking, feeling and doing behaviour enabling it to get matched with the existing social norms or behaviour of the majority in the group or society.

Types or forms of Conformity

In general, people may be found to demonstrate two types of conformity in their social behaviour known as (i) private conformity and (ii) public conformity.

1. *Private conformity*, in the opinion of Insko et.al. (1983), is said to occur, when individuals are truly persuaded that the group is right and when they willingly and privately accept the norms of the group as their own beliefs. In this way, private conformity is quite private in the sense that here we may witness the private acceptance of the social norms on the part of an individual. This phenomenon was extensively studied by Sheriff (1935). Let us know about it.

Sheriff's classical experiments on private conformity

Muzafer Sherif, a Turkish Socio-psychologist, carried out an experiment in 1935 for studying the phenomenon of conformity. This experiment was carried out in two phases. There were three participants in the study. In the first phase of his experiment, Sheriff asked each of the three participants one by one to pay attention to a dot (single point) of light while sitting alone in a totally dark room. This dot was on a wall in a quite stationary condition (with no movement) at a distance of 15 feet from the place of participants. However, on account of a phenomenon of optical illusion known as *auto-kinetic effect* it got observed by the participants moving in jagged circle. It occurred on account of a lack of reference point for its observation in the complete darkness of the room. The task of each participant, in the first phase of the study, was to make 100 judgments as to how far the dot of light was moving in inches. At the conclusion of the first phase of the study when participants individually made their estimates, it was seen that there existed a quite significant variation in the estimates of the length of the movement of the dot on their part.

In the second phase of this experiment conducted after a few days, these three participants were again engaged in doing the same task but with a difference. This time they did not participate as individuals but as members of a three-person group. Here they could enjoy the hearing of one another's estimates of the movement of the dot. This development naturally affected their individual beliefs/ estimates and soon their responses began to converge to the point of providing a single unanimous response i.e., establishing a group norm for the estimation of the length of the light.

The findings of the experiment helped Sheriff conclude that individuals, formerly placed in an individual situation and having judgment of a thing in their own ways, tend to arrive at a common judgment after being placed in a group situation and accept this common judgment as a group norm. Later on, as an extension of his experiment, Sheriff, repeated the experiment with the individuals in individual situations all alone and found them responding in terms of the established norms instead of providing their own estimates of the length of the light. They, thus, in fact behaved under the influence of private conformity by accepting the group estimate (group norm) as their own estimate (own norm).

Private conformity: The type of conformity in which individuals willingly and privately accept the norms of the group as their own beliefs.

2. *Public conformity* true to its naming is a public show of one's conformity. In this type of conformity, people are found to work under pressure. They go along with majority opinion and publicly behave as demanded by the majority or social norms while privately considering that the group or social norm is not right. In such conformity, thus, there is nothing like personal or private acceptance of a certain view point or a way of doing something on the part of the concerned individuals. Arch's classical experiments on conformity may be said to be good examples of such conformity. Let us know about them.

Public conformity: The type of conformity in which individuals while working under pressure publicly behave in tune with the majority opinion or social norms.

Asch's classical experiments on public conformity

There arise numerous occasions in the people's social life when they are found to go with the opinion of others especially the majority in believing and doing what they say in spite of having a contrary view about it. It reminds us of a folk story where four miscreants planned to befool a merchant selling a cow baby. They appeared before him one by one to tell that the animal he was selling was a goat baby and not a cow baby and finally got him agreed to sell it in the price of a goat baby. Here we may see that the merchant acted under the pressure of the social influence demonstrating conformity with the majority opinion regarding the animal identity in spite of having a contrary view/ belief about it. The American socio-psychologist Solomon Asch (1951) is credited to conduct quite useful experimental studies in studying the nature and impact of the phenomenon of such type of conformity. In one of his study carried out with a group of eight male college students, the experimental setting and working took its shape in the manner as laid down below.

- One among the eight participants was selected as the real or main participant for studying the phenomenon of conformity. The remaining ones of the participants worked as the confederates/ helpers of the researcher in the conduct of this study. However, they were there in the experiment for doing the same task as assigned to the main participant with no knowledge about their presence as confederates of the researcher.
- All of these eight participants were told at the start of the experiment that they were participating in an experiment on visual judgment.
- In terms of their seating arrangement the real or main participant was provided the space and turn for participating in the experiment only after all the seven participants (the confederate of the researcher) were done with their job.
- During the experiment, participants were presented first with a standard line drawn on a white card. After that a second white card was presented before them consisting of three comparison lines marked as A, B and C as given in the figure 13.1.

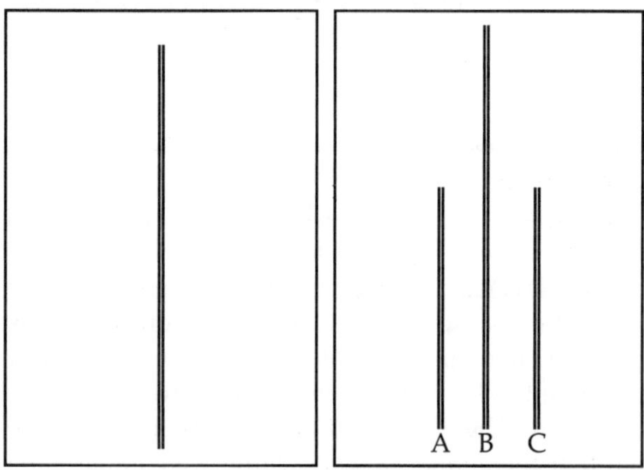

Fig. 13.1: Three Comparison lines in Asch Experiment

- The participants' task in the experiment was to tell in the presence of all the other participants loudly which one of the three comparison lines had the same length as the standard line. The real or main participant had to do it after all the seven participants (acting as confederates) had done their job in this concern.
- The task in this experiment was quite simple. There existed a line (the middle one B in the figure 13.1) among the three comparison lines equal in length to the standard line with no ambiguity of any kind in its recognition as such. However, the manipulation in this experiment was done on four accounts (i) the judgment was made public, every participant had to announce it in a loud (quite hearable) voice well before all the other participants, (ii) the real or main participant was given the last place, he had to announce his judgment after hearing the judgments of others, (iii) the researchers had instructed the other participants acting as the confederates/helpers to provide the incorrect response-picking up the same incorrect line say the third one C in the figure 13.1 and (iv) For providing a check on suspicion on the party of the real or main candidate where six out of the seven confederates were instructed to pick up the same incorrect line say the third one C, the one participant had to pick up the line A for his incorrect response.
- At the conclusion of the experiment it was noted that the real or main participant also provided the same incorrect answer -line C as given earlier by the majority of the confederate participants of the study. Obviously, the conformity-agreeing with the opinion and beliefs of the others here emerged in the behaviour of the real participant by getting influenced through the majority opinion of others.
- For deriving further conclusion on the type of conformity visible in the behaviour of the real participant, Asch in another experiment asked the participants to report their answer on a paper, instead of saying it in a loud voice in front of the others. The rate of conformity was significantly dropped distinguishing clearly between public conformity and private conformity.

Through his experiments Asch, thus, tried to conclude that the individuals (just as the real or main participant of his study) show a good amount of conformity in their behaviour under pressure (influenced and affected by the majority opinion of the group). In public, or in the presence of others, there is a less possibility of going against the majority opinion, and it forces them to conform, even though in real sense they might have been disagreeing with it at their heart (like the real or main participant of the Asch's study who became a victim of public conformity even when he disagreed with it at his heart).

Factors affecting Conformity

The socio-psychologists and researchers have identified a number of factors that either increase or decrease the level of social influence in a given social situation, and in this way, directly or indirectly, contribute towards the conformity of the people to the views of others in the group. We may name and discuss some of these significant factors as below.

1. **Cohesiveness:** Cohesiveness of a group refers to the type of unity, togetherness and degree of attraction visible in the attitude and behaviour of the members of the group towards each other, the group as a whole and its goals and norms. The research studies in social psychology have revealed the significance and importance of cohesiveness in bringing conformity of the individual members towards the group goals and norms. In principle, the more cohesive is the group (i.e., the more interdependent its members are, and the more attraction they feel for their group and its goals) the more likely they are to conform.
2. **Group Size:** Size of the group also matters in deciding the fate of the conformity on the part of group members. In general, the bigger the groups in size the greater are the chances of witnessing conformity on the part of group members simply for the reason that in a large group we may expect a quite big number for exercising social influence or group pressure on the individual members to go along with majority and abide by the group norms. The presence of even three members in the group may work well for making an individual conform and go along with majority even if he has a reverse opinion on this account. We have already witnessed the happening of this phenomenon while discussing the Asch experiment on comparison of lines.
3. **Group Unanimity:** The presence or absence of unanimity among the members of the group also plays a leading role in deciding the nature of the fate of conformity. As a general rule, greater is the unanimity among the members of the group in relation to some issue or compliance of social norms more are the chances of witnessing increase in the amount of conformity. In fact, unanimity in the group is always found to work as a great pressurizing force on the individual members to conform. However, when there is some voice of dissent the conformity gets decreased in the same proportion. Even a single dissent exercised on a part of an individual member (irrespective of his status, knowledge and skill etc.) may provide sufficient strength and confidence to other members to think about their conforming or not conforming to the majority decision or group norms.
4. **Self-esteem and confidence of the individuals:** The level of self-confidence and self-esteem of the people also work as a significant factor for their conformity in one or the other social situations. It has been generally found that the people possessing high self-esteem and more self-confidence are less likely to conform than those lacking in the possession of these traits. Where one's self-confidence and self-esteem provides them sufficient strength and an open mind to express their own views, and doing something other than the majority, the lack of self- confidence and self- esteem leaves a little scope for the individuals to differ and non-conform.
5. **Status of the individual:** What is true for self-esteem and self-confidence is also equally applicable for the status of an individual in the group or society to conform or not conform to the majority opinion or group norm. The lower the social position or status of a person in the group, more are the chances of showing conformity behaviour on his part. Reverse is also true. The people with high social status or position in the group are more likely to show a lesser degree of conformity as they have power and scope forgoing against the majority and social norms.
6. **Nature of the social norms**: The nature of conformity on the part of individual members also depends much on the nature of the social norms prescribed for their behaviour in one or the other social situations. In reference to the maintenance of social behaviour, socio-psychologists have mentioned two types of norms-namely descriptive norms and injunctive norms. Descriptive norms, true to their naming, describe what people in general do in a particular social situation such as putting waste or used material in the containers meant for this purpose at the public places. On the other hand, injunctive norms clearly specify what is desirable / approved behaviour or undesirable/ unapproved behaviour in one or the other social situations, i.e., one should not litter at public places. Both types of these norms add to influence the conformity in peoples' behaviour but with a difference. The injunctive norms carry a much stronger appeal accompanied with a hidden warning for conforming to the

socially desirable behaviour and hence prove more effective than the descriptive norms in inducing conformity in the behaviour of people.

Principles or Factors Governing one's Conformity
- Cohesiveness
- Group size
- Group unanimity
- Self-esteem and confidence of the individuals
- Status of the individual
- Nature of social norms
- Cultural and age factors
- The need for individuation
- Situational factors such as public v/s private response, and nature of the task and level of competence.

7. **Cultural and Age Factors:** Cultural effect as well as age factors are also found to exercise their roles in affecting and influencing the level of conformity of the people. Regarding the cultural effect, it is observed that the conformity of the people varies in accordance to the nature and impact of culture they belong. In general, cultures that are collectivist in nature exhibit a higher degree of conformity than the individualistic cultures. Accordingly, people belonging to rural, backward and tribal cultures are found to be more prone to conformity than the urban and western culture-influenced people and communities in India.

Regarding the impact of age factor on conformity it has been found that the individuals younger in age especially children are more prone to conformity than the people older in age due to lack of experience and status. In fact, there is a quite direct relation between one's age and level of conformity. Older the age, lesser is the likelihood to conform easily to the opinions and beliefs of others.

8. **The Need for Individuation:** There are individuals who have a quite strong urge or inherent desire to maintain their individual identity for expressing their own opinion, holding their own belief and behaving their own way by choosing not to go with others. They resist the majority decision even they find themselves all alone in the group or community for taking a different stand. In this way, the level of conformity maybe seen to get decreased or increased or on account of the presence or absence of such individuation demonstrated on the part of the members of the group. Sometimes, these individuals are really the talented ones who know more and possess ability to provide quite unique and useful ideas for the group and thus may be found to resist the majority decision for pressing their own for the benefit of the group or society. The other times, they may be found to be going against the majority and behaving in a different manner only for the sake of bringing them into limelight and becoming popular for having courage to go against majority and social norms.

9. **Situational factors:** In addition to the above more prominent and common factors involved in influencing and affecting the increase and decrease in the level of conformity on the part of people there are certain other specific and situational factors found effective for the purpose. These may be briefly stated as below:
   (i) **Public v/s Private Response:** In the situations when group members are required to provide their judgment or express their views publicly in front of others, they have great pressure on them to conform-going with the majority of group norms. On the contrary, when they are supposed to engage in expressing their views or opinions privately for example casting their vote through secret ballot, they feel free to express their personal opinion or exercise their own individual judgments with no outside group pressure. In this way, situations when members of the group are supposed to provide their responses publicly or privately cast a great impact over the nature of their conformity behaviour in one or the other social situations.
   (ii) **Nature of the task and level of competence:** Nature of the tasks and competency possessed on the part of the members in the group for performing these tasks also adds to the increase and decrease in the conformity level of the individuals. In the situations, when, the tasks or behaviour to be performed on the part of individuals are vague or difficult, then it makes or say forces them to conform to the views and suggestions of others or go with majority. However, when the tasks are simpler and easy to handle the people may feel competent to go it alone and in such a case the need to conform is found to be greatly decreased. In this way, the nature of the task or behaviour to be performed can work as one of the potent factors in influencing and affecting the nature of conformity in one or the other social situations.

To Sum Up

The term conformity stands for a form or mode of social influence putting pressure on the individuals to bring changes in their behaviour in tune with the existing social norms or behaviour of the majority in the group or our desire to be liked and accepted by others.

In general, people may be found to demonstrate two types of conformity in their social behaviour known as private conformity (privately accepting the norms of the group as one's own beliefs), and public conformity (publicly behave as demanded by the majority or social norms). While the phenomenon of private conformity was extensively studied by Sherif through his classical experiment in 1935, the phenomenon of public conformity was studied by Solomon Asch through his classical experiment in 1951.

There are certain factors that are known to either increase or decrease the level of social influence responsible for making the people conform. These factors affecting conformity may be named as cohesiveness, group size, group unanimity, self-esteem and confidence of the individuals, status of the individual, nature of social norms, cultural and age factors, the need for individuation and a variety of situational factors such as public v/s private response, and nature of the task and level of competence.

Compliance

Concept and Meaning

The other important socially influenced behaviour in our social world is compliance. According to Merriam Webster Dictionary the term compliance has been defined as "the act or process of complying to a desire, demand or proposal". In demonstrating a complying behaviour, the individual or group of individuals is found to comply or submit to the request or proposal made to them by someone who is interested in getting it done so. It is in this sense, that American Psychological Association (2007) has described the term compliance as "change in one's behaviour due to the request or direction of another person".

Compliance: A form of social influence aimed to bring changes in people's overt behaviour to comply with the request or proposal made to them by others.

Featured with the above-cited explanation provided to the term compliance, the behaviours like below may be well exemplified as the socially influenced compliance behaviour of the people in one or the other social situations.

- You respond to the request made by an old lady to help in picking up her dropped stick.
- Children may be found to cry and engage in tantrums for agreeing their parents and elders to their justified or unjustified demands.
- You may act and respond in the way as asked by your friends or acquaintances for doing favour to them
- The customers may be found to buy one or the other things when a salesman with his art makes a pitch and then asks them to make the purchase.
- You see an advertisement appealing in its own way for purchasing a product, and you make up your mind for its purchase by ordering it online.
- We all stand when our national anthem is played whether at a public place or community gathering.

Principles or Factors Governing one's Compliance

The socio-psychologists like the famous American scholar Robert Cialdini (1994, 2006), working and experimenting in the field of social influence, have mentioned about the following basic principles/ factors that usually govern the compliance behaviour of the people.

1. **Friendship or Liking**: Degree of trust or faith imposed on someone may safely draw others to say yes for one's request or proposal. It is why, the individuals are more willing to comply with requests from their near ones, relatives, friends or others in comparison to the requests coming from strangers or the people not trusted and liked by them. Accordingly, we show a lot of compliance to the proposals put up by insurance agents, shopkeepers, and others in our one or the other types of deals and transactions who are trusted and liked by us most.
2. **Commitment or Consistency**: Commitment made by us on one or the other accounts with someone on one or the other issue or deal works as a good internalized pressure for honoring it on our behalf. Accordingly, when we settle a price for the purchase of a piece of land or any other commodity, it becomes obligatory on our part to maintain the continuity of our

'*yes*' for the commitment once made in this connection. Similarly, whenever people show their commitment to one or the other social cause or make public their views on one or the other policy matter, there remains a lot of consistency in their behaviour. In this way, the commitment made or *yes* said by somebody for the request or proposal of others has a greater possibility of its honoring/ complying well till the time it remains consistent with the earlier commitment. However, any new proposal or request which is inconsistent with the earlier commitment definitely may face uncertainty in its compliance.

3. **Scarcity:** The need decides the value of a thing. How useful and essential is to say *yes* or comply with the request or proposal of others on one's part decides the fate of it being honored or denied on one's part. When there is shortage or scarcity of a particular commodity, in the market, the purchasers are more inclined to agree with what is proposed by the sellers, even if it seems to be somewhat unreasonable to them otherwise. The people who feel scarcity of the resources or opportunities may be found to say *yes* for the hard-pressed proposals and service rules and comply with a lot of things to be asked by their employers in their service tenure.
4. **Reciprocity**: What we do to others as good or bad gets returned to us usually in the same proportion on one or the other ways. Reciprocity in fact, thus, is the rule of nature and it applies equally to our social relations and interactions. Accordingly, in general, people may be found to comply more with a request or proposal from someone who has done some favour to them in the past or is obliging them at present in comparison to those who do not fall in the list of favouring them in such a way.

Principles or Factors Governing one's Compliance

- Friendship or liking
- Commitment or consistency
- Scarcity
- Reciprocity
- Social validation
- Authority

5. **Social Validation**: The social validation of a behavioural act increases the possibility of its repetition on our part. When we see others comply with a certain type of request or proposals made to them on this account with a satisfactory return, we have almost no hesitation in going their way in the compliance of the similar requests or proposals. In such a case, the fear of getting wrong and uncertainty about our decision seems to be vanished in a greater degree and we willingly agree to get along with others for the compliance of request or proposals of others. The social validation we get by seeing others to get benefitted through the compliance of a request or business proposal motivates or in a way persuades us to engage in such complying behaviours on our part.

6 **Authority:** From early childhood we may be seen to comply with what is asked or desired by our parents, elders, and teachers the well-known authorities holding such a position of influencing and guiding our behaviour to a compliance path. It goes for us in the similar way, after getting maturity on our part. All of us, in general, are found to comply more in a greater degree with what is asked or desired by the people who hold some recognized legitimate authority than someone who does not hold such position.

Techniques of Compliance-Making People Comply

Making people comply with the request or proposal made to them is really a great art. It involves a lot of labor and skilled performance on their part as we witness through what is done by a number of compliance professionals such as salesmen, insurance and property agents, counselors, and coaches etc, or many of us in the capacity of the parents, teachers and administrators. In practice, the task of making others say *yes* for the request or proposal made to them needs the employment of a number of specific tactics and strategies such as exemplified below.

1. **The Foot-in-the-door technique:** In case you want to get beyond a door, it may begin by putting first a portion of your body in to the way. If you succeed, it may help you to have more success in getting entry to the room. Much in the same way, in using the technique Foot-in-door for gaining compliance in one or the other social situations from others, a beginning is made by an individual for placing a small request and when this is granted, it is further escalated to the point of achieving what is aimed. For example, in a working situation, your coworker may ask if you fill in for him

for a day. After you say yes, he may then further submit if you could just continue to fill in for the rest of the week. The trick here goes well in most of the cases for a simple reason that once the target person complies to the small request, it becomes a little hard for him to say no to its extension. Surely, he would not like to disfigure his good image by showing inconsistency to his initial response and accordingly the desired success in availing conformity/yes to a proposal or request from the desired target can be properly availed on our part.

Foot-in-the-door technique

A technique used for getting people to comply with our request by first getting them agreed to our small request, and then extend its dimension to the point of achieving what is aimed.

The technique is well applied by shopkeepers to sell their products to the customers. For this purpose, they initially request them to have a taste of their product. After having their compliance, they further request them to buy some amount of their product in the quantity of their choice. More often, it gets compliance on the part of the customers as they feel obliged to some extent by tasting their product and want to maintain their gentleman image.

2. **Law-ball technique:** In making use of this technique, for getting agreed people to accept a proposal or deal, the target customers are first lured by offering relatively lower price along with some additional discount for the purchase of a product. However, once the customers accept the offer, they get it changed in one or the other ways for leaning the deal more favourably to their side. You may have experienced it while purchasing something from the shopping malls, or booking a car or flat.

Law-ball technique

A technique used for making people comply with our proposal or deal first luring them by quoting lower price or offering sizable discount and then making them agreed to pay more by putting one or the other reasons.

Besides the marketing and business deal, we may very well witness the use of this compliance technique in our day-to-day life and social dealings. Initially, the people may be offered to pay a lesser amount for becoming a member of a social club or getting honored for their donation to a social cause by a big celebrity, but after getting their yes and completing the necessary formalities, they may be informed about some or the other changes such as the fees has been recently raised or some local authority will be honoring them on this occasion. In all such cases, however, the results are more commonly found in the favour of the success of this technique, perhaps for the reason that once an individual has made an initial public commitment to a course of action, he or she is reluctant to withdraw, even when the ground rules are changed (Burger and Cornelius, 2003).

3. **The Door-in-the-face-technique:** This technique of gaining compliance on the part of a requester or proposer runs contrary to the one discussed already in the name of "The Foot-in-the-door technique". Here, instead of beginning with a small request and then presenting a larger one, people seeking compliance are found to initiate or start with a quite heavy request or demand and then, after this is rejected, covert it to a lighter or smaller one–the one actually in their plan for being accepted. The dealers and sellers often are found to make use of this tactic for pushing up the price desired on their part to get accepted by the target customers. It may also happen with us while selling our plot of house. We place a quite heavy price much above the market rate with a clear visibility of being rejected by most of the purchasers. After then, we get engaged in the negotiation with a clear aim of lowering our quoted price to a level on which we actually desire to sell it.

The Door-in-the-face-technique

A technique used for getting compliance of our request by first initiating with a quite heavy demand and then after its probable rejection, convert it to a lighter one.

4. **The Foot-in-the-Mouth technique:** Nobody would like to harm or bite his own foot even when it happens to be in his or her mouth. Its recognition as its own makes them behave in a friendly way. Similarly, people generally prefer to oblige their friends, relatives and acquaintances by getting agreed to their request or proposal. It is such recognition on the part of a request maker that helps him first to seek or establish good relationships with the target persons and then put his request before them for the compliance (much like putting his foot in their mouths) with a

reasonable certainty that it will not be refused (bitten by them). This type of compliance behaviour thus works quite straightly on the principle of reciprocity. The existence of good relationship is reciprocated in a proper way i.e., the presence of mutual trust between the requester and responders. Accordingly, friends usually help friends and acquaintances accede to each other's request when they need so and it is this relationship which is well exploited in the use of the technique *Foot in the mouth* for gaining compliance of others on the part of the request makers or proposal submitters. In this connection, the statements like we are all students, women, resident of the same province, followers of the same faith or religion, the people of the same caste, province, country or say human beings may be well used by the request makers for getting people agreed to say yes to their proposal of one or the other kind.

Foot-in-the-mouth technique

A technique used for getting compliance to our request by initiating some type of relationship with the target people aimed to increase their feelings of obligation to comply.

5. **That's-not-all technique:** This is another useful technique based on the principle of reciprocity- do some extra favour and get a quick favour in return. The shopkeepers, insurance agents, property dealers, and even the public school-owners, may be found to make use of this technique quite often for luring the target persons for complying with their proposals. In practice how this technique gets employed, let us illustrate it with an example.

Remember some of your purchasing deals? You were in the market for purchasing a laptop of a particular brand. The shopkeeper showed you the quoted price of the company for this purpose. You asked him for paying some discount. As a result of negotiation, he finally offered you a low price. But it was not the end or that's all. Meanwhile while you were making up your mind to say yes or no, a small incentive was also offered to you further for sweetening the deal in the form of free antivirus software for a year with the hope that this would help him close the deal. And it really worked. You got agreed perhaps for feeling obliged through the extra concession and reciprocated it by accepting the deal.

6. **Deadline Technique:** The deadline technique of promoting compliance to a desired behaviour represents a technique in which target persons are told that they have only limited time to take advantage of some offer or deal. Many of the shopkeepers and property dealers may be found to make use of this technique in the promotion of their sale. They provide a deadline for the concession available on their product/ flat by advertising a specific time limit for this purpose. Here they also clearly specify that after this deadline, the said item will be available at its original price. Here it is but natural that everybody would be in a hurry to avail the concessional items in a low price instead of paying for them more after the expiry of the time limit. It is also here to be seen that no shopkeeper can afford to sell the items without getting its due profit on them. Therefore, in most of the cases neither the sale is a real one and not the time limit as announced by them in their advertisements. However, the trick used for promoting the sale works a lot. It may attract so many customers and lure them to rush for the purchase of the items within the time limits even when they have no urgent need or liking for its purchase then and there.

Obedience

Concept and Meaning

The third important socially influenced behaviour, falling after the previously discussed behaviours- conformity and compliance is obedience. In terms of its formal definition, it refers to a type of socially influenced behaviour in which people are found to obey or submit to the orders or commands from others for doing what is demanded from them without questioning the authority who issues these orders.

Obedience: A form or type of socially influenced behaviour in which people are found to obey or submit to the orders from others for doing what is demanded from them without questioning the authority who issue these orders.

Forms of obedience

Like conformity and compliance, obedience behaviour can also take different forms depending up on the nature of the order or command providing authority as well as the one who is obeying this command.

- Obedience on the part of children to their parents, family members, teachers and elders.
- Obedience on the part of employees and workers from their employers and masters.
- Obedience on the part of police and military personnel to their seniors in ranks.
- Obedience on the part of followers of a faith or religion to its beliefs, rituals and doctrine.
- Obedience on the part of the members of a community or citizens of a country to the prescribed norms and laws.
- Obedience on the part of the members of a gang to their leader.
- Obedience on the part of the ignorant and unknowledgeable to the experts and knowledgeable
- Obedience on the part of human being to God or Nature as the supreme power.
- Obedience on the part of individuals to the self-imposed restrictions helpful to their existence, survival and well-being.

Milgram's study on obedience

A series of quite useful social psychology experiments for studying phenomenon of obedience were conducted by Yale University psychologist Stanley Milgram (1963, 1965).In one of his experiment, he tried to measure the willingness of study participants to obey an authority figure who instructed them to perform acts that conflicted with their personal conscience. The experimental setting, procedure and outcomes of his experiment may be briefly summarized as below.

- In his experimental study there were three types of individuals designated as experimenter(the researcher himself), the participants of the study (on which experimenter performed the experiment) and the confederates (the experimenter's own people). For the role of subjects or participants he selected 40 male volunteers (20–50 years old) from a wide variety of backgrounds with the help of advertisements.
- At the beginning of the experiment, experimenter informed the participants that they were taking part in an investigation into the effects of punishment on learning. They had to play the role of teachers and their job in this experiment was to make the other volunteers alike them to play the role of teacher. In terms of experimental setting, the experimenter and the participant of the study both were required to sit in the same room (referred to as control room) the experimenter sitting behind the participant for issuing instructions to him from time to time. The confederates volunteer (acting as learner) was required to sit in the adjoining room (referred to as shock room) for making him non-visible to the participant (playing the role of a teacher).
- Experimenter in the gathering of all the participant volunteers (acting as teachers and learners) explained that the teacher's job would be to sit in the control room along with the experimenter and to read out a list of word pairs to the learner. After the teacher reads the list once, it would be the learner's job to remember which words went together. For instance, if the word pair was *red-carpet*, the teacher would say the word *red* on the testing trials and the learner would have to indicate which of four possible words (*bird, hairs, wall* or *carpet*) was the correct answer by pressing one of four buttons in front of him. In case the learner makes a mistake in recalling the correct word, he would be liable for the punishment in the form of receiving an electric shock. For inflicting punishment to the learners, teachers were required to begin with the smallest possible shock (15 volts) but with each mistake the shock was to be increased by one level (an additional 15 volts) extended to 450 volts.
- Once the learner (who was, of course, actually an experimental confederate) was alone in the shock room, he unstrapped himself from the shock machine so actually there was nothing like feeling shocks for the wrong responses. Moreover, for responding on their part the learners were equipped with a tape recorder possessing a prerecorded series of responses of the learner that the teacher could hear through the wall of the room for every step taken by him in his testing and shock providing task.
- The teacher heard the learner say "ugh!" after the first few shocks. The teacher was told to go on increasing the shock level each time the learner made a mistake. With the increase of the level of shock, the responses of the learner also get intensified indicating the grief and pains they are feeling at their end. For example, exclaiming at 150 volts "Please, get me out from here, my heart is bothering me now". At 180 volts, the learner shouted that he could no longer stand the pain. As the shock reached about 270 volts, the learner's protests became more vehement, and after 300 volts the learner declared that he was not going to answer any more questions. From 330 volts, onwards, just

silence was there from the side of the learner. The experimenter responded to participants' questions at this point, if they asked any, with a scripted response indicating that they should continue reading the questions and applying increasing shock even when the learner did not respond.

- At this point and even before that the participants playing the role of teachers indicated their desire to stop the experiment and check on the condition of the learner. However, most of them continued after being assured they would not be held responsible for what they have been asked to do. If at any time a particular participant/teacher indicated his desire to halt the experiment, he was verbally encouraged to continue. If the participant still wished to stop after all the verbal prods, the experiment ended in the case of that particular pair of the teacher and learner. Otherwise, it was only called to end after the participant/teacher had given the maximum 450-volt shock three times in a row to the paired learner.
- Milgram was interested in his study to find out the overall impact of the instructions issued or orders passed by an authority on the obedience behaviour of the target persons. How far they may go blindly to obey the authority and what works in influencing their behaviour to such an extent. Prior to the study, forty psychiatrists that Milgram consulted told him that the lesser than 1 percent of subjects would administer what they thought were dangerous shocks to the learner. However, the results of the experiment were quite contrary. Under the presence of the experimenter (the authority figure) and his insistence to continue to increase the shock level, 65% of the participants continued giving the shock to the learner all the way up to the 450 volts maximum, even though that shock was marked as "extremely dangerous" and there had been no response heard from the participant for several trials (more enough to create suspense about their being alive).
- Through such findings of his study, Milgram tried to conclude that people may be found to obey the orders of an authority figure blindly, if they willingly or otherwise accept the authority of the person issuing them instructions or orders; remain present before them for watching their behaviour and issuing orders; and making them assured that they will not be held responsible for any damaging outcomes of their obedient behaviour.

Exercising resistant or control over destructive obedience

Destructive or blind obedience and subjugation to an authority figure proves quite dangerous and destructive to the wellbeing of the individual or group of individuals who fall victim to such undesirable obedience. It definitely needs to be controlled or resisted by letting the tendencies of blind obeying reduced in their nature and outcomes. In general, the following strategies may be recommended for being applied for the purpose.

1. **Individuation**: The use of this strategy demands that the individual be entrapped or engaged in destructive obedience behaviour realize that one is himself responsible for what he does with others irrespective of who orders him for doing it and whatever assurance is given to him for feeling safe on this account. There are instances, where the police officials engaging in the encounter of the political rival at the orders of the political authorities had to bear consequences through the enquiries set up and judicial judgments appeared against them at the later stage. No one stood for protecting them for their destructive obedience in these cases. Similarly, it should be quite clear to the people who commit heinous crimes and offences under the influence of destructive obedience that they will have to bear the brunt when they are caught and held responsible for their acts with a least consideration that somebody was there to order them for doing all this. For this purpose, the individuals, in general, from their early childhood should be exposed to these bitter truths for helping them to realize that one is fully responsible for the harm produced by following the improper commands and not the authority.
2. **Exposure to the Disobedience Models:** Observational learning and modeling is considered a quite effective technique for learning or relearning of one or the other things related to our social life. It can be appropriately used for making the people realize and learn that beyond some point, unquestioning submission to destructive commands is inappropriate. How to resist the pressure of the commanding authority and tactfully or bravely demonstrate a destructive disobedience behaviour (refusing to obey the destructive commands) can, thus, be properly emphasized through exposing individuals to the actions of disobedient models.
3. **Appropriate upbringing of the children:** The developmental age period is the best period of

individual's development and growth. The traits of the personality helpful for the individuals to resist pressure of destructive obedience get inculcated among the growing children through their proper bringing up and handling of them by their parents, elders and teachers. The democratic and appropriately expressive environment available to them helps much in the development of desirable personality traits for enabling them to resist pressure of destructive obedience. In facing such situations, then and there we may find them questioning the expertise and motives of the commanding authority figures and taking their own decision of what should be obeyed or what not.

4. **Reinforcing the destructive disobedience behaviour:** The individuals who demonstrate courage to disobey the commands and orders of mass destruction and improper inhuman treatment and similar other improper and inappropriate ones should be praised, rewarded and provided recognition in public. It will help not only to boost their morale but also prove an example for others to stand against the destructive commands.

To Sum Up

The term obedience refers to a type of socially influenced behaviour in which people are found to obey or submit to the orders or commands from others for doing what is demanded from them without questioning the authority who issue these orders.

Much like conformity and compliance, obedience behaviour can also take different forms depending on the nature of the order or command providing authority as well as the one who is obeying this command. It has been usefully studied through a series of quite social psychology experiments conducted by Yale University psychologist Stanley Milgram during the period, 1963-1965.

Destructive or blind obedience and subjugation to an authority figure proves quite dangerous and destructive to the wellbeing of the individual or group of individuals who fall victim of such undesirable obedience. It definitely needs to be controlled or resisted by following the strategies like Individuation (feeling when one realizes that one is himself responsible for what he does); Exposure to the Disobedience Models; Appropriate upbringing of children; and Reinforcing the destructive disobedience behaviour.

ASSESSMENT QUESTIONS

Section I: Essay Type Questions

1. What is Social Influence? Throw light on its meaning and concept in detail.
2. Define the term social influence and discuss about its different forms and ways (such as conformity, compliance and obedience) in brief.
3. What is conformity? Throw light on its meaning and concept as one of the modes and forms of our socially influenced behaviours.
4. Define the term conformity and discuss about its various types and forms.
5. What are private and public conformity? Distinguish between them.
6. Discuss about the Sheriff's classical experiments on private conformity and Asch's classical experiments on public conformity.
7. What is a conforming behaviour? Why and when do we choose to conform? Discuss.
8. While throwing light on the concept of conformity, name and discuss about the role of various factors affecting conformity.
9. What is compliance? Throw light on its meaning and concept as a socially influenced behaviour in detail.
10. Discuss in detail about the role of the various principles or factors governing one's compliance.
11. What is compliance? Discuss in detail about the various techniques of compliance-making people comply.
12. Throw light on the application and use of the following techniques of compliance.
    (i) The Foot-in-the-Door technique
    (ii) Law Ball technique
    (iii) Door-in-the-face technique
    (iv) The Foot-in-the-Mouth technique
    (iv) That's not all technique
    (v) Deadline technique.
13. What is obedience? Throw light on its meaning and concept as one of our socially influenced behaviours.
14. While defining the term obedience, discuss about its various forms or types.
15. What is our obedience behaviour? How was the phenomenon of obedience studied by Stanley Milgram through his experiments on obedience? Discuss.

16. What is destructive obedience? How it can be restrained or controlled? Discuss.

Section II: Short Answer Type Questions

1. What is social influence?
2. Name the different three forms and ways of social influence.
3. What is conformity? Name its two different types.
4. What is private/public conformity?
5. Tell in brief about the Asch's classical experiment on public conformity.
6. Mention in brief about the Sherriff's classical experiment on private conformity.
7. Name any four factors affecting one's conformity.
8. What is compliance as a social influence behaviour?
9. Name any five principles or factors governing one's compliance.
10. Tell in brief about scarcity/ reciprocity/ commitment/ friendship or liking as a factor governing one's compliance.
11. Name any five techniques of compliance-making people comply.
12. Tell in brief about any one of the following compliance technique.
    (i) The Foot-in-the-Door technique
    (ii) Law-Ball technique
    (iii) Door-in-the-face technique
    (iv) The Foot-in-the-Mouth technique
    (iv) That's not all technique
    (v) Deadline technique.
13. What is obedience as a social influence behaviour?
14. Name the different forms of obedience behaviour
15. Tell in brief about Milgram's study on obedience.
16. What is destructive obedience?
17. Mention about any one measure employed for exercising restraint or control over the destructive obedience.

Section III: Objective Type Questions

1. Who among the following is famous for performing a classical experiment on private conformity?
   (a) S.C. Asch
   (b) Muzafer Sherriff
   (c) Stanley Milgram
   (d) None of these
2. Who among the following is famous for performing a classical experiment on public conformity?
   (a) S.C. Asch
   (b) Muzafer Sherriff
   (c) Stanley Milgram
   (d) None of these
3. Who among the following is famous for performing a study on obedience?
   (a) S.C. Asch
   (b) Muzafer Sherriff
   (c) Stanley Milgram
   (d) None of these
4. Which one of the following is not a factor governing one's compliance?
   (a) Reciprocity
   (b) Availability of the things or opportunities in abundance
   (c) Authority
   (d) Social validity
5. In one of the social situations, beginning is made by an individual for placing a small request and when this is granted, it is further escalated to the point of achieving what is aimed. It is an example of the compliance technique named :
   (a) The Foot-in-the-Door technique
   (b) Law-Ball technique
   (c) Door-in-the-face technique,
   (d) The Foot-in-the-Mouth technique,

Answers

1 (b)	2 (a)	3 (c)
4 (b)	5 (a)	

14

Meeting Life Challenges

Learning Objectives

After going through this chapter, you will be able to:

- Define the term frustration
- Know about the meaning and nature of frustration
- Discuss the causes of frustration
- Throw light on the reactions to frustration
- Define the term internal or psychological conflict
- Know about the meaning of the term internal or psychological conflict
- Mention the types of internal or psychological conflicts
- Discuss the ways and means of resolving internal or psychological conflict
- Define the term stress
- Know about the meaning of the term stress
- Elucidate and state what are stressors
- Explain and discuss the stressors as External or Environmental and Internal or Psycho-social
- Know and tell what is the stress cycle
- Discuss and describe about the effects or outcome of stress
- State about the mechanism of adaptation to stress
- Know, what is coping
- Throw light on the general and formal coping strategies or techniques
- Discuss the promotion of positive health and wellbeing
- State about acquisition of life skills on one's part
- Discuss the acquisition of positive health on one's part

Introduction

Life is not a bed of roses. It is a continuous struggle for the satisfaction of one's needs physical and psychological for seeking one's adjustment to his self and the environment in which one can have all possibilities of facing odds and suffering from reverses ending in one or the other types of frustrations, conflicts and stresses. A number of such bolts from the blues may emerge in one's life accidently or incidentally in the form of natural calamities, deaths of near and dear, road accidents or result through one's own mistakes, failures and wrong doings. Irrespective of the source of their emergence, all of such happenings in one's life play a quite substantial role in placing one or the other types of challenges before him for coming out from such a mess, protecting him from their ill consequences and aftereffects and seeking ways and means for remaining mentally and physically healthy and socially O.K. For meeting out these life challenges one needs to be equipped with the essential know-how and why of the types of frustrations, conflicts and stresses, creeping in one's life at one or the other time along with the measures to take control of them in an appropriate way. Besides this, the handling of the life challenges and adversities also require from us to concentrate over the measures helpful in the promotion and development of positive health and well-being by acquiring the necessary life skills. In the present chapter we would try to know and discuss about these.

Frustration

Meaning and Definitions

Man is ambitious by nature. He has aspirations and desires to be fulfilled. He plans and strives hard for their realization, but it may be possible that despite his best planning and efforts he may not get the desired success. At times he finds himself in a state of confusion with all the paths ahead blocked. With repeated failures, he reaches a state or condition of frustration defined in the manner as below.

Carroll: Frustration is the condition of being thwarted in the satisfaction of a motive. (1967, p. 33)

Good: Frustration means emotional tension resulting from the blocking of a desire or need. (1959)

Gilmer: When there is some interference with our goal directed behaviour, the result is frustration. (1970, p. 304)

Coleman: Frustration results when our motives are thwarted, either by some obstacle that blocks or impedes our progress towards a desired goal, or by the absence of an appropriate goal. (1970, p. 82–83)

Barney and Lehner: Frustration refers to failure to satisfy a basic need because of either condition in the individual or external obstacles. (1953, p. 28)

Frustration: Condition resulted through the repeated failure in the satisfaction of one's basic needs or attainment of a cherished goal.

These definitions reveal that (*i*) frustration is that stage or condition in which failure dominates the attempts; (*ii*) in a state of frustration one feels a major obstacle in the satisfaction of one's basic needs or in the attainment of one's cherished goal; (*iii*) the significance of the goal and strength of the blockade increases the degree of frustration; and (*iv*) the cause of frustration lies both in the individual himself and his environment.

Causes of Frustration

The causes of frustration may be studied under major heads—external factors and internal factors.

A. External Factors

External factors are also called environmental factors. These are the situations or conditions present in one's environment. They affect the individual from outside. The main external factors are as follows:

1. **Physical factors:** Natural calamities, obstacles or events in their physical world such as hailstorms, floods, droughts, earthquakes, fire accidents, etc. These cause frustration in an individual.
2. **Social and societal factors:** Social forces and the social environment may also block the path of an individual either in the attainment of some important goal or in the satisfaction of one's basic needs and desires. In this way, they become the potential source of frustrating motivated individuals. For example, a particular society or community may impose a bar on the marriages of school mistresses which may cause frustration in a young school mistress who is in deep love with a handsome boy and desires to marry him. Similarly, a young man of bright career may feel frustrated when he is denied admission to a course on the grounds that he does not fulfill the condition of being a permanent resident. Social factors also include the part played by other persons in blocking the desires of the motivated individuals. A child may feel frustrated when he is denied permission to go to a movie with his friend, or to a dance or picnic.

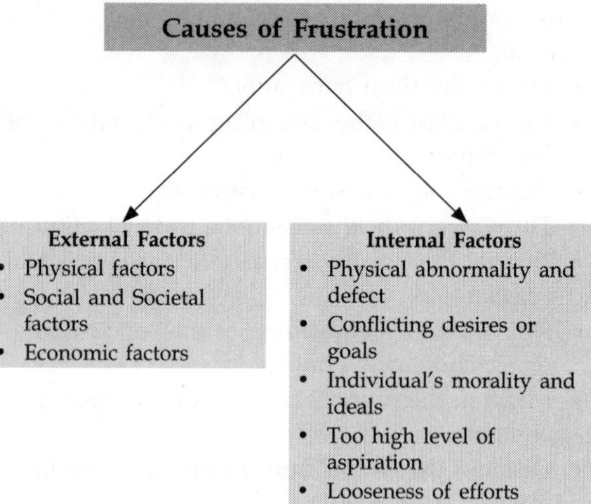

Fig. 14.1: Causes of Frustration

3. **Economic factors:** Economic and financial factors contribute much in frustrating individuals. Instances are there when a young man committed suicide as a result of the frustration suffered by a long interval of unemployment, or a mother killed herself and her children by jumping into a well due to the utter frustration caused by the continuous denial of basic need—food. Similarly, revolts against the social or political set-up are often the result of frustration suffered due to severe economic deprivation.

B. Internal Factors

Internal factors are those which frustrate an individual from within. These are also called personal factors as the person himself is the cause of such frustration. The main factors in this category are as below:

1. **Physical abnormality or defects:** Too small or too big a stature, very heavy or lean and thin body, an ugly face or dark complexion, some glandular or bodily defects (such as

being squint-eyed, blind, deaf or dumb) may constitute a source of frustration. Deficiency in one's intelligence or backwardness in a particular subject may also frustrate an individual who is motivated to learn a particular course or choose a particular vocation.

2. **Conflicting desires or aims:** Frustration is also caused by the mutually conflicting desires or aims. For example, a man wishes to marry a girl whom he loves but he also wishes to avoid it since it interferes with his ambition of going abroad for higher studies. However, he has to make a choice and, a choice of one at the cost of the other may becomes a cause of frustration for him. A similar frustration may be felt by a young woman who aspires to become a mother but avoids it due to the fear of losing her job or it affecting her career.
3. **The individual's morality and high ideals:** An individual's moral standards, code of ethics and high ideals may become a source of frustration to him. He is always caught between his superego and Id. At the same time when his ego fails to maintain a balance between the two he becomes frustrated. Due to the weight of the moral standards of his conscience, he possesses the unnecessary feeling of guilt or an unusual fear of punishment. For example, he may like to become friends with a girl but his moral standards do not allow him to do so. Similarly, one may be denied to smoke, to see an adult movie, only because of one's code of ethics or high ideals. The inhibitions and the possible conflicts may give rise to emotional tension in him. Consequently he may feel frustrated.
4. **Level of aspiration too high:** One may aspire very high in spite of one's incapabilities or human limitations. For example, a young man may aspire to become the captain of a cricket team in spite of the fact that he does not even know how to play this game. Such aspirations are bound to result in frustration.
5. **Lack of persistence and sincerity in efforts:** Frustration may be caused by one's own weakness in putting continuous and persistent efforts with courage, enthusiasm and will power at one's command. A person may read a book with no sincere willingness to understand it. After some time he takes another book and does the same thing with it as well. He complains that he is not able to grasp anything after reading too much and thus gives reasons for the feeling of inadequacy that ultimately lead to frustration.

Reaction to Frustration

Frustration, depending on its intensity and nature, results in various types of reactions of the individual. Some have frustration tolerance to the extent that they bear the consequences with a little injury to self or society, while others, or former in special situations, become violent and thus demonstrating two types of aggression named as external and internal.

1. **External aggression:** "This aggression", as Carroll observes, "may be directed towards either the person or persons who caused the frustration or towards the substitute or substitutes." (1967, p. 34). Consequently, a clerk in his frustration of not getting promotion may quarrel with his officer or rebuke his wife or beat his children. A boy experiencing frustration in the playground may try to hit the boy denying him the chance of carrying the ball or may use his younger brother or parents as substitute for relieving his tension.
2. **Internal aggression:** It is an aggression that is turned inward towards the self. Instead of releasing one's emotional tensions by attacking others, one resorts to the attack of one's self. Instead of blaming others, the individual blames himself. Although self-criticism does not do any harm, excessive aggression towards the self is destructive for the self. Eventually, the person becomes neurotic or tries to find escape through suicide. As far as the well-being of the individual is concerned, this inward aggression is far more dangerous than outward aggression.

To Sum Up

Frustration refers to a condition reached on account of repeated failure experienced by an individual in the attainment of his basic needs or realization of an important goal. The causes of frustration may be external (lying in the external conditions or environment) or internal (lying within the individual).

Under frustration people may react differently, depending upon their own nature as well as the intensity of the frustrating experiences. They may react violently with varying intensity by resorting to aggression towards their self or the things and persons, whom they consider responsible for their frustration. They may also demonstrate adjustable reactions like increasing trials or improving their efforts, adopting compromising means, surrendering and accepting their defeat or withdrawing them from the frustration giving situations.

Internal or Psychological Conflicts

Meaning and Definitions

The term conflict is variously used. There may be conflicts between the ideologies of two sects, cultures, religions and organisations. Conflicts may also arise between husband and wife; father and his son; and teacher and the taught. They may also show their presence among brothers and sisters, members of an organisation or community, states of a country and countries of the world at large. Apart from these external or outer conflicts, there are inner or internal conflicts within a man which are more dangerous to his well-being. These conflicts are called psychological conflicts. Lets us know about these.

Douglas and Holland: Conflict means a painful emotional state which results from a tension between opposed and contradictory wishes. (1947, p. 216)

Barney and Lehner: Psychological conflict is a state of tension brought by the presence in the individual of two or more opposing desires. (1953, p. 30)

L. S. Shaffer (1961): Conflict may be defined as a state of affairs in which two or more incompatible behaviour trends are evoked that cannot be satisfied fully at the same time.

Coleman: Conflict is the anticipated frustration entailed in the choice of either alternative. (1970, p. 83–84)

Internal or psychological conflict, in the light of the above definitions, may be (*i*) a painful state or condition of an individual; (*ii*) intense emotional tension during this state; (*iii*) the result of the presence of two or more desires or wishes in the individual; and (*iv*) due to being at the crossroads, not able to choose between the two opposing desires, the individual becomes tense and restless.

> **Internal Conflicts:** Indecisiveness in making choices between opposing or contradictory desires.

In view of the above characteristics, *the term conflict may be defined as a painful tense state of an individual aroused on account of the indecisiveness in making a choice between two or more opposing or contradictory desires.*

Types of Internal or Psychological Conflicts

1. **An Approach–approach conflict:** In this type of internal conflict, an individual is faced with the problem of making a choice between two or more positive goals almost equally motivating and important. For example, a child may have to choose between reading an interesting novel or going out to play cricket. A young man may experience such conflict in choosing between two equally qualified beautiful and respectable girls for marriage. The conflicts of this type are of little danger and temporary in character since a step taken towards the realisation of one goal leads to the automatic diminishing of attraction for the other.

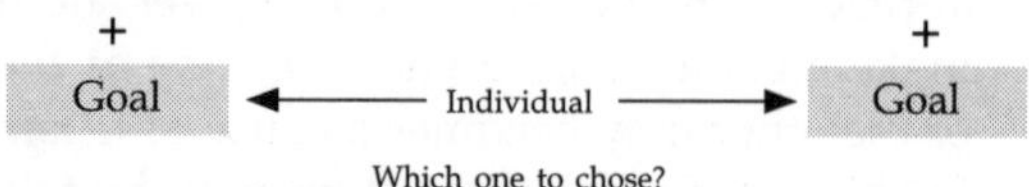

Fig. 14.2: An Approach–Approach Conflict

However, there are occasions when one feels great difficulty in making a choice between two positive desires. For example, a young girl may be devoted to her family and at the same time desire to marry a boy of another caste whom she loves which is not acceptable to her parents. Similar complexity arises in the cases where one is torn between duty and ambition, between loyalty to one's mother and to one's wife, or between present satisfactions and future prospects.

2. **An Avoidance–avoidance conflict:** In this type of conflict, an individual is caught in a situation where he must choose between two or possibly more negative courses of action. He is torn between two unattractive goals. In other words, he is faced with a choice where he cannot win either way.

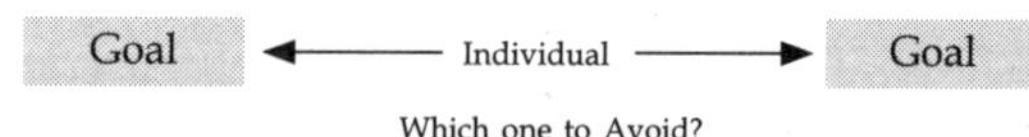

Fig. 14.3: An Avoidance–Avoidance Conflict

For example, a child who does not want to study and at the same time does not wish to displease his parents by failing in the final examination may experience such conflict. Similarly, a boxer may have to choose between his fear of defeat at the hands of his rival or, if he does not fight, the loss of the respect of his admirers. It is like being caught between the devil and the deep sea. Due to the threat involved in such a situation both the choices are equally unattractive and hence the natural tendency to escape from them or to do nothing. Here when one is compelled to take a decision, he is likely to suffer the conflict of avoidance–avoidance type. Usually, this type of conflict is more serious than the approach–approach type of conflict.

3. **An Approach-avoidance conflict:** In this type of conflict, one is faced with a problem of choice between approaching and avoiding tendencies at the same time. In such a conflict, an individual is both attracted to and repelled by the same goal or course of action. An individual may be motivated towards a kind of behaviour or activity which he perceives to be wrong, evil and degrading, but at the same time the attraction of behaviour is so strong that he becomes restless without doing it. To marry or not to marry, to tease or not to tease, to purchase a scooter or not to purchase it, are some of the situations that may repel and attract an individual simultaneously.

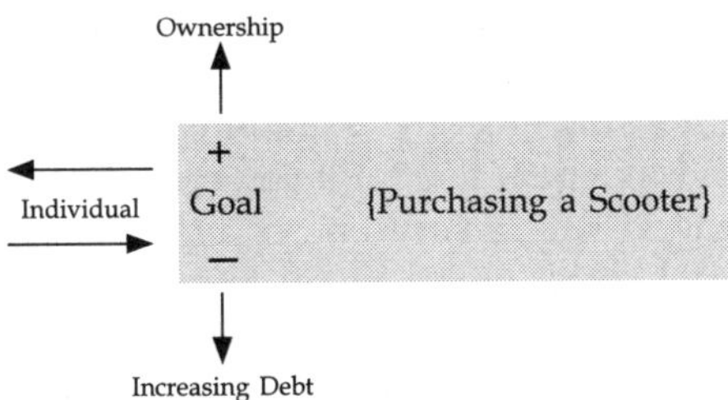

Fig. 14.4: An example of approach-avoidance conflict

Approach-avoidance type of conflicts are, distinctly, the most serious of the types discussed here as they bring about the most severe emotional tension and give rise to anxieties and complexes.

Resolution of The Internal or Psychological conflicts

We have seen in the above discussion that sometimes we may come across some conflicting desires producing very taxing and complicated situations before us. Here the choice becomes quite difficult for us, which in turn, may give us a lot of anxiety and stress. At this stage, we badly need some measures of conflict resolution broadly summarized in the manner given below:

1. First of all, accept each desire as it arrives without judgement or resistance.
2. Then, remove any barrier or resistance for making your own choice out of the two conflicting desires. This barrier many times is resulted through the heightening of your own emotion. Remove the emotional blockade by adopting relaxation technique like meditation, recreational or play therapy, etc.
3. Now think with a cool mind, the goals of your life, the main purpose you want to serve and which one of the two desires is helpful to you in serving your life goals, (not necessarily the immediate or temporary goals.), running in tune with your inner voice and may also appear socially as well as morally sound.
4. Then opt for one of the desires and follow it with your full zeal and enthusiasm, seeking a lot of satisfaction and pleasure in doing and living with it.
5. Initially, you may choose to postpone the task of choice-making. But it should be a quite temporary phase merely for taking time in getting calm and relaxed. However, it is essential to make deliberate attempt for the proper resolution of the conflict. You may find that you can do so in many of the conflicting situations as exemplified below:
   - If one wants to stay seated as a way of maintaining one's comfort but wants to get up as a way of getting a drink, he must search in his own context for potential ways of getting a drink without getting up.
   - In case these arises a conflict for a working teacher between watching a cricket match and setting a question-paper on a holiday. The potential for compromise here lies in either limiting the time for viewing the cricket match, *i.e.* viewing the half game or only the important scene or managing time for both by sacrificing rest and sleep.
6. The key to the resolution between conflicting desires of opposite nature, thus, lies in seeking a balanced compromise in one way or the other. However when the desires are equally attractive or repulsive, then the choice-making may provide a great challenge to the individual concerned. At this stage, he has to analyse the greater amount of benefit received carefully or risk involved in opting one at the cost of other desire. Sometimes it may necessitate seeking advice from elders, experienced and trusted ones and other times one has to gamble or seek direction from the Almighty. However, once a decision is made, it should be followed in its strict sense to save the energy that gets wasted due to indecisiveness and half-hearted follow-up.

To Sum Up

Internal or psychological conflict refers to a painful condition or emotionally tense state of an individual due to the presence of the two equally opposed and contradictory wishes at the same time. Generally, the conflicts may be of the types like Approach-approach conflicts, Avoidance-avoidance conflicts and Approach-avoidance conflicts.

The key to the resolution between conflicting desires of opposite nature lies well in seeking a balanced compromise between them in one or the other appropriate way.

Stress

Meaning and Definitions

The term stress is used in a number of ways in our day-to-day life to represent our internal state of psychological upset or disequilibrium caused by one or the other factors named as stress. As examples of this use, we can cite the following:

- "Ramesh has been under a lot of stress since he got fired."
- "The bank staff experienced acute stress during the ordeal of the robbery."
- "The people who live in Ladakh and North Kashmir experience considerable stress due to extreme cold in the winter season."
- "Stress is known to cause high blood pressure, ulcers and heart attacks."

Taking clues from the above-cited uses and meaning of the term stress, Morgan et. al (1986) have tried to define the term stress in the manner given below:

We define stress as an internal state which can be caused by physical demands on the body (disease conditions, exercise, extremes of temperature and the like) or by environment and social situations which are evaluated as potentially harmful, uncontrollable, or exceeding our resource for coping.

This definition given by Morgan and others makes us think that there are some internal and external factors that may give birth to particular stressful situations proving harmful to our well-being. The nature and amount of the harm caused to our self, in this case is definitely greater than the usual amount of the wear and tear caused by day-to-day anxieties, worries, struggles, disappointments and failures. The scholars Malott and Whaley (1983) highlighted this fact in their definition calling stress as "*conditions that cause tissue damage far beyond the daily wear and tear of living*". It explains the reason why stress is known to cause fatal diseases like high blood pressure, ulcers cancer and heart attacks.

Stress: An internal condition causing tissue damage far beyond the daily wear and tear of living.

However, it is also true that stress does not merely result in physiological or bodily damage. It also causes a wound in one's psyche resulting in the heavy loss to one's mental health to the degree that it becomes too uncontrollable and unmanageable on the part of the individual by adopting normal courses of coping and adjustment.

In this sense, *we can define stress as an internal condition or state of an individual caused by one or the other internal or external factors (termed as stressors) affecting his bodily condition and psyche in a harmful way to the extent that it becomes difficult on the part of the individual to control or manage it by normal course of adaptation or damage control exercises.*

What are stressors?

In its simple meaning, the term stressors stands for all that causes stress to an individual. In the technical sense, however, it refers to "*a type of stimulus that occurs in sufficient amount to cause stress.*"(Malott and Whaley, 1983)

This definition provides a special status for the stress-inducing situation. Each and every stimulus that causes day-to-day irritations or adjustment problem is not qualified for being named as stressor. In a general way, every one of us is faced, many times each day, with one or other minor stress situations. Breakfast or lunch is not served in time, the bus is not available, the supply of electricity or cooking gas is very poor, the Internet connection is not working, etc. Such situations are very common to everyone and may cause some or the other type of frustration or disappointment resulting in irritation, sadness or annoyance. But all such happenings are very much situational, momentary and manageable. These do not result in the serious setbacks or inflict heavy damage and wounds to one's body and psyche by being uncontrollable or unmanageable on the part of the suffering individual. These become stressors only when they occur in such a large scale with a greater intensity to cross the limit of one's normal wear and tear capacity inflicting a heavy physiological and psychological damage resulting in agony, pain, displeasure and unhappiness to him and others.

Stressor: Any stimulus that occurs in sufficient amount to cause stress

In physical sense, we may equate it to the normal wear and tear caused by the normal traffic on a crossing bridge. However, in case an eighteen-wheel truck or electric train is allowed to move on the bridge, then it may cause stress in a real sense to the bridge by crossing the normal wear and tear capacity of the bridge. Such situation may occur in one's life by facing one or the other hazards and calamities of life like losing a job, money or property, a severe illness or the death of someone close, financial liabilities beyond one's income, marital discord, etc.

In this way, stressors, as we must know about them, are those stimuli that cause a serious damage to our body and psyche by crossing our limit to normal wear and tear capacity of the unhappy events in day-to-day life.

Types of stressors

Stressors in general may be classified into two broad categories, external or environmental, and internal or psycho-physiological. Let us know something about them.

External or environmental stressors

Environmental stressors are those environmental stimuli that may be found to cause a heavy stress on the suffering individual. Here the stress-inducing stimuli is external, *i.e.* lying outside the individual's environment.

- These environmental stressors are found in the maladaptive and uncongenial environmental conditions at one's home, family, neighbourhood, community and workplaces. The mutual rivalries, fighting, clashes and struggles, improper behaviour and unnecessary criticism, the disappointing and frustrating living or working conditions all may give birth to stress-producing events.
- Major changes or transitions in life, which compel one to cope in a totally new way, may, also, prove a big source for the stress producing situations. We may include in such sources all the nature- and man-made catastrophes. The occurrence of earthquakes, floods, fire breaking incidences and accidents, death of near and dear ones, loss of property and finances, robbery and cheating, terrorist attacks, communal violence, etc. may be said to be the glaring examples of the stress-inducing situations in people's life.

Internal or psycho-physiological stressors

These stressors are found within the individual himself having a particular type of mental setup, ways of behaving and bodily conditions. We may explain them as below:

- Some persons are characterized to possess a particular type of behaviour more prone and susceptible to stress than the other people. Friedman and Rosenman, (1974) have named them as persons having Type A personalities. They always remain in a hurry and are noted to be very competitive, highly motivated, ambitious, workaholics, easily angered and very time conscious.
- There are persons who have a very weak psyche, with damaged self-confidence. They are always anxious, fearful and negative in their thinking. The heaven is always going to fall on them. They invite all types of anxieties, worries and pressures and stresses for the reasons unknown to them.
- Some people by nature imbibe very little stress tolerance capacity. A few minor things and decisions in life contrary to their wishes may tear them into pieces. Their capacity of wear and tear is too low and thus, they may be found to feel stressed even in the minor change and adjustment problems of their day-to-day life.
- Physiological factors may contribute in a significant way as a producer and precipitator of the stress conditions. Depending upon the stress bearing capacity the state of our body characterized with poor health, defective sensory action organ systems, illness and fatal diseases, sleeping disorder, alcoholism and drug addiction may prove a constant source of stress-inducing situation to the affected persons.
- Unhappiness and frustrations caused by one or the other factors may prove a strong psychological base for generating and fuelling the stress inducing situations in the concerned individual.

Stress cycle

Stress, as we have discussed, is produced or generated through a unique play or interaction between the factors or things lying within the individual himself and his environment. These factors termed as stressors are thus responsible for the stress one suffers in a particular situation. In case, the induced stressful situation persists for a longer time, then this induced and persisted stress is turned into distress for the suffering individual. This distress then itself begins to work as a source of greater stress for the individual resulting into more distress, unhappiness and sorrow.

In this way, we have a stress cycle involving stress inducing conditions, induced stress, the evil effects of stress resulting into distress, the distress felt then working as a source of greater stress which, in turn, ends in more and more distress to the suffering individual. Diagrammatically, we can represent such stress cycle in the way as shown in Fig. 14.5.

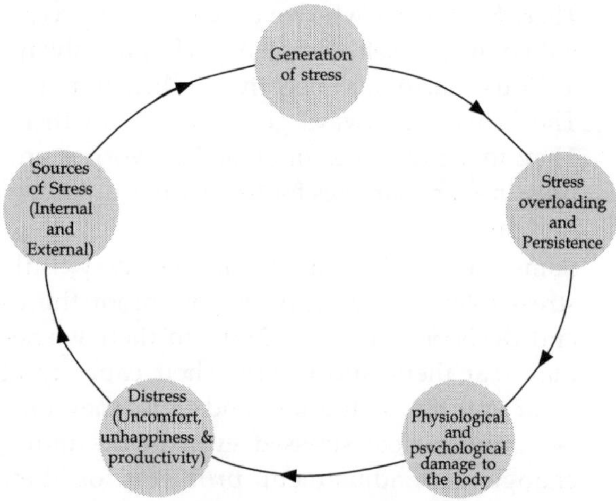

Fig. 14.5: A stress cycle

Effects or outcomes of stress

Stress when surpasses one's limit of tolerating, it (termed as one's stress tolerance capacity) becomes a great harmful factor causing considerable damage to the body and the mind of the suffering individual. *We can here define one's stress tolerance as the amount of stress one can tolerate before breaking down under the pressure of stress (Much in the same way as the load and exhaustion a bridge can tolerate before demonstrating the sign of collapse).* When stress becomes overloading, at first, it results in less severe damage resulting in overall unhappiness, un-comfort and un-productivity to the suffering individual to the extent of the loss of life. We can describe these immediate and long-term effects of the stress on the body and mind of the individual in the way given below.

A. Immediate Effects of Stress

1. **Behavioural changes:** The affected individual shows marked behavioural changes characterized as below:
   - Showing visible signs of nervousness, helplessness, exhaustion and paralysed thinking
   - Showing a state of panic reaction, running here and there, or unable to decide and do anything
   - Developing overeating behaviour
   - Resorting to smoking and alcoholism
   - Exhibiting restlessness and sleeping disorder problem
2. **Physiological changes:** In this respect, the related symptoms may be as under:
   - Level of muscular tension is increased.
   - There is an abnormal change in the rate of heart beat and blood pressure.
   - There arise problems related to digestion and elimination.
3. **Emotional changes:** As immediate reaction to stress one may experience a lot of emotional disturbance and abnormality in the emotional output in the manner given below:
   - There is sudden arrival of negative emotions on the scene in an abnormal and excessive amount in one's emotional outlet, *i.e.* sudden outburst of anger, fear, jealousy and hatred.
   - Showing a high state of anxiety restlessness and depressions.
   - There happens a problem related to lack of interest in love-making and social intimacy.
4. **Cognitive changes:** In this respect, initially, one may be found to exhibit the following symptoms:
   - He shows a marked distortion in one's ability to attend or concentrate on a particular thing or idea with an unusual increase in distractibility and decrease in concentration.

Table 14.1: Effects or outcomes of stress

	Immediate effects of stress	Long-term effects of stress
Behavioural changes	• Nervousness, panic reactions, exhaustion, paralysed thinking • Alcohol consumption and smoking • Restlessness and sleeping disorders	Serious behavioural disorders like forgetfulness, obesity Excessive alcohol consumption and drug addiction
Physiological changes	• Increase in muscular tension • Abnormal change in heart beat and blood pressure • Problem related to digestion and elimination	A known victim of high blood pressure, migraine, hypertension, heart disease, skin diseases, ulcer and even cancer
Emotional changes	• Victim of the outburst of anger, fear, jealousy and hatred • High state of anxiety, restlessness and depression • Problems related to lack of interest in love-making and social intimacy	Serious emotional disorders like chronic anxiety and depression, fears and phobias, personality changes and mental illness
Cognitive changes	• Increase in distractibility and decrease in concentration	Serious cognitive disorders e.g. memory problems, obsessive thoughts and sleep disorders

B. Long-term effects of stress

In case if the stress inducing conditions persist for a longer time, it may lead to the worsening of the condition of the individual in the manner given below:

1. **Behavioural changes:** The affected person becomes a victim of serious behavioural disorders e.g. forgetfulness, obesity, alcoholism, drug addiction, etc.
2. **Physiological changes:** The affected person becomes a victim of serious physiological disorders, ailments and diseases on account of notable decrease in his immune system. In its evil effects, one's stress makes one more susceptible to infectious agents by temporarily suppressing his immune system. As a result an individual may be seen to catch cold soon after a period of stress (such as final examination). When persisting long, the stress reactions may result in making the affected person a known victim of high blood pressure, migraine, hypertension, heart disease, ulcer, skin diseases and even cancer.
3. **Emotional changes:** The affected person becomes a victim of serious emotional disorders such as chronic anxiety and depression, fears and phobias, personality changes and mental illness.
4. **Cognitive changes:** The affected person becomes a victim of serious cognitive disorders such as memory problem, obsessive thoughts and sleep disorders.

In this way, the resultant effects and outcomes of stress are quite serious and unpleasant for the well-being of the affected person. There remains no joy and happiness to him in his life. He becomes quite cut-off from the social interaction and productivity in his work output. Gradually, his life becomes miserable to him and a matter of burden to others eventually pushing him to his untimely death.

Adaptation to stress

The individual after receiving alarming signals about the impact of stress-tries to resist the negative effects of the stress inducing situations by resorting to the mechanism of adaptation or adjustment in the manner outlined below.

Biological adaptation

The body adopts the required resistance measures by mobilizing its reserves to deal more effectively with the stressor, visible in the form of changes in the nervous and endocrine systems like increased muscle tonus, pumping of stored sugar into the blood stream, change in breathing, perspiration and secretion of glands.

Psychological adaptation

In addition to biological adaptation a mechanism of psychological adaptation is also employed by the person concerned in dealing with the situations resulted through the stress-inducing factors. Such adaptations, as Coleman (1970) observes, may be classified as (1) task-oriented adaptation and (2) ego defence-oriented adaptation.

1. In the task-oriented adaptation to stress situation, one feels confident to handle it by bringing changes in oneself or one's environment or both, whatever the situation warrants. The adapted behaviour, here, then may take the following forms :
   (*i*) Attacking behaviour
   (*ii*) Withdrawal behaviour
   (*iii*) Compromising behaviour

   Let us illustrate the mechanism of the task-oriented adaptations through its various forms with the help of particular instance where a female child becomes victim of severe stress on account of feeling rejected and improperly treated in comparison to her brother. In this case, she may resort to one of the following types of adaptation mechanism:
   (*i*) She may build up a high level of hostility being discharged in delinquent behaviour.
   (*ii*) She may simply resort to withdrawal rather than attack the source of frustration. Consequently, she will be limited to herself by being an introvert and passive person.
   (*iii*) She may compromise with the situations by thinking that she is a girl and has to adjust in a male-dominated society, where the sons are likely to get more affection, attention and protection and therefore, she need not be perturbed.
2. **Ego defence-oriented adaptation:** Such type of adaptation comes into picture where one gets stressed by feeling a threat to one's integrity or phenomenal self. Here, the stressed individual often resorts to ego defence mechanisms involving attack, withdrawal or compromising stand.

   As a result, the person may defend himself by attacking and blaming others for his mistakes. He may escape from the painful truth by denying it or by pushing it to his unconscious or he may bargain a compromise by admitting it in his consciousness in such a distorted way that it no longer hurts.

Coping with stress

The well-being of a person facing stressful situation well lies in his ability of coping with such stress.

The question here may arise what we mean by the term coping used as an encountering strategy to reduce or eliminate the effect of stress.

What is coping?

Lazarus and Folkman (1984) define coping as *"Constantly changing cognitive and behavioural efforts to manage external and/or internal demands that are appraised as taxing or exceeding the resources of the person."* We may clearly note that the latter portion of the stated definition reads as "external and/or internal demands that are appraised as taxing or exceeding the resources of the person" is nothing but an expression used for describing one's internal state of stress.

In consequence thus coping is nothing but the sincere efforts made by an individual to manage or control the stress he faces in a given situation.

General coping measures or strategies

In managing or controlling the situations resulting through the stress experienced by an individual the adoption mechanism (biological as well as psychological) already emphasized in this very chapter may serve a quite useful purpose. To say or suggest more in this connection, we may think of classifying the needed coping strategies for meeting the stressful situations in the categories mentioned below. (Cohen and Lazarus, 1979)

1. **Direct action response:** The individual tries to change or manipulate his/her relationship indirectly to the stressful situation, such as escaping from/removing it.
2. **Information seeking:** The individual tries to understand the situation better and to predict future events that are related to the stressor.
3. **Inhibition of action:** Doing nothing. This may be the best course of action if the situation is seen as short term.
4. **Intra-psychic or palliative coping:** The individual re-appraises the situation (for example, through the use of psychological defence mechanisms) or changes the 'internal environment' (through drugs, alcohol, relaxation or mediation).
5. **Turning to others** for help and emotional support.

Formal coping strategies or techniques

So far in this text, what we have discussed in the name of the adaptation and coping measures represent those generalized ways and means that are employed by the affected persons in a quite spontaneous and informal way for dealing with their stress-inducing situations. However, for dealing more effectively with the stress, the affected persons usually need some well-organized formal management strategies for coping with their stress. These techniques used singly or in combination may be outlined as below:

1. **Information-providing techniques:** Here attempts are made to provide appropriate information to the person about the nature of his problem and solution possible on this account. In the opinion of Messer, David and Meldrum Claire (1995:278), two main types of information can be here provided (i) procedural, which gives factual information about the sequence of events that the person is likely to experience; and (ii) sensory information about the sorts of feelings and sensations that the person is likely to experience. In providing such information to the people, it is always advisable to furnish the information in a manner consistent with the preferred coping style of the person concerned. While, the persons having a carefree and avoidant style are to be given more general information, those having a sensitive and non-avoiding attitude are benefitted through specific procedural and sensory information.
2. **Biofeedback techniques:** In employing such techniques, the people are given appropriate medicines or treated through needed devices for providing them relief from the pain or stress inducing situations. In this way, the focus of the used techniques here purely lies in treating the symptoms of stress rather than the stressor itself.
3. **Relaxation techniques:** In these techniques of managing stress, efforts are made to make use of the technique of progressive relaxation. The technique involves alternately tensing and relaxing various muscle groups while attending closely to the sensations the person is feeling when his muscles are tensed versus when they are relaxed. In this way, the person is made to learn to become sensitive to the relaxed state of his muscles in contrast to the state of tension. The methods utilized for such progressive relaxation are varied in their nature and level of difficulty such as laughing or breathing deep exercises to meditation or hypnosis. The intention of such interventions is to replace the anxious response with a response that is incompatible with anxiety.
4. **Cognitive restructuring techniques:** These techniques employ a number of specific methods (based on cognitive behaviour therapy) for the purpose of bringing desired changes in an individual's negative and pessimistic thinking

or ways of responding. The main assumption with these techniques is the view that stress suffered by an individual is often caused by the erroneous or negative thinking and "self-talks" and therefore, a suitable change needs to be brought out in one's thinking and way of interacting with the self. One must keep himself occupied with positive thinking and provide constructive and positive suggestion to his self for his welfare and improvement. As a result, a cognitive restructuring training is always focused on replacing one's negative thinking and harmful self-talks with positive thinking and constructive internal dialogues aimed to bring desired changes in his emotional responses and behaviour. For employing this stress management technique, Messer David and Meldrum Claire (1995:278) suggest a three-phased training to the individuals in the way given below:

Phase 1. They are taught the rationale of the method and given an understanding of the effects of cognition on behaviour.

Phase 2. Here they are taught a number of cognitive behavioural techniques (for example, replacing anxiety-provoking 'self-talks' with new and more positive ways of talking to yourself about stressful situations).

Phase 3. In this concluding phase, they rehearse these techniques.

5. **Systematic desensitization technique:** This technique is based on the assumption that a stressful situation is caused on account of oversensitivity of an individual towards a thing or practice. It we resort to its systematic desensitization, then a thing or practice may cease to function as a source of stress for the individual concerned. Morgan et al (1986) have illustrated the use of this technique with an example involving a young woman having intense fear or phobia of hypodermic syringes and needles. The procedure and steps involved are summarized here as below:
   - The patient was taught to relax during the therapy session.
   - The patient was made to form a variety of images of the feared objects or situations ranked from strong to weak in terms of the amount of fear they produce.

(Here in this case the therapist used real syringes and needles arranging their presentation in such a sequence that the first stimuli produced no fear and the latter stimuli produced more and more fear.)

   - Having learnt to relax in the presence of a weak stimulus the next stronger stimulus in the series was presented in the patient until she learnt to relax when this one was present.
   - This process continued until the patient could touch herself with a needle and remain relaxed.

6. **Modeling technique:** The practice to employ this stress management technique has been stemmed from the work of Bandura (1969). In his social learning theory, he has demonstrated the use and impact of modeling in learning or acquiring some or the other behaviour by observing and imitating the behaviour of a model. Accordingly, in applying this technique, the individual suffering from the stress-related problem is exposed to a model (for example on a video or film) who is coping successfully with the same stress-related problem. How this model is coping with stress, can now be learnt and practiced by the suffering individual for doing away with his stressful problem.

To Sum Up

Stress may be defined as an internal condition or state of an individual coupled with the stressors affecting his bodily conditions and psyche in a harmful way. Stressors may be classified into two broad categories-external or environmental and internal or psycho-physiological.

Effects or outcomes of the stress may be described as immediate and long-term effects.

The process of coping with stress resulting in reducing or eliminating the effects of stress may be carried out through (i) adoption mechanism (biological as well as psychological) and (ii) utilizing the formal coping strategies or techniques like information processing, biofeedback, relaxation, cognitive restructuring, systematic desensitization and modelling techniques.

Promoting Positive Health and Well-being

One has to be sufficiently capable of standing against the odds and reverses for facing the challenges of life. In this concern, the discussion carried out so far in this chapter in the form of dealing with the frustrations, conflicts and stresses, caused to him on this account, may help a lot. However, it needs to be supported by the measures to help the individuals get sufficiently equipped with the deterrence in the form of not yielding to the pressure created by the adversity of life. Such deterrence can be available to them by focusing on the things like below.

- Acquisition of appropriate life skills helpful in meeting the challenges of life
- Maintenance of an overall positive health covering Physical, Mental, Emotional, Social, Moral and Spiritual aspects of one's personality and well-being

Acquisition of Life Skills

The term life skills here stands for the acquisition of well-meaning skills or special abilities for living one's life in its full form by facing the challenges or hurdles created in one's life for one or the other reasons. We may name and discuss some of the important ones as below.

1. *Self-care and maintenance:* One should possess enough stress-bearing capability by maintaining his immunity or resistance level in a proper form. One should be strong enough in terms of his physical, mental and emotional functioning and it can only be achieved through a process of self-caring and maintence i.e., concentrating over the maintence of a proper level of one's physical, mental, emotional and social health accompanied with the learning of well meaning skills for bearing stress and anxiety ridden situations. The simple learning of suitable breathing technique or any other relaxation and distraction method may help the people well at the time of a tense moment. Similarly, the acquisition of environmental adaptation skills may also help the people for not getting disturbed or annoyed with the presence of usual noise, light, pollution level or scarcity and non-availability of one or the other things in one or the other situations.
2. *Interpersonal relationship managing skill:* The skill related to managing interpersonal relationship stands for one's ability or capacity to manage the mutual relationship existing between people living and working in a social or professional set up. According to Baron. R (1997: 17) the term managing interpersonal relationship means "to establish mutually satisfying relationship and relate well with others." The acquisition of this skill may help people in establishing and maintaining a good relationship with others. The fair and proper relationship existing among the people reduces the chances of getting them clashed and in case somehow it happens, then, there remains all possibility of coming to terms with ease.
3. *Problem-solving skill:* The term of problem-solving skill may be defined as the skill or ability helpful not only in facing a problem with the necessary confidence but also solving it in a systematic and scientific way. The acquisition and employment of this skill is much needed on our part in one or the other situation. It may be well seen that there are a lot of disturbances and difficulties arising in one's life on account of the emergence of one or the other types of problems creating a lot of tension, anxiety and stress for him and the others related to him. Therefore, one should try to get him equipped with the desired ability or skill of problem solving.
4. *Decision-making skill:* The decision-making skill refers to a skill or ability equipping one with skill or ability to take timely decision in a proper way by paying needed consideration over the available alternatives, resources and existing circumstances. Equipping with such ability may help the people in protecting them from becoming victim of indecisiveness resulting into one or the other types of psychological conflicts, frustration and stress in their life.
5. *Time management skill:* Everybody now in this modern age remains in hurry, complaining about the lack of time resulting in causing a lot of frustration, and stress for them in the different social situations. However, on the other hand, it may also be clearly observed that those who seem to perform a number of day-to-day tasks and professional activities are doing them with necessary precision and fruitful outcomes with less tension and stress in comparison to others. Why this difference? It is the time management skill possessed or not possessed by the individuals that is responsible for this difference. The equipping of time management skills makes one capable of utilizing the available time in a most appropriate way by distributing it for doing one or the other tasks according to its need and importance, its nature and time taken for its execution.
6. *Stress management skill:* The stress arising situations are almost inevitable in one's life. Therefore it is appropriate for one to get equipped with the stress management skill. As a term the stress management skill may be defined as a skill or ability helpful in dealing effectively with stress-inducing situations instead of breaking under pressure or showing signs of helplessness and hopelessness. The acquiring and employing of this skill may help the people in developing necessary stress

tolerance capacity and coping with the stress in the needed way in a stress-induced situation.

7. *Self-sufficiency skill*: One should be sufficiently self-sufficient and independent in terms of fulfilling his basic needs. He should try to acquire skills and abilities that may help him in getting economically sound by earning his livelihood in a satisfactory way. Economic self-sufficiency equips an individual to face a number of challenges that may creep in his life due to shortage of funds and non-availability of financial sources.
8. *Skill of Assertiveness:* Assertiveness may be defined as an ability or skill possessed by an individual to manage his behavioural functioning in such a way as to asset or stand up well in a particular situation in saying and doing what he wants to say and do without hurting or annoying others. In this way acquisition of this skill may help people in getting the desired freedom for the expression of their inner self instead of remaining tense or stressed on account of facing internal conflict or external sensor.
9. *Emotional self*-control: The emotional self-control skill may be defined as the ability or skill helpful in exercising desirable control over one's emotions for getting along well with one's self and others. In this way, its acquisition may prove quite beneficial for the people in seeking needed adjustment to the self and others including the things and situations lying in one's environment. It makes one cool in the trying situation and thus may prove a boon in facing the odds in one's life.
10. *Flexibility skill*: The skill of flexibility may be defined as the ability or skill helpful in enabling an individual to bring needed changes in his behavioural functioning according to the demands of changed situations. It thus provides sufficient adaptable capacity and quality for the people in getting them adjusted according to the needs of the circumstances brought out through one or the other reverses or requirements imposed on them in one or the other situations.
11. *Positive and Rational Thinking:* The skill of positive and rational thinking may be defined as an ability or skill helpful to the individual for carrying out a much needed rational thinking characterized with a lot of constructiveness, creativity, and positivity in his thinking and doing. It helps him in a great way for achieving his set goals with a lesser fear of failures and getting entrapped in the vicious circle of stress-related problems.
12. *Optimism*: Optimism refers to an ability or skill possessed on the part of individuals helpful in providing strengths and confidence for facing the odds of life with a firm belief that there is a morning for every dark night. The people possessing such optimistic outlook for perceiving the reverses and difficulties in their life thus may be found to pass through the crisis and challenges of life with needed patience and courage.

Acquisition of Positive Health

One may fall ill, catch cold or become a victim of several viruses and spreading diseases easily than the others. He may also get easily upset on account of some minor reverses. It is all on account of the poor defense he possesses in terms of his weaknesses with regard to his physical, mental, emotional, social, moral and spiritual health-the various keys of his overall well-being. Accordingly, if we want to be better prepared in terms of our defense to fight and stand against the odds and challenges of our life, we have to take care of the development and maintenance of an overall positive health covering physical, mental, emotional, social, moral and spiritual aspects of our personality and well-being. Let us see what can be done on this account.

1. *Looking towards the Food and Liquid Intake:* One should be quite careful about his food and liquid intake-in reference to the type of balanced diet one needs according to his or her age and the type of work one does in his or her daily routine. Proper attention should also be paid over the cleanliness, purity and quality of water one drinks. The use of other types of artificial drinks such as cola, soda, alcohol etc. should be avoided. The drinking of tea and coffee should also be within limits. Besides this, one should develop healthy habits of being regular and punctual in his food and liquid intake and the manner in which it is consumed on his part.
2. *Looking towards the intake of air:* One should be quite careful about the quality of the air one breathes by protecting oneself from the health hazards of the pollution and poisonous gases.
3. *Caring for the regular exercise and physical fitness*: Physical fitness is quite essential for the maintenance of overall positive health, Therefore, needed attention should be paid by individuals in doing physical work and activities, and engaging in exercise, and physical fitness programs including yoga activities with a proper schedule and precautions needed for this purpose.

4. *Maintenance of positive attitude*: It is one's attitude that gives direction to one's behaviour in the desired way for the attainment of overall positive health on his part. Therefore sufficient care should be taken by individuals for imbibing the appropriate positive attitudes towards the things, people, and events going on in one's environment.
5. *Maintenance of positive thinking:* It is very well said that nothing is good and bad, it is one's thinking that makes it so. Therefore, enough attention should be paid over the development and maintenance of the ability or skill of positive thinking on one's part. It is one's positive thinking that remains hopeful and optimistic at the time of facing adversities and reverses in one's life.
6. *Emotional Management*: The proper management of one's emotions is quite essential for developing a proper level of emotional health among the individuals but it also adds to their physical, mental, social and moral health. Therefore needed care is to be taken for acquiring the skill of managing the emotions of their own and others in a proper way on the part of individuals.
7. *Social abilities and social support:* Getting socially developed for developing a proper level of social health. Attention should be paid over the imbibing of the needed social abilities and skills for carrying out proper interaction and relationship with others. The maintenance of such social relationships and friendships may prove quite helpful to individuals for getting informational, physical, material and emotional support required on their part in facing one or the other challenges in life.
8. *Moral and Spiritual Development:* Caring for imbibing with the needed ethical sense and moral values and spiritual enlightenment does not add only to one's moral and spiritual health , but it also proves quite helpful in contributing towards their overall positive health and well-being. The moral and ethical principles imbibed on his part helps him well in facing life's crises and challenges. Similarly his faith in God and Universal goodness helps him be steady on the path of seeking development and in the other dimensions of his personality as well as getting him suitable support at the time of facing the challenges of life.

To Sum Up

The task of acquiring positive health and well-being requires on the part of the individuals to learn the art and skill of (i) the acquisition of a set of appropriate life skills helpful in meeting the challenges of life, and (ii) maintenance of an overall positive health covering all aspects of their personality and well-being.

In the former category of essential life skills we may include the acquisition of skills like: Self-care and maintenance, Interpersonal relationship managing skill, Problem solving skill, Decision making skill, Time management skill, Stress management skill, Self-sufficiency skill, Skill of Assertiveness, Emotional self-control, Flexibility skill, Positive and Rational Thinking, and Optimism, etc.

The development and maintenance of an overall positive health requires on one's part the need to care for things like: proper food, liquid and air intake; regular exercise and physical fitness; maintenance of positive attitude and thinking; emotional management; acquisition of social abilities and social support; and moral and spiritual development, etc.

ASSESSMENT QUESTIONS

Section I: Essay Type Questions

1. What is frustration? Discuss its possible causes.
2. Define frustration and throw light on its possible effects or accompanying reactions.
3. How do people in general react with their frustrations? Discuss.
4. What are internal or psychological conflicts? Discuss their main types with examples.
5. Throw light on the following types of internal conflicts with examples.
   (i) An Approach-Approach conflict
   (ii) An Avoidance-Avoidance conflict
   (iii) An Approach-Avoidance conflict
6. Discuss the possible measures for controlling and resolving the conflicts of desires developing in an individual.

7. What is stress? Discuss its possible causes and sources.
8. What are stressors? Discuss their various types with examples.
9. Discuss the nature and mechanism of stress cycle.
10. Define stress and throw light on its possible immediate and long term effects or outcomes.
11. What is stress? What possible measures may an individual take in adapting to stress?
12. What is coping? Discuss the possible coping strategies for dealing with and managing stress.
13. Discuss the ways and means of promoting positive health and well-being by taking care of (i) the acquisition of essential life skills and (ii) acquisition of positive health habits.

Section II: Short Answer Type Questions

1. Define the term frustration/internal conflicts stress/stressors.
2. What makes a person frustrated? State in brief.
3. Name two things each associated with internal and external causes of frustration.
4. Give one example each for demonstrating the nature of simple reactions and violent reactions to frustration.
5. Give an example of approach–approach conflict/ Avoidance–avoidance conflict/Approach–avoidance conflict.
6. Tell about two things related to the resolution of internal conflicts.
7. Give two examples each of external and internal stressors.
8. What is a stress cycle?
9. Name a few important physiological outcomes of the persisted stress.
10. Name two changes or effects of stress related to the areas specified below:
    (i) Behavioural aspect
    (ii) Physiological aspect
    (iii) Emotional aspect
    (iv) Cognitive aspect
11. What is biological adaptation to stress?
12. What is psychological adaptation to stress?
13. What is coping?
14. Name any three formal strategies or techniques of coping with stress.
15. What is bio-feed/ relaxation/ systematic desensitization or modelling technique for managing stress?
16. Name any five life skills that need to be acquired for promoting positive health and well-being among individuals.
17. Name five essentials habits of daily living for promoting positive health and well-being.

Section III: Objective Type Questions

1. To marry or not to marry, to purchase a scooter or not to purchase is an example of:
   (a) Approach–Approach conflict
   (b) Approach–Avoidance conflict
   (c) Avoidance–Avoidance conflict
   (d) None of these

2. An internal condition or state causing tissue damage far beyond the daily wear and tear of living is referred to as:
   (a) Anxiety (b) Frustration
   (c) Stress (d) Conflict

3. A female child becomes a victim of severe stress on account of feeling rejected and improperly treated in comparison to her brother. In consequence, she develops a high level of hostility being discharged in delinquent behaviour. Tell what type of adaptive mechanism she is resorting to.
   (a) Task-oriented adaptation
   (b) Ego-defense oriented adaptation
   (c) Biological adaptation
   (d) None of these

Answers

1 (b) 2 (c) 3 (a)

15

Abnormality of Behaviour and Psychological Disorders

Learning Objectives

After going through this chapter, you will be able to:

- Tell, what is normal and abnormal behaviour
- Know about the criterion for deciding normality and abnormality of people's behaviour
- Decide the appropriateness of the criterion for deciding the abnormality of behaviour
- Throw light on the various causes or factors responsible for the abnormality in behaviour
- Discuss the various types of psychological disorders identified and named as : (i)Anxiety Disorders, (ii) Obsessive-Compulsive and Related Disorders, (iii) Trauma and Stressor-Related Disorders, (iv) Somatic Symptom and Related Disorders, (v) Dissociative Disorders, (vi) Depression Disorders, (vii) Bipolar and Related Disorders, (viii) Schizophrenia Spectrum and Other Psychotic Disorders, (ix) Neuro-developmental Disorders,(x) Disruptive Impulsive-Control and Conduct Disorders, (xi) Feeding and Eating Disorders, and (xii) Substance-Related and Addictive Disorders.

Meaning of the term normal and abnormal behaviour

The term 'normal' seems to be derived from the word 'norma' which means a carpenter's square or rule. A norm, therefore, became a rule, pattern or standard, and it was in this sense that the term 'normal' was introduced into the English lexicon. The term 'abnormal' with its prefix *ab* (away from) thus came to signify the deviance or variation from the normal. Anything not normal must, therefore, be abnormal. But there is some difficulty in deciding what is normal. In the basic or medical sciences, it is easy to decide what is normal. In examining the temperature of the body, blood pressure, the amount of sugar in the blood, pulse rate, beating of the heart, etc., are standard universal norms. On a psychological front, however, we can't have an ideal model of man or ideal behaviour to be used as a standard norm.

As a result, the problem of deciding what behaviour is or is not normal has proved to be a difficult one. However, several attempts have been made for establishing criteria for describing what is normal or abnormal. Let us know about them.

Criterion for deciding Normality and Abnormality of People's behaviour

1. *Ethical or moral criterion*: According to this criterion, a person is considered to be abnormal if she lies or she acts in an immoral manner. This criterion is solely based on the value judgements made by people who observe behaviour. For being taken as normal, the behaviour should be appropriate and desirable from the view point of ethics or morality. This description of normality and abnormality carries the following defects:
   - (i) The major problem with this perspective is that morality is not an absolute concept. What is 'moral' or 'immoral' may change from place to place and from time to time.
   - (ii) A person who is known to have high morality may show signs of known behavioural disorders, while many people who are labelled as psychologically deviant may not exhibit any immoral behaviour. To be affected with anxiety or depression cannot be labelled as immoral. Therefore, in any way, morality can't be made a criterion for deciding a behaviour as normal or abnormal.
2. *Criterion of social conformity:* According to this criterion, those, who conform to societal norms are considered normal and those who do not care for them are labelled abnormal. This view is

based on the assumption that normality is what the majority of people approve of or follow. For example, if wearing short hair, tight jeans, or a sleeveless blouse gets social approval, it may be taken as normal or else it would be labelled abnormal. Hence, if we adopt social conformity as the sole criterion of deciding the behaviour as normal or abnormal, we will have to change our decision from place to place or culture to culture and in the same culture or place from time to time as we can't resist changes in attitude towards what is socially acceptable and normal.

3. *Criterion of ideal or perfection:* According to this criterion, normal behaviour is equated with perfect or ideal behaviour. A few persons attain a level of perfection difficult to be attained by the masses. They become ideals and serve a model for labelling as normal. A major flaw in this criterion lies in the fact that there exists nothing like absolute ideal or perfection. The judgement is purely subjective, for example, one may think the life and behaviour of Gandhi as ideal but for the activists and revolutionaries not he but Subhash Chandra Bose or Bhagat Singh may be the ideals. Besides, this approach is based on what ideal behaviour ought to be and not what it is. The model of ideal varies from situation to situation and, in a situation, from time to time. The behaviour which is considered ideal for a particular age in a particular situation may altogether be labelled abnormal in a different age or in a different situation.
4. *Legal criterion:* According to this criterion a law abiding citizen is normal but the one who violates the law is labelled abnormal. Behaviours like murder, rape, burglary or prostitution come from this legal definition arid are definitely labelled antisocial or abnormal. But what is legal or illegal is again a matter of controversy. In a dynamic society, laws change fast. Hence, they are not absolute but change from society to society, place to place and even from time to time. Moreover, the mere absence or presence of a few evidences may declare an act or behaviour legal or illegal. Therefore, the legal criterion cannot be made a reliable or valid criterion for the judgement of normality or abnormality.
5. *Pathological or medical criterion*–According to this criterion, the normality or abnormality of the behaviour depends upon the functioning of the nervous system. In this way all abnormal people are affected with some mental illness or disease. Consequently, they should be sent to the mental hospitals as patients for treatment by persons who are trained to cure them. This view has a wide appeal and has been responsible for arousing a mass feeling that abnormal behaviour is somehow an indication of an illness or disease.

However, the inadequacy of this criterion has now also been proved. Most people who are found to be mentally disturbed do not suffer from the 'diseases' or 'illnesses' in the usual sense of these terms. They show no signs of structural damage or dysfunction in their nervous systems. Therefore, it may be seen clearly that the pathological or medical criterion does not make a reliable and valid criterion for the definition of normality or abnormality.

6. *Psychological criterion:* According to this criterion, psychological functioning— whether defective or normal— is the deciding factor of the abnormal or normal behaviour. Eysenck (1960) writes, "Abnormality then is not in terms of people suffering from mental diseases produced by definite causes; it *is* rather in terms of defective functioning of certain psychological systems."

In this way, according to this criterion, abnormal people are definitely psychologically handicapped individuals Their abnormality, whatever kind or form it may be, is linked with some malfunctioning of certain psychological systems. There are definitely certain psychological causes or factors like anxiety, conflicts and stresses, fears and phobias, maladaptive attitudes and ways or thinking and reasoning, defective ways of coping and adjustment with the self and environment that may cause one or the other types of abnormalities in people's behaviour. However, on a close analysis of this criterion we may find that, whatever strength may be visible in the claim of the psychological criterion, the abnormality of behaviour cannot be exclusively called an exclusive product of psychological or sociological causes. In any case, biological or physiological factors may not be ruled out in the explanation of the behaviour of abnormal people.

Criteria of Deciding Abnormality of Behaviour

- Ethics or moral criterion.
- Criterion of social conformity
- Criterion of ideal or perfection.
- Legal Criterion
- Pathological or medical criterion
- Psychological criterion

The conclusion about the appropriateness of the criterion for deciding the abnormality of behaviour

All the first four criterion–ethical, social conformity, ideal or perfection and legal, laid down for deciding the normality and abnormality of people's behaviour are purely subjective. They may vary from society to society and no objective and universal criteria can be laid down for the normality and abnormality by depending merely on these criteria.

With regard to the effectiveness of other criteria named as (i) pathological or medical criterion, and (ii) psychological criterion, we may say that both of them in their own ways possess a reasonable capacity of defining the normality and abnormality of one's behaviour. However, we can't depend also upon any of them exclusively in deciding an individual as normal or abnormal. In some cases, pathological or medical approach helps in the diagnosis of abnormality, while in the other, the abnormality, in the absence of any organic cause, may be detected through the malfunctioning of certain psychological systems.

Causes or Factors Responsible for the Abnormality in Behaviour

The causes or factors responsible for the abnormality in one's behaviour may be broadly classified as (i) Heredity Factors, (ii) Biological Factors (iii) Psychological Factors, and (iv) Sociological Factors. Let us know about their roles.

Hereditary factors

Heredity consists of all that is transferred to the offspring from the immediate parents in the form of genes and chromosomes at the time of the conception of the child in the womb of the mother.

Role of Chromosomes: Abnormalities among human beings are transmitted both by the sex-linked chromosomes and the autosomes. A few examples are as under.

- One possible genetic anomaly is a missing sex chromosome. This abnormality, called Turner's Syndrome, produces a person who has the superficial anatomical appearance of a female but usually has subsequent immature sexual development.
- The presence of extra sex chromosomes also cause abnormality diagnosed as Klinefelter's Syndrome. Here the affected person has too many female chromosomes instead of the usual composition XY. Such an individual has the superficial appearance of a male and usually a normal sized penis, but very small testes, and may also possess many female characteristics, such as developed breasts, feminine face and voice, little body hair. Such males are always sterile, usually suffer from emotional difficulties and may show symptoms of psychosis and antisocial behaviour.
- The presence of extra chromosome in any pair of the twenty-two autosomes (three instead of the usual two) has been found to cause Mongolism—a severe form of mental retardation in which the individual has slanting eyes, a flat face and other characteristics that produce a superficial resemblance to Mongoloids.

The Role of Genes: Defective genes transferred to the offspring are in many ways responsible for the transmission of abnormalities such as below:

- *Ataxia:* It causes lack of coordination and inability to maintain balance while standing or walking.
- *Huntington's Chorea:* This degeneration is marked by speech impairment, intellectual impairment and emotional disturbance.
- *Idiopathic epilepsy.*
- *Muscular Dystrophies:* A disorder involving paralysis of muscles.
- *Neuralatrophy:* A disorder of peripheral nerves.
- *Alzheimer's disease and Pick's disease*: Both relate to pre-senile psychosis in which atrophy of the cerebral cortex occurs. In Pick's disease, brain degeneration occurs in localized foci, mostly in the frontal areas while in Alzheimer's disease degeneration is diffused throughout the brain.
- *Schizophrenia.* A functional disorder in which heredity plays a part of strong predisposing factor.
- *Psycho-physiological disorders:* Certain psychophysical disorders like hyperthyroidism, peptic ulcers and essential hypertension have been found to possess strong hereditary bases.

Physiological or Biological factors

A number of physiological or biological factors of one or the other nature exemplified and mentioned below may be found to play a quite substantial role in causing abnormality of behaviour among the people.

1. *Structure of the body (Physique):* In a normal course one should remain reasonably satisfied

with his somatic structure or physique in order to get adjusted with his self and the environment. Any serious deviation from the norms, whether in terms of height, weight, body proportions or appearance, may create a serious adjustment problem for the individual and this in turn may develop malfunctioning or disorders of the behaviour.

2. *Endocrine system:* The endocrine system plays an important role in the growth and development of the body and mind. Any defect in their functioning leads to significant physiological anomalies which, in turn, provide fertile ground for the growth of disorganized personalities. For example, over-activity of the secretion of adrenal glands may cause a woman to grow beard and develop a masculine physique and may exhibit the physical and sexual maturity of an adult in a three or four-year-old child. Similarly, pituitary gland imbalances may lead to increase in height (seven to nine feet in height), dwarfs (two to four feet in height), a gorilla-like appearance and abnormal sex characteristics and behaviour. The abnormalities so produced are liable to be made an object of ridicule, jest, social isolation and harsh and unfair treatment which, in turn, can cause a variety of abnormalities in the behaviour of the affected persons.
3. *Microorganisms:* These are disease-producing bacteria. Some microorganisms may infect the brain along with the body as in pneumonia, malaria and syphilis while the others may affect the brain directly as in meningitis.
4. *Toxic chemicals:* The chemicals such as lead, methyl alcohol, carbon monoxide, carbon tetrachloride and intoxicating drugs and other material produce toxicity. They affect the functioning of the brain and may result in behavioural disorders.
5. *Physical injury*: Physical injury and trauma may cause damage to the brain either directly or through interference with its blood supply and thus may result in brain disorders—structural or functional.
6. *Malnutrition:* Severe malnutrition during early embryonic and infantile stage has been found to lower body resistance, affect brain structure and growth of intelligence. Post mortem studies of the malnutrition death of infants have revealed the content of their brain cells to be sixty per cent less than that of the normal content. Pellagra, a mental disorder, is found to be caused by vitamin deficiency. In the same manner, the deficiency of certain vitamins, glucose and hormones has been found to cause many abnormalities—structural or functional.
7. *Deficiency of oxygen:* Anoxia—a deficiency of the oxygen supply to the tissues—has been found to cause many abnormalities. Human nerve cells are very sensitive to lack of oxygen and may result in structural damage to the brain or life-long mental deficiency or affect drastically the complex mental functions such as immediate memory.
8. *Sleep deprivation:* Sleep deprivation is considered an important biological factor causing abnormality under stress. The prolonged sleep deprivation brings typical abnormal symptoms in the behaviour of an individual such as irritability, feeling of persecution, inability to concentrate and periods of disorientation and misperceptions, illusions and hallucinations. In some cases it may also bring about certain neurological changes and autonomic nervous system effects.

Physiological or Biological factors causing abnormality in behaviour

- Structure of the body
- Endocrine system
- Microorganisms
- Toxic chemicals
- Physical injury
- Malnutrition
- Deficiency of oxygen
- Sleep deprivation

Psychological factors

Besides hereditary and biological factors, there are psychological causes that are responsible for the development of abnormal behaviour and mental illness in the manner as given below.

1. *Psychological deprivations of the early age:* Psychological deprivation during infancy and early childhood contributes significantly towards the causation of abnormal behaviour in the manner exemplified and briefed as below.

- *Oral deprivation:* The individuals who are deprived of the opportunity of seeking gratification from sucking behaviour in infancy may be found to be emotionally unstable and disturbed at the later stage.

- *Parental deprivation:* Loss of parental affection has been found to play a very significant role in the development of maladjustment and abnormality.
- *Anal deprivation:* Anal frustrations on account of the early and rigorous toilet training of early age are reported to cause emotional difficulties and behavioural problems in later life.

2. *Faulty learning and horrible experiences*: Most of the patterns in our behaviour are the result of our learning and experiences. In the case of learning of habits, attitudes, interests or other acquired traits and physical mental, emotional and social competencies, where the adequate and right learning results in adjustment, inadequate and faulty learning creates difficulties in one's adjustment. Let us take for example the understanding of sex behaviour. The child may learn that sex is shameful or fearful. He may think that he is not fit for normal sex behaviour. Such faulty acquisition, misconceptions and wrong understanding of sex-related information are found to contribute to learning maladaptive behaviour such as homosexuality, inadequacy, withdrawal tendency etc., which may further result in serious dis-organization of the personality. Similarly, certain painful experiences, especially in the early age, are bound to leave psychological wounds that never completely heal. Sometimes such experiences like an encounter with a vicious dog or a bull, sexual assault, or experience with a gang of robbers may be sufficient to establish a conditioned fear response which may result in certain types of abnormalities and mental illnesses.

Psychological factors causing Abnormality in behaviour

- Psychological deprivations of the early age (such as oral, parental and anal deprivation)
- Faulty learning and horrible experiences
- Defective family environment and strict parental attitude
- Psychological stresses and self-devaluation

3. ***Defective family environment and parental attitude:*** Undesirable parental attitude and uncongenial family environment full of defective models, conflicts and stress situations prove a potent source for the causes of abnormal behaviour. In all such defective situations in the family environment, the child fails to get favourable conditions for his adequate adjustment and development. He neither gets balanced love and affection nor adequate safety, security and resources for the satisfaction of his essential needs. He is therefore always starved of one or the other of his physical or emotional needs. Predisposed in this manner, the unfortunate happenings concerning the treatment towards him and the members of the family are bound to make his behaviour and reaction patterns quite deviant from the normal and thus he drifts towards abnormality and mental illness.

4. *Psychological stresses and self-devaluation: Stress refers to* a psychic condition of an individual subjected to constant failures, frustrations, tensions, conflicts and pressures. The central factor causing maladjustment and disorders in the stress situations is the feeling of self-devaluation. One loses faith in one's integrity, abilities and capacities, and thinks himself, unworthy, unwanted and good-for-nothing.

Sociological factors

The sociological factors rooted in the social and cultural environment of an individual are also seen to cast desirable or undesirable impact up on the behaviour of the individuals since their early childhood. It is a well accepted fact that much of our abnormal behaviour is an acquired disposition or learned behaviour. As a result of what an individual experiences or for what he becomes conditioned to through formal and informal contacts in his socio-cultural environment, his behaviour patterns get fixed accordingly. Consequently, the abnormalities and mental disorders are the cause and result of the defective and unfavourable socio-cultural environment. Most of the maladaptive and abnormal behaviours like antisocial behaviour, alcoholism, drug addiction, sexual deviations and disorders, neurotic and psychotic disorganisations, if analysed, may be found to possess deep-rooted socio-cultural causes. A number of devastating situations such as (i) problems arising in the earning of one's livelihood, (ii) the deprivation and disadvantages suffered on account of caste, language, and minority status, (iii) ill effects of industrialization, urbanization and modernization, (iv) the shadow or ill influences of cultural and social evils, (v) marital discord and family instability, and (vi) natural or national calamities may prove a sufficient cause for the creation and perpetuation of the abnormality and mental disorders among the individuals.

To Sum Up

In its simple meaning the term normal stands for a set of rule, pattern or standard, while abnormal for the deviance or variance from the normal. However for taking decision about the abnormality of people's behaviour the society is adopting a number of criterion named as Ethics or moral criterion, Criterion of social conformity, Criterion of ideal or perfection, Legal Criterion, Pathological or medical criterion, and Psychological criterion. Among these six criteria, the first four are quite subjective in their nature and therefore the last two are more often employed for taking decisions about the abnormality of one's behaviour or psychological disorders.

Regarding the factors responsible for developing abnormality or psychological disorders among individuals we may broadly classify them as Heredity factors (incorporating the roles of chromosomes and genes), Biological or physiological factors (e.g. body structure, endocrines, microorganisms, malnutrition, physical injury, sleep deprivation, etc.), Psychological factors (e.g., early age psychological deprivations, Faulty learning and horrible experiences, Defective family environment and parental attitude, Psychological stresses and self-devaluation), and sociological factors (e.g., the deprivation and disadvantages suffered in the society, the ill influences of cultural and social evils, marital discord and family instability, and natural or national calamities, etc.).

Psychological Disorders

The abnormalities found in the behavioural functioning of the people may lead them to be inflicted with one or the other types of psychological disorders. For their better identification as well as treatment, there have been a number of attempts from time to time to classify them in one way or the other. For this purpose, at present juncture, we have at our disposal:

- The DSM-5 (The Diagnostic and Statistical Manual of Mental disorders-Fifth Edition) developed by American Psychiatric Association (APA) in 2013 and
- ICD-10 (International Classification of Diseases, 10th version) brought out in 1994, by World Health Organization (WHO)

The readers, here are advised to go through any standard text of abnormal psychology for getting acquainted with the entire range of the types of mental disorders, diseases and abnormalities in the people's behaviour found worldwide as mentioned in both of these classification systems.

However, for their simple knowing about the various types of psychological disorders found in the people, in this chapter we would like to discuss them under the following heads.

- Anxiety Disorders
- Obsessive-Compulsive and Related Disorders
- Trauma-and Stressor-Related Disorders
- Somatic Symptom and Related Disorders
- Dissociative Disorders
- Depressive Disorders
- Bipolar and Related Disorders
- Schizophrenia Spectrum and Other Psychotic Disorders
- Neuro-developmental Disorders
- Disruptive, Impulsive-Control and Conduct Disorders
- Feeding and Eating Disorders
- Substance-Related and Addictive Disorders

Anxiety Disorders

Behavioural disorders designated as anxiety disorders represent the type of behaviour dominated by anxiety reactions which interfere with the individual's personal and social adjustment. The anxiety involved here is a free-floating anxiety characterized as predominantly irrational and disproportional. It is irrational in the sense that no relevant or justified explanations can be given by the individual for his anxiety reactions. Similarly, it is disproportional in the sense that quite often, a very minute danger or stress situation gives rise to disproportionately strong anxiety reactions in the individual.

An individual suffering from anxiety disorder may also exhibit the typical physiological symptoms like mild nausea, loss of appetite and some loss of weight; heart palpitations, feeling of heartburn, elevated blood pressure and increased pulse rate, suffocation and difficulties in breathing; cold sweat, headaches, muscle tension or pain, dryness-of the mouth, trembling of hands and lips and frequent sighing; Speech disorder, sleep disturbances, and sexual dissatisfaction; inappropriate eating habits, chronic mild diarrhea, frequent urination and difficulties in digestion; and excessive use of alcohol, tranquilizing drugs or sleeping pills.

A case of Anxiety Disorder

An 18-year-old girl was referred to a psychiatric clinic. She first came to the attention of the authorities eight months earlier, when she attempted suicide. At the time of interview, she was found to be under considerable tension. The anxiety lessened somewhat in the face of repeated encouragement and reassurance. Eventually, she told a story which revolved for the most part around her father. She said that he had told her that her mother had frustrated him sexually. At another time, he kissed her, but she denied any further advances. She admitted having frequent dreams and nightmares most of which involved the father. Her anxiety became so great that she insisted that her mother should sleep with her. Before going to bed, she went through a ritual of barricading the bedroom door. She could sleep as long as her mother kept an arm over her. At the same time she was afraid of the mother and occasionally hesitated to eat anything she had prepared, and was sometimes so fearful that she remained awake all night in order to watch her mother. The problem got intensified by the father's advances when he attempted to molest her and by the mother's passive reaction to the situation. The girl had deeply ambivalent feelings about both her father and her mother. In spite of her repeated expressions of fear and hatred for the father, she was found to be preoccupied with thoughts of him both in her waking fantasies and her dream life

(Source: Adapted from Kisker, 1977, p. 197).

There are many types of anxiety disorders such as (i) Generalized Anxiety Disorder, (ii) Panic Disorder, (iii) Phobias, and (iv) Separation Anxiety Disorder.

Generalized Anxiety Disorder refers to a type of anxiety disorder in which one's thinking and feeling related to one's anxiety is so generalized that it may lead to prolonged, vague, unexplained and intense fears not necessarily attached to any particular object. He fears, worries and has an intensive apprehension for one or the other things with no reason attached to his fear or apprehension. The length to which he may go for finding things to worry about is remarkable. As soon as one cause for worry is removed, he finds another until his kith and kin lose patience with him.

Panic Disorder: This type of anxiety disorder is more severe than the generalized anxiety disorder in the sense that here the anxiety reactions are more intense, frequent and damaging in their nature and consequences. The range of getting one panicky is also quite wide. One may demonstrate signs or symptoms of the state of panic reactions for a host of things and situations characterized with the symptoms like losing sense of thought, losing control over motor responses, suffering from shortness of breath, chest pain, dizziness, trembling, and choking to the extent of utter helplessness in protecting himself from the faced danger.

Phobia: Refers to a type of anxiety disorder in which a person experiences persistent, intense, irrational fear of a specific situation or object. In spite of his rational knowledge that his fear is unrealistic and overwhelming, he is forced to experience great apprehension and anxiety symptoms while in contact with the phobic object or situation. Some of the common phobias with their technical names and inherent meaning are listed below:

Acrophobia	–	fear of high places.
Agoraphobia	–	fear of open places.
Aichmophobia	–	fear of short and pointed objects.
Algophobia	–	fear of pain.
Astraphobia	–	fear of storms, thunder and lightning.
Claustrophobia	–	fear of closed spaces or confinement.
Hemotaphobia	–	fear of the sight of the blood.
Hydrophobia	–	fear of water.
Lalophobia	–	fear of (public) speaking.
Mysophobia	–	fear of dirt or contamination.
Nyctophobia	–	fear of darkness.
Ochlophobia	–	fear of crowds
Pathaphobia	–	fear of disease or illness.
Photophobia	–	fear of intense light.
Pyrophobia	–	fear of fire.
Thanato phobia	–	fear of death.
Toxophobia	–	fear of being poisoned.
Xenophobia	–	fear of strangers.
Zoophobia	–	fear of animals or some particular animal.

It is clear that phobias may involve any situation or object surrounding one's life. Moreover, they have no respect for age, intellectual level or social position. Henry III of France had a peculiar phobia concerning eggs and became terrified at the sight of them. Schopenhauer, the German philosopher, had a fear of razors and thereby preferred to singe his beard rather than shave it.

**A Case of Ochlophobia–
The Fear of Crowds**

A young woman had ochlophobia–fear of crowds. Whenever there were many people about her, she was afraid that she would be crushed or die from suffocation. In spite of the knowledge that her fear being irrational, she was not able to travel by train or bus, go shopping to a market, attend social parties or visit movies. This kept her a virtual prisoner in her home. On free association, her phobia was traced to her early childhood. As a child she had been granted permission to watch the circus parade go by her house but was strictly warned not to follow it into town. On account of the excitement she forgot this and followed the parade into the centre of the town where she soon found herself crowded on all sides. She became frightened and began to cry. A kind gentleman helped her out of the crowd to a front row. After a time her fear subsided and she returned home. Due to fear she could not discuss her terrifying experiences with her parents. The entire experience was repressed into the unconscious, giving rise to an irrational fear of crowds. Due to its free association, the early experience was recalled and the knowledge of the source of fear gradually helped her to get rid of her phobia.

Source: Adapted from Page, 1970, p. 142.

Separation Anxiety Disorder: This type of anxiety disorder is developed among the children on account of an intense fear of getting separated from their near and dear to which they are closely attached such as motherscare takers or to whom they are dependent on the satisfaction of their physical and psychological needs. The children suffering from this disorder show a lot of anxiety, restlessness, and apprehensions of one or the other nature on getting separated from their attachment figures even for a short duration. They need them everywhere for their protection and caring, and thereby cry and show their resentment in or the other ways for resisting their separation in one or the other situations.

To Sum Up

Anxiety disorders represent the type of psychological disorders in which people are found to demonstrate a behaviour dominated by anxiety reactions which interfere with the individual's personal and social adjustment. The anxiety involved here is a free floating anxiety characterized with the exhibition of the one or the other typical physiological symptoms. *There are many types of anxiety disorders such as (i) Generalized Anxiety Disorder (an intensive fear or apprehension for one or the other things with no reason attached to it), (ii) Panic Disorder (showing more intense, frequent and damaging anxiety reactions), (iii) Phobias (experiences of a* persistent, intense, and irrational fear of a specific situation or object such as water, fire, height, darkness etc.) *and (iv) Separation Anxiety Disorder (a severe anxiety shown on* account of an intense fear of getting separated from the object of attachment).

Obsessive-Compulsive and Related Disorders

Obsessive behaviour represents maladaptive behaviour or disorder in which an individual is haunted with the persistent recurrence of unwelcome, absurd and disturbing idea or thought. For example, a wife may have an obsessive idea of stabbing or poisoning her husband, a mother of hurting her little girl, a son of wishing his mother's death, a husband of pushing his wife down a flight of stairs. Although the person realizes the absurdity and irrelevance of such thoughts, still he is unable to get rid of them. The more desperately he tries to rid himself of them, the more they persist.

Obsessive behaviour, in the step further, becomes compulsive behaviour. Compulsion is in fact an overt manifestation of the obsessive thought or an idea. In other words compulsions are obsessions translated into action. Compulsive behaviour, in this way, may be defined as maladaptive behaviour or disorder in which a person is seen to perform repeated acts of unreasonable and irrelevant nature such as washing his hands again and again, checking the alarm clock several times to ensure it has been wound, or returning to his house again and again to be certain that the door has been locked or following an elaborate ritualistic sequence in detail before going to sleep. Such patterns of behaviour are maladaptive in the sense that they are unnecessary and irrational. Even the person realizes the absurdity of his compulsive acts, but he feels uncomfortable unless he performs the compulsive act.

A Few Examples of obsessive-compulsive behaviour

- An adolescent boy was found to have a unique obsessive- compulsive behaviour concerning fire, technically known as *pyromania*. He was preoccupied with the idea of fire and possessed an overwhelming urge to set fires without caring for the consequences. He admitted setting innumerable fires causing damage to properties and lives but could not give any reason for his strange criminal behaviour.

- A pretty young woman of a rich family was found to be suffering from an obsessive compulsive behaviour, kleptomania (uncontrollable urge to steal). Whenever she attended dinner parties she could not resist herself from putting selected spoons in her handbag. She had a sort of record of 300 stolen spoons. At one time when 'She was seen picking the spoons by a friend and asked why she did it, she felt humiliated but replied, "I don't know why it happens but something compels me to do it."
- Samuel Johnson suffered from an obsessive-compulsive behaviour, *'coprolalia'*. He had a strong urge to utter obscene words for which he was often humiliated. He had no explanation for his strange conduct.
- A principal of a Girls college was found to suffer from an obsessive-compulsive behaviour related with contamination and cleanliness. She used to wash her hands and take baths several times a day. After going outside it was necessary for her to change her clothes. Whenever a visitor came to her drawing room, she had the room cleaned and sprayed with disinfectant.
- A middle-aged man was found to suffer with an obsessive- compulsive-behaviour related with the drinking of tea. He could not drink his tea for fear that a pin might have been dropped into it. He was forced to pour his tea back and forth several times to make certain that it did not contain any pin.
- A school boy, thirteen years of age, was brought for help on account of his obsessive-compulsive rituals. When he urinated, he had to wash four times, if he had to put on his socks, he washed seven times, and if he touched something with one hand, he had to touch it with the other, He could give no reason for observing such methodical ritual.

Recently, DSM-5 has mentioned in its system of classification about some new variety of obsessive-compulsive disorders terming them as related disorder in the name of (i) hoarding disorder,(ii) trichotillomania (hair-pulling disorder),(iii) excoriation (skin picking) disorder and (iv)body dysmorphic disorder. Let us know about them.

Hoarding Disorder: Individuals suffering from the obsessive-compulsive disorder named as Hoarding disorder are found to feel that they must save items, and they become very distressed if they try to discard them (APA.2013). These people in fact have inherent craving for collecting and accumulating a host of things and as a result it is common for them to wind up with numerous useless and valueless items, from junk mail to broken objects to unusual clothes. Their compulsion to remain away from giving up their possessions, results in an extraordinary accumulation of items that clutters their lives and living areas.

Trichotillomania (Hair-Pulling Disorder): The people suffering from trichotillomania repeatedly pull out hair in the form of pulling one hair at a time from their scalp, eyebrows, eyelashes, or other parts of the body (APA, 2013). Despite taking resolution not to engage in such behaviour and trying to reduce or stop the hair-pulling for the time being, the sufferers may be helpless in getting rid of this practice

Excoriation (skin-picking)Disorder: Much alike the practice of hair pulling from a particular body part, the people suffering from skin picking disorder are engaged in using their fingers to pick on skin from one area of their body, most often the face. Keep picking skin on one of the area of their body results in significant sores or wounds (APA, 2013). It turns into an obsessive-compulsive behaviour in the sense that the affected person is habituated to do it again and again despite the agonies, impairment and embarrassment suffered, resolutions made and attempts done by him for leaving this bad practice.

Body Dysmorphic Disorder: Individuals suffering from the obsessive-compulsive disorder named as body dysmorphic disorder are found to become preoccupied with the belief that they have a particular defect or flow in their physical appearance. Actually, the perceived defect or flaw is imagined or greatly exaggerated in the person's mind.The perception or belief that there is definitely something wrong with their body part or appearance, drive the individuals to engage in obsessive-compulsive acts such as repeatedly checking themselves in the mirror, grooming themselves, picking at the perceived flaw, comparing themselves with others, seeking reassurance, or performing other similar behaviour activities.

It is also quite common to witness the people suffering with Body Dysmprphic disorder to experience difficulties, distress, impairment and embarrassment on account of their repetitive undesirable behaviour.

To Sum Up

Obsessive-Compulsive Disorders represent the type of psychological disorders in which an individual is found to perform repeated acts of unreasonable and irrelevant nature (e.g.) washing his hands again and again, or checking the alarm clock several times to ensure it has been wound, etc.), even, when he himself realizes the absurdity of his compulsive acts.

Recently, DSM-5 has mentioned in its system of classification about some new variety of obsessive-compulsive disorders terming them as related disorders in the name of (i) hoarding disorder (compulsion to hoard things in a huge way with their no use), (ii) trichotillomania (hair-pulling disorder), (iii) excoriation (skin picking disorder) and (iv) body dysmorphic disorder (preoccupying with the belief of having a particular defect or flow in the physical appearance).

Trauma-and Stressor-Related Disorders

Trauma is a lasting adverse effect on an individual caused by an event that involves threat or danger. According to the DSM-5, trauma can result when an individual directly experiences an adverse event, witnesses that event, or learns about it from others. The people caught in a nature-made catastrophe, like flood, fire, violent storms (tsunami), rock sliding, accident, earthquake, or the man-made catastrophe such as terror attack, indiscriminately shooting incidents, bomb blast, molestation and rape, robbery, and warfare etc. are more often subjected to a type of disorder called as *Posttraumatic Stress Disorder (PTSD)*

Posttraumatic Stress Disorder (PTSD)

The type of psychological disorder that results when an individual directly or indirectly experiences an adverse event (e.g. flood, fire, violent storms, a fatal accident, earthquake, bomb blast, robbery, and warfare etc.)

The symptoms visible among the Posttraumatic Stress Disorder (PTSD) affected are listed in DSM-5 into four clusters named as below.

1. Recurrent experiences of the event, as in memories, dreams, or flashbacks
2. Amplified arousal, including sleep disturbances and reckless behaviour
3. Avoiding thoughts, places, and memories about the event
4. Negative thoughts, moods, or feelings (APA, 2013)

Somatic Symptoms and Related Disorders

Somatic symptom and related disorders is the name given to the type of disorder in which the suffering individual is found to show and feel one or the other types of physical symptoms of an ailment or disease on account of psychological difficulties. These symptoms can't be traced to a specific physical or biological cause. Thereby, the medical tests performed for diagnosing their physical difficulties and health problems are either normal or fail to explain the reasons for their pain or illness. In such a situation, it is natural for them to become worried and distressed about their health because they don't know what is behind their health problems. It is to be noted here that among the people suffering from one or the other types of somatic symptom and related disorders, the symptoms are similar to a specific physical disease, their pain or suffering on this account is also real and may last for several years, but their cure and treatment is always psychological rather than medical.

Types of Somatic symptom and related disorders

There are several types of somatic symptom and related disorders such as *Somatic Symptom Disorder, Illness Anxiety Disorder, Conversion Disorder, and Factitious Disorder.*

Somatic symptom disorder (SSD) : As the name suggests, somatic symptom disorder is a form of mental disorder in which there is a predominant presence of one or more physical or bodily symptoms including pain related to one or the other physical ailment or disease unexplained through medical diagnosis. The presence of these somatic symptoms is quite alarming and provides a lot of anxiety and stress to the affected person in terms of thinking always about his health-related somatic symptoms and try to consult one or the other doctors for this purpose. It is also to be seen that people with SSD are not faking their symptoms. The distress they experience from pain and other somatic symptoms they experience are real, regardless of whether or not a physical explanation can be found. And the distress from symptoms significantly affects their daily functioning and provides them a lot of inconvenience in their adjustment and living.

Illness Anxiety Disorder: People with this type of somatic disorder are persistently worried and preoccupied with a concern that they have or will be affected by a serious illness or disease. Here the concern of their supposed illness and health is so great that can't think beyond it. The topic of their conversation and interaction with the people always hangs around their illness. They are often frustrated when medical examinations are negative and feel convinced that the doctors have erred. The concern about their health and the resulted anxiety level is so high that a minor body complaint or appearance of a somatic symptom such as a slight headache may be adjudged and believed on their part as a sign of brain tumour. Not only this, but they may also be gripped with excessive anxiety when they read, listen or come across the illness of others. They begin to adjudge and assume that they are also most likely to suffer from the same in a short while. Any diagnosis and advice from the doctors is unable to rid them from such sort of anxiety and fear about their health and illness.

A question may arise about the difference between the somatic symptom disorder and illness anxiety disorder as the affected persons in both these disorders are found to be anxious and concerned about their health and illness. The difference lies in the way this concern is expressed. In the somatic symptom disorder, one expresses his concern by telling and worrying about the somatic symptoms related to some health problem or illness. On the other hand, in the illness anxiety disorder, it is some or other types of illness present or assumed to be coming in future that becomes the focus of one's anxiety quite greater in its intensity and frequency. Moreover, where in somatic symptom disorder, the presence of somatic symptoms is a must in illness anxiety disorder somatic symptoms are not present or if present, are only mild in intensity.

Conversion disorder: This type of somatic disorder is reflected and diagnosed through one or the other types of functional neurological symptoms visible in the behaviour of the people with no satisfactory medical explanation available for it. That is why this order has also been designated as Functional Neurological Symptom Disorder. These symptoms may include conditions like (i) Weakness or paralysis, (ii) Abnormal movements (such as tremor, unsteady gait, or seizures), (iii) Blindness, (iv) Deafness, (v) Difficulty in walking or standing, and (vi) Loss of sensation or numbness.

The affected person is found to show such symptoms all of a sudden mostly on account of getting exposed to a stressful situation. Regarding their ill effects, the symptoms or deficits associated with conversion disorder are found to cause a greater degree of clinically significant distress or impairment in social, occupational, or other important areas of functioning of the affected people.

Factitious Disorder: The term factitious disorder stands for the type of disorder that is artificially created or developed on the part of the affected individual with no valid medical or organic cause available for it. It is in this sense a deceptive behaviour and self-imposed disorder in which the affected people themselves create or build symptoms for one or the other illness or injury.

The diagnostic criteria for Factitious Disorder noted in DSM 5 are:

- Falsification of physical or psychological signs or symptoms, or induction of injury or disease, associated with identified deception.
- The individual presents himself or herself to others as ill, impaired, or injured.
- The deceptive behaviour is evident even in the absence of obvious external rewards.
- The behaviour is not better explained by another mental disorder, such as delusional disorder or another psychotic disorder.

To Sum Up

Somatic Symptom and Related Disorders represent the type of disorders in which the people are found to show and feel one or the other types of physical symptoms of an ailment or disease on account of psychological difficulties with no trace of a specific physical or biological cause. However, the symptoms are similar to a specific physical disease, their pain or suffering on this account is also real and may last for several years, but their cure and treatment is always psychological rather than medical. There are several types of somatic symptom and related disorders such as (i) *Somatic Symptom Disorder (The affected people showing* the predominantly presence of bodily symptoms including pain related to some physical ailment unexplained through medical diagnosis) , *(ii) Illness Anxiety Disorder (The affected people are* persistently worried and preoccupied with a concern that they have or will be affected by a serious illness or disease), (iii) *Conversion Disorder* (one or the other types of functional neurological symptoms such as blindness, deafness etc. visible in the behaviour of the people with no satisfactory medical explanation) *and (iv) Factitious Disorder* (self-imposed disorder in which the affected people themselves build symptoms for one or the other illness)

Dissociative Disorders

Dissociation may be known as a disconnection between a person's thoughts, memories, feelings, actions or sense of who he or she is. In a normal course of our functioning it may happen with us in a mild form at one or the other times such as day dreaming, getting lost in a book, movie or sight-seeing resulting in cutting connection with what is happening around us. It becomes a problem and abnormality turning into a type of disorder when it gets intensified in its severity, and consequences.

In this sense the term dissociative disorders stands for the form or type of disorders in which individuals are found to show a greater degree of the severity in cutting connection between their self and reality existing at present or experienced by them in their past. In dissociative disorders, the affected individuals, thus, may be found to experience a variety of problems concerning their memory, identity, emotion, perception, behaviour and sense of self, strong enough to disrupt every area of their mental functioning.

With regard to their causation, it has been observed that most often these are the results of the one or the other types of trauma experienced by them in their past in the form of a rape victim, the victim or observers of the nature or man-made catastrophes, incidents or accidents.

There are three types of dissociative disorders named as (i) Dissociative identity disorder, (ii) Dissociative amnesia, and (iii) Depersonalization/ Derealisation disorder. Let us know about them.

Dissociative identity disorder well known as multi-personality disorder refers to a type of dissociative disorders in which the affected people are found to live in two personalities and shift from one to another for dissociating them from their own real identity without their awareness.

Accordingly, they are found to feel as if they have within them two or more entities, each with its own way of thinking and remembering about them and their life. Their way of thinking including attitudes and preferences for one or the other things may suddenly shift and then shift back. Criteria for diagnosis of Dissociate identity disorder according to APA (2013) include:

- The existence of two or more distinct identities or personality states.
- The distinct identities are accompanied by changes in behaviour, memory and thinking. The signs and symptoms may be observed by others or reported by the individual.
- Ongoing gaps in memory about everyday events, personal information and/or past traumatic events.
- The symptoms cause significant distress or problems in social, occupational or other areas of functioning.

Dissociative amnesia refers to a type of dissociative disorder in which the person suffers from abnormal forgetfulness by not being able to recall information of one or the other types of information or happenings about oneself. This loss of one's memory is not resulted through on or the other physical causes such as head injury or the consequence of some neurological dysfunction. Such memory loss may be witnessed occurring among the affected individuals in varied forms such as: (i) Localized (unable to remember an event or period of time), (ii) Selective (unable to remember a specific aspect of an event or some events within a period of time), (iii) Generalized (complete loss of identity and life history), and (iv) The state of fugue in which the people are found to travel a distance from home and workplace or do certain acts by assuming other identity but are unable to recall what they have done.

Regarding its causation, the cases of dissociative amnesia are more often linked with the things happening with them in their past in the form of childhood trauma, and particularly related to emotional neglect, abuse and sexual assault as well as the enormous stress felt in their present.

Depersonalization/derealization disorder is that type of dissociative disorder in which people are found to be affected with one or the other types of two abnormalities in their behaviour referred to as (i) Depersonalization, and (ii) De-realization.

Depersonalization here refers to a type of disorder in which the affected individuals are found to experience a dream like state making them feel separation or detachment from their mind, self or body. It alters their perception about the self and consequently, they may feel as if they are outside their bodies and watching events as an observer that are happening to them.

The term *derealization,* on the other hand, refers to a type of disorder in which the affected individuals are found to experience their detachment or separation from reality lying before them. In fact here their sense of reality is temporarily lost or changed to perceive it in some other unrealistic way. Accordingly, they may feel as if things and people in the world around them are not real or they may have a distorted perception of the things in an unrealistic or unusual way.

To Sum Up

Dissociative Disorders stands for the type of disorders in which individuals are found to show a greater degree of the severity in cutting connection between their self and reality existing at present or experienced by them in their past causing them to experience a variety of problems concerning with their memory, identity, emotion, perception, behaviour and sense of self, strong enough to disrupt every area of their mental functioning. There are three types of dissociative disorders named as (i) Dissociative identity disorder (people living in two personalities and shifting from one to another for dissociating them from their own real identity without their awareness, (ii) Dissociative amnesia (people suffering from abnormal forgetting by not being able to recall information or happenings about themselves), and (iii) Depersonalization/ Derealisation disorder (individual experience a dream-like state making them feel as if they are outside their bodies and watching events as an observer that are happening to them or to experience a distorted perception of the things in an unrealistic or unusual way).

Depressive Disorders

Depressive disorders are characterized by *disproportionate* reactions to distressing stress situations like the death of a loved one, an occupational failure or a financial set-back. In such distressing stressful situation, there is nothing abnormal to have feelings of grief and despair in a reasonable amount. It is when these feelings become exaggerated in intensity and duration and begin to interfere with personal or social adjustment of an individual that they turn into depressive behavioural disorder.

Moreover, time is found to be a great healing factor in normal depressive reactions. The memories of normal stress situation become hazy with the passage of time, coupled with the creation of new interests. Life becomes worth living once more. However, when these reactions turn in to a state of depressive disorders, the depressed mood does not return to normal even after a reasonable period of time as it ordinarily does in normal depressive reactions. Here the symptoms concerning depression of mood are also severe. The patient may have intensive feelings of dejection, discouragement and sadness. There is a high level of anxiety and apprehensiveness and extreme feelings of self-condemnation. The person is unable to concentrate and his level of activity and initiative is lowered. In its more severe form, the anxiety and desperations are heightened to such an extent that the person is unable to work, and sits in despair viewing the dark side of life alone and sometimes thinks of committing suicide.

Depression may be viewed as hostility or anger directed against the self instead of being turned outward. Instead of blaming others, the person blames himself for the loss and the distressing situation. This consciousness of guilt raises his level of anxiety and apprehensiveness and forces him to relieve his tension through the mechanism of self-criticism and a relatively continued mood of depression. Thus the formula for getting affected with depressive disorders is self-condemnation plus an external loss precipitated in the case of predisposing personality traits as inability to express hostility and aggression directly and outwardly, submissiveness, dependence, sensitivity to criticism and self-criticism. Here, the person may be viewed as punishing himself by feeling responsible for the loss or for the distress situations.

Now concentrate over a case of depressive disorder stated below in the box.

A Case of Depressive Disorder

A young woman was found to be suffering from depressive disorder. Hardly had she been married for one year when her husband died of poisoning by drinking milk he had taken at night before going to bed. A lizard was found in the milk pot and this convinced the young woman that she was to blame for the death of her husband. She often thought that she had murdered her husband since she had not covered the milk pot while boiling the milk. Thus instead of experiencing normal grief or sadness, she developed depressive disorder.

The dynamics of neurotic depressive behaviour in the above case study reveals that the process starts when there is considerable emotional loss for which the person thinks the self responsible. He begins to condemn himself and is overwhelmed with the feelings of intense guilt. The depression then employed is a defense which satisfies the person when he inflicts punishment on himself through a continued period of depression. In some cases it turns out to be the last resort and is adopted as an illness especially when the person sees no silver lining among the dark clouds of despair and frustration in his life. The seriousness of this illness increases with the intensification of despair when many patients attempt suicide.

To Sum Up

Depressive Disorders represent those psychological disorders in which people are found to show *disproportionate* reactions to distressing stressful situations (like the death of a loved one, an occupational failure or a financial set-back) strong enough to interfere with their personal or social adjustment. There is a high level of anxiety and apprehensiveness and extreme feelings of self-condemnation. In its more severe form, the anxiety and desperation are heightened to such an extent that the person is unable to work, and sits in despair viewing the dark side of life alone and sometimes thinks of committing suicide.

Bipolar and Related Disorders

Bipolar and related orders belong to a category of mental disorders in which people are found to experience changes in their mood, energy and ability to function at a greater degree in a bipolar way-travelling from one extreme to another extreme of their positive and negative states of functioning. In other words, people with bipolar disorders may have periods in which they may be in the pleasant state of being overly happy, excited and energized and other periods of unpleasantness feeling very sad, hopeless, and sluggish. Bipolar disorders are also named as manic-depressive disorders meaning thereby that they are characterized with the presence of the states of mania as well as depression on an alternative basis (with a possibility of the neutral state in between).

The state of mania is associated with the elation of mood and excessive excitement. The individual here is high in spirits, overactive and bursting with energy. Manic behaviour is of three degrees: hypomania, acute-mania, and hyper-acute or delirious mania.

Hypomania is a relatively mild form of excitement which manifests itself through a state of apparent happiness coupled with unusual restlessness or nervousness. Acute mania is a more severe form of manic behaviour than hypomania. Here restlessness or excitement is more marked and elation more extreme. Hyperacute or delirious mania is a most extreme form of manic behaviour. The individual becomes very restless and excited. He experiences hallucinations and delusions of both persecution and grandeur and loses all contact with reality. In his wild excitement, he may shout and laugh constantly, tear his clothes and is likely to become dangerous both to self and to others.

The state of depression in a bipolar disorder is usually poles apart from the state of mania. Here the individual remains in low spirits, feels discouraged and sad. He loses interest in things around him and may even neglect appearance and body care. There is a severe lack of useful energy. Loss of appetite, loss of weight and constipation and lowering of sexual desire are common in this depressive state.

In their behavioural functioning, people with bipolar disorders experience extreme states of mania and depression typically occurring during distinct periods of days to weeks, called mood episodes proving quite damaging to them and others in their interaction.

The bipolar and related disorders for their diagnosis and treatment purpose are further categorized as: bipolar I, bipolar II, and cyclothymic disorder.

Bipolar-I Disorder represents that form or type of bipolar and related disorders in which the state of manic behaviour in the form of acute and hyper-acute mania dominates the scene. People with bipolar I disorder thus experience an extremely high excited and erratic behaviour with manic "up" periods that last at least a week and may be so severe that one needs medical care. It may be followed by neutral mood or more commonly with the extreme 'down' periods of depressive mood lasting at least 2 weeks.

Bipolar-II Disorder represents that form or type of bipolar and related disorders in which the suffering individual is diagnosed with having at least one major depressive episode and also at least one hypomanic episode. People may return to their usual functioning between these episodes. In this way, in this disorder one also has erratic highs and lows, but it is not as extreme as bipolar I

Cyclothymic Disorder represents a milder form of bipolar disorder in which people may experience many mood swings with hypomania and depressive (ups and down) symptoms that occur frequently but with less severe symptoms than those found in bipolar I and II disorders.

To Sum Up

Bipolar and Related Disorders represent those psychological disorders in which people are found to experience changes in their mood, and ability to function at a greater degree in a bipolar way-travelling from one extreme to another extreme of their positive state (known as mania) and negative state (known as depression) of functioning. While in the state of mania they experience the elation of mood and excessive excitement, the state of depression, on the other hand is marked with the feelings of discouragement and sadness. The bipolar and related disorders for their diagnosis and treatment purpose are further categorized as: bipolar I, bipolar II, and cyclothymic disorders.

Schizophrenia Spectrum and Other Psychotic Disorders

Psychotic disorders are more "serious disorders" of the mind and in this sense represent major mental illness. A psychotic behaviour is characterized by a serious form of personality disturbance in which the patient shows periodic or prolonged loss of contact with the world of reality. The legal and social term "insanity" is frequently used for psychotic disorders. A person who is judged insane is considered unable to act consciously and therefore, lawyers often plead the insanity of their clients for saving them from being punished for crimes committed by them. Among these disorders, exhibiting change in the functioning of the brain, schizophrenia is known to lead to all other types of psychotic disorders in terms of its frequency and damaging consequences. Let us know in detail about it.

The term schizophrenia literally means splitting of the mind. Here splitting of the mind does not mean a split personality as in amnesia and multiple personality, but a marked separation of the self from reality. "The term schizophrenia." according to Coleman (1970:275),"is now used to include a group of psychotic reactions in which there are fundamental disturbances in reality relationships and in emotional and intellectual processes."

Schizophrenics as a rule manifest a number of symptoms, the significant ones of which are:

1. Lack of coherence in the thought process
2. Disorganised patterns of thinking and feeling
3. Apathy, absence of feeling
4. Disorganised patterns of speech
5. Peculiarities of movements or bizarre actions
6. Autism—preoccupation with private fantasy
7. Withdrawal from reality or seclusiveness
8. Neglect of conduct and personal habits
9. Delusions and hallucinations

Types of schizophrenia: For the purpose of diagnosis as well as treatment, the schizophrenic disorders may be sub-divided into four major types-Simple, Hebephrenic, Catatonic, and Paranoid.

Simple schizophrenia: Simple schizophrenia is characterized by an attitude of indifference, or in advanced stages by extreme apathy. The disorder usually begins with a decreased interest in normal activities of life during adolescence or early adult life and then gradually develops into loss of ambition, emotional indifference and withdrawal from social relations. The individual becomes increasingly indifferent and seclusive and begins to obtain his satisfaction through day-dreaming and eventually sinks into an apathetic state. At this stage he does not care at all. There is nothing to wish for, nothing to fight for. He has no connection with realities to assume responsibility and is content to lead a simple, irresponsible, indifferent and dependent life.

Hebephrenic schizophrenia: Hebephrenia represents withdrawal in an extreme form. The patient no longer remains interested in the world around him. His silly and inappropriate giggling, weeping or laughing behaviour does not result from external stimuli but from stimuli from within the imaginary world in which he lives. In severe cases the withdrawal and regression is so extreme that the person behaves in many ways like an infant. It is an incurable stage and the patient continues to exist on the level of his choice in the strange world of his own creation.

Catatonic schizophrenia: The catatonic schizophrenia is diagnosed mainly on the patient's behaviour fluctuating between stuporous depression and wild excitement. Consequently, his motor behaviour may be inhibited (stupor) or alternately he may break out into an inexplicable burst of over-activity (catatonic excitement). During, his periods of stupor the patient may remain for hours in a bizarre posture. For example, he may sit, stand, or keep his limb in a particular position for hours or he may manifest symptoms like muscular rigidity (rigidity of the muscles and a general resistance to movement), waxy flexibility (remaining in any position in which he is put), echopraxia (mimicry or imitation of what others do), echolalia (automatic repetition of words said by another) and negativism (resisting even the simplest request). He may repeatedly carry out complicated stereotyped movements such as hanging the parts of his chair in a certain sequence symmetrically with both-hands or walking endlessly up and down the ward; some steps in one direction and an equal number of steps in the other. In the excited phase of catatonia, the patient becomes extremely over active, agitated, aggressive and destructive. During such periods he may shout, throw himself around, tear his clothes, assault others, or injure and mutilate himself. The violence of the catatonic patient is unbridled. In addition to the motor symptoms, catatonic patients display typical schizophrenic thinking and affect. They may frequently experience fears, hallucinations and delusions involving ideas of grandeur and of persecution.

Paranoid schizophrenia: The term paranoid literally means 'beside oneself.' Consequently, a paranoid person is one who believes person himself to have a special relationship with other people. Accordingly, paranoid schizophrenia is diagnosed mainly by the disorders of thought content involving systematic delusions and hallucinations frequently of persecutory nature resulting in loss of critical judgement and an unpredictable behaviour. In the beginning, the individual who develops paranoid schizophrenia feels unworthy and suffers from the feeling of inferiority. He resorts to defense mechanism of blaming others for his failure to achieve. He carries this defense to extremes by distrusting everyone to the extent that he feels certain that they have designs against him. Suspicions of others gradually grow into ideas of reference and ideas of reference, in turn, become delusions of persecution.

Hallucination and the delusions of persecution of the paranoid schizophrenic may take many forms sometimes of very peculiar nature. The patient falsely believes that an event has a particular significance for him individually. He may believe that the events described by the news reader on the television are oblique references to his own life; the newspapers say things about him in code; there is a special meaning for him in the nods and glances exchanged by others on the train.

The persecutory beliefs and the element of mystery combine to produce a preoccupation with plots to kill or injure the patient. A businessman was sure that his partner was trying to get rid of him and take over the company. Another patient used to wear a rubber suit at home to protect himself from the rays of an "influenced machine" which a spiteful neighbour was directing against him. A labourer declared that some people were going to lower him into hot acid and make hot iron out of him. The more interesting case is of a woman patient who remarked that "one of the doctors has stolen my mind out of my head and he is going to use it to make a lot of money".

The paranoid schizophrenic is inclined to be very verbal about his or her ideas and beliefs. Such patients are generally alert, agitated, talkative, aggressive but also confused and afraid. At times when they believe that someone wants to destroy them, they destroy them first in order to save themselves. The hostile attitude and aggression shown by some of the paranoid patients reflects such trends. However, as the personality deteriorates with time, the paranoid schizophrenics tend to become withdrawn and apathetic rather than aggressive.

To Sum Up

Schizophrenia Spectrum and Other Psychotic Disorders represent those psychological disorders falling in the category of psychotic disorders which are judged as more "serious disorders" of the mind and in this sense a state of major mental illness. The term schizophrenia literally means splitting of the mind. Accordingly, schizophrenia spectrum and other psychotic disorders represent the group of those psychotic disorders in which people experience fundamental disturbances in reality relationships and in emotional and intellectual processes. For the purpose of diagnosis as well as treatment, the schizophrenic disorders may be sub-divided into four major types: (i) *Simple schizophrenia* (characterized by an attitude of indifference, or in advanced stages by extreme apathy), (ii) *Hebephrenic schizophrenia* (representing withdrawal in an extreme form), (iii) *Catatonic schizophrenia* (diagnosed mainly on the patient's behaviour fluctuating between stuporous depression and wild excitement), and (iv) *Paranoid schizophrenia* (diagnosed mainly by the disorders of thought content involving systematic delusions and hallucinations frequently of persecutory nature).

Neuro-developmental Disorders

In this category we may include the disorders and disabilities such as Mental retardation, ADHD, Autism and Learning disabilities. On account of bringing mental malfunctioning as well as getting developed from the early childhood during the developmental period, these are referred to as neuro-developmental disorders.

Mental retardation

Mental deficiency, retardation or sub-normality may be understood as a retarded, sub-normal or deficient growth and development of one's mind or brain exhibiting subnormal intellectual capacities or inadequate adaptation to the environment on account of inherent or external factors. From the very beginning right from the early childhood, the developing children are found to be inflicted with one or the other types of mental deficiency and sub-normality. On the basis of the intelligence tests findings, individuals suffering from such deficiency or sub-normality were previously classified as dull, moron, imbecile and idiot. These have been now replaced by describing them as individuals with mild, moderate, severe and profound retardation. The new classification is based on the consideration of deficiency in adaptive behaviour along with the considerable low scores on an intelligence test.

Mild retardation: A majority of approximately eight-five per cent of the retarded belong to this category. In adult life, these individuals attain intellectual levels comparable to that of the average ten year old child. They show signs of delayed development early in life, and learn to walk, talk, feed and toilet themselves a year later than the average. They may be identified in schools as slow learners and are frequently required to repeat early grades. Speech disturbances are common among them. In comparison with normal individuals, the mildly retarded exhibit immature behaviour, have poor control over their impulses, lack judgement, and fail to anticipate the consequence of their actions. Their sexual behaviour and adjustment, in spite of the normal sexual development and fertility, is unpredictable and leads to a variety of problems and difficulties.

The mildly retarded individuals generally do not show any organic pathology and require little supervision. They are considered to be educable. With early diagnosis, parental assistance, and aid of special classes, they can be expected to reach a reasonable degree of educational achievement and to make an adequate social and economic adjustment in the community.

Moderate mental retardation: Approximately ten per cent of the totally mentally retarded belong to this category. In adult life these individuals attain intellectual level similar to that of the average six year old child. Physically they appear clumsy, suffer from motor in-coordination and present an affable, dull and somewhat vacuous personality. As a result of their inadequate development and deficient capacities and abilities they are regarded as 'trainable' instead of being 'educable' like the mildly retarded. From early infancy or childhood they show signs of retardation in almost all areas of development, and though they manage to speak, their rate of learning is too slow. They are unable to do any work that requires initiative, originality, abstract thinking, memory or consistent attention, and cannot be expected to acquire the basic skills of reading and writing. However, with early **diagnosis,** parental help and adequate training and support, most of the moderately retarded can achieve considerable independence in all spheres of life. Nevertheless, they require constant supervision and support and need institutionalization depending on their general level of adaptive behaviour.

Severe mental retardation: Nearly 3.5 per cent of the total retarded individuals-mostly children and adolescents—belong to this category. They never attain an intellectual level greater than that of the average four year old child. The mortality rate due to high susceptibility to disease is quite high among these individuals. They are grossly retarded in development from birth or infancy on-word and show severe motor and speech retardation. Sensory defects and motor handicaps are common. The majority of them display relatively little interest in their surroundings and many of them never master even the necessary skills and functions like feeding and dressing themselves, or bladder and bowel control. The severe mental retardates are neither 'educable' nor 'trainable' and the majority of them remain dependent on others throughout their lives. They need care and supervision of others with a great need for institutionalization. They may profit with proper care, timely treatment and specialized training and managing their own physical well-being and doing manual labour.

Profound mental retardation: This group makes 1.5 per cent of the total mentally retarded population. If is characterized by the most severe symptoms of mental retardation. The individuals belonging to this category never attain in adult life an intellectual level greater than that of the average two year old child. They are severely deficient both in their intellectual capacities and adaptive behaviour. The symptoms associated with them arc retarded growth, physical deformities, pathology of the central nervous system, mutism, severe speech disturbances, motor in-coordination, deafness and convulsive seizures. They are unable to protect themselves against common dangers and are unable to manage their own affairs and satisfy their physical needs. Their life span, as a result of their low resistance, is too short. Such individuals are completely dependent on others and need the care and supervision given to an infant. Essentially, they need to be institutionalized as their condition deteriorates on account of the biased attitude of the parents and stress demands of their environment.

Attention-Deficit /Hyperactivity Disorder (ADHD) refers to a neuro-behavioural disorder of the childhood often visible before the age of 6 or 7 through the symptoms of excessive inattentiveness, hyperactivity and impulsivity (often also accompanied with the problems of deficient and aggressive behaviour). The children, themselves are not responsible for learning or developing these symptoms in their behaviour. The disorder is almost caused through some dysfunction in their brain and neurological functioning. In turn, it makes them lose control over their ability for inhibition or self-regulation resulting into ADHD behavioural problems chronic enough for causing major difficulties in one's life areas like home, school, work or social situations.

An example of an ADHD child 'Danny'given below may reveal to you exactly what ADHD is.

> Danny, a 9-year-old boy, was referred to us because of his difficulties at school and at a home. Danny had a great deal of energy and loved playing most sports, especially baseball. Academically, his work was adequate, although his teacher reported that his performance was diminishing and she believed he would do better if he paid more attention in class. Danny rarely spent more than a few minutes on a task without some interruption: He would get out of his seat, riffle through his desk, or constantly ask questions. His peers were frustrated with him because he was equally impulsive during their interactions: He never finished a game, and in sports he tried to play all positions simultaneously.
>
> At home, Danny was considered a handful. His room was in a constant mess because he became engaged in a game or activity only to drop it and initiate something else. Danny's parents reported that they often scolded him for not carrying out some task, although the reason seemed to be that he forgot what he was doing rather than that he deliberately tried to defy them. They also said that, out of their own frustration, they sometimes grabbed him by the shoulders and yelled "Slow down!" because his hyperactivity drove them crazy.
>
> **Source:** Durand and Barlow (2013:486)

Autism: Usually evident before age three and mainly caused through the brain dysfunction, autism refers to a pervasive developmental disorder that may bring serious impairments and disabilities in the communication, social, emotional and cognitive behaviours of the affected children. It is usually demonstrated by them in terms of their social aloofness and bizarre activities like repetitive and unusual responses to sensory experiences and affects adversely their educational performance and adjustment in life.

Autistic children are found to exhibit quite typical characteristics in their overall behaviour and personality. In terms of their cognitive behaviour they may suffer adversely in learning skills such as reading, writing and computation and sensory deficits like over or under responsiveness to light noise, touch or pain. The most distinguishable characteristics or symptoms of autism are related with the deficits and disorders concerning communication skills, social skills, emotional behaviour and adaptive skills. Many of these children are also seen to exhibit marked peculiarities and disturbances in their behaviour like rigidity or resistance to change, temper tantrums, repetitive stereotyped and self- injurious behaviours.

The following example may illustrate well the characteristic features of Autism

> **Autism: A Mother's Perspective**
>
> Autism is when your two-year-old looks straight through you to the wall behind you-through her father, her sister, her brother, or anybody else. You are a pane of glass, or you are her own personal extension, your hand a tool she uses to get the cookie she will not reach for herself. Autism is when your eight year old fills a carton with three-quarter-inch squares of cut up paper to sift between her fingers for twenty minutes, half an hour, longer. Autism is when your eleven year old fills sheet after sheet with division - division by three, by seven, eleven, thirteen, seventeen, nineteen.... But that's enough, there are many books about autism now, anyone can read, the symptoms. I read the image for what the symptoms can't convey: this child was happy. It is not happiness to want nothing but what you have? Craving, the Buddha taught, was the source of all misery, detachment, the road to the serene equilibrium of nirvana. But nirvana at eighteen months? That's too soon.
>
> **Source** - Claria Claiborne Park *"Existing Nirvana"*, The American Scholar, 67: 2 (1998), 30.

Learning Disorders or Disabilities

Learning disorders or disabilities are associated with those children who suffer seriously from the impaired learning inefficiency to the extent that they essentially require special attention, care and remedial programs for the rectification of their learning problems and disabilities. In general, the two types of learning disabilities of the students named as Dyslexia and Dyscalculia need to be studied and known more on the part of the teachers and trainers.

Dyslexia is a type of learning disability or disorder causing problem to the suffering individual in the acquisition and application of a language related to one or the other language skills like reading, writing, listening, and speaking causing considerable harm to his educational progress and adjustment in life. Dyslexia may exist among the students in its various forms and types such as (i) primary or hereditary dyslexia, (ii) secondary or developmental dyslexia, (iii) trauma or accidental dyslexia. Apart from this, it can also be classified as visual dyslexia, auditory dyslexia and dysgraphia or kinaesthetic dyslexia.

Dyscalculia is a type of learning disability or disorder causing problem to the suffering individual in the acquisition and application of the abilities to calculate or compute in mathematics causing considerable harm to his educational progress and adjustment.

In seeking treatment of children with dyslexia and dyscalculia it should be well remembered that learning disabilities caused on account of dyslexia and dyscalculia may vary widely in their nature and occurrence. We can't prescribe the same remedy for all the cases related to dyslexia or dyscalculia. Therefore, in the treatment of the children suffering with dyslexia or dyscalculia we may witness a number of specialized techniques for the education and adjustment of the suffering children depending upon the nature of learning problems suffered by the children on this account.

To Sum Up

Neuro-developmental Disorders represent a group of disorders and disabilities such as Mental retardation, ADHD, Autism and Learning disabilities. Here the term mental retardation stands for a retarded, sub-normal or deficient growth and development of one's mind or brain exhibiting subnormal intellectual capacities or inadequate adaptation to the environment on account of inherent or external factors. On the basis of the intelligence tests, the mentally retarded were previously classified as dull, moron, imbecile and idiot. However, based on the consideration of deficiency in adaptive behaviour along with the considerable low scores, they are now classified as the individuals with mild, moderate, severe and profound retardation on an intelligence test.

Attention-Deficit/Hyperactivity Disorder (ADHD) refers to a neuro-behavioural disorder of the childhood often visible through the symptoms of excessive inattentiveness, hyperactivity and impulsivity. The disorder is almost caused through some dysfunction in the brain and neurological functioning. In turn, it makes them lose control over their ability for inhibition or self-regulation resulting in ADHD behavioural problems chronic enough for causing major difficulties in one's life areas like home, school, work or social situations. Caused through the brain dysfunction autism refers to a pervasive developmental disorder bringing serious impairments and disabilities in the communication, social, emotional and cognitive behaviour of the affected children. It is visible among them through their social aloofness and bizarre activities and affects adversely their educational performance and adjustment in life.

Learning Disorders or Disabilities refer to those psychological disorders in which individuals are found to suffer seriously from the impaired learning inefficiency to the extent that they essentially require special attention, care and remedial programs for the rectification of their learning problems and disabilities. In general, the two types of learning disabilities of people named as dyslexia and dyscalculia are more common and needs special attention. In this concern where, dyslexia is a type of learning disability that causes problem to the suffering individual in the acquisition and application of the language skills like reading, writing, listening, and speaking, dyscalculia, on the other hand, creates problems in the acquisition and application of the abilities to calculate or compute in mathematics.

Disruptive, Impulsive-Control and Conduct Disorders

It may be quite natural for children to act impulsively and violently and to become disruptive, defiant and act in socially undesirable ways at one or the other times for a short while in the form of short-lived episodes. However, when these conducts or behaviours become much more severe and longer lasting affecting their social interaction, and proving harmful to them and others, then they may turn into problematic behaviour and behavioural disorders named as disruptive, impulse-control and conduct disorders.

In a formal way, the term disruptive, impulsive-control and conduct disorders refers to a group of disorders or abnormalities in behaviour classified as (i) Oppositional defiant disorder, (ii) Conduct disorder, and (iii) Intermittent explosive disorder.

Oppositional Defiant Disorder: Children with this type of disorder are found to show the typical age-inappropriate opposing and defiant behaviour in a quite hostile way in the manner as below:

- They often loose temper, get angry, irritated and resentful on one or the other account most of the time on unreasonable grounds with an angry and irritable mood.
- They often argue with the authority figure, and refuse to comply with the request or rules and thus wilfully and deliberately try to annoy others.
- They are found to possess an attitude or feelings comprised of vindictiveness.
- They do not realize or convinced in any way the inappropriateness of their angry, defiant and oppositional behaviour. Rather they try to argue and convince others about the appropriateness of their otherwise inappropriate behaviour.

Conduct Disorder: It refers to the type of age-inappropriate behaviour more serious than the opposition defiant behaviour shown by the children involving the breakage of social rules and regulations on their part off and on, more frequently and vigorously other than the normal way. In this way, one or the other types of anti-social acts or behaviours, when committed in a more severe, and deliberate form for inflicting pain, loss and injury to others including animals and properties may describe a child to be inflicted with the conduct disorder. We may cite the following as examples of the acts or conducts associated with such type of disorder.

- Acting aggressively toward people and animals (such as bullying, physical fights, use of a weapon to cause harm),
- Destroying public and private property of others wilfully and deliberately for the purpose lying with them.
- Doing unlawful acts such as theft, lying, deceiving, robbery, chain snatching, vehicle lifting, kidnapping etc.
- Violating norms and rules enforced in the family, school, play grounds or other places of their social interaction and activities in a more frequent, deliberate and severe form such as playing frequent truancy from the class and school, running away from the home, etc.

Intermittent Explosive Disorder: This type of behavioural disorder is the severest and more damaging in its occurring and consequences than the oppositional defiant and conduct disorders. The impulsive actions and aggression led reactions or responses here are quite inflammatory and explosive just like the explosion resulted through a bomb blast that occurs in the behaviour of the affected individuals more frequently and untimely. The distinguished features of the behaviour demonstrated on the people with this type of disorder may be named as (i) quite impulsive in nature,(ii) much more out of proportion to the event or incident that triggered them, (iii) resulting much loss to the people as well as others to whom reactions or responses are addressed in the form of causing damage, distress, and serious problems of adjustment and interactions.

To Sum Up

Disruptive, Impulsive-Control and Conduct Disorders found in the children refers to a group of disorders or abnormalities in behaviour classified as (i) Oppositional defiant disorder (characterized with the typical age-inappropriate opposing and defiant behaviour in a quite hostile way), (ii) Conduct disorder (characterized with serious anti-social acts deliberately committed to inflict pain, loss and injury to others including animals and properties) and (iii) Intermittent explosive disorder (characterized with the impulsive out of proportion aggressive behaviour involving reactions or responses that are quite inflammatory and explosive just like the explosion resulted through a bomb blast occurring more frequently and untimely).

Feeding and Eating Disorders

Feeding and eating disorders may be known as the illnesses or disorders in which people experience severe disturbances in their eating behaviours and related thoughts and emotions. People with eating disorders typically become pre-occupied with food and their body weight. There are three main types of eating disorders: anorexia nervosa, bulimia nervosa and binge eating disorder.

- *Anorexia nervosa* is an eating disorder in which people pursue extreme thinness and lose dangerous amounts of weight. The central features of this disorder are a drive for thinness, intense fear of weight gain, and disturbed body perception and other cognitive disturbances. Typically, the disorder begins after a person who is slightly overweight or of normal weight has been on a diet and females are more affected with this disorder than males. In terms of its outcomes, people with this disorder are found to develop various medical and health problems such as Skin metabolism and heart-related problems and particularly amenorrhea (the absence of menstrual cycles in women).

- In a perfect similarity with Anorexia nervosa, *Bulimia nervosa* is also dominated with a morbid fear of gaining weight. However, for becoming thin instead of resorting to rigorous fasting, people with bulimia nervosa while avoiding regular meals on one hand before others go on frequent eating binges quite often secretly and then force themselves to vomit or take other extreme steps to keep from gaining weight. The binges are often in response to increasing tension and are followed by feelings of guilt and self-blame. In terms of consequences, people with Bulimia nervosa are found to be affected with a number of psychological problems (particularly related to anxiety, depression, obsession-compulsion and mood disorders) and medical problems associated with their teeth and gums, indigestion and intestine disturbances and menstrual periods cycles problem in women.
- *Binge-eating disorder* is an eating disorder in which people have frequent binge-eating episodes but do not display inappropriate compensatory behaviours. Although most overweight people do not have binge-eating disorder, two thirds of those with binge-eating disorder become overweight. Unlike anorexia nervosa and bulimia nervosa, this disorder is more evenly distributed among males and females.

To Sum Up

In the eating disorders named as Anorexia, Bulimia nervosa and Binge eating disorder, the affected individuals demonstrate a high degree of abnormality in their eating behaviour. In all these disorders people live with a morbid fear of gaining weight. However, while in *Anorexia nervosa* people pursue extreme thinness and lose dangerous amounts of weight; in Bulimia nervosa instead of extreme fasting, people when eating binges, quite often secretly force themselves to vomit or take other extreme steps to keep from gaining weight. In Binge eating disorders, the people while avoiding regular meals go on with frequent binge eating episodes but with no vomiting.

Substance-Related and Addictive Disorders

In the category of substance-related and addictive disorders, we may include, abnormality and behavioural disorders named as alcoholism and drug addiction, Let us know about them.

Alcoholism

Alcoholism is usually referred to excessive drinking or dependence on alcoholic beverages, which people drink for many reasons and in many ways, situations and styles. They should not all be considered alcoholics. The World Health Organization-WHO (1969:228) has defined alcoholics as "excessive drinkers whose dependence on alcohol has attained such a degree that they show noticeable mental disturbance or an interference with their mental and bodily health, their **interpersonal relations and their smooth social and economic** functioning, or who show the prodromal (beginning) signs of such developments."

The habit of alcoholism: The habit of excessive drinking dependence on alcoholic beverages is perpetuated gradually. E.M. Jellinek (1942), an authority on alcoholism has pointed out the following four stages in the development of alcoholism.

Pre-alcoholic phase*:* This initial phase lasts from two months to two years. The beginner, who drinks for social reasons or merely on account of curiosity, finds that it relieves him of anxiety and tension and as a result learns to use alcohol as a relief measure. Gradually, he begins to experience an increased tolerance for alcohol and needs a large amount to reach the same stage of sedation. This phase is characterized by a gradual shift from infrequent or light to frequent or heavy drinking.

Prodromal phase: At this stage alcohol begins to be **used** more as a drug and less as a beverage with dependency on it increasing and manifested through the following behavioural phenomena:

- The individual becomes preoccupied with drinking, worrying where and when he will have his next drink.
- He feels guilty about drinking and usually avoids references to alcohol in conversations. At the same time he feels a strong urge to drink and thereby often resorts to surreptitious rather than open drinking.
- There is a sudden onset of 'blackouts' for some of the periods of drinking.
- There is considerable memory impairment. One may remain conscious at the time of drinking but later unable to recall the events.

The crucial phase: The third stage is alarming. The dependency on alcohol increases to the extent that there is a danger of an individual losing everything that one values. He may drop friends, lose jobs and leave the members of his family including children and wife but not giving up the habit of drinking. The behaviour compels one to withdraw from the social environment ending in the isolation further making him drink heavily at any time. In this phase drinking is sought to be rationalized as a source of comfort. The need for liquor becomes a constant source of worry, detrimental to diet combined with the harmful effects of alcohol deteriorates his health, lowers his sexual drive and makes him hostile towards the persons and environment completely ruining his harmony and peace.

4. *The chronic phase*: This is the most crucial stage where the individual lives only to drink. His bodily systems become so conditioned that these must be supplied with alcohol or he suffers withdrawal reactions. In case alcohol is not available, he is ready to consume any of the liquid-containing alcohol like shaving lotion, hair tonic, spirit or a medical preparation. He loses control upon his behaviour and prolonged bouts of intoxication often lead to marked ethical deterioration (character disorders), complete neglect of personal appearance and concern for others, impairment of mental processes and even alcoholic psychoses in some cases. In comparison with the crucial phase, the chronic phase, results in the loss of tolerance for alcohol usually when even a small amount leads to intoxication. At a more advanced stage, the alcoholic admits defeat and unless he receives treatment is unlikely to give up drinking.

The effects of alcoholism

Alcoholism may result in severe disturbances of physiological, psychological and social functions as given below:

1. *Physiological damage:* Almost every tissue and organ of the body is adversely affected by alcohol. Since an alcoholic largely depends upon alcohol as a major source of food, he neglects his diet. Consequently, he suffers from vitamin and nutritional deficiencies. A drastic reduction in the intake of protein causes cirrhosis of the liver. Prolonged consumption of alcohol can damage the endocrine glands or cause heart failure, hypertension, shrinking and inflammation of the lining of the stomach, and capillary hemorrhage. It can also lead to the lowering of overall resistance to disease as a result of which the life expectancy of an alcoholic is considerably reduced. The incidence of death in the case of alcoholics may occur on account of depression leading to suicide, inter-current infection especially from respiratory injections, liver or cardiac failure, and inhalation of vomitus etc.
2. *Psycho-physiological damage:* This damage may result in a number of neurological and psychotic disorders (brain syndromes) such as pathological intoxication, delirium tremens, alcoholic hallucinosis, alcoholic deterioration and KorsaKoff's syndrome.
3. *Behavioural damage:* Alcoholism may result in one or the other kinds of behavioural damage in the manner like below:
    - It can cause severe deterioration in the thought processes and damage intellectual functioning. Sufficient intoxication may lead an individual to 'black out' causing inability to remember what he said or did. Motor behaviour is adversely affected on account of the deterioration in motor coordination, balance, speech and the power of sensation and perception.
    - It may cause severe personality or character disorders. There is likely to be a deterioration of personal habits, a lack of regard for one's appearance, self-image and self-respect. Following release of inhibitions, impairment of judgement, loss of emotional and motor control, disturbance in self-evaluation and indifference to self caused by intoxication, Alcoholics easily drift towards irresponsible behaviour and anti-social acts.
    - Intoxication adversely affects the sex behaviour of an individual who is likely to lose interest in the family. Sexual incapacity caused by alcoholism may further deteriorate the situation. Frustration, lack of inhibitions and defective intellectual and moral judgement may result in sexual deviations and crimes.

Drug addiction

Drug addiction is a state of acute intoxication, detrimental to the individual and to society, produced by the prolonged and excessive use of a drug, natural or synthetic, and characterized by (a) an intense craving or compulsion to obtain or consume it regardless of consequences; (b) a tendency to increase the dosage with time; (c) physiological and psychological dependence on the effects of the drug; and (d) manifestation of particular withdrawal symptoms on abrupt discontinuation of the drug.

Drugs – types and effects

Depending upon the nature of their effects, drugs may be classified as stimulant, sedative and deliriant (mind blowing).

Stimulant drugs: These drugs stimulate the brain and sympathetic nervous system resulting in alertness and increase in response and motor activity. The major drugs of this category are nicotine, cocaine, caffeine, and amphetamines like benzedine, dexedrine and methedrine.The addiction to stimulant drugs makes an individual dependent, physiologically and psychologically, on its ever increasing doses for the continuous stimulation of sense organs. In the long run it results in severe loss of appetite and weight, constipation, increased anxiety and irritability, sleep deprivation, gradual impairment of intellectual functioning and periodic episodes of delirium.

Sedative drugs: These drugs slow down the activities of an organism and diminish the responses of the brain and nervous system. As a result they are used as pain relievers and sleep inducers and may be classified as narcotics and hypnotics. The major narcotic drugs are opium, morphine, heroin, codeine, Demerol and methadone and hypnotic drugs include barbiturates like amytal, Nembutal, seconal, and non-barbiturates like bromides, and paraldehyde chloral hydrate. The prolonged use of sedative drugs leads to increasing tolerance and physiological as well as psychological craving for them. The immediate effects are pleasant and there is relief from pain and lessening of voluntary movements followed by euphoria. But these effects are short-lived and are followed by a negative phase of craving for more of the drug and the consequent ill effects.

The sudden withdrawal of sedative drugs results in dangerous withdrawal symptoms like restlessness, nervousness, excessive perspiration, nausea, vomiting, diarrhea, severe headache, marked tremors, cardio-vascular collapse and painful muscular cramps. In the case of hypnotics the withdrawal reactions may lead to epileptic seizures and delirium. If not treated in time, the seizures can cause death.

3. *Deliriant or mind-blowing drugs:* These drugs produce transient states resembling psychoses resulting in marked confusion, distortion in thought processes, delirium, illusions and hallucinations. Marijuana produces a euphoric state involving increased self-confidence and a pleasant feeling of relaxation characterized by floating imagination. There is a considerable distortion of the sense of time and space. In some cases the individual becomes irritable. There is a marked impairment in the motor and intellectual functioning but the users usually think that their efficiency has increased. This false sense of adequacy gives rise to incidents of reckless driving and other anti-social episodes. In many individuals the intoxication of marijuana may produce acute psychotic reactions as found with hallucinogenic drugs. The most popular mind blowing or hallucinogenic drug is LSD – 25 or lysergic acid diethylamide. Other hard drugs of this category are mescaline (an alkaloid and the active ingredient of peyote), psilocybin (a crystalline powder from the mushroom) and bufotenine. The outward symptoms of LSD and other hallucinogenic drugs addiction bear a strong resemblance to the behaviour of schizophrenic patients. There, is marked confusion, muddling in one's thinking and development of visual and auditory hallucinations. There is a false sense of well-being and the patient gradually develops a high tolerance and dependence.

Another drug of this category which is most abused is meth-amphetamine (speed) taken in the form of intravenous injection. Prolonged use of this drug results in malnutrition, brain damage, disturbance of the heart rhythm, and a dangerous impulsive, paranoid unpredictable behaviour.

To Sum Up

Substance-Related and Addictive Disorders represent the category of psychological disorders which include the disorders caused through the harmful intake of alcohol and drugs (commonly known as alcoholism and drug addiction). Here, alcoholism refers to that type of abnormality in people's behaviour in which they are found to resort to excessive drinking or dependence on alcohol beverages to the extent of causing severe physiological, psychological and social damage to their life. On the other hand, drug addiction represents a state of accurate intoxication detrimental to the individuals and to society resulted through the prolonged excessive use of a drug classified as stimulants (such as nicotine, cocaine, caffeine, and amphetamines), sedatives (such as opium, morphine, and heroin) and deliriants or mind blowing (such as marjuna, LSD-25 and meth-amphetamine or speed).

ASSESSMENT QUESTIONS

Section I: Essay Type Questions

1. What is normality or abnormality of behaviour? Discuss in brief the following criterion of distinguishing between the normal and abnormal people.
   (i) Ethical and moral criterion
   (ii) Criterion of social conformity
   (iii) Criterion of ideal or perfection
   (iv) Legal criterion
2. Name the different criterion of deciding the normality and abnormality of people's behaviour. Derive conclusion about the suitability of these criterion.
3. Throw light on the various causes or factors responsible for the abnormality in behaviour.
4. What do you understand by the term psychological disorders? Discuss any one of these psychological disorders in detail.
5. What are anxiety disorders? Distinguish among.
   (i) general anxiety disorder
   (ii) panic reactions
   (iii) phobias
   (iv) separation disorders
6. What are Obsessive-Compulsive and related disorders? Provide some instances of the people demonstrating such disorders in their behaviour.
7. Throw light on the following types of newly known obsessive-compulsive related disorders.
   (i) Hoarding disorder, (ii) Trichotillomania ,(iii) Excoriation and (iv) Body dysmorphic disorder
8. What are Trauma and Stressor-related disorders? Discuss Post-traumatic stress disorder.
9. What are Somatic Symptoms and Related Disorders? Distinguish among their different forms known as (i) Somatic symptom disorder, (ii) Illness anxiety disorder, (iii) Conversion disorder, and (iv) Factitious disorder
10. What are Dissociative Disorders? Distinguish among their different forms named as (i) Dissociative identity disorder, (ii) Amnesia, and (iii) Depersonalization disorder.
11. What are Depressive Disorders? Explain.
12. What are Bipolar and related disorders? Discuss the states of mania and depression in detail.
13. What are Schizophrenia Spectrum and other psychotic disorders? Discuss in brief.
14. What are Neuro-developmental Disorders? Discuss in detail about one of following disorders.
    (i) Mental retardation, (ii) ADHD, (iii) Autism, and (iv) Learning disabilities.
15. What are Disruptive Impulsive-Control and Conduct Disorders? Tell in brief about Opposition defiant, Conduct, Intermittent and Explosive disorders.
16. What are eating disorders? Tell about anorexia nervosa, bulimia nervosa and Binge eating disorder in brief. How are these caused?
17. What are Substance-Related and Addictive Disorders? Discuss about them in brief.

Section II: Short Answer Type Questions

1. Tell in simple words what is normal and abnormal.
2. Name the different criterion of describing normality and abnormality of people.
3. What is the ethical or moral criterion/ social conformity/ideal or perfection/legal/ psychological criterion of terming individuals as normal or abnormal?
4. Name the three psychological disorders each caused through the influence of chromosomes and genes.
5. Name two factors responsible for causing psychological disorders falling in the biological, psychological and sociological categories.
6. Name any four phobias experienced by the people.
7. What is the hair pulling/skin picking disorder?
8. What is Post-traumatic stress (PTSD) disorder?
9. What is Illness anxiety/Factitious disorder?
10. Give an example of the Amnesia/ depersonalization disorder?
11. What is the state of mania/depression in bipolar disorder?
12. What is schizophrenia/ affective disorders of psychotic origin/ paranoid disorder?
13. What is Mental retardation/ADHD/Autism/ Learning disability?

14. What is Opposition defiant/Explosive behaviour?
15. What is anorexia nervosa/bulimia nervosa/ Binge eating disorder?
16. Point out three ill effects of alcoholism/drug addiction.

Section III: Objective Type Questions

1. Which one of the following is not termed as a biological factor to cause abnormality in people's behaviour?
   (a) Sleep deprivation
   (b) Anal deprivation
   (c) Structure of the body
   (d) Micro organisms
2. An individual is found to show an intensive fear of high places. He is grasped with the phobia named as:
   (a) Agoraphobia (b) Acrophobia
   (c) Astraphobia (d) Algophobia
3. Which one of the following is not a newly added disorder in the category of Obsessive-compulsive disorders?
   (a) Hoarding disorder
   (b) Trichotillomania
   (c) Eating disorder
   (d) Body dysmorphic disorder
4 The amnesia disorder falls in the category of disorders named as
   (a) Anxiety Disorders
   (b) Depressive disorders
   (c) Dissociative disorders
   (d) Neuro-developmental disorders

Answers

1 (b) 2 (b) 3 (c)
4 (c)

16

Therapeutic Approaches

Learning Objectives

After going through this chapter, you will be able to:

- Know and discuss the various medical or somatic therapies named as Drug or Chemotherapy, Shock Therapy and Psycho-Surgery
- Differentiate between the nature and use of medical and psychological therapies.
- Explain the use of psychoanalytic or psychodynamic therapy
- State the use of client-centred psychotherapy
- Discuss the use of various types of behaviour therapies known as (i) Counter Conditioning, (ii) Desensitization Method, (iii) Aversive Conditioning, (iv) Modelling, and (v) Method of Positive Reinforcement
- Throw light on the nature and use of various types of cognitive therapies designated as (i) Rational Emotive Therapy (RET), (ii) Beck's Cognitive Therapy (CT), and (iii) Cognitive Behaviour Therapy (CBT)
- Explain the nature and use of the Humanistic-Existential Therapy
- Throw light on the nature and use of other alternative therapies designated as (i) Group Therapy, (ii) Family Therapy, (iii) Dramatic Therapy, and (iv) Meditation Therapy
- Tell about the rehabilitation of the mentally ill.

Introduction

Abnormal behaviour and the accompanying mental disorders or illnesses are undesirable and harmful to the individual as well as to the society. Every care therefore needs to be taken to avoid the occurrence of such behaviour and disorders through preventive measures. However, the cases of abnormality in behaviour or mental illness are bound to occur and therefore, suitable curative measures are to be taken essentially for helping the maladjusted and sick individuals. Mental illness or abnormality in behaviour is an individual as well as situational problem and it is not possible to lay down a general treatment. Moreover, the illness needs to be treated in terms of superficial symptoms as well as at the root causes. Therefore, the problem of the treatment of mental patients or abnormal should include medical, and psychological procedures. In this way the therapies of abnormal behaviour may be grouped into two broad categories:

A. Medical or Somatic therapies

B. Psychological or psychotherapies

A. Medical or Somatic therapies

The medical or somatic therapies are concerned with the physiological treatment of abnormal behaviour and mental illness. Some of the main measures in this category are drug or chemotherapy, shock therapy and brain surgery.

Drug or chemotherapy

There has been a widespread use of psycho-therapeutic drugs derived from chemical substances in the treatment of mental illness. These drugs can be grouped into the following categories—(i) major tranquilizers, (ii) minor tranquilizers, (iii) anti-depressives, (iv) sedatives, and (v) hallucinogenic.

Let us know about the uses and importance of all such drugs.

- Major tranquilizers (e.g. Chlorpromazine, and reserpine) are used with psychotic patients but may be found useful in the case of alcoholic and senile patients also. They diminish anxiety, agitation, aggressive behaviour, hallucinations and delusions and thus help to control various psychotic symptoms without impairing intelligence or clarity of consciousness.

- Minor tranquilizers like meprobamate and chlordiazepoxide reduce anxiety, apprehension and tension in the neurotic and psychosomatic patients.
- Anti-depressive drugs like phenelzine, isocarboxazid, imipramine, and amitriptyline diminish apathy and lethargy and are therefore widely used in controlling depressive reactions.
- Sedative drugs like phenobarbital, reduce anxiety, over-activity and insomnia. Sedatives carry side effects such as interference with clarity of consciousness, and causing drowsiness and therefore in many cases, the use of tranquilizers is widely recommended in place of sedatives.
- Depressants like lithium carbonate are mainly used in the treatment of agitated depression.
- Anticonvulsant drugs like trimethadione, sodium diphenyl hydantoinate are found to be effective in controlling several types of epilepsy.
- Hallucinogenic drugs such as LSD and mescaline, are useful in the treatment of schizophrenic patients particularly children.

The use of drugs has been effective in reducing the severity of symptoms and making the management of the patients convenient in the hospital or at home. It has made possible for many patients to function in the community instead of remaining in the hospital. The drugs make many more patients accessible to psychological and sociological treatment.

However, the use of drugs has many limitations and drawbacks. The drugs and the dosage vary for different illnesses and patients. Therefore matching drug and dosage to meet the needs of a given patient in a particular situation is an uphill task. Moreover, the drugs may also carry side-effects. The advantages are not also enduring as the drugs tend to 'mask' symptoms rather than to come to grips with the actual causes of abnormal behaviour. Hence, drug therapy cannot be taken as a complete treatment for an abnormal behaviour and mental disorder and has to be supplemented with other physical or psychological measures.

Shock therapy

It involves an artificial induction of deep comas, convulsions **or** both by shock inducing drugs or electric current. The more popular therapy in this concern is Electro Convulsive Therapy (ECT), also referred to as Electro Shock therapy (EST). In this therapy, convulsion is produced by passing electric current through the brain of the patient. For this purpose he is placed on a comfortable bed and electrodes arc placed on each side of his head and an alternating current, usually between 100 and 200 volts, is passed between them for a period of about two seconds. Patients are generally given muscle relaxant before administering ECT. While inducing current, the shoulders and limbs of the patient are held lightly by nurses and attendants and a rubber gag is placed between his teeth to prevent injury during the convulsion. About five to ten ECTs are given two to three times a week depending upon the requirement of the situation. There is confusion and loss of memory during the period immediately before and after treatment, but it gradually returns in a few weeks. The ECT has been found helpful for depression, involutional melancholia, mania, schizophrenia and other psychotic reactions. It is quite popular for controlling cases of agitated depression and schizophrenia and is found useful for patients who do not respond well to drug therapy.

Psycho-surgery

It involves surgical operation of the patient's brain and aims to destroy or isolate certain maladaptive cell complexes in the frontal areas of the brain responsible for undesirable emotional responses and mental disorders. The removal of maladaptive cell complexes in the frontal lobes or the cutting of nerve pathways between the prefrontal lobes of the brain and the thalamus or hypothalamus by the surgical operations results in reducing the emotional torment of disturbing thoughts, apathy, delusions and hallucinations. Consequently, psychosurgery may be found useful with a wide range of mental patients including schizophrenics, involutional melancholic, anti social personalities, alcoholics, manic depressives and patients suffering from stubborn obsessive and other severe neurotic reactions.

Psychosurgery as a method of treatment of the mental patients involves considerable risk and negative consequences. It may reduce or even impair the patient's intellectual abilities. There may be temporary or permanent organic complications including convulsions, aphasia, increased appetite and rectal or vesical incontinence. In some cases brain surgery may lead to death. Therefore, in all cases psychosurgery should be the last resort and its use restricted to patients with whom everything else has been tried and failed, so that any improvement at all may be considered a great gain.

To Sum Up

The treatment of abnormality and psychological disorders may be classified into two broad categories namely, somatic or medical therapies, and psychological or psycho therapies.

Somatic or medical therapies are concerned with the physiological or medical treatment of the affected individuals. Some of the main measures belonging to this category are drug or chemotherapy, shock therapy and brain surgery. In the use of drug therapy it may be seen that various drugs prove effective in reducing the severity of symptoms and make the management of the patient convenient in the hospital or at home. But the drugs also carry severe side-effects and the treatment does not remove the actual causes of abnormality or disorder. Drug therapy has therefore to be supplemented by other measures.

The therapy known as shock therapy involves an artificial induction of deep comas, convulsions or both by shock-inducing drugs or electric current. The more popular therapy for this purpose is Electro Shock-therapy (EST) in which a convulsion is produced by passing electric current through the brain of the patient. It is quite popular for controlling cases of agitated depression and schizophrenia and is found useful for patients who do not respond well to drug therapy.

Psychosurgery involves surgical operation of the patient's brain for reducing the emotional torment of disturbing thoughts, apathy, delusions and hallucinations. However, it involves considerable risk and negative consequence and should be taken as a method of last resort.

B. Psychological or Psychotherapies

The majority of cases of behavioural disorders or mental illness may be adjudged as products of severe maladjustment caused by psychological factors. Physical or medical treatment in such cases does not prove very useful. Such patients need psychological treatment for solving their psychological difficulties and achieving better personality adjustment. This form of psychological treatment is known as psychotherapy.

Psychotherapy is a difficult term to define. However, it may be understood as a method of treatment of psychological problem or disorder of an individual (known as patient) by a trained person (known as therapist) through a behavioural approach in the form of establishing a psychological relationship with the patient for the purpose of solving the patient's emotional difficulties and promoting adequate personality growth and adjustment.

The main objective in psychotherapy is to bring about changes in the patient's perception of himself and of his environment and thus resulting in positive enduring changes in his behaviour for achieving adequate adjustment and regaining better mental health. For the realization of this objective a number of systematic approaches to psychotherapy, differing in goals and procedures, have been evolved. These are psychoanalytic therapy, client centred therapy, behaviour therapy, cognitive therapy, humanistic-existential therapy and some other alternative therapies as group therapy and yoga therapy. Let us know about them. But before doing this let us know about the therapeutic relationship existing between the therapist and client/patient.

Psychotherapy: A method of treatment of psychological problem or disorder used by a therapist through a behavioural approach in the form of establishing a psychological relationship with the patient with the purpose of solving his emotional difficulties for achieving adequate adjustment and mental health.

Therapeutic relationship

In a therapeutic treatment, particularly employing psychological methods, the success of a particular treatment method depends much on the appropriate relationship existing between the therapist and client/patient. Therapist has to win over the client for knowing about the needed things regarding his past and present along with the history and nature of his problem. The client should have the required faith in the therapist and his method of treatment. Since, it is the client who needs to be helped in a distressing situation, and he is completely dependent on the therapist for getting him rid from the faced problem, it is the therapist who has to own the responsibility of maintaining the required degree of the interrelationship existing between the two. For exercising his role in a proper way on this account, a therapist, in general, is required to be imbibed with the traits and characteristics as briefed below.

1. The therapist must be genuinely and not superficially in relationship with his client. He should be what he is. Anything going on

in him, which is relevant to the relationship, can be seen by his client. He should be able to bring a direct personal encounter with his client, meeting him on a person to person basis.

2. The therapist should have the capacity for empathy. To sense the client's inner world of private meanings as if it were his own, without losing the "as if" quality, is empathy. He should also be able to communicate some of the significant fragments of that understanding. By showing *empathy,* by sensing and reflecting their clients' feelings, therapists can help clients experience a deeper self-understanding and self-acceptance. As Rogers (1980:10) describes his own experience on this account in the following way:

Hearing (active listening) has consequences. When I truly hear a person and the meanings that are important to him at that moment, hearing not simply his words, but him, and when I let him know that I have heard his own private personal meanings, many things happen. There is first of all a grateful look. He feels released. He wants to tell me more about his world. He surges forth in a new sense of freedom. He becomes more open to the process of change. I have often noticed that the more deeply I hear the meanings of the person, the more there is that happens. Almost always, when a person realizes that he has been deeply heard, his eyes moisten. I think in some real sense he is weeping for joy. It is as though he were saying, "Thank God, somebody heard me. Someone knows what it is like to be me."

3. The therapist must experience a warm, positive, acceptance towards what is in the client. He must praise and respect his client as a person and thus pay a positive regard. As far as possible, this positive regard should be unconditional.
4. The therapist needs to acts in such a way that his client may perceive the genuineness of the acceptance and empathy which the therapist experiences for him. The perception of such a psychological climate in the relationship by the client results in the constructive personality growth and desirable changes in the behaviour of the client.
5. The therapist should act in his words and deeds in such a way as to win the confidence of his client for revealing and disclosing the things related to his personal world and the problem he is facing. In fact he should have a strong positive image in the public on this account. He should never exploit the trust and confidence of the client in any way.

Psychoanalytical or Psychodynamic Therapy

The founder of the psychoanalytical or psychodynamic therapy was Sigmund Freud who developed the theory and technique of psychoanalysis. Freud believed that earlier conflicts, desires, painful or anxiety-arousing experiences, though repressed and unconscious, are responsible for the present abnormal behaviour of an individual. He used the technique of free association and dream analysis for tracing the real causes of the present problem by uncovering the repressed conflicts.

In the technique of free association, the patient is made to lie on a couch, with the analyst (therapist) sitting out of his range of sight. The patient is asked to 'free associate', that is, to speak freely about whatever comes into his mind, no matter what it is and to go on talking about his thoughts and feelings as subsequent associations reveal themselves. He is expected to talk frankly. He must not hold back past or present events, attitudes towards the therapist or fantasies, no matter how unpleasant or embarrassing they may be.

In case the patient remains silent or claims that 'nothing comes to mind' it may be his resistance to treatment. He is told that all thoughts and feelings are important to the treatment process. If he insists that he is really trying, it may be postulated that the resistance is caused by unconscious parts of his mind. Such resistances themselves provide clues to the patient's conflicts.

Dream analysis is another major technique used in psychoanalytical therapy for uncovering unconscious motivation and repressed conflicts. During sleep, the defenses of the ego are lowered, allowing repressed material to reach the conscious. For this reason, dreams, to some extent, may be taken as the 'royal road' to the unconscious. Expressing his views in this concern, Freud asserts, that one's dreams, are loaded with repressed material, although in symbolic form. The manifest content of the dream is the actual dream and its events, but the latent content is the hidden, symbolic meaning of those events that would, if correctly interpreted, reveal the unconscious conflicts that were creating the nervous disorder. (Freud, 1900)

Consequently, through the analysis of material produced by means of free association and patient's dreams, the analyst begins to get all the clues about the possible underlying causes of the behavioural disorder of his patient. For the most part, the analyst has to rely for his subject matter on the verbal responses based on the memories of the patient. Later on, some more direct evidences become available. The patient's personality is reflected in the way he behaves during the analytic period. His habitual patterns of behaviour his way of looking at things, his likings and love, his prejudices and bias, may all affect the way in which he deals with his analyst. His total behaviour is to be analysed by the therapist for going deep into his problem.

Many times, on account of the phenomenon of transference the patient's attitudes and behaviour towards his therapist is unrealistic. During the interaction in the process of psychoanalytical therapy, the patient and therapist develop a complex emotionally charged relationship. As a result, the patient usually transfers his deepest emotions to the analyst, the analyst becoming the love object or the hate object depending upon the early experiences of the patient with his parents or other important persons. For example, a female patient may view the analyst as an ideal husband and lover or may exhibit feelings she had as a child towards her father. The mechanism of transference is important in effecting the cure of the patient as it allows letting go of repressed feelings towards persons resembling husband, lover or father figures. The analyst intelligently establishes rapport and relationships for the uncovering of the unresolved conflicts and repressed feelings and tries to make interpretations based on the emotional attitude and behaviour shown by the patient towards the analyst.

In brief, the psychoanalytical therapy rests on the following assumptions and techniques.

- Abnormal behaviour of the patient is the result of the repressed desires or conflicts experienced earlier in one's life.
- Through free association and recalling day to day dreams the patient is given art opportunity to uncover his unconscious desires and repressed conflicts.
- The mechanism of transference helps in the task of uncovering the conflict as it is once again made into an interpersonal one, this time between the patient and the therapist.
- The analysis of free association, dreams, transference and overall behaviour of the patient helps in knowing the abnormal behaviour of the patient.
- The therapist tries to show the patient how some early experiences affected his emotional life and finally helps him to achieve new and more adaptive modes of adjustment in order to lead a normal life.
- Finally, the therapist tries to break the bond of interpersonal relationship between himself and his patient in order to make the patient face the realities of life and solve his problems independently (after developing an impressive insight into his problem) without any emotional support from the therapist.

The prevalent mode of psychoanalytical therapy has been modified in many ways from orthodox psychoanalysis propagated by Freud and his followers in the manner such as below.

- The couch is gone, and the client (the term used now in place of the Freud's term patient for the individual seeking therapy) may sit face to face with the therapist and he or she may also stand or walk about.
- Rather than remaining quiet until the client says something or revealing, the modern psychoanalyst is far more directive, asking questions, suggesting helpful behaviour, and giving opinions and interpretations earlier in the relationship, which helps speed up the therapeutic process.
- The treatment session now may go on two to four times a week for two or more years. These sessions are more likely to be focused on current situations, interpersonal relationships and other sources of conflict. The therapist may also take advantage of such treatment adjuncts as play therapy, art therapy, group therapy and hypnosis instead of being dependent upon free association and dream analysis only.
- Today's psychoanalysts also focus less on the "id" as the motivator of behaviour, instead looking more at the "ego" or sense of "self" as the motivating force behind all actions. Some psychoanalysts also focus on the process of transference more than on other typical aspects of traditional psychoanalysis, leading to the more general method called psychodynamic therapy. Psychodynamic therapy is typically shorter in duration than traditional psychoanalysis.
- Even so, all the psychodynamic techniques require the client to be fairly intelligent and verbally able to express his or her ideas, feelings and thoughts effectively. People who are extremely withdrawn or who suffer from the more psychotic disorders are not good candidates for this form of psychotherapy. People, who have non-psychotic adjustment disorders, such as anxiety, somatoform or

dissociative disorders, are more likely to benefit from psychodynamic therapy (Ciccerelli & White, 2012)

Client-centred psychotherapy

This is also known as non-directive therapy and is the outcome of the philosophy and experiences of an American psychologist Carl Rogers (1902-1987) who had full faith in the worth and competencies of the human individual. His assumption was that people are innately good and effective. They have an innate tendency for self-actualization, that is, to realize their potentials. As the self has an innate tendency towards self-actualization, the most important evaluation should come from the self of a person. In case where a person accepts evaluation from others and if these evaluations are negative or conditionally positive the result is conflict between self-evaluation and the evaluation of others. This type of conflict may give rise to undue anxiety and tension and thus in due course cause abnormalities. For example, a newly married normal girl may develop abnormal behaviour by considering herself worthless after being repeatedly criticized by her mother-in-law or husband.

Consequently, Rogers' therapy demands from the individual to return to his basic nature of evaluating himself positively. It believes that the client (the term used for a patient) is quite competent to resolve his conflict as he has within himself resources for self-actualization and healthy adjustment. He needs only a deep affectionate relationship with the therapist to learn how to use his resources. Rogers' therapy involves very strong conviction about the client's worth and his basic urge for self-actualization. The therapist is there not to direct but merely to help the client direct himself for his healthy adjustment. On account of this non-directive role of the therapist, Rogers' therapy is known as non-directive therapy. It is known as client-centered therapy (and more recently as person-centred therapy) because it revolves totally around the client or the person seeking therapy as may be seen in some of the following steps associated with this therapy.

1. In Rogers' therapy, the client himself approaches the therapist for help in order to get rid of some psychological stress. During the first interview, the therapist instead of solving his difficulty himself assures him of his help in working out the client's own solutions.
2. In the next interview, the client is encouraged to talk about his most deeply felt emotions as freely as possible. In this way, the negative feelings that have been bottled up inside the client come out into the open. Here the therapist does not intervene but creates suitable therapeutic conditions which would facilitate the client to talk in a more honest arid emotional way about himself and his problem.
3. The next move is concerned with helping the client to gain an insight into his emotional conflicts. It involves acceptance, recognition and clarification of the feelings of client by the therapist. Here attention is paid to the emotional aspect rather than to what the client says. The therapist tries to provide an environment for removing the emotional conflicts which are blocking self-actualization by selecting and focusing on statements and feelings expressed by the client. It is a sort of help rendered by the therapist to the client for learning suitable ways to evaluate himself and his environment in a true perspective.

As a result, the client gains insight by (i) understanding the causes behind his behaviour, (ii) recognising and accepting his self in its real position, and (iii) working towards his positive self-growth and better adjustment.

4. After gaining insight into his problem, the client is helped in seeking some minor positive actions for the solution of his problem. Here also the therapist is not to direct or lead but to recognize and render clarification about the possible courses of action. The minor positive actions bring satisfaction and develop self-confidence paving the way for more positive action and thus helping the client in his self-actualization.
5. Finally, there comes a stage when the client, after gaining confidence in his self, feels that he does not need further therapeutic interviews. As such the decision for ending the therapeutic relationship comes from the client. At this stage, he is known to acquire his original drive for self-actualization by learning positive ways of understanding and promoting his self.

Evidently, from beginning to end, Rogers' therapy is centred round the client. He is the main actor who has to play the leading role. The therapist encourages and sets the therapeutic environment for helping him, to discover ways of self-actualization by gaining insight into his problem, removing discrepancy between his real self and his idealized self-image and developing confidence in his self for healthy adjustment.

As far as the suitability of the therapy is concerned, Rogerian therapy may not, in fact, be appropriate for a severe psychological disorder. It may, however, work well with mildly disturbed people if handled properly by a therapist in appropriate environment of interpersonal relationship.

To Sum Up

Psychoanalytical therapy assumes that repressed desires or conflicts experienced earlier in one's life are the real source of the causation of abnormal behaviour. The analysis of material produced by means of free association, dreams and other measures helps in getting clues for the underlying causes of behaviour disorder. The therapist then tries to acquaint the patient with the effect of his early experiences and helps him to achieve new and more adaptive modes, of adjustment. On the other hand, *Client-centred psychotherapy* is centred around the client. It creates proper therapeutic environment for helping him to discover ways of self-actualization by gaining insight into his problem, removing discrepancy between his real self and his idealized self- image and developing confidence in his self for his healthy adjustment.

Behaviour therapy

The basic assumption underlying behaviour therapy is the belief that behaviour in all its forms and shapes is learned. The abnormal behaviour grows out of maladaptive or defective learning. Therapy, in turn, becomes an attempt to provide corrective learning experiences through the use of the same kinds of learning techniques that people use to learn any new responses.

As a term thus, behaviour therapy denotes the use of experimentally established principles of learning for the purpose of changing un-adaptive or abnormal behaviour. As far as the origin of the maladaptive or defective learning is concerned, it is traced either in classical conditioning as advocated by Pavlov or in operant conditioning as explained by Skinner. Based on these two approaches, various methods of behaviour therapy (discussed ahead) have come into existence.

1. *Counter-conditioning*

One may learn maladaptive or abnormal behaviour through conditioning. As a result, a person may show fear responses in the presence of certain normally neutral stimulus objects and events. When that happens we say that he has developed some unrealistic fear or phobia. Fear of animals, height, water, darkness, closed or open places, all such phobias may be seen as a result of defective learning or improper conditioning. The treatment of such behaviour lies in its counter-conditioning.

For illustration, let us take the case of a child who has developed a generalized fear of rabbits through conditioned fear responses. In this case, the treatment may be worked out by associating some pleasant or favourable responses with the presence of a rabbit. The child may be given his most liked eatables or allowed to listen to the most enjoyable tune or play the game in the presence of a rabbit. The rabbit may be kept at some distance and then gradually moved closer on successive occasions. The fear responses can thus be gradually eliminated.

The sexual dysfunctions like frigidity, impotence and early ejaculation may also be treated by the process of counter-conditioning. Most often such dysfunctions are the result of anxiety which causes sexual inhibition. Thus the treatment process involves conditioning as below:

- To attempt sex relations only when there is a minimum of anxiety, for example, in situations in which there is a clear desire,
- To attempt sex relations only when desirable support, cooperation or assistance is available from the sex partner.

Gradually the reaction of anxiety to sexual experiences may be eliminated because they will now not be permitted to happen, and adequate sexual responses may in time be strengthened resulting in the treatment of a particular sexual dysfunction.

2. *Desensitization methods*

Conditioned anxiety responses are the root causes for the development of many abnormalities in the behaviour of individuals. The treatment of such abnormalities may involve a variety of techniques designed to increase the individual's capacity to tolerate an anxiety-provoking situation. Two such techniques are described, below:

(i) *Systematic desensitization:* This technique was developed by Joseph Wolpe, an American psychologist. It aims to reduce levels of anxiety related to an anxiety-provoking situation progressively through some well-planned systematic steps like relaxation, outlining hierarchy of individual's anxieties, and desensitization.

- In this initial stage, attempts are made to develop an anxiety hierarchy. For this purpose, the patient's anxieties are studied and ranked according to the intensity of anxiety to the different stimuli ranging from most to least frightening. Side by side, in the earlier session of therapy, the patient is made to learn the art of relaxation of the muscles of the body.

- When the patient has mastered the relaxation technique, the desensitization process begins The patient is made to relax completely in a, comfortable chair or a couch with his eyes closed, and asked to imagine and experience the scene in the hierarchy which is the least anxiety-provoking and progressively reaches the scene which is highest in the hierarchy. The motor relaxation is viewed by Wolpe as antagonistic to anxiety. The patient imagines and experiences the scene with little or no anxiety, and thus his sensitivity to the imagining of such experiences is de-conditioned. Treatment is terminated when the patient reaches a stage of relaxing completely and imagining vividly and without any anxiety the scenes which evoked the greatest anxiety before the commencement of the treatment.
- There may be certain variations of the desensitization procedure. Instead of imagining a situation, the patient may be exposed to the real stimuli which evoke anxiety. This is termed as desensitization in vivo. In such a procedure, a patient who has a fear of humiliation at making mistakes may be made to commit minor errors and then progressively more serious ones in the presence of the therapist in each instance until all feelings of anxiety disappear. In another variation, desensitization may be done using a tape-recorder or video film eliciting anxiety-provoking situations.

(ii) ***Flooding or implosive therapy:*** In this method of desensitization, the patient is exposed immediately to the greatest anxiety-provoking situation. He is not gradually introduced to the anxiety-provoking situations starting from the least to the most as in systematic desensitization but is encouraged to face the frightening or distressing situation and remain there, regardless of how much anxiety *is* generated, until a spontaneous decrease in anxiety takes place. A child who fears rabbits may be confronted with a rabbit through a videotape or by way of real-life situation. It may be seen that his peak anxiety does not last very long and he eventually gets used to it and feels that his fear was irrational.

3. *Aversive conditioning*

Aversive conditioning involves the modification of behaviour patterns through pain or punishment. This treatment has proved effective in overcoming obsession thinking, compulsive acts, homosexuality and other sexual deviations, alcoholism, over eating, smoking, drug dependence, gambling, etc. The method consists of administering a noxious stimulus {resulting in an unpleasant response) to the patient in an appropriate time relation to the stimulus to which aversive conditioning is desired. The assumption of such treatment is that the patient will gradually learn to avoid abnormal pattern of behaviour and prefer a more desirable and normal one. For example, in treating a man for homosexuality, the aversive conditioning would involve an introduction of a punishment (electric shock or some other punishment) while he is made to look at the picture of an attractive male but would be permitted to look at the picture of a female or some sexually attractive parts of a female figure without being punished.

Similarly, in the treatment of chronic alcoholism aversion conditioning may be achieved with the help of a drug *Antabuse*. The person who is a chronic alcoholic is persuaded to take the drug. A drink of alcoholic beverages, after taking the drug, results in strong unpleasant and uncomfortable physical reactions like increased pulse rate, difficulty in breathing, severe headache and nausea. The repetition of such unpleasant experiences results in the avoidance of alcoholic beverages.

4. *Modelling*

Modelling is a therapy technique in which a patient's behaviour is modified as a result of observing the appropriate and normal behaviour of other people used as models. One may use modelling therapy for eliminating a child's fear of rabbits by making him observe that the other children are playing with the rabbits without fear. Similarly, one's phobia of snakes may also be overcome through modelling therapy. Such patients may be made to observe both real and filmed incidents of people (models) and snakes in which people (models) may be seen approaching the snakes gradually with no signs of anxiety and fear.

Modelling as a technique may also be used for learning more adaptable and desirable ways of personal and social adjustment. People may also be helped in the treatment of sexual dysfunctions by means of films or live models depicting practical techniques and normal sex behaviour.

5. *Method of positive reinforcement*

In this method, carefully selected rewards and schedules of reinforcement are used to modify a patient's behaviour in the direction of socially desirable well-adaptive behaviour. Anorexia nervosa, a condition in which the affected person refuses to eat, has been found to be successfully treated by arranging for eating to be followed by a proper schedule of positive reinforcement or rewards such as to be allowed to go to a movie, play a favourable game, use of a radio or provision of good company etc.

A technique known as 'token economy' is also used as a method for treating abnormal behaviour. It is based on the principle of positive reinforcement. In this method, plastic or metal tokens are used as rewards for reinforcing the positive and desirable behaviour shown by patients. These tokens may, later, be exchanged for special privileges such as television viewing, single room accommodation, to obtain special food, magazines or novels etc. This token economy as a behaviour modification technique has been found most effective in improving and modifying the behaviour of people in institutions or hospitals.

To Sum Up

Behaviour therapy denotes the use of experimentally established principles of learning for the purpose of changing maladaptive or abnormal behaviour. Based on the classical conditioning or operant conditioning, it involves important methods like counter conditioning, desensitization, flooding, aversive conditioning, modelling and method of positive reinforcement. In *counter conditioning*, the maladaptive or undesirable behaviour learned through conditioning is de-learned and replaced through desirable behaviour by making it to learn through the same mechanism of conditioning. In the use of *desensitization,* attempts are made to employ a variety of techniques (such as systematic desensitization and flooding or implosive therapy) designed to increase the individual's capacity to tolerate an anxiety-provoking situation. In *aversive conditioning* the employed technique involves the modification of behaviour patterns through pain or punishment. In the use of the technique of *modeling* the patient's behaviour is modified as a result of observing the appropriate and normal behaviour of other people used as models. The use of the *Method of positive reinforcement* involves the employment of the appropriate rewards and schedules of reinforcement to modify a patient's behaviour in the direction of socially desirable well-adaptive behaviour.

Cognitive Therapies

Cognitive therapies, true to their naming, focus on one's cognition-the ways of thinking, reasoning and drawing conclusions for identifying and treating abnormality and mental illnesses of the people. There are three types of therapies available in this category, named as below:

(i) Rational Emotive Therapy (RET), (ii) Beck's Cognitive Therapy (CT) and (iii) Cognitive Behaviour Therapy (CBT)

Rational Emotive Therapy (RET)

The earliest one among the cognitive therapies used for the treatment of abnormality and mental illness was a therapy named as Rational Emotive Therapy (later on named as Rational Emotive Behaviour Therapy) developed by Albert Ellis in the 1950s. The cognitive approach he adopted for this purpose was based on the following assumptions.

- Our cognition-the thought process determines our feelings and behaviour. The abnormality of behaviour and mental illness is the outcome of the faulty cognitions about the self, others and the things lying in the environment.
- What makes our cognition-the way of our thinking, reasoning and interpreting of the things defective and erroneous is thus the root cause of the abnormality in our behaviour and mental illness. According to him it is one's irrational thinking-the ways of perceiving, and interpreting the things in his unique defective way that puts him into trouble of getting entrapped in the vicious circle of distress and related problems. Take the case of perfectionist and pessimist. Both of them are attributed with irrational thinking and beliefs. When they face a small failure, they might perceive it as a quite big one like the heaven has fallen on them. They become distressed, and begin to think and believe negative things about them, others and the things lying in their environment leading to more distress and creating more problems for them.
- The treatment of the abnormality of behaviour and mental illness thus lies in taking care of one's irrational and erroneous thinking and beliefs that are responsible for arousing them emotionally in a negative and undesirable way. For this it is needed to help them in bringing necessary changes to their thought process and belief system leading them to remain emotionally balanced-necessary for their living a balanced life. In this way, we may see that

this form of cognitive therapy is an opportunity for the patient to learn of his current distortions and successfully eliminate them.

The procedure and steps adopted for treatment in RET

Step1: Employment of ABC (Antecedent–Belief–Consequence) analysis

Albert Ellis developed a model named ABC for analyzing and identifying the problem of the patient. Let us know about it.

(i) The term *Antecedent* or *Activating event* in ABC model stands for the events or happenings that caused a psychological problem or distress to the patient. The therapist tries to know about them through a variety of means and information collected from the patient, family members and other possible sources.

(ii) The term *belief* here stands for the types of irrational beliefs held by the individual through his irrational and erroneous thinking about his self, others and the things lying in his environment. These beliefs are quite far from reality and therefore cannot be supported by the empirical evidences. As examples of such beliefs we may cite the erroneous assumptions held by the individuals like below:

- Feeling excessively upset over other people's mistakes or misconduct.
- Believing that you must be perfectly competent and successful in everything to be valued and worthwhile
- Believing that one should be loved and liked by everybody all the time
- Believing that it is catastrophic when things are not the way you want them to be.
- Believing that one will be happier if one avoids life's difficulties or challenges

The holding of one or the other types of such beliefs or outlook is associated with the evaluation of the role of one or the other antecedent events in causing the felt distress or problem. These irrational beliefs are assessed through a variety of means such as interviews, questionnaires, inventories, attitude scales etc.

(iii) The term *consequence* here stands for the eruption of negative feelings, emotions and behaviours resulting through the distorted perception of the antecedent event on account of one's erroneous and irrational beliefs having no connection with reality.

Step 2: Providing therapeutic treatment

Ellis believes that it is not the antecedent or activating event (A) that causes negative emotional and behavioural consequences (C), but rather it is the distorted and unrealistic interpretation of these events on the part of an individual resulting in the formation of his irrational belief system (B) that leads to a particular type of problematic consequences (C).

According to Ellis, thus, the eradication of the problem lies in adopting measures for bringing necessary changes in one's belief system. Therefore, after identification of the irrational beliefs, attempts are made by the therapist to work with the patient/client in the task of challenging and refuting the negative thoughts. For this purpose, although both direct as well as non-directive questioning in a Socratic dialogue mode may be used yet most of the therapists prefer to make use of the latter for better results. The non-directive questioning provides a gentle, non-probing and non-threatening mode for the required disputation of the client's irrational beliefs and thoughts. For example, a therapist may ask the client (who is depressed on account of the irrational belief that he/should be loved or cared by everyone in all situations) why should everybody always do this for you? Why do you need such caring? It helps the clients/patients to think and ponder deep into their unrealistic beliefs and illogical way of thinking and emotive responding. On the basis of the more realistic evidences available to them they begin to re-interpret the things in a more realistic light. Eventually it helps the client to develop more rational beliefs and healthy coping strategies for leading meaningful emotionally balanced normal life.

Beck's Cognitive Therapy

As a cognitive approach for addressing the behavioural problems and psychological distress especially related to depression and acute anxiety among individuals, the Psychologist Aaron Beck developed a therapy named as Cognitive therapy (CT) through his work conducted in the 1960s. His approach in this regard while resembling in a number of ways to the earlier discussed Rational Emotive Therapy differed mainly as below.

In adopting cognitive approach for explaining the distortions in the ways the clients/patients look at things while Ellis (1957) suggested that it happens on account of irrational and unrealistic thinking, Beck (1967) proposed the cognitive triad for this purpose.

This cognitive triad quite typical to the people with depression is visible among them in its three forms of negative thinking namely negative thoughts about the self, the world and the future. These thoughts occurring in a stream-like fashion tend to be automatic in depressed people as they occur spontaneously one after another such as I am quite poor in my studies; my parents and teachers hate me; I can't finish any task in time; it seems that I am a worthless person; I have no friends to share my concern, etc. Quite often these negative thoughts persist even in the face of contrary evidence or assurance to an individual, and work as a strong attribute for leading one to utter depression.

In addition to the presence of the above-mentioned triad of irrational automatic negative thoughts there are two other mechanisms that may contribute significantly towards the causation of depression, namely (i) Negative self schemas, and (ii) Errors in Logic (i.e. faulty information processing)

The term Negative Self-Schemas refers to a set of negative beliefs and pessimistic expectations about themselves possessed on the part of the depression prone individuals learned and acquired by them through their earlier experiences mostly related to their childhood and traumatic in nature These may include (i) parental rejection, neglect or abuse, (ii) publicly ridiculed in school or community, (iv) victims of bullying, exclusion from the peer group, or sexual assault, (iii) occurring of sad events such as death of a parent or sibling, etc.

The possession of a thought pattern in the form of unrealistic negative thinking coupled with a bunch of negative self-schemas and self-image lowers self esteem and self-confidence of the people to such an extent that they are bound to make logical errors in their thinking by focusing selectively on certain aspects of a situation while ignoring equally relevant information in this regard. Beck named it as a process of cognitive distortion in which one is found to suffer from the problem of carrying out his thinking in a quite distorted and illogical way for arriving at some conclusion about his self, others and world quite erroneous and far from reality. It leads to the formation of a dysfunctional cognitive structure in depression or anxiety-prone individuals making them victims of depression or anxiety disorders as when some more precipitating factors appear in their day to day life.

The treatment of mentally ill persons in Beck's cognitive therapy consists of first identifying the nature of the problem and the possible causes attached to it. It then calls for the adoption of indirect questioning technique for the soft, non-threatening disputation (challenging) of the client's dysfunctional cognitive structure composed of the distorted irrational thinking and beliefs. The responding to question - "why everybody should care about you" may help the client in doing away with his cognitive distorted structure erected through his erroneous belief that "he should be always cared and looked after by others".

Cognitive-Behavioural Therapy

It is aimed to bring needed changes in one's cognitive behaviour-thinking and drawing conclusions for feeling and acting in a desirable way. Cognitive behavioural therapy takes a double-barrel approach for dealing with behavioural problems and disorders. Where, on one hand, it aims to bring desirable change in people's way of thinking, side by side, on the other it also works towards altering the way they act.

In this way, this treatment approach helps in deriving two-sided benefits of both the cognitive as well as behavioural approaches for treating abnormal behaviour (i) by making people aware of their irrational negative thinking and to replace it with new ways of thinking and (ii) training them to practice the more positive approach and way of living in their life.

1. The beginning in the use of this approach is made to bring needed changes in the irrational negative attitude and thought process of the problem-ridden individual. In general, people suffering from depression, anxiety and mood disorders, for example are found to be grappled with pessimistic and negative thinking, and over generalized self-blaming behaviour such as "I am worthless, I will not be able to face the interview board, the other candidates are far better than me, they are looking so relaxed and confident, I will get surely nervous in answering the questions, so on and so forth".
2. To change such self-defeating, over-blaming, and pessimistic behaviour of the individuals, into a desirable one, therapists now try to teach the affected people to restructure their thinking and behaving positively in stressful situations. The first task in this concern is to replace, negative self-talk with positive, confidence and assurance. He can thus help them in restructuring their thought process. It can then be followed, to train them to act in a desirable way guided through their restructured thinking.

In practice, the use of cognitive-behavioural therapy has been found quite encouraging and helpful for a number of people suffering from anxiety, depression and mood disorders. While going through such treatment, the affected people get valuable opportunity to replace their negative thinking and self-defeating pessimistic behaviour with more realistic appraisals of themselves and practice behaviour that helps them in getting rid of their problems. How cognitive behavioural therapy is practiced and what gains are available with the use of this therapy may be made clear by going through the following description provided by Myers, David G.(2014:556).

> In one study, people with obsessive-compulsive behaviours learned to re-label their compulsive thoughts. Feeling the urge to wash their hands again and again, they would tell themselves, "I'm having a compulsive urge". They would explain to themselves that the hand-washing urge was a result of their brain's abnormal activity, which they had previously viewed in PET scans. Then, instead of giving in, they would spend 15 minutes in an enjoyable, alternative behaviour, such as practicing an instrument, taking a walk, or gardening. This helped them "unstuck" their brain by shifting attention and engaging other brain areas. For two or three months, the weekly therapy sessions continued, with re-labeling and refocusing practice at home. By the study's end, most participants' symptoms had diminished, and their PET scans revealed normalized brain activity. Many other studies confirm cognitive-behavioural therapy's effectiveness for those with anxiety, depression, or anorexia nervosa.

To Sum Up

Cognitive therapies focus on one's cognition-the ways of thinking, reasoning and drawing conclusions for identifying and treating abnormality and mental illnesses of the people. There are three types of therapies available in this category, named as Rational Emotive Therapy, Beck's Cognitive Therapy and Cognitive Behaviour Therapy. In the Rational Emotive Therapy effort is made to help the patients to bring necessary changes in their irrational and erroneous thoughts and beliefs leading them to live an emotionally balanced normal life. In Beck's cognitive therapy, work begins with the identification of the nature of the problem and its probable causes. It is then followed by the adoption of indirect questioning technique for the soft, non-threatening disputation (challenging) of the client's dysfunctional cognitive structure composed of the distorted irrational thinking and beliefs. *Cognitive behavioural therapy* helps in deriving two-sided benefits of both the cognitive as well as behavioural approaches for treating abnormal behaviour by (a) making people aware of their irrational negative thinking and to replace it with new ways of thinking and (b) training them to practice the more positive approach and way of living in their life.

Humanistic-Existential Therapy

Humanistic-existential therapy represents a blend of two types of therapies known as humanistic therapy and existential therapy. Humanistic therapy is governed and guided through the key ideas and principles inherent in the humanistic perspective postulated by the humanists like Abraham Maslow and Karl Rogers. Humanistic perspective views human nature as basically good, with an inherent potential to maintain healthy, meaningful relationships and to make choices that are in the interest of ones self and others. These choices help one to satisfy his basic needs including the need for self actualization-striving for a goal true to one's nature or becoming his true self (e.g. becoming musician, dancer, technician etc). Whenever there is any hurdle in their realization, it results in one's maladjustment and cause abnormalities in one's behaviour. Actually, the humanistic perspective mainly emphasizes that "not being one's true self" is the main source of problems and the therapist should try to help the client in getting out of this mess for living a meaningful life.

The existential therapy is directed and shaped on the basis of ideas and principles inherent in the philosophy and perspective of existentialism. Existentialism believes in the very existence and well-being of the individuals. It advocates the need of exercising free will on the part of individuals for making choices in life for making their life meaningful. For this purpose it assumes that people should live peacefully with no incalculable loss in their life by having love and respect for themselves and others. They should also own responsibility, and show creativity in performing the tasks of their own choices. Failure in one or the other such aspects may breed anxiety, despair and frustration in one's life. More over these may also be caused on account of one or the other ill happenings in one's life such as death of some dear one, accidental and incidental losses or fear of eventualities such as death etc. In this way, in view of the existential therapists, the central problems people face are embedded in anxiety over loneliness, isolation, despair, and, ultimately, death. In dealing with such aroused anxiety and depression, therapists are needed to provide the client opportunity for their free expression, creativity, love and authenticity for making his life meaningful.

In adopting a synthesis of both the humanistic and existential therapies a therapist is found to help the clients in getting rid of their problems through a well planned and organized therapeutic program with the assumption mentioned below.

The clients need to be helped by making them perceive and remove the obstacle in the path of the satisfaction of their basic needs as well as a quite important need related to their self-actualization (becoming true to their self). Similarly, they may also be helped in identifying the nature of their anxiety or frustration and the things responsible for its eruption and then dealing with it successfully by adopting the suitable means. In attaining both these objectives the therapists attempt to help the clients first by creating a therapeutic relationship that is warm and accepting and that trusts that they are capable of identifying and dealing with their problems and then helping them in the manner as below:

(i) To help them in freeing themselves from disabling assumptions and attitudes responsible for their problems so that they can live fuller lives.
(ii) To emphasize growth and self-actualization rather than curing diseases or alleviating disorders.
(iii) To help them not to see anxiety nor despair as a symptom of a disorder, but view it as a normal part of experience, accept them and use their energy to help them make authentic or genuine choices about their life and to take responsibility for their future experiences rather than just reacting to circumstances.
(iv) To provide opportunities for exercising creativity, love, authenticity, and free will on the part of the clients for helping them come out from the state of acute anxiety, stress, frustration and despair and enabling them to live meaningful lives in the face of uncertainty and suffering.
(v) To help the clients achieve a dimension of self-respect, self-motivation, and self-growth to facilitate their early and meaningful recovery.

To Sum Up

Humanistic-existential therapy while adopting a synthesis of the humanistic and existential therapies helps the clients in getting rid of their problems through a well planned and organized therapeutic program focusing on (i) their perceiving and realization of the their basis needs including the need related to their self-actualization, and (ii) identifying the nature and cause of their anxiety or frustration and then dealing it with successfully by adopting the suitable means.

Other Alternative Therapies

All these treatment methods have one-to-one relationship involving one helping person (the therapist) and one person coming for help (the patient). There are other behavioural approaches such as group therapy, family therapy and dramatic therapy that involve two or more persons in seeking and providing treatment help. In addition, there are some good approaches available on this account from the ancient civilization such as Yogic meditation therapy in Indian Culture. Let us know about them.

Group therapy

In contrast with such one-to-one relationship group therapy demands the involvement of a group (two or more persons) at a time with a single or several therapists. According to Kisker (1964:388), "Group therapy is a method of treatment in which a number of people are treated at one time or in which group dynamics are used in the treatment of one person."

In group therapy, a group usually consists of six to twelve members who meet one or more times a week. This group is somewhat homogeneous with respect to age, sex and type of disorder. Usually the group is led by a therapist. The different therapeutic measures like psychoanalytical therapy, client-centred therapy and behaviour therapy used in individual therapy may also be successfully used in group therapy which may take several forms. There are differences in objectives, approaches and techniques. Some groups are conducted in the format of individual therapy, others are essentially educational, featuring the presentation of certain materials which the members discuss and apply to themselves. A few groups are largely inspirational, others seek to promote insight to release experiences or problems, pent up emotions or unconscious impulses to facilitate self-discovery or to teach social skills.

In modern group therapy a group situation known as 'encounter group' is used for the treatment of maladaptive behaviour. In such a group the patients are encouraged to behave in an unguarded fashion. They get immediate and open feedback from fellow members and the therapist or the group leader. In some encounter groups the members engage in group activities like singing, games, physical exercises, physical intimacy, dance, dramas and other entertainment programmes. The idea behind such group activities is to induce fatigue or pleasure in order to break resistances for the closer group interaction, and proper catharsis or sublimation of their unconscious improper motives.

Group therapy has many advantages over the individual therapy, the foremost being the economy in terms of time, labour and financial resources as the treatment may be given to a number of patients in group affected with the same disorder. Beyond this, the group therapy provides an environment for the learning of desirable social skills and unlearning of maladaptive behaviour through the use of group dynamics. It also permits persons with common problems to support and help one another.

However, group therapy does not necessarily work well with all types of disorders and patients. For example, some people find it impossible to talk about themselves and their problems in a group. In some cases of agitated depression or psychotic disturbances, the group encounter may prove dangerous. As a result, there is a need for considerable skill on the part of therapist who deals with a group of patients. It is his competency, art of group dynamics, and understanding between him and his patients which prove helpful in bringing encouraging results of group therapy.

Family therapy

Family therapy is a variation of group therapy in which two or more members of a family are treated together as a unit. The family group in this therapy may consist of a troubled married couple, or it may be a set of parents and one or more of their children. Sometimes it is the whole family being treated in a clinic or in its natural habitat—the home.

Family therapy has grown out of the realization that each member of a family is influenced by every other members. Usually, unhealthy intra-familial relationships are responsible for the maladaptive abnormal behaviour of an individual. On the other hand, an abnormal family member may prove a potent factor in turning the environment of family uncongenial and thus paving the way for making other members maladjusted and abnormal.

A proper treatment procedure must care for the related factors in one's family along with his treatment. In order to bring about a desirable modification in the behaviour of an individual we have to take care of the intra-familial relationships within his family. If we attempt to change the patient without changing the others in the family, we may find family circumstances conspiring to keep him as he is. That is why, many patients who improve in the hospital or clinic are found to manifest a reappearance of symptoms when they return to their families.

Family therapy is a challenging and promising approach. It helps the family members to discuss their attitudes with each other and acquire insight in the intra-familial relationship. It brings desirable changes in the whole family interaction, ensuring that changes in one person will not be counteracted by the behaviour of others. This approach brings all or a large portion of the family under study and thus helps in maintaining the family's equilibrium and allows the family to work its adjustment problems as they occur.

The treatment through family therapy often reveals that the patient who first seeks help or is referred for help is not necessarily the most maladjusted. He may be the victim of the maladjustment or defective interpersonal relationship of his parents or other members of the family. For example, difficulties in the marital relationship of parents may cause difficulties in parenting and it may, in turn, cause behavioural abnormalities in the children. In such cases, improvement in marital relationship of the parents through a well planned family therapy always brings desirable improvement in the behaviour of a child patient.

Dramatic therapy

Dramatic therapy uses the enactment of roles and incidents, when problems are acted out instead of being talked about. Role playing and psychodrama are examples of such therapy.

In role playing, the patient acts out the behaviour of an individual in a certain situation. In doing so he either repeats his own previous behaviour or gives indication of his possible behaviour in that situation. In this way, role play gives the patient and therapist an opportunity to gain insight into the patient's behaviour. It also provides an opportunity and stage to achieve catharsis and to practice more adaptive ways of one's behaviour. Psychodrama involves a more elaborate procedure than role play for acting out behaviour. It generally involves five elements on the pattern of a dramatic setting: a stage, the therapist in the role of director, the patient as a hero, helping characters (other persons or therapists) and the audience. The patient is made to act out his problems. All concerned persons are made to participate in the spontaneous acting out of problem situations related to the patient's life.

Meditation Therapy

Mediation, as a term, refers to a process of mediating-focusing attention on something so vital as on one's breath or on one's thought, recited mantra or a particular object lying in one's environment aimed to attain the needed relaxation, and thought control in one or the other situations. Historically, the practice of meditation is known for its origin in eastern cultures more than four thousand years ago. Our great Rishies and even the general public had adopted the meditation practice in their regular daily routine. In Patanjali's yoga system it was the highest stage of one's concentration and yogic sadhna. However, in the present modern days, the credit for its more popularizing and exporting to the western cultures goes to one of our meditation practitioner Maharishi Mahesh Yogi. Referred to as transcendental meditation, Mahesh Yogi's brand of meditation has been widely accepted in Europe, USA and throughout the world. As far as transcendental meditation is concerned, the most common mental device used in this meditation is the repetition of a mantra. The mantra is a simple sound selected by the instructor as a mental concentration device. One such sound, "om" or "ahhom" has been popular. Other mental devices that have been used in meditation include the *mandala* (a geometrical figure), *nadam* (imagined sounds), and *pranayama* (breathing). A general procedure for making use of transcendental meditation is laid down below.

Procedural steps

- Choose a calm and quite pollution free environment and place for doing meditation
- Sit in a comfortable position with eyes closed on a mat or chair (the standing position is also acceptable).
- Concentrate on deep breathing while at the same time repeating the mantra.
- Soon, you will feel that the sound of the mantra is disappearing and your mind is experiencing more subtle thought levels and finally arriving at the source of the thought and when it happens you may think yourself in deep meditation.

Apart from the above-stated transcendental meditation, other forms of meditation practices originated from the Patanjali's Yoga system include Vipasana meditation, Chakra Yoga, Mudra yoga, Kundalini Yoga, and Sudarshan Kriya Yoga (SKY).

All these forms of yogic meditations have experimentally proved quite effective as an appropriate therapy or method of treatment of abnormality, mental disorders and illness particularly associated with acute anxiety, depression, stress, frustration, aggression, social deviance and substance abuse.

To Sum Up

The other useful therapies put up in the group of psychological therapies may be named as group therapy, family therapy, dramatic therapy, and meditation therapy. *Group therapy*, here, stands for a method of treatment in which a number of people are treated simultaneously or in which group dynamics are used in the treatment of one person. In modern group therapy a group situation—encounter group—has proved effective in treating behavioural disorders. *Family therapy* is a variation of group therapy in which two or more members of a family are treated as a unit. In *Dramatic therapy* the method of treatment involves enactment of roles and incidents. Here the problems are acted out instead of merely talking about them. Role playing and psychodrama are examples of such therapy. In Mediation therapy the attention of an otherwise agitated, depressed or anxiety-ridden patient is focused on something so vital as on one's breath or on one's thought, recited mantra or a particular object lying in one's environment aimed to attain the needed relaxation, and thought control in one or the other situations. The two of the most common meditation practices employed in this therapy may be named as transcendental meditation (popularized by Mahesh Yogi) and the therapies based on the Patanjali Yoga system.

Rehabilitation of the Mentally Ill

Dealing with the problems of behavioural abnormality or mental disorder and illness of the clients does not end with their treatment by making use of one or the other therapies or treatment measures discussed above in this chapter. It is one part of the care or attention that is needed to be paid over them. It helps them in getting rid of the problems and difficulties they were facing as well as securing their recovery from the mental ailments and other related behavioural problems. But the work is still incomplete. It needs to be supplemented with the adoption of suitable rehabilitation measures for helping them in reaching their optimal level of independent functioning in society and for improving their quality of life. The needs of helping them on this account may be quite varied and multi-dimensional depending up on their nature of ailments or problems being suffered on their part. Accordingly, the rehabilitation measures adopted for the patients of severe problems such as schizophrenia, bipolar disorder, acute anxiety disorder, and depression, needs to be somewhat differing from the cases of milder ailments such as generalized anxiety and phobia or the sufferers of behavioural problems such as socially deviant behaviour, substance abuse or mental retardation etc. However, one thing is common and sure for all types of these cases, that all of them need to be helped in getting enabled for living an independent and happy social life. For this purpose, they need to be trained and oriented for becoming satisfactorily independent in terms of their physical, economical and social living. Therefore, the rehabilitation measures or means employed for their welfare may include the things like below.

1. They should be oriented about the adoption of *appropriate health habits* in terms of doing regular physical exercises, and yoga activities, being careful about their food, and sleeping habits in proper tune with the type of ailment or problem suffered by them.
2. For their proper socio-psychological adjustment they should be provided opportunities to acquire the needed skills such as *communication skills, life-saving skills, emotional management skills* etc. There should also be due attempts for getting them accepted and integrated in their familiar socio-cultural environment by educating the family and community for the needed awareness and positive attitude towards them through the means like family therapy and community awareness.
3. For seeking economical independence they should be trained in acquiring the needed *occupational and vocational skills* for helping them earn their livelihood by seeking their self-employment or jobs in one or the other sectors.

To Sum Up

Rehabilitation of the mentally ill refers primarily to modification of the environment in order to provide a life situation in which the patient has a reasonable chance of making a successful adjustment. Various socio-therapeutic measures carried out by the psychiatric social worker with the help of voluntary and non-voluntary social welfare agencies help a patient in his overall adjustment by bringing desirable changes in his physical, social, educational, professional and therapeutic environment. Moreover, these measures prove effective in providing systematic care of the patients after their discharge from the hospital in terms of follow-up treatment and proper rehabilitation.

ASSESSMENT QUESTIONS

Section I: Essay Type Questions

1. What is medical or somatic therapy? Discuss in detail the various methods used for medical or somatic therapy for the treatments of mental disorders or abnormalities in behaviour.
2. Discuss any two of the following medical or somatic therapies in detail.
   (i) Drug or chemotherapy
   (ii) Shock therapy
   (iii) Psycho surgery
3. What are psychological therapies? Discuss any two among the various types of therapies designated as psychological therapies used for providing treatment to the affected individuals.
4. Discuss in detail the psychoanalytic or psychodynamic therapy used for the treatment of abnormality or mental disorders.
5. What is client-centred psycho-therapy? Describe in detail.
6. What is behaviour therapy? Discuss any two of the following behavioural therapies in detail
   (i) Counter conditioning
   (ii) Systematic desensitization
   (iii) Flooding or impulsive therapy
   (iv) Aversive conditioning
   (v) Modelling
   (vi) Method of providing positive reinforcement

7. What is cognitive therapy? Discuss in detail any one of the cognitive therapies used for the treatment of abnormality or mental disorders.
   (i) Rational Emotive Therapy (RET)
   (ii) Beck's Cognitive Therapy (CT),
   (iii) Cognitive Behaviour Therapy(CBT).
8. What is Humanistic-Existential therapy? Discuss its employment for treating abnormality and mental disorders.
9. Discuss in brief the use of following therapies.
   (i) Group therapy
   (ii) Family therapy
   (iii) Dramatic therapy
   (iv) Meditation therapy
10. Throw light on the rehabilitation of mentally ill individuals.

Section II: Short Answer Type Questions

1. What is medical or somatic therapy?
2. Tell in brief about Drug or chemical therapy/ Shock therapy/Psycho surgery used for the treatment of mental disorders or abnormalities in behaviour.
3. What is psychological therapy?
4. Name any four psychological therapies used for the treatment of abnormality or mental disorders.
5. What is behaviour therapy?
6. Name the various methods used for providing behaviour therapy to affected individuals.
7. Tell in brief about Counter conditioning/ Systematic desensitization/ Flooding or impulsive therapy/ Aversive conditioning/ Modelling/ Method of providing positive reinforcement for the treatment of mental disorders and abnormalities.
8. What is cognitive behavioural therapy?
9. Tell in brief about Rational Emotive Therapy/ Beck's Cognitive Therapy/ Cognitive Behaviour Therapy.
10. What is Humanistic-Existential Therapy?
11. Tell in brief about the use of Humanistic-Existential Therapy.
12. Mention in brief the use of Group therapy/ Family therapy/ Dramatic therapy/ Meditation therapy.
13. Tell two things about the ways and means employed for the rehabilitation of mentally ill.

Section III: Objective Type Questions

1. Rational Emotive Therapy (RET) is called what type of psychological or psycho-therapies?
   (a) Behaviour therapy
   (b) Cognitive therapy
   (c) Client centred therapy
   (d) Humanistic-existential Therapy
2. Which one of the following is not a method or techniques used in the employment of Behaviour therapy?
   (a) Desensitization
   (b) Modelling
   (c) Aversive conditioning
   (d) Psychoanalysis
3. Who is the propagator of the therapy known as Rational Emotive Therapy?
   (a) Carl Rogers
   (b) Albert Ellis
   (c) Aaron Beck
   (d) None of these
4. A technique known as 'token economy' is also used as a method for treating abnormal behaviour. It is based on
   (a) The principle of positive reinforcement
   (b) Aversive conditioning
   (c) Counter conditioning
   (d) None of these

Answers

1 (b) 2 (d) 3 (b)
4 (a)

17

Psychology and Life

Learning Objectives

After going through this chapter, you will be able to:

- Know and discuss about the human-environmental relationship
- Throw light on the effects of physical environment surroundings particularly the noise, pollution, crowding and disasters on human behaviour
- Discuss about the effects of human behaviour on physical environment
- Know and discuss two of the major concerns or problems of our society namely (i) poverty and (ii) aggression & violence
- Know about the role of psychology in the maintenance of our physical health
- Mention about the impact of television and mass media on our behaviour

Introduction

Psychology defined as a science of behaviour is related with our life activities in its various ways and forms particularly in terms of the manifestation of our behaviour in relation to our self, others and outside world. How we perceive and react to our own self, thus, may be found to affect our life activities in a considerable way. The self-esteem and confidence built and self-regulation exercised on our part in our behavioural functioning is seen to play a quite mentionable role in this direction. Similarly, the quality and characteristics of our interaction with others on an individual basis or in the group also cast a significant effect on our life activities. You have known all about it in the discussions carried out in the earlier chapters of this text. In addition what lies in our outside environment-physical and socio-cultural and our relations-ways of behaving and responding to this environment also play a key role in affecting our life activities in a reciprocal way, i.e. our behaviour and life activities affect the environment and what happens in the environment plays a key role in affecting our behaviour and life as a whole-including our health, social life and overall well-being. In this chapter we would be discussing many of the things related to these aspects. Let us begin with the discussion of our relationship with the available environment for our living and exercising behavioural activities.

Human-Environmental Relationship

Beyond us lies the surrounding environment-physical and socio-cultural available for our interaction and life functioning. The physical environment in this concern is said to include nature as well as man-made entities. In the list of nature-given entities we may include the things and objects available to us with the courtesy of nature such as earth and space, soil, water, air, mountains, rivers, minerals, rivers, oceans and their treasures, sun and moon light, weather conditions and climate etc. The man-made environmental entities include all what has been constructed or built by the humans within the available natural environment such as dams, power projects, bridges, roads, railway tracks, cities, houses, factories, parks and gardens, and artificially created pools, ponds and lakes etc.

Socio-cultural environment refers to all what is available to us in our surroundings for our social interaction and cultural transmission from the social and cultural agencies such as family, neighborhood, peers and friends, community, school and other higher educational institutes, social and religious institutions, information and entertainment agencies including media and online transmission etc. Both these environmental forces-physical and socio-cultural, exercise a great impact in shaping our behaviour and personality for living our life in one or the other ways. Here at present, let us focus our discussion to analyze the extent to which our behaviour is affected through physical environment and vice versa.

Effects of Physical environment and surroundings on Human Behaviour

There are a number of elements, situations and conditions, objects or stimuli in one's physical environment-natural and built up or man-made that have enough potentiality of influencing, directing and controlling one's behaviour in one way or the other. A few of such physical environment determinants may be named as below:

- The geographical location and the nature of the land, soil, and climate of the place
- The quantity and quality of the food, water, air etc, available to the people living in a particular region
- The nature of the essential living material facilities like clothes, shelter, means of transport, livelihood, and other essentials for living
- Pollution free or polluted environment
- The impact of incidents and accidents as well as natural inequalities and calamities like storms, earthquakes, droughts, tsunamis, fires, and floods, etc
- The availability or non-availability of the company of the nature in the form of animals, birds, plants, forests, rivers, mountains, sea beaches etc.

Each one of the above-mentioned factors related to one's physical environment-natural or built up is quite effective in influencing one's behaviour. We may cite a number of examples in support of this claim.

The hilly people who live a hard life on account of the odd circumstances generated by the extreme weather conditions and other unfavourable physical facilities are found to possess a typical type of hardworking nature, persistence and endurance in their behaviour in comparison to those who are favoured by their physical environment in the form of the availability of easy means of livelihood and living. Experimental evidences have properly established that the behaviour of the individuals is affected in a positive and negative way depending up on the favourable or unfavourable physical environment and working or living conditions available to them. In any establishment, factory or institution we may notice a tremendous difference in the behaviour and work culture of the employees depending up on the favourable and unfavourable physical environment and facilities available to them for their working. Annoyance generated on account of the unsatisfactory physical and working conditions may breed frustration, anxiety, aggression and other maladaptive behaviour tendencies among the behaviour of the workers and other employees.

Moreover, how do we sense, perceive, and interpret a situation or behave in a particular way at a particular moment is dependent upon our reactions and responses to the stimuli available in our physical environment and surroundings. While the desired and favoured physical facilities and situations in our environment provide us pleasant experiences and lead us to desirable rewarding behaviour, the unpleasant experiences generated through lack of facilities and unfavourable physical conditions may give birth to the traits of undesirable behaviour. You may yourself perceive the induced difference in your behaviour by experiencing the sudden stoppage of the working of the ceiling fan, cooler or air conditioner on account of electricity failure.

For the illustration of the negativity and adverse impact resulted through unfavourable situations or factors lying in our physical environment let us consider and discuss the role of a few of such unfavourable environmental factors, such as (i) Noise, (ii) Pollution, (iii) Crowding, and (iv) Natural Disasters.

Noise and its Effect on Human Behaviour

A sound is turned into noise for an individual when it is so high in its intensity and unpleasantness that it becomes increasingly irritating or annoying for him. In all its forms and modes-mild or severe it may cause inconvenience and create problems of one or the other nature to the sufferers. Besides casting harmful effects on their physical health (e.g., hearing loss, increase in blood pressure, and causing heart problems etc.) it may equally and to say bit more affect their mental health and behaviour in a quite adverse way in the manner summarized below.

1. It brings a quite harmful effect on the sensation, perception, attention and decision-making mechanisms of the individuals. In turn, it may create problems for them in gathering proper information from their surroundings, misinterpret a situation, and wrongly respond to the stimuli resulting in the creation of a number of behavioural and interactional problems.
2. On account of proving a big distraction and interfering force, noise causes a great loss in one's concentration or focusing up on the task in hand. They have to fight a war against the resistance or obstacle put up by the effect of noise in their work environment and thus their

level of performance related to the task in hand is bound to suffer a heavy loss. Besides, reducing the level of achievement, it may cause distaste or apathy towards the task, affect their motivation, and may result in frustration and anxiety-ridden problems.

3. Noise may adversely affect the process of communication going on between individuals. In this situation, there is all possibility of the misinterpretation of the communicated message resulting in the wrong doing and spoiling of the interpersonal relationships.
4. The most severe and damaging effect of noise that has been experimentally studied or personally experienced lies in the fact that it leads to a variety of abnormality and disorders in one's behaviour such as irritability, aggressive tendencies, violent behaviour, dissatisfaction, despair and frustration and other mental health problems.

Pollution and its effect on Human behaviour

The term pollution according to the Oxford Language Dictionary stands for the presence or introduction into the environment of a substance which has harmful or poisonous effects. In our environment such pollution may exist in a number of forms such as air pollution, water pollution, and soil or land pollution. Although nature is kind enough to bless us with the purest possible form of air, water and soil for our living, we human beings are responsible of polluting them in one or the other ways.

Air pollution, in this concern, is created and enhanced by us through (i) producing smoke by burning one or the other stuff including the burning of remains and waste of the fields by the farmers and that of the household by the house holders; (ii) smoke generated through factories, and indoor smoke generated by smoking cigarette, cigar or beedi, (iii) smoke generated through the use of vehicles, (iv) throwing and allowing household and industrial wastes or garbage including non-biodegradable such as plastic, tin or any metal container to become a source of air pollution, (v) spreading dust, building material and other types of impurities during construction work, and (vi) becoming a source of major pollution through the leakage of chemicals, poisonous gases and radioactive material from industrial plants or storage such as which happened in the case of the unfortunate Bhopal Gas tragedy in our country in 1984.

Similarly, we pollute sources of water-an another precious gift of nature through our unwise acts like throwing all types of waste, chemicals, garbage, dead bodies etc in the river, ponds, lakes or wells.

The soil which is utilized by us for the growing of vegetation and food products is also put under heavy intoxication by treating with harmful chemical fertilizers and spreading of insecticides as well as allowing dangerous chemicals and waste of factories and households sewer water and human waste to get absorbed in the fields growing contaminated food products consumed by all of us.

Pollution created in all the above-mentioned forms at any place or period proves quite harmful and hazardous to the well-being of we all humans not only in terms of casting damaging impact on our physical health but our psychological well-being and mental health is also adversely affected in a variety of ways particularly in terms of the impairment of the functioning of our nervous system, and emotional disturbance and turmoil felt by us on this account. Accordingly, pollution may be found to cast a damaging effect on all of our essential psychological processes-sensation, perception, attention and concentration, mood and emotionality, motivation, learning, memory as well as communication and our interpersonal relationships. In this concern, air pollution may cause us a lot of inconvenience and uncomfortable situation by chocking our breath, spoiling our mood through foul, bad and unpleasant smell resulting in a lot of obstacles in our behavioural functioning, including our performance at work, and interaction with others. You may be experiencing it many ways while encountering with the pollution generated through running vehicles, dust and other suspended particles reaching your face and noise, the smell and sensation experienced through the rotten wastes and garbage lying on the land and spreading in the river, ponds or lake water.

Much like polluted air, the polluted water and soil infected and intoxicated with harmful chemicals, and poisonous substances may equally prove quite harmful for the physical and psychological health of the individuals. In addition to the damaging effects of water and land pollution, experienced in our breathing, we are also targeted through the liquid we drink and the food stuff we consume by eating the fish and other sea food, vegetables and fruits poisoned through the polluted water and soil.

The psychological effects of the pollution caused through the transport vehicles, heavy industrialization and leakage of gas, chemicals and other harmful substances have been experimentally studied variedly in our country and abroad. Their findings have brought into lime light that the people affected through such pollution were found to demonstrate a considerable decrease in the ability to concentrate at a task, lowering of their motivation and performance level, increase in their anxiety and stress level, developing restlessness and aggression in their ways of behaving and interacting with others, as well as serious disturbance in their memory, reasoning and decision making. In the case of pregnant mothers and developing children, the infection from one or the other types of pollution have been found to prove quite costly in terms of causing mental deficiencies and retardation, and giving birth to a number of psychological disorders and ailments.

Crowding and its effect on Human behaviour

The term crowd or crowding, as discussed already in chapter 11 of this text, stands for the collection of a large number of people at a place temporarily for a spell of time period without any particular common goal or target to achieve. The presence of a large number of people at the railway station platforms or passing through the stairs of metro stations, gatherings at the places of religious fairs and festivals, people roaming in busy marketing places, a group of people witnessing the show of a magician at the road side, or greeting some influencing or famous personality such as cine actor or leader appearing before them walking on their way, etc. may be cited as some examples of the term crowding.

The meaning of the term crowding in the above said manner is emphasized chiefly for getting it distinguished for the term group. However, in our day to day functioning, the term crowding may also be used for a large number of like-minded people gathered at a particular place for some common purpose as the audience in a cinema hall, passengers travelling in a bus or railway coach, students studying in a room, visitors in a visiting gallery, devotees in a religious place, etc.

In both its meaning there is one thing that is common and it is the presence of a large number of people at a time at a specified place and time. Whenever, the number of people in their gathering in a specified area exceeds more than the normal limits of one's capacity-known as crowding tolerance capacity, he or she may fall victim to the negative consequences of crowding. These consequences may affect the people's health and well-being both in physiological and psychological terms. We are here more concerned of the psychological consequences. Let us know about them in brief.

Crowding may lead to people experiencing a lot of unusualness, suffocation, restlessness, anxiety and stress in its various forms and resulting outcomes.

- In some situations, it proves a great obstacle in paying needed attention to the stimuli for proper responding and attending to a task or behavioural act thus affecting the performance and behavioural responses of the people in an adverse way.
- In other situations, it may become a source of spoiling their mood, experiencing a lot of unpleasantness, feeling them anxious, desperate and frustrated, developing stress and thus leading them towards one or the other types of abnormalities in behaviour and mental disorders.
- It may also make them react in a much agitated and aggressive way giving birth to quarrels and fighting.
- A number of negative incidents like chain snatching, pick pocketing, abduction, sexual harassment may also be visible at a time of mass crowding. The anxiety and stress generated on this account may also be seen responsible for a number of psychological problems among the victims.

In this way, the phenomenon of crowding may be found responsible for de-stabilizing the behavioural equilibrium of the people in one or the other forms resulting in one or the other behavioural problems or disorders.

Disasters (Natural or Man-Made) and their impact on Human behaviour

Although nature blesses us with so many essentials and comforts for our existence and living, yet there are also possibilities of it getting furious on one or the other accounts such as disturbances in its natural functioning. Its fury causes us to experience sad and horrible events in the name of forest fires, floods, cyclones, tsunamis, earthquakes and volcanic eruptions. All of these events and happenings prove quite damaging and devastating for our well-being to the extent of losing everything in our possession including the life of our near and dear ones as well as also of our own. Such type of nature's fury resulting in hazardous consequences is termed as natural disaster, catastrophe or devastation. Apart from such natural source of disasters, people are also haunted, and victimized through accidental and man-made disasters. We can name them as road or rail accidents, aeroplane crash, terror attacks, bombing by the enemy country etc.

The consequences of all such disasters are limitlessly damaging to the sufferers or victims. They may get deprived of all their material possession–houses, properties, shops, industrial establishments, hard-earned money, animal stock and crops leaving no means for their sustaining and living a life. Many of them become homeless, orphans and bankrupt. They may lose their one or the other limbs, get paralyzed or inflicted with one or the other serious diseases on account of the unhygienic ailing conditions followed after the disasters. The loss of lives of the near and dear ones adds much to their grief. It is one side of the story. The other one in terms of suffering psychologically is equally and even much more devastating to them. Let us see how.

What happens or suffering physically for the loss of one or the other valuable possession including lives, cast a deep wound on the psyche of the victims in the form of painful traumatic experiences and memories. Besides clouding with a lot of anxiety, frustration, depression and stress in their living, they also become haunted with a lot of negativity resulting in one or the other types of emotional and behavioural problems, and mental disorders as the side effects of the trauma experienced by them. Psychologists and researchers have tried to know about the effects on the psyche of the survivors by conducting a number of post-traumatic studies. One of such studies was conducted in our country on the victims of Bhuj (Gujarat) earthquake in January, 2001 concluding in the manner as below.

> Many of the affected persons have been forced to develop unusual abnormalities in their behaviour like, intense sleep disturbances, anxieties, and depressions, fears and phobias related to loud noises, multi-storey buildings, work place, home and school avoidance, recollection of smell, images, sounds, etc.

A prominent abnormality and psychological disorder generated through the traumatic experiences related to disasters and devastating events among the victims has been identified and named by the psychologists and psychiatrists as Post Traumatic Stress Disorder (PTSD). According to American Psychiatric Association (2013), persons affected with this disorder are characterized with the symptoms categorized as below.

1. *Intrusion:* They are found to be surrounded with the intrusive thoughts such as repeated, involuntary memories, distressing dreams, or flashbacks of the traumatic event.
2. *Avoidance:* They try to avoid people, places, activities, objects and situations that may trigger distressing memories and feel quite perturbed even at the time of talking about these happenings.
3. *Alterations in their cognition and mood:* There may be quite mentionable alteration in their cognition and mood such as (i) Inability to remember important aspects of the traumatic event, (ii) distorted beliefs about oneself or others, (e.g., "I am bad," "No one can be trusted") (iv) distorted thoughts about the cause or consequences of the event leading to wrongly blaming self or other, (v) ongoing fear, horror, anger, guilt or shame (vi) much less interest in activities previously enjoyed, (vii) feeling detached or estranged from others, or (viii) being unable to experience positive emotions (e.g., happiness or satisfaction).
4. *Alterations in arousal and reactivity:* They may be found to suffer from behavioural problems such as (i) being irritable and having angry outbursts, (ii) behaving recklessly or in a self-destructive way, (iii) being overly watchful of one's surroundings in a suspecting way, (iv) being easily startled and (v) having problems regarding their concentrating or sleeping.

To Sum Up

There are a number of elements, situations and conditions, objects or stimuli in one's physical environment that have enough potentiality of influencing, directing and controlling one's behaviour in one way or the other. While the desired and favoured physical facilities and situations in our environment provide us pleasant experiences and lead us to desirable rewarding behaviour, the unpleasant experiences generated through lack of facilities and unfavourable physical conditions may give birth to the traits of undesirable behaviour. We may witness this fact in a quite clear way by observing the adverse effects of the factors like noise, pollution, crowding, and disasters on our behaviour and overall functioning.

We may see that noise, in its all forms mild or severe may cause a great inconvenience and create a number of problems of one or the other nature to all of us. Besides casting harmful effects on our physical health (e.g., hearing loss, increase in blood pressure, and causing heart problems etc.) it may equally and to say bit more affect our mental health and behaviour in a quite adverse way to the extent of causing a variety and giving birth to a number of psychological disorders and ailments.

Pollution in all its forms such as air pollution, water pollution, and soil or land pollution proves quite harmful and hazardous to our well-being not only in terms of casting a damaging impact on our physical health but our psychological well-being and mental health is also adversely affected through its damaging influence. In this concern, it has been experimentally proved that it adds to increase in people's anxiety and stress level, develops restlessness and aggression in their.

Crowding the presence of a large number of people at a time at a specified place and time- is found to affect people 's health and well-being both in physiological and psychological terms in a quite adverse way. In terms of bringing psychological consequences and affecting people's behaviour, crowding may lead to them experiencing a lot of unusualness, suffocation, restlessness, anxiety and stress, aggression and violence provoking stimuli sufficient enough for de-stabilizing their behavioural equilibrium in one or the other forms resulting in one or the other behavioural problems or disorders.

The consequences of Disasters (Natural or Man-Made) are limitlessly damaging to the victims. What happens on suffering physically by them in terms of the loss of one or the other valuable possession including lives, cast a deep wound on the psyche of the victims in the form of painful traumatic experiences and memories. Besides clouding with a lot of anxiety, frustration, depression and stress in their living, they also become haunted with a lot of negativity resulting in one or the other types of emotional and behavioural problems, and mental disorders as the side effects of the trauma experienced by them. A prominent abnormality and psychological disorder generated through the traumatic experiences related to disasters and devastating events among the victims has been identified and named as Post Traumatic Stress Disorder (PTSD).

Effects of Human Behaviour on Physical environment

We have seen how the factors, situations and events going on in our physical environment affect our behaviour and life activities. However, the relationship between environment and human behaviour, as emphasized earlier, is two sided. Our behaviour and life activities also cast a sizable impact in providing a direction and shape to what exists and goes on in our environment. Actually, our habits, attitudes, ways of living and working are responsible for the up keep of our physical environment healthful and positive for us in its all forms and shapes. The reverse is also equally true. We do a great damage to our environment and almost make it our enemy instead of a friend or a blessing by resorting to bad manners, improper habits and ways of living and doing harmful acts in the manner as summarized below.

1. Our habits and actions are responsible for creating as well as raising the level of all types of pollution-noise, air, water, land or soil in its all damaging and worst form such as (i) Loud horns on roads, and playing full volume music or audio voices on mikes, anytime anywhere for one or the other excuses, (ii) Polluting air through smoke making, spreading dust or throwing garbage, use of plastic and tin packing, making use of air conditioners and refrigerators, and leakage of the gas and radioactive substances, (iii) polluting rivers, lakes and ponds by throwing all types of wastes, sewage water, industrial chemicals, dead bodies etc, and (iv) polluting land or soil through insecticides and harmful chemicals.
2. Our behaviour and actions are responsible for soil erosion and ecological imbalances such as: (i) Merciless cutting of the trees or deforestation, (ii) unplanned huge construction of houses, industrial establishment, dams, bridges etc. and (iii) hunting and killing of wild animals.
3. Crowding is also found to vitiate the goodness and positivity of the physical environment. On this account our actions, habits, and traditions may be seen working as a potential cause. Our carelessness about maintaining social distance and disrespect to other's personal space also adds much in enhancing crowding and its negative effects.
4. Many of the disaster created events or situations may be clearly found to bc thc handiwork of the undesirable and improper acts of human beings. Accordingly, negativity in our behaviour in the form of uncontrolled aggression, revengeful attitude, utter selfishness and carelessness may be found to be the sole factor in vitiating the harmony, peace and positivity of the environment through the sad events of road rages and accidents, indiscriminate shooting and killings, terrorist acts, and war mongering. Even for the fury of the nature visible in the form

of one or the other catastrophes, our actions in the form of interfering in the work of the nature and disturbing the ecological balance, as well as paying no heed about the warning bell raised for the incoming natural disasters may be found responsible for its occurrence and its causation to more harm to us.

To Sum Up

Besides getting affected through the factors, situations and events going on in the physical environment our behaviour is found to cast a sizable impact in providing a direction and shape to what exists and goes on in our environment. Actually, our habits, attitudes, ways of living and working are responsible for the up keep of our physical environment healthful and positive. The reverse is equally true as it is our behaviour that turns our physical environment as our enemy by causing damage to it by engaging in acts like (i) creating as well as raising the level of all types of pollution-noise, air, water, land or soil, (ii) causing soil erosion and ecological imbalances, (iii) crowding a place to the unreasonable amount, and (iv) becoming a cause of a number of nature and man-made disasters.

Psychology and Social Concerns

Not only the physical but the socio-cultural environment consisting of the functioning of the various socio-cultural agencies, their practices, attitudes, stereotypes, prejudices, discriminations, as well as one or the other social concerns and problems prevalent in the society at one or the other time may affect and influence human behaviour as well as our life as a whole. We have discussed about many of these aspects previously in this text. At present here in this chapter we would be focusing our discussion only on the two most important social concerns and problems, namely (i) poverty and discrimination, and (ii) Aggression and violence being faced by our society at present. These problems may have their specific reasons for their occurrence and thus may need different types of measures in terms of their economic, social, political or legal/constitutional solution. However, we will be thinking about it from a psychological angle. Let us take them one by one.

Poverty as a major social concern

Poverty is a quite major concern and problem being faced by our society and country at present as majority of the citizens are forced to live below the poverty line.

As a term poverty has been defined in the Merriam Webster Dictionary as "the state of one who lacks a usual or socially acceptable amount of money or material possessions."

We see that, here, in this definition one's poverty has been interpreted in two senses-one in its usual form and the other as socially acceptable. It leads us to conclude about the two distinct types or forms of the poverty of the people, families and communities. We can name them as (i) Absolute poverty and (ii) Relative poverty.

- Absolute poverty, in terms of the usual or most common interpretation of the term poverty, stands for the type or form of the poverty of the people, family and community in which they are found to suffer from the complete lack of the means necessary to meet their basic needs. However, here also the differences may arise in terms of the interpretation of the term basic needs. When taken in its narrower and closer meaning, it usually stands for meeting one's most basic personal needs such as food, clothing and shelter. However, with the change in the socio-economic status of the people and families we may find that in the list of basic needs, now it is quite common to enlist needs like access to clean drinking water, sanitation and healthcare, better housing, better education for the children, proper road and transportation facilities, etc. In this type of poverty, the basis on which, we label a person, family, or community as poverty ridden is the same. It remains quite independent of their permanent location or era.
- Relative poverty, on the other hand, stands for the type and form of poverty that is relative. It is said to occur when a person or family is unable to meet a minimum level of standard of living, compared to others in the same time and place. The basis on which we define relative poverty varies from place to place and time to time. For example, in a locality where most of the residents are living in the properly constructed brick houses, the families having thatched roof houses are likely to be termed as poverty-ridden families but not when some of the people and families in the same locality and time period are bound to live in tents or even forced to live on pavements.

Now the question that arises is how to take a decision about state of poverty of people and family in a particular society at a particular time period. It is taken on the basis of drawing an index of poverty that may be found to differ from place to place and time to time at the same place. Every state and country, therefore, may be found to draw an index or poverty line grounded on the income and facilities being enjoyed for living by its people for determining how many of its people are living in poverty.

In whatever ways the poverty of the people gets defined or picks up its absolute or relative form, one thing is quite certain that its impact and consequences are always quite damaging and devastating for the suffering people, families and the community as a whole. Known as a curse in itself, poverty leads to cause one or the other types of deprivation and discrimination resulting in a variety of personal and social disadvantages as discussed below.

Discrimination as a term in the social context is used for a section of the society, community, group of people, and individuals being put to disadvantages or deprived of their due rights and privileges by the group of people who enjoy majority, power and status in the society. In context of poverty, we may see the poverty-ridden people and families suffering from a lot of discrimination in one field or the other against the rich and wealthier section or group of the society. Their poverty becomes a sole cause of putting them under a lot of deprivation and disadvantages.

By the term deprivation associated with disadvantages suffered on account of the poverty we here mean the state in which the individuals are found to be deprived from getting their due share in respect of the available facilities, and opportunities for their proper living and progress in comparison to the other people of the same society who are richer and wealthier. Let us know about such sort of deprivation and disadvantage suffered by these poverty-ridden people.

In fact, proper economic conditions and wellbeing have greater value in today's materialized world. Every facility of life and opportunities for one's welfare and development are closely linked with one's prosperity in terms of wealth, money and sound means of earning livelihood. Poverty is taken as a great curse causing all types of deficiencies, deficits and obstacles in one's living, growing and adjusting to one's self and the environment. One's poverty or paucity of economic resources may be found to put up a number of hurdles in the satisfaction of his basic needs, his proper progress and development and adjustment to his self and the environment.

In the circumstances of such economic deprivation, *i.e.*, poverty, the children and other members of the family can't get adequate means even for the satisfaction of their most essential basic needs like food, water, rest and sleep etc. They don't get shelter for living and clothes for wearing. The youngsters are compelled to earn the livelihood or to help their elders in parental occupation. When they venture for schooling, they have no money for the school fees, books, dress or other educationally essential materials. In such a deprived condition, how, can we think about their all-round development and adequate adjustment? All their efforts and energies are thereby concentrated on doing away with their economic deficiencies just to keep themselves alive and adjust in this world of high material values. In this way their whole behaviour and personality is shaped into their struggling nature essential for their needed economic existence and survival. In contrast to the poverty-ridden children and individuals there is an affluent layer of society who has everything for the satisfaction of its basic needs and progress. The children belonging to such strata are born with a silver spoon in their mouth and as a result do not have to bear the wrath of economic deprivation. Therefore, it is but natural, that such inequalities and wide variation in the economic level of the different layers of the society would be ultimately creating widespread dissatisfaction, conflicts and tensions in the mind of those who suffer on account of such inequalities, deficiencies and deprivation.

The Ill Consequences of Poverty

Poverty and economic deprivation brings a lot of inconvenience and hardships and adverse outcomes for the sufferers briefed in the manner as below.

Physical and social adversities

Their poverty of economic deprivation may result in severe physical and social consequences such as:

- The death or suicide on account of the starvation and lack of economic support.
- Malnutrition problems suffered on the part of pregnant mothers, and children leaving a quite damaging effect on the health and well-being of mothers and developing children.
- Occurrence of severe health problems, diseases and untimely loss of lives on account of the lack of essentials such as proper sanitation, clean water, healthcare and medical facilities.
- Access to good schools, healthcare, electricity, safe water, proper transportation facilities, and other critical services remains elusive for living a worthy life for a number of people and families living below the poverty line in a particular society.

- The blockage and obstacles suffered in the path of the proper development and progress in life from early childhood on account of lack or denial of educational facilities, skill learning and opportunities for seeking employment (self or otherwise), etc.
- Compelling the parents to make their children serve others in the form of child labour, slaves, and prostitutes.
- What is termed as class struggle is absolutely the fight between haves or haves notes, the so called poor and rich. It is the typical consequence of poverty of the section of a people who believe that they are poor on account of the haves-enjoying economic, social and political power. As inequality increases, heightened poverty is likely to cause increased tensions in society visible in the form of increase in the rate of crimes, terrorist or Naxalite activities etc.
- One thing is also quite typical with the impact of poverty on people, families and communities, that one's inflicted with it, it becomes quite difficult for coming out from its vicious circle. Poverty is a difficult cycle to break and often travels from generation to generation. For those able to move out of poverty, progress is often temporary. Sudden economic shocks, food insecurity, and climate change may threaten their gains and push them back into poverty.

Psychological consequences and adversities

Poverty and economic deprivation has been found to cause some typical psychological adversities and negative outcomes to the sufferers in the ways such as:

- Becoming a major cause of affecting and diminishing their level of aspiration, motivation, and zeal and enthusiasm for work and progress in life.
- Affecting their perception about the self in a negative way and thus making them suffer from the problems of lack of confidence, lowering of their self-esteem and self-efficacy. Accordingly they may be found to believe in factors like luck, fate, good and bad stars, instead of their abilities and hard work.
- They are found to be a great victim of maladjustment, depression, anxiety, stress and frustration on account of the discrimination, deprivation, and paucity suffered by them in their life on one or the other accounts and thus may live the life of utter hopelessness, powerlessness, having a lot of fear and uncertainty about their future.
- They may be found to suffer from emotional problems generated through the resentments and dissatisfaction creeping among them on account of the discrimination and deprivation suffered on their part in one or the other ways. Their social behaviour is then also adversely affected resulting in certain types of aggression and withdrawal tendencies in their social interaction.
- Their cognition and cognitive functioning is also adversely affected. The maladjustment suffered in their socio-cultural environment and the growing conflicts and tension arising among them on account of their economic deprivation and discrimination proves a great obstacle in their concentrating on a task, and applying their thinking and reasoning to interact properly in a given situation.

The above mentioned ill consequences of poverty makes us remind about taking appropriate timely measures for the reduction and alleviation of poverty of the people, family and community. The problem is quite serious and big in size. It needs the multi-dimensional efforts from international, national, regional, local and individual platforms.

Efforts for dealing with the Issue of Poverty

For eradication and providing necessary help to the needy poor people and community, well intended efforts are always needed. The problem, on account of its multi-dimensional nature, however, needs multi-dimensional efforts and involvement of the all concerned stakeholders for its proper tackling in the ways briefed as below.

1. *Self efforts:* In many of the forms, people and their acts are responsible for making them remain in their poor state. Hence, it is their own responsibility for doing away with things contributing towards their poverty. One is the best solver of his own problems, and thereby the personal contribution of the people regarding their poverty eradication always carries enough weight. Accordingly, in case, if people decide to educate and skill themselves for gaining meaningful employment, work with all their sincerity in doing their job, avoid getting affected with bad habits such as alcoholism, drug addiction and indulging in meaningless disputes, violence and criminal behaviour, then, much can be achieved by them with their own efforts for reducing and eradicating their poverty.
2. *Help and assistance from others:* Outside help and assistance is also greatly needed for the eradication or alleviation of poverty. In

this concern where at the local level, the governments of the respective countries need to do their best, at the international level the responsibility lies on the shoulders of International agencies like The United Nations and the World Bank. The work done by the NGOs (non government welfare organizations) in this direction at the national and international level should also be encouraged and more and more help should come from the well to do citizens. The efforts made in this direction may include the variety of measures such as mentioned below.

(i) To provide the poverty-ridden people (BPL families) essentials for their living through free distribution or grains, pulses, cooking oils, cooking gas etc, through a well accessible rationing system and to see that there should not be any death on account of starving.

(ii) To make arrangement for them the next essentials for their living such as clean drinking water, electricity, living houses, means of transport, medical facilities, legal assistance, and educational opportunities to their youngsters on totally free or at very concessional or affordable prices.

(iii) To introduce schemes and programs to provide them opportunities to get employed in the private and public sectors and also for starting their own work for their sustaining as well as adding to their income for the eradication of their poverty.

(iv) To take measures for getting them aware of the things that are responsible for their own poverty problem such as their bad habits of smoking, gambling, taking drugs, and consuming alcohol, stealing, pick pocketing, and engaging in unnecessary quarrelling, fighting and harming each other, and then spending money on police and court cases.

(v) To empower them educationally, socially, politically in context of seeking social justice, equity and equality on the lines as prescribed in our Constitution.

The efforts done on the international front for poverty alleviation

On the international level, quite useful efforts are made by the UN Agencies such as UNICEF, and World Bank for helping poor countries and individuals. On this account, we may make special mention of the World Bank which has an ambitious target of reducing poverty to less than 3% of the global population by 2030. Some of its actionable plans in this direction to eliminate poverty include the following:

- Installing wells that provide access to clean drinking water
- Educating farmers on how to produce more food
- Constructing shelter for the poor
- Building schools to educate disadvantaged communities
- Providing enhanced access to better healthcare services by building medical clinics and hospitals

Measures Employed in Our Country for poverty alleviation

Right from gaining independence, adequate measures and attempts have been made by the Government of India. in close cooperation of the state governments, for the eradication of poverty. Through its Poverty Alleviation Programs, it is trying to reduce the rate of poverty in the country by providing proper access to food, monetary help, and basic essentials to the households and families belonging to the BPL (below poverty line) category. At present, the major programs and schemes under operation for the alleviation of poverty may be briefed as below.

1. *Jawahar Gram Samridhi Yojana (JGSY):* The main aim of this programme is the development of rural areas Infrastructure- i.e., roads to connect the villages to different areas, and also other social, educational (schools) and infrastructure facilities such as hospitals. Its secondary objective is to give out sustained wage employment to the rural people.
2. *National Old Age Pension Scheme (NOAPS):* The scheme provides pension to all old people who are above the age of 60 who could not fund for themselves and did not have any means of subsistence. The pension rate has now been revised from Rs 200 to 2000 a month.
3. *National Family Benefit Scheme (NFBS):* It aims to provide a sum of Rs.20000 to the beneficiary who will be the next head of the family after the death of its primary bread earner.
3. *National Maternity Benefit Scheme (NMBS):* This scheme provides a sum of Rs 6000 to a pregnant mother who is aged above 19 years in three instalments. The sum is provided normally 12-8 weeks before the birth in three instalments and can also be availed even after the death of the child.
4. *Annapurna Scheme (AS):* It aims to provide 10 kg of free food grains to the eligible senior citizens who are not registered under the National Old Age Pension Scheme.

5. *Integrated Rural Development Program (IRDP):* It aims to raise the families of identified target groups (small and marginal farmers, agricultural labourers and rural artisans) living below the poverty line through the development of sustainable opportunities for self-employment in the rural sector.
6. *Pradhan Mantri Gramin Awaas Yojana (PMGAY):* It is aimed to provide affordable housing to rural people by 2022.
7. *Mahatma Gandhi National Rural Employment Guarantee Act, 2005 (MGNREGA):* It is aimed to provide at least 100 days of guaranteed wage employment in a financial year to all families of rural areas whose adult members opt for unskilled labour-intensive work.
8. *Pradhan Mantri Jan DhanYozna (PMJDY):* It is aimed to guarantee access to financial services, such as basic saving and deposit bank accounts, insurance coverage of Rs 2 lakh and Life Insurance cover of Rs 30000.
9. *Self-Employment Program (SEP):* It is aimed to provide financial assistance to urban poor for setting up gainful employment ventures/ enterprises suited to their skill, training and aptitude.
10. *Deendayal Antodaya Yozna: National Urban Livelihoods Mission (DAY-NULM)*: It is aimed to enable poor to access gainful employment and employment through skill training and placement, subsidy to urban poor, shelters to urban homeless, social mobilization, and institutional development.
11. *Pradhan Mantri Kisan Samman Nidhi Yozna (PMKSNY):* It is aimed to provide income support to the farmers and their families. Under this scheme, all small and marginal farmers will be provided with income support of Rs.6000 per year in three instalments which will be deposited directly to their bank accounts.
12. *The Pradhan Mantri Garib Kalyan Yojana (PMGKY):* It is aimed to provide free food grains to BPL families - 5kg of wheat/rice and 1 Kg of pulses per family.
13. *Pradhan Mantri Shram Yogi Maan-DhanYozna (PM-SYMY):* It is aimed to provide an assured monthly pension of Rs 3000/- per month after attaining the age of 60 years to the workers in the unorganized sector such as street vendors, rickshaw pullers, agricultural workers, mid-day meal workers, construction workers, or workers in similar other occupations.
14. *PM Jan Arogya Yojana (PMJAY), Ayushman Bharat program:* It aims to provide medical facilities for the poor by opening 1.5 lakh health centers across the country and providing an insurance cover of Rs 5 lakh, targeting the poor, deprived rural families and identified occupational categories of urban workers' families.
15. *Training of Rural Youth for Self-Employment (TRYSEM):* It aims to help unemployed rural youth between the age of 18 to 30 years to acquire skills for self-employment.
16. *Sampoorna Grameen Rozgar Yojana (SGRY):* The programme is self-targeting in nature and aims to provide employment and food to people in rural areas who live below the poverty line.
17. *Pradhan Mantri Kaushal Vikas Yojana (PMKVY.* It aims to enable a large number of Indian youths to take up industry-relevant skill training that will help them in securing a better livelihood.
18. *Start Up India Scheme (SUIC):* It aims at developing an ecosystem that helps in the promotion and nurturing of entrepreneurship across the country.
19. *Stand Up India Scheme (SUIS):* It aims to facilitate at least one SC or ST borrower and at least one women borrower to take bank loans between Rs 10 lakh and Rs. 1 crore per bank branch for setting up a green field enterprise.

To Sum Up

Poverty is a quite major social issue and problem for all the societies and nations of the world all over the globe. As a term it stands for the state of one who lacks a usual or socially acceptable amount of money or material possessions. The decision about the state of poverty of people and family in a particular society at a particular time period is taken on the basis of drawing an index of poverty and then drawing a poverty line. The families or individuals having an income below this threshold value are considered to be under the below poverty line (BPL). In its simple meaning, the poverty line is the minimum income required to purchase the basic goods and services that are essential to satisfy the basic human needs in one or the other social setup.

Poverty is a curse in itself. In all its forms and shapes, it results into quite devastating and damaging consequences not only for the affected individuals, families and communities but the society and humanity as a whole also has to bear the blunt of these consequences. For poverty eradication and providing necessary help to the needy poor people and community, well-intended efforts are always needed. In this concern, at present, a number of useful programs and schemes are under operation for the alleviation of poverty in the country.

Aggression and Violence prevalent in the Society

Aggression and violence of one or the other nature prevalent in the society is also a quite big issue and major concern. In its all form and shapes it creates a great hurdle in the peaceful living and general welfare/well-being of the members of the society along with impeding development and progress of the society/nation in a big way. Regarding the types of violence rampant in our society we may particularly name them as: (i) Domestic Violence, (ii) Child Abuse-Violence against children (iii) Sexual Violence against the women, and (iv) Violence committed by Naxalites, and terrorists.

Although, in our country now we have appropriate legal, constitutional and defense measures for dealing with these problems, yet for knowing the roots for the eruption of these problems and seeking measures to deal with them from psychological angle, let us try to look at what the psychologists mean by the terms aggression and violence.

According to psychologists, human aggression may be understood as a type of specific behaviour demonstrated by an individual with a clear intention of inflicting physical or psychological injury to other individual.

Depending up on the nature of the aggression and intention reflected in the aggressive behaviour of the aggressors, aggression has been identified to exist in its two distinct forms or types named as (i) Hostile Aggression and (ii) Instrumental Aggression. Let us know about them.

Hostile aggression: True to its word meaning, this type of aggression involves a lot of hostility in the behaviour of the aggressor towards the victim. Here the aggressor may be seen to make use of verbal or physical stimulus with a sole purpose of inflicting harm or injury to the victim in a verbal or physical form. The intent of the aggressor here is to make the victim suffer and the reinforcement is the pain and suffering that is caused.

> **Hostile Aggression:** A type of aggressive behaviour that stems from the feelings of anger and resentment and performed by an individual with a sole purpose of inflicting pain or injury to the targeted individual.

A good example of hostile aggression occurs in a cricket tournament when the cricket bowlers throw a high inside fastball at the batsmen who have angered them. They do so for a clear intention of taking revenge by inflicting injury and making the opponents suffer and thus feel satisfaction on this account. This kind of aggression is often considered quite nearer to the term violence in its nature and consequences.

Instrumental Aggression: In its word meaning, this type of aggression works as an instrumental or means in the hands of the aggressors for achieving their goal or purpose. In social world the individuals may be seen to utilize this type of aggression for registering their win or success against the individuals or group in competition.

> **Instrumental Aggression:** A type of aggressive behaviour demonstrated by an individual with the aim of using it as a means to achieve some goal instead of intending it for inflicting harm on the targeted individual.

Thus, the primary consideration, here for resorting to aggression on the part of the individuals is not to inflict any injury or harm to the opponent (as happens with hostile aggression), but to avail success in their attempts for registering a victory or success against the individuals or group in competition. In comparison to the hostile aggression, instrumental aggression is more commonly utilized by the individuals in different social situations especially in the field of sports, business and work places for getting ahead of their competitors. It is less condemned than the hostile aggression. However, it may be equally dangerous and harmful to the victims.

> **To Sum Up**
>
> As a term, aggression may be understood as a type of specific behaviour on the part of the individuals called aggressors in which they are found to make use of a well thought-out and planned stimulus (verbal, physical or both) with a clear-cut objective of inflicting physical or psychological injury or harm to other individuals (referred to as victims) who are unwilling as well as unprepared for receiving such treatment from the aggressors.
>
> Aggression has been identified to exist in its two distinct forms or types named as Hostile aggression and Instrumental aggression. In the former type of aggression, the aggressors make use of verbal or physical stimulus to harm and injure others with an intention of making the victims suffer instead of winning or showing their Excellency, or Superiority over others in one or the other performance areas. The instrumental aggression on the other hand, works as an instrumental or means in the hands of the aggressors for achieving their goal or purpose.

Aggression and Violence

As mentioned earlier in the discussion about the nature and consequences of the type of aggression known as hostile aggression, this type of aggression falls quite nearer to the term violence used in the world of social situations. Both are performed with a sole intention of causing harm or injury to others. Both are compulsorily characterized with the presence of certain negative and volatile factors named as anger, resentment, frustration or revenge etc.

Violence: An unruly unsocial behaviour demonstrated by an individual or group in the form of uncontrolled aggression full of anger and resentment towards the target individual, group or a social situation.

However, the amount and intensity of such volatile elements is quite out of proportion in violence in comparison to the aggression of any sort. In addition, there always remain greater opportunities and possibilities of more damages and ill consequences through the outcomes of violence in comparison to the aggression (hostile and instrumental). The aggressor here is seen to demonstrate a quite uncontrolled volatile behaviour full of anger and hostile feelings towards the target individual or group in the likewise social situations. In the demonstration of such uncontrolled behaviour, there is a direct violation of the code of conduct and specified rules and norms prevailing in the social system on the part of the individual or group engaged in violent behaviour for inflicting harm and damage to the well-being, life, and properties of the target individuals or segments of the population belonging to that social system.

To Sum Up

Aggression many times may turn into violence. Both aggression and violence have many things in common such as having an intention of harming and injuring others, and characterized with the presence of certain negative and volatile elements named as anger, resentment, frustration or revenge etc. However, harm-inducing behaviour and the amount and intensity of the volatile elements is quite out of proportion in violence in comparison to the aggression of any sort appearing in the form of out of rules uncontrolled behaviour displayed on the part of the violent individuals or groups towards the target individuals, groups or their properties.

Theories of Aggression (What makes people aggressive?)

Theories of aggression represent the type of approaches adopted by the researchers and psychologists for providing one or the other types of explanations for the aggression of the individuals in their social life. In this concern, we here would like to concentrate only on the two widely accepted theories named as Frustration theory of Aggression and Social learning theory of Aggression.

Frustration Theory of Aggression

Frustration, as we know, represents a feeling of helplessness that develops within individuals when one or more of their motivated or goal-directed behaviours are blocked and they are deprived of success or from realizing their target. In this situation, they are found to feel a lot of resentment and anger that can push them to engage in an aggressive behaviour. This is the basis of the Frustration theory of aggression, first proposed by Dollard and his colleagues at Yale University in 1939. In its original version, this theory made the following two bold assertions in its explanation of people's aggression.

(i) Frustration always leads to some form of aggression, and

(ii) Aggression always stems from frustration

As a result, in a variety of social situations, we may generally come across the presence of a significant frustration-aggression relationship. However, the viewpoint put forward in this original version of Frustration theory, soon came under attack by arguing that frustration always leads to aggression is not true. Not all frustration leads to aggression. Research and experience repeatedly show that:

- People often cope with their frustration or express it in non-aggressive ways, and
- In a number of cases, frustration may lead to depression and a withdrawal behaviour.

Revised version of Frustration-Aggressive Theory

In a reformulation of the frustration-aggression theory Leonard Berkowitz (1978, 1989) theorized that although frustration does not necessarily result in aggression, yet it is quite capable of creating a readiness or heightening the predisposition for aggression. For aggression to actually occur, certain stimuli associated with aggression must be present. These stimuli are cues that the frustrated person associates with aggression. An example of this phenomenon in animals according to Cox (2007) would be the "red flag" for the enraged and frustrated bull.

The newer version recognizes that certain aggression could have causes other than frustration and that frustration could lead to behaviours other than aggression (e.g., withdrawal). It further conveys that the response to frustration can be modified by learning. Thus, an individual can learn to have some other, more productive and less aggressive response to frustration. Berkowitz (1989) even went so far as to accept the idea that a cognitive evaluation of the situation influences the extent to which frustration produces these negative feelings. People feel upset and attack their frustration causers after analyzing that the outcomes are not merely accidental and they have been deliberately and wrongfully kept from attaining their goal. In this way, increased arousal and anger triggered by frustration, result in aggression only when socially learned cues signal the appropriateness of aggression in the particular situation. If the social learned cues signal that aggression is inappropriate, it will not result.

To Sum Up

Frustration Theory of Aggression is a theory of aggression which in its original form (proposed by Dollard and his colleagues) conveyed that "all of our aggression is the result of frustration and that frustration always leads to aggression". However, now in its revised version (put up by Leonard Berkowitz) it conveys that it was not necessary for frustration to result in aggression and aggression does not carry frustration as an only cause for its occurrence. Our increased arousal and anger triggered by frustration, result in aggression only when socially learned cues signal the appropriateness of aggression in a particular situation.

The General Aggression Model (GAM): A Modern Theory of Human Aggression

According to the General Aggression Model (GAM) presented by Anderson and Bushman (2002), there are two sets of factors that are responsible for initiating aggressive behaviour at their own separately or in combination. These may be named as (A) situational factors (factors relating to the current situation) and (B) personal factors (factors relating to the people involved).

A. Situational Factors: In this category of factors or variables, influencing aggressive behaviour, we may include the factors or variables such as:

(i) Frustration,
(ii) Some kind of provocation from another person (e.g., an insult),
(iii) Exposure to other people behaving aggressively (aggressive models - real or those shown in the media),
(iv) Anything that causes individuals to experience discomfort–such as high temperature, physical pain, drill, disrespectful treatment and even a boring classroom lecture or public address.

B. Personal Factors: These factors or variables represent the variability of different kinds found among human beings. Some of the personal factors that are known for causing aggression in us are as follows:

(i) Traits that predispose some individuals towards aggression (such as high irritability, antisocial personality, impulsivity, etc.).
(ii) Attitudes and belief about violence (e.g., believing that it is acceptable and appropriate).
(iii) A tendency to perceive hostile intentions in other's behaviour and
(iv) Specific skills related to aggression (e.g., knowing how to fight or how to use various weapons.

According to the General Aggression Model, these two sets of factors–situational and personal, in turn, lead to overt aggression. However, here much depends on individuals' interpretations (appraisals) of the current situation and restraining factors (e.g., the presence of police or the threatening nature of the intended targeted person). Thus it is their such cognitive appraisal that makes them engage either in thoughtful actions, which might involve restraining their anger, or impulsive action, which can lead to overt aggression actions (Branscombe and Baron, 2017:368).

To Sum Up

The General Aggression Model (GAM)–A Modern Theory of Aggression (presented by Anderson and Bushman), conveys that there are two sets of factors–situational (related to the current situation) and personal (related to the people involved) that are responsible for initiating aggressive behaviour among the people. These two sets of factors, in turn, lead to overt aggression through their impact up on three basic psychological processes (i) arousal (increase in physical arousal or excitement), (ii) affective states (arousal of hostile feelings and their outward signs), and (iii) cognition (bringing hostile thoughts, beliefs and attitudes about aggression in mind).

The Social Learning Theory of Aggression

According to this theory of aggression, aggression much like other social behaviour is a learned phenomenon. It has the roots in learning theories and perspectives like classical and operant conditioning and most predominantly in "The social theory of learning" put forward by the eminent psychologist Albert Bandura (1973). In his social learning theory, he has emphasized that the aggressive behaviour is learned and acquired by the individuals by observing the behaviour of their role models in one or the other social field. The process of such observational leaning on the part of an individual, thus, just begins with the watching of the role models behave aggressively in one or the other social situations. This behaviour gets imitated as there is a strong tendency among humans to imitate a behaviour which attracts or serves their purpose. As a result, the individual behaves aggressively in the same way in a similar social situation as watched by him in the behaviour of his role model. After imitation, the next role for learning aggression on the part of an individual is played by him depending on the type of reinforcement he receives for his imitative behaviour. In case, he is checked and punished for his aggression, then the story of its learning, i.e., imbibing in the behaviour of the individual ends. But if his aggression is tolerated, gets unnoticed or appreciated or rewarded in any way, then it has all possibility of getting imbibed by him in his social behaviour. In this way, according to social learning theory, aggressive behaviour in social life on the part of the individuals is acquired in two consecutive phases, first by modeling (observation and imitation of the behaviour of models) and then its subsequent positive reinforcement. Reinforcement or reward received on an initiated aggressive behaviour matters much in the learning of aggression because it has enough capability to convey or teach the principle that "aggression pays". In addition to what the individuals learn through direct experiences (by remaining present and witnessing the events in the social situations), the learning of aggression through watching of the aggressive behaviour of a role model can also go on effectively with the help of vicarious (indirect) experiences such as (i) watching their aggressive behaviour on television, computer, or movie screen, and (ii) its subsequent consequences-rewarding or punishing.

To Sum Up

The Social Learning Theory of Aggression, originated from Bandura's Social learning theory that emphasizes that most of what we learn (including the aggressive behaviour) is acquired through our observational learning i.e., observing and imitating the behaviour of people considered role models by us. Accordingly, individuals learn not only how to aggress, but also when and against whom to aggress.

Causes or Determinants of Aggression

Based on the views expressed by researchers and psychologists in their proposed theories of aggression, the causes or factors associated with human aggression may be broadly grouped into three categories, namely, (A) Personal Factors or Determinants of Aggression, (B) Socio-cultural Factors or Determinants of Aggression, and (C) Situational Factors or Determinants of Aggression. Let us learn about them in brief.

Personal Factors or Determinants of Aggression

The Person-centered determinants or causes lying within the individuals may involve the following:

- Typical personality make up (e.g. being A Type person and having some specific personality traits correlated high with aggression)
- Gender differences (showing males as more prone to aggression than females)
- Personality disorders (e.g. chromosomal abnormality-the presence of an extra Y chromosomes in males and the possession of the trait narcissism on the part of individuals) and
- Alcohol consumption-the excessive drinking on the part of individuals

Socio-cultural Factors or Determinants of Aggression

Under the category of socio-cultural determinants, we may include the factors or causes such as:

- Social discrimination and exclusion
- Socio-cultural norms and practices prevailing in society
- Sexual jealousy
- Harmful effects of violence shown on television, films and other smart devices
- The damaging effect of the available violent pornography

Situational Factors or Determinants of Aggression

Under the category situation-centered determinants of aggression, we may include the environmental conditions prevailed at the site of social encounter in the shape of:

- Heat generation and temperature recorded at the site.
- The nature and impact of the noise level, and crowding at the social event or encounter site.
- The frustration suffered by the individuals due to one or the other reasons.
- Happening of the direct provocation incidents or accidents at the site.

Prevention and Control of Aggression or Violence

It is a well known fact that the prevention and control of a problem well lie in the causes or factors responsible for its emergence. We have already discussed the various points of view and theoretical perspectives as well as the various factors or determinants responsible for the aggression and violence of the people. A proper analysis of these perspectives and determinants of aggression may help us in knowing about what needs to be done for its prevention and control. For this purpose, let us begin with a look at the factors or determinants discussed in this chapter under the heads - Personal, Socio-cultural and Situational factors.

Personal factors are very much person-specific and therefore there is hardly any scope in exercising restrain or control over many of them. However, something for the prevention and controlling the improper habits like alcohol consumption can be usefully done. Regarding reduction of the impact of *socio-cultural factors* in inducing or increasing aggression, we can say that efforts can be well initiated for the discontinuance of certain practices, norms and traditions, such as discrimination, exclusion, deprivation and disadvantages suffered in the society on the part of certain individuals and groups on one or the other accounts, along with the needed reduction in the harmful effects of sexual jealousy, media violence and violent pornography. Regarding the reduction of the impact of the *situational factors* on aggression of the people such as heat and temperature, noise, crowd, frustration, direct provocation, heightened arousal, easy availability or accessibility of weapons, the measures like below may be well adopted.

(i) Making efforts to hold social events, or having social encounters at the places where problems related to uncomfortable heat and temperature, noise, crowd do not arise or if arises then efforts can be successfully made for not allowing them to become a cause of aggression or violence.

(ii) The situations involving or resulting in the frustration, heightening of emotional arousal and provocation of the individuals participating in the social events or taking part in the social encounters in one or the other forms should be avoided as well as restrained in a proper way.

(iii) The easy availability and accessibility of sharp-edged weapons, fire arms including revolvers and pistols should be properly restrained by enacting the necessary laws for their restricted use as well as imposing ban on their public display and illegal possession.

Now take the case of different perspectives and theoretical explanations provided for the aggression and violence of people. Here we may come to a well-recognized conclusion that aggression-irrespective of its nature and type, is a learned phenomenon. For its prevention and control we should, therefore, look for the measures and techniques that may prove helpful firstly in the stoppage of its learning and secondly for its subsequent unlearning if it gets intruded somehow in our social behaviour. Taking cognizance of these two important considerations, we can name and discuss the different measures or techniques adopted for the prevention and control of aggression or violence of the people in the manner as below.

1. **Making use of Punishment as Retaliation or Deterrence:** It essentially includes the delivery of some or other type of aversive consequences through a variety of means such as inflicting heavy fines, putting the accused in prisons, or solitary confinements, or providing physical punishments of one or the other nature for their undesirable acts of aggression and violence. Although use of such strategy is somehow decried in the case of growing children and first time wrong doers, yet it is needed for working as an essential deterrence for the prevention of the uncontrolled undesirable acts of aggression and violence in the society.

2. **Controlling and Management of Anger by making use of Self-regulation, or Catharsis:** It is anger that fires aggression in most situations. It therefore needs on our part to adopt adequate measures for exercising restrain and control over it through some suitable means such as self-regulation and catharsis. Luckily enough nature has equipped us with a valuable gift-an

effective internal mechanism, known as self-regulation or self-control for restraining our anger and overt aggression (Baumeister, et.al. 2005). It is therefore our utmost duty to have positive implicit attitudes toward regulating our own emotions, for enabling us to restrain our anger and aggression in a needed way.

In the use of catharsis technique for controlling aggression, individuals are provided an opportunity to let their bottled aggressive feelings and resentment come out through some appropriate outlet such as (i) ventilating their suppressed aggression by acting it out actively-hitting or whopping the self, boxing or punching an inanimate target while screaming, or (ii) expressing their feelings to others (verbally or in writing) and opening up their mind for getting the pent-up tension released.

3. **Unlearning of the Aggressive Behaviour:** It is now a well accepted fact that aggression on the part of individuals is a learned behaviour in all its forms and shapes. For doing away with this problem, one needs to get to unlearn by resorting to the techniques of de-conditioning, extinction and de-valuation.

   In making use of the techniques of *de-conditioning*, where the undesirable aggressive behaviour of the individuals is subjected to turn into a quite unpleasant experience for them, the demonstration of unaggressive and rule-abiding behaviour on their part should be made an encouraging pleasant experience in its outcome.

   In the use of the *Elimination or extinction of undesirable behaviour technique,* the erring individuals may be made to go through some direct or vicarious experiences to feel heat of the devastating experiences of aggression committed by the concerned people individually or collectively. When they see how aggression on the part of the individuals, including celebrities, star performers and highly praised social groups may prove fatal to the persons in their interaction, innocent ones, as well as also ruining their own career and future, it may help them in learning a good lesson for saving them from the attractive trap of acting rudely and aggressively in their social encounters

4. **Training in Social Skills:** One of the reasons why individuals indulge in aggression is that they lack some form of social skill. It is their lacking in social skills that may create problems for them in their proper self-expression, problem solving, interaction and communication with others as well as to express their anger or annoyance constructively and nonviolently. Thus, there is an urgent need of helping such individuals in their learning of needed social skills. For this purpose, if we try to teach them such techniques as how to communicate anger or criticism in constructive ways, how to negotiate and compromise when conflicts arise, and how to apologize when they need to, it may considerably help in the prevention and control of aggression (Christensen, et al., 2014).

5. **Reducing Frustration and Apprehensions of the Sufferer:** Frustration, in all its dimensions, as discussed earlier in this text, is regarded as one of the major sources of individual or collective aggression. It is the frustration-the blocking of his goal by someone-that directs his behaviour towards aggression. Similarly, a violent agitation, aggression or violence on mass scale may be seen to take place in society when the individuals playing here the role of aggressors reach a stage of frustration of not getting their due share without doing so. The frustration among the individuals as well as in public may also creep in by the fear and apprehensions spread in society as a result of undesirable and criminal acts such as committing dacoity, destroying of property and taking lives of others. In all such situations, there is a need for taking suitable measures to reduce the frustration and apprehensions of individuals and the group who is subjected to such fear, apprehension and frustration.

6. **Inculcating an Attitude or Habit of Maintaining Peace and Harmony:** The maintenance of positivity in one's behaviour may prove a strong deterrence for the entrance of negativity in one's mind and behaviour. We may see that the people or the society which adheres to the principle of non-violence and peace may contribute much in the reduction of aggression and violence in the society. We have in our country a good example of such desirable behaviour demonstrated and path shown by the Father of the Nation, M.K. Gandhi. We should help ourselves to bring a desirable change in our outlook and attitude to remain peaceful at the time of provoking situations and believe in the maintenance of peace and harmony in the society. A quite good habit and practice adopted for this purpose may consist of begging apology (admission of wrong doing

plus a request for forgiveness) for our harsh and otherwise undesirable behaviour towards others and accepting other's apology on this account. It makes parties in conflict cool and somewhat satisfied and helps them to develop a situation to forgive and forget about the anger or aggression-provoking incidence.

To Sum Up

Aggression is a learned phenomenon. For its prevention and control we should, therefore, look for the measures and techniques that may prove helpful firstly in the stoppage of its learning and secondly for its subsequent unlearning if it gets intruded somehow in our social behaviour. Accordingly, in the prevention and control of aggression and violence among the individual and groups, the measures and strategies proving helpful may be cited as :

- Making use of punishment as retaliation or deterrence,
- Controlling and management of anger by making use of self-regulation or catharsis
- Unlearning of the Aggressive behaviour through the use of the techniques such as de-conditioning
- Reducing frustration and apprehensions of the sufferer.
- Making use of the apology and forgiveness to maintain desired peace and harmony

Our Health and Psychology

For our well-being and proper functioning we need to be physically as well as mentally healthy in all aspects. Knowledge and understanding acquired through the study and application of psychology helps us much in our functioning as a healthy person. In chapter fifteen of this text we have discussed how the knowledge of psychology helps us in knowing and dealing with the abnormality of our behaviour, and mental disorders affecting our mental health. Here we want to focus more on the physical aspect of our health. Much like our mental health, our physical health is also guided and directed by one or the other much related psychological factors. Our psyche and its functioning in the form of sensing, perceiving, interpreting the perceived stimuli for taking judgment in a situation, our thinking, reasoning, and problem-solving ability play a very dominant role in our doing and behaving with regard to the up keep of a good physical health. Similarly our attitudes and beliefs and lifestyle adopted towards health-related aspects also matters much in this direction. Much can be done by taking care of them. Let us see how.

1. First of all let us see what is of utmost importance for keeping us in good health. Certainly it is the quality of intake in terms of what we eat, drink and breathe. The next in this sequence comes the execution of our daily routine related to elimination processes, cleaning of our teeth and taking bath, doing other necessary routine day to day and occupational work, exercising and other health maintaining physical activities, taking rest and sleep at the proper time in a proper way etc. The degree to which all these mentioned aspects remain in operation in an appropriate form and rhythm, we may be found to lead a healthy disease-free life. The reverse is also true, we may be facing a lot of health problem and unhappiness on account of the carelessness or helplessness shown in the execution of one or the other health maintenance activities.

   Now question may arise-what makes us careful or careless in attending to what is needed to leading a healthy and disease-free life. Certainly it is our own lifestyle, our thought processes, attitudes and beliefs that we hold towards the health related aspects. In fact our thinking, attitudes, beliefs and lifestyle in their positive and negative form in one way or the other lead or compel us to be careful or careless in connection with the quality of our food, water and air intake, rest and sleep, exercise and physical activities, and other routines of our daily life, and avoiding or indulging in health-injuring activities such as smoking, alcoholism and substance abuse. Psychology as science of behaviour may play a significant role in bringing needed change in the outlook, thinking, habits, attitudes and beliefs of the people in picking up healthful habits and temperament for adopting a lifestyle helpful to them in leading a healthy disease-free life.

2. The degree to which one remains happy or unhappy, stressed or relaxed in one's life is found to affect the wellness or illness of one's health. The conflicts arising and frustrations or set back suffered by us on one or the other accounts in our life may be seen to prove a big source of our health impairment and illness. Besides, the natural calamities and accidental bad incidences in our life, our inability or mismanagement in the handling of our emotions in the needed way during our social interaction in daily and professional life

also plays a significant role in playing a major role for creating a lot of anxiety, conflicts and stress in our life. Actually, stress generated in any way, is always found to work as a potential threat for the health and well-being of the affected persons. The knowledge and understanding reached through the study of psychology now may help individuals in managing their anxiety, frustration and stress in a suitable way for protecting them from falling victim of the health impairment and illnesses.

3. A branch of psychology, known as positive psychology, tells us how the positivity in our thinking, and feeling behaviour affects the nature of our doing behaviours resulting to us in our all over happiness and positivity in our life. Thus, it recommends for being happy in all situations and adopting a positive approach of looking at the things and the situation in a bright way rather than having unnecessary anxiety and worries over what is happening or will happen. We may use our self-experience to see how our positive thinking, "all is well" attitude, and auto suggestions that we are getting improved day by day may help us in getting rid of our health problems and achieve early recovery from illness with the help of the treatment prescribed by the doctor.
4. The studies performed in health psychology-a branch of psychology reveal that it is the thinking, attitude, lifestyle and specific personality traits like optimism, self-esteem, self-confidence and a burning desire of achieving the targets of significance in one's life that helps him for keeping appropriate zeal and enthusiasm to make efforts for living a healthy and disease-free life and also as well to get early recovery after falling ill sometimes. Actually there is found a reciprocal relationship between the psychological factors lying within the individual and the status of his physical health. Where the poor state of one's physical health or his illness may become a source of number of behavioural and adjustment problems, (e.g. people become abnormal in their behaviour in their illness) the behavioural and adjustment problems may also make one a victim of a number of health problems including serious illness. A number of psychosomatic disorders ailments such as migraine, peptic ulcer, asthma, hypertension, skin, eating and sleep disorders, urinating problems, sexual frigidity in women and impotency in men have been known to have their occurrence only on account of the psychological problems rather than having some well identified organic cause.

In this way, we may see that there exists a close relation between the physical health and psychological functioning of human beings. It is why the persons equipped with the knowledge and understanding of the psychology-especially the health, positive and clinical psychology may help us well in the preservation, promotion and maintenance of our physical health including the treatment and early recovery from physical ailments.

To Sum Up

Knowledge and understanding acquired through the study and application of psychology helps us much in our functioning as a healthy person. In this respect, it does not only help in knowing and dealing with the abnormality of our behaviour, and mental disorders affecting our mental health, our physical health is also guided and directed by one or the other much related psychological factors. It has been experimentally proved and observed in our daily life experience that there exists a close relation between the physical health and psychological functioning of human beings. It is why the persons equipped with the knowledge and understanding of psychology-especially health, positive and clinical psychology may help us well in the preservation, promotion and maintenance of our physical health including the treatment and early recovery from physical ailments.

Impact of Television and Mass Media on our Behaviour

Our behaviour and personality is shaped as a result of what we learn or acquire through our direct or indirect experiences. According to social or observational learning theory, proposed by Albert Bandura (1973), the behaviour and actions exhibited on the part of the celebrities, and stars on the screens of television and movies, may work as the model behaviours for being imitated and imbibed on the part of the people in a way of vicarious experiences gained by them on this account. Now-a-days, this scope of learning through vicarious or indirect experiences has been quite widened with the arrival of modern age technology. Children from a quite early age now have full access to a huge amount of audio-visual material available to them on their smart phones, tablets, laptop and computer's screen.

The psychological effects of their observation of the things, and events displayed on the screen is quite deeper much more than gained through the reading of good or bad literature or listening to the instructions given to them on this account.

The exposure to such content, events and behaviour displayed on the screens of these devices, may reward the viewers in both ways-positive and negative. We can learn so many useful things helpful in making us better in our social communication and interaction with others, learn so many good habits, use their services for providing online education to the learners or telling about the national welfare schemes, observe and practice a number of skills such as doing yoga activities, dancing, using one or the other appliances, etc. However, the evil effects of such exposure are not also lesser in any way. In a usual way, the evils are more easily caught and imbibed by us than learning the lessons of good behaviour and morality. It is why we may see, that the lessons of bad and undesirable behaviour are now being increasingly imbibed by the observers, especially the younger ones in their actions. The incidences of engaging in quite abnormal and serious anti-social and criminal activities such as bank robberies, ATM breaking, chain snatching, vehicles lifting, aggression and violence including brutal sexual assaults, planned murders, kidnapping and extortion of money, terrorist activities and mass destruction etc, are many times found to be tutored or engineered through what is learned from the acts performed and incidences shown on the screens of television, movies and smart devices. Truly, it is quite alarming and red signal to the welfare of the society as well as to the individuals engaging in these activities. There is a need of taking well meaningful steps and measures for saving the people especially the growing children from the evil effects of such devastating negative effects of the television and other mass media means.

To Sum Up

The exposure to the contents of the actions, events and behaviour of others especially our elders, celebrities, and stars displayed on the screens of television, smart phones, and modern technological devices affects our behaviour to a great extent both in positive as well as negative ways. We can learn so may useful things helpful in making us better in our personal and social life. However, the evil effects of such exposure are also not lesser and in a way much more than the good impact. It is why we may see, that the lessons of bad and undesirable behaviour are now being increasingly imbibed by observers, especially the younger ones in their actions through their exposure to TV and mass media. There is, therefore, much need of taking suitable measures for saving the growing children from these evil impacts.

ASSESSMENT QUESTIONS

Section I: Essay Type Questions

1. Discuss about the inter-relationship between human behaviour and physical environment.
2. How does our behaviour affect the things going on in our physical environment? Discuss in detail with examples.
3. Throw light on the effects of physical environment surroundings particularly noise, pollution, crowding and disasters (natural and man-made) on human behaviour.
4. What are the major concerns or problems faced by our society? Discuss any one of them in detail.
5. Throw light on any one of the following major social concerns.
   (i) Poverty, (ii) Aggression & violence
6. Explain how the knowledge and understanding of the subject psychology can play a major role in the maintenance of our physical health.
7. Discuss in detail the role played by television and mass media influences in shaping people's behaviour.

Section II: Short Answer Type Questions

1. Provide two examples of how our behaviour is influenced by noise/pollution/crowding/nature-made disasters/man-made disasters.
2. Provide two examples for explaining how our behaviour affects the things and events happening in our physical environment.
3. Name three major causes of poverty in our society.
4. Name three major schemes or programs launched by Indian Government for addressing the poverty issue.
5. Name the major types of aggression and violence proving a big concern for our society.
6. Give two instances each of the nature of violence committed by terrorists and naxalites in our country.
7. Provide two examples to illustrate how our physical health gets affected by our attitudes and beliefs.
8. Give two examples to illustrate how our behaviour is affected with the influence or impact of our exposure to television and mass media.

Section III: Objective Type Questions

1. Which one of the following is not an after effect of noise?
   (a) Hearing loss
   (b) Increase in blood pressure
   (c) Causing heart problems
   (d) Mental retardation
2. Which one of the following is not a program initiated by Government of India for addressing the issue of poverty?
   (a) Integrated Rural Development Program
   (b) National Old Age Pension Scheme
   (c) Beti bacho, Beti padhao Scheme
   (d) National Family Benefit Scheme
3. Which one of the following is not a factor or cause for aggressive behaviour?
   (a) Mental conflicts
   (b) Sexual jealousy
   (c) Gender differences
   (d) Noise
4. The General Aggression Model (GAM) has been presented by
   (a) Albert Bandura
   (b) Anderson and Bushman
   (c) Freud
   (d) Carl Rogers

Answers

1 (d) 2 (c) 3 (a)
4 (b)

18

Developing Psychological Skills

> **Learning Objectives**
>
> After going through this chapter, you will be able to:
>
> - Name and know about different types of psychological skills are required for developing one as an effective psychologist.
> - Discuss about the psychological skills categorized as General skills and named as Intellectual Skills, Personal Skills, and Observational Skills.
> - Throw light on the nature and use of the psychological skills are categorized as Special skills and named as Communication Skills, Psychological Testing Skills, Interviewing Skills, and Counselling Skills.

Introduction

As a student of psychology you must not only have knowledge and understanding about the contents of psychology, but should also be acquainted with the applied aspects of the subject psychology along with the acquisition of certain essential skills related to the subject psychology referred to as psychological skills. It is more true and essential for those who want to make use of their knowledge and understanding of the subject psychology as a professional in the field of psychology. All professions, in their applied aspect, require or expect from the persons working in one or the other field to be equipped with two types of essentials-one pertaining to the theoretical understanding of their work done in their area and the other related to the skills needed for its practical application. The same is true for the persons who want to work as professional psychologists in their career choice in the name of psychological researchers, educational psychologists, clinical psychologists, social psychologists, guidance and counselling professionals, sports psychologists, etc. For getting developed as one or the other types of psychology professionals, thus, one has to imbibe himself with certain types of essential psychological skills besides having necessary understanding about the principles of psychology. Let us try to discuss about the type of psychological skills required and their acquisition on the part of the psychological professionals in this chapter.

Types of Psychological Skills Required for Developing as an Effective Psychologist

A skill in its formal way according to Merriam Webster Dictionary may be defined as a learned power or ability of doing something competently. As an acquired ability through direct and indirect experiences of a skill, thus, may make us quite competent to perform a particular task or activity in a highly successful way. That is why one always needs to be sufficiently skilled for performing a particular task in an utmost satisfactory and successful way. Imperatively, if you want to opt for psychology as your career, you besides acquiring sufficient knowledge and understanding about the psychology principles, need to be equipped yourself with the various types of psychological skills required for developing you as an effective psychologist.

These so called psychological skills may be divided mainly into two distinctive categories, named as below.

(i) General Skills, comprising of a group of intellectual skills, personal skills and observational skills.

(ii) Specific Skills comprising the group of communication skills, psychological testing skills, interviewing skills and counselling skills.

Let us discuss them one by one.

General Skills

General skills are those skills which are supposed to be possessed by all persons working as a professional psychologist irrespective of the field of their working such as health, clinical, educational, industrial, environmental, sport, forensic, etc. They very well reflect the personality of a professional psychologist and their possession is essential for terming him or her as a psychologist in an effective way. The skills named as intellectual, and personal skills are generally included in the category of general psychological skills. We may identify and name these skills in the way briefed as below.

Intellectual skills

We may include one or the other cognitive and emotional intelligence skills in this subcategory of psychological skills helpful for the psychologists in their professional activities. The persons equipped with these skills are found to imbibe the qualities and characteristics like below in their demonstrated behaviour and functioning as psychologist.

- They possess a quite satisfactory level of basic intelligence in terms of the use of their thinking, reasoning, problem solving, decision making, critical and thought-analysing ability, intellectual curiosity, and creativity accompanied with a lot of flexibility in their cognitive functioning.
- They are found to be sufficiently equipped with emotional intelligence skills for properly understanding and interacting with others with the possession of qualities like empathy, active listening, self-control, patience and tolerance, respect for other's feelings, point of views, values or diverse opinions, and thus having an adequate capacity of managing emotions of the self and others in a needed way in one or the other interpersonal interactions.

Personal Skills

We may include in this sub-category of psychological skills, the abilities or personality characteristics that are quite personal and individual in nature such as below.

- Awareness about the self in terms of knowing his strengths and limitations
- Habits and lifestyle helpful in keeping one physically and mentally healthy, well organized and adjusted in his personal and professional life including properly attentive towards time management, personal hygiene, physical fitness and appropriate dress
- Imbibed with the useful personality characteristics such as inclination and desire to help others, honesty in dealing with others and sincerity towards responsibilities, believing in ethical and moral values, spirit of fighting with the odds and stress tolerance, imbibed with reflecting skill to have introspection and examination of his own actions and activities for giving them the needed push and direction for behaving with the self and others
- Possession of the needed sensitivity to diversity-individual and cultural differences. In this regard it should be well remembered that the professional psychologists essentially need to be equipped with this necessary skill or ability as one of their personality characteristics. They have to work in diversified environmental situations-physical as well as socio-cultural and interact with people who belong to diversified socio-cultural backgrounds, have a wide variety of individual differences in terms of their abilities, potentials, and ways of thinking, feeling and behaving.

Observational Skills

It is well said that for the welfare of one's own and others, one should be able to open his ears and eyes well in sensing and interpreting what is happening in his surroundings or the environmental situations or events going on at one or the other times. This saying may prove equally true in the case of professional psychologists who are supposed to draw conclusions by sensing and judging the things happening in the environmental surroundings and with the people whose behaviour they are supposed to study. Here they have to remain quite alert and attentive for making use of their all sensory, perceptual, reasoning and inferential abilities for a keen observation of the things related to the behaviour of the people along with the environmental factors affecting their behaviour in a given situation. Their observation here may take a variety of forms or shapes depending upon the nature of the happenings of the behavioural events-natural or induced, or the way or mode adopted for such observation. These may be named and briefed as below.

Naturalistic observation: Here the professional psychologists try to study the behaviour of the people as it occurs in its natural way or reflected in their day to day behavioural activities in a usual fashion by making use of the suitable means for its observation.

Induced or controlled observation: Here the psychologists or researchers try to study the behaviour of their clients or subjects of the study by inducing or creating conditions for the occurrence of a particular type of behaviour such as anxiety ridden, aggressive, helping or pro-social behaviour for its systematic and scientific study in the laboratory like controlled conditions or in the way as studied under the naturalistic observation mode.

Participant Observation: In this type of observation, the psychologists try to observe the behaviour of a group of people by joining them as an associate or participant in any of their group activities. For example, he may join the group of children in their play activities or accompany them on tour and excursion activities to closely observe them for investigating about one or the other aspects of their social behaviour. This may provide good opportunity for the observation of the behaviour of the individuals. However, it suffers from a serious limitation as the presence of an observer may obstruct the natural and spontaneous flow of the behavioural activities of the participants under study.

Non-participant observation: This type of observation tries to do away with some of the defects or limitations of the participant observation. Here the psychologists observe the behaviour of the people in such a way that they may not have any idea that their behaviour in any way is being observed. For this purpose, as an observer they may take their position in such a place and in such a way that while the individuals under observation may not see them, they can clearly watch and hear, if possible, all about their behaviour in action. There may be a screen or a curtain of such a nature as can help for real observation while hiding their presence. The use of some modern equipment like secret cameras, video recording, audio recording etc, may also serve such purpose. While sitting at quite a far distance, the observer may also take the help of a telescope for a clear but secret observation. Whatever means and methods may be employed by the psychologist, his motive in such an observation is always to come in contact with the natural and spontaneous behaviour of the subjects without making them aware of his presence.

The task related to the observation of the behaviour of the individuals under study and the environmental situations in which this behaviour is occurring is not as simple as it seems. Besides, adopting a quite systematic and well planned procedure and means and equipments for the observation and recording of the observed events, it requires certain types of specific abilities, temperamental characteristics as well as precautions observed and efficiency exhibited in the observation and conclusion drawn on the part of the observer professionals. We may name some of the important ones as below.

- Remaining alert and attentive in making use of sensory and perceptual abilities for focusing on the targeted things related to people's behaviour and their environment.
- Maintaining the required curiosity for knowing more and more or collecting information about the target in observation
- Keeping patience, optimistic attitude and the needed sincerity as well as objectivity in the observation of the objects or goals of observation
- Making use of the needed devices and techniques or resources for carrying out the task of observation in a most effective way
- Following all the needed formalities for the observance of ethical and moral code for carrying out observation and maintaining secrecy of what is known through such observation
- Remaining truthful about the observational findings by remaining ready for their evaluation or verification on the part of others observers
- Carrying out the task of observation by following the systematic steps like (i) Planning and Preparation for Observation, (ii) Observation of the targeted Behaviour and related environmental surroundings in a proper way, (iii) Analysis and Interpretation of the observed results, (iv) Providing opportunities for the Generalization of the findings of observation.

To Sum Up

Psychological Skills required for developing one as an effective psychologist may be broadly classified as General skills (comprising of a group of intellectual, personal and observational skills) and Specific Skills (comprising the group of communication skills, psychological testing skills, interviewing skills and counselling skills).

In the category of general skills where, *Intellectual skills* reflect the abilities and capacities of an individual with regard to the possession of cognitive and emotional intelligence helpful for the psychologists in their professional activities, the *personal skills,* in this concern, reflect the abilities or personality characteristics of an individual that are quite personal and individual in nature. *Observational skills,* on the other hand, stand for the skills helping the professional psychologists to be equipped with a keen insight and ability to observe and study properly the things and happenings in their environmental surroundings and with the people whose behaviour they are supposed to study.

Special Skills

The skills including in this category represent the skills that are quite specific and special in nature for helping the concerned professional psychologists in carrying out their specific professional activities in an appropriate way. We may name them as (i) Communication skills, (ii) Psychological testing skills, (iii) Interviewing skills, and (iv) Counseling skills.

Each one of these group of skills, is meant for the execution of certain specific tasks and thus may be seen to serve the specific purpose of some specific group of professional psychologists, e.g., counseling skills are meant for the use of the professionals who get engaged in the task of counseling their clients, and psychological testing skills are required on the part of professionals who engage in the task of assessing or evaluating the psychological abilities or competences of their subjects or clients such as educational psychologists, clinical psychologists, sports psychologists, etc. However, it does not mean that these so called special skills are totally exclusive and meant for working in an area. In their applied sense, actually they all are mutually well inclusive and thus may prove quite useful as well as essential for the psychologists working in different areas. Let us discuss about the nature and use of these specific skills one by one.

Communication Skills

Communication skills are very much needed on the part of all professional psychologists who need to get engaged in their interaction with the individuals or subjects of the study for gathering information from them of one or the other particular nature through a well-meaning process named communication. Let us know about what we mean by the term communication and the related communication process.

Communication, in its literal sense, stands for the act of communicating. One can communicate his ideas, thoughts, feelings, etc. or transfer any type of information and knowledge to others through this act. For this purpose, he may also take the help of some instruments, appliances or devices like telephone, telegram, fax, e-mail, radio broadcasting, and telecasting. In this sense, communication may be taken as a one-sided transaction of a piece of information, knowledge, ideas, thoughts, and feelings from a person (source of transmission) to another person or persons at the receiving end. However, its meaning cannot be limited to such a one-way transmission. It is always a two-sided affair. The two individuals-psychologist and the client/subject as the source of transmission and its receiver are found to equally share and participate in the communication process. The etymological derivation of the term communication also supports the above line of thought. As is commonly known, the term has been derived from the Latin word *Communis* meaning 'common'. In this sense, as a verb the term stands for an act of sharing commonness or common understanding and experiences with others. It is in this sense, that the term communication has been defined by Edger Dale (1961) as "*the sharing of ideas and feeling in a mood of mutuality.*" In this way, in its broader meaning, the term communication stands for a process of sharing or exchanging information, thoughts, and feelings between the two individuals- psychologist and client/subject playing the roles of the source of communication and receiver through some mutually agreeable or known media (verbal or non-verbal). We can understand well about the process of communication through a cycle illustrated in Fig.18.1

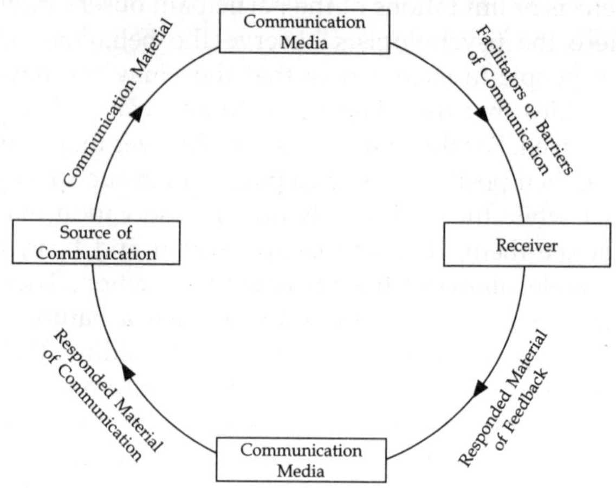

Fig. 18.1: The process of communication.

The success in a process of communication depends on the successful workability of its elements or components. In this connection here we may note that much depends up on the cooperation and efforts going on between the psychologist himself and the client/subjects playing the roles of the source and receiver in the ways as required from them from time to time during the process of communication. The next is the content of communication, what is asked, enquired, or responded on the part of both parties during the communication process and then the media-such as verbal and non-verbal used for carrying out the message from both sides including care taken for handling of the intervening variables such as facilitators and barriers in the process of communication in a proper way.

In this way, while taking care of all the elements of components involved in the process of communication, a psychologist should concentrate on the following aspects for getting him well-equipped with the skill of communication.

1. Since, communication is a two-sided process therefore, the psychologist should always be quite careful in the establishment of an interlinked inclusive environment in which he and his client or subject should mutually share information having no hesitation or reservation on their part with a reasonable trust, and feeling of respect towards each other.
2. In the communication taking place between two parties, it is quite essential that what is conveyed by one as a source or sender should be grasped or understood well by the other as receiver in the way as intended on the part of the sender. The content as well as media of communication (verbal or non-verbal), therefore need to be well cared for on the part of both the parties under conversation or communication. In making use of the media, the things that need more attention on the part of the psychologists may be briefed as below.
   - While making use of the verbal media for communication with his client he should try to make use of the language spoken and understood well on the part of his client or audience under conversation. On his part he should try to pay needed attention on the appropriateness of mode of his speaking or communicating with the clients orally or in written form in a needed way through the use of common language.
   - The importance or value of the use of non-verbal media in communication should be given due weight on his part. He should try to acquire necessary expertise on his part for conveying as well as receiving communicated information, thoughts and feelings through non-verbal means such as facial expression, eye movements, gestures, postures or movements of the body. Many times, a number of things not getting revealed through the verbal media-words spoken or written, come under notice through the signs and symptoms inherent in the non-verbal communication related to body language, style of dressing and mannerism of others.
   - Besides this he should acquire necessary ability related to active listening-attending properly what is conveyed to him through the word spoken or on or the other non-verbal means. In addition, he should try to gain proficiency in understanding and grasping the direct or indirect meaning conveyed in the written mode of expression.
   - He should try to provide due importance to the factors playing the role of facilitators or barriers in communication. The favourable situations such as calm and quiet environment, tension-free mutual interaction, proper climate and weather conditions may play wonders in enhancing the effectiveness of the communication process. On the other hand, unfavourable conditions or situations in the form of noise, non-availability of proper physical facilities, mutual conflicts and tensions, improper climate and weather conditions may play havoc by disharmonizing the process. The psychologist in his communication with the clients should try to gain expertise in organizing favourable conditions by having provision for as many facilitators as possible. However, on the other hand, the barriers must be taken by him as the negative and detrimental force and, as such, every effort should be made by him for keeping them totally away or reducing their impact on the communication process.

Psychological Testing Skills

The professional psychologists including the research psychologists working in various areas such as educational, clinical, counseling, industrial and business management have to make use of one or the other types of psychological tests for assessing or knowing about one or the other things related to the psychological potential, abilities and behavioural functioning of their clients or subjects for one or the other purposes. In this concern, a particular psychological test is developed for the assessment of a particular psychological attribute of the persons being tested.

It can't be used for carrying out the assessment of the persons with regard to other psychological attributes. It has necessitated on the part of the test developers to develop a variety of tests for being used to assess a wide variety of psychological attributes of human beings belonging to a common set-up and environmental conditions. In general, the psychological tests so developed may be classified into the categories mentioned as below:

1. ***Achievement tests:*** Used in assessing what a person has achieved, acquired or learnt.

2. ***Personality tests:*** Used in assessing personal qualities or characteristics referred to as personality traits.
3. ***Aptitude tests:*** Used in assessing different aptitudes capable of predicting one's success in the area of the particular aptitude such as mechanical, artistic, clerical, managerial etc.
4. ***Interest tests:*** Used in the assessment of the varying interests possessed by an individual such as interest in gardening, literary interest, interest in social work, etc.
5. ***Attitude tests or scales:*** Used in assessing the attitude of the persons towards a thing, an idea, a person, philosophy, custom, tradition, etc.
6. ***Intelligence tests:*** Used in assessing the intelligence or level of cognitive functioning of the individuals.
7. ***Emotional intelligence tests:*** Used in assessing the level of emotional intelligence possessed by the individuals.
8. ***Mood and motivation tests:*** Used in assessing the nature of the mood and motivational levels of the individuals.
9. ***Adjustment inventories or tests:*** Used in assessing the level of one's adjustment towards self and environment.
10. *Personality Inventory:* Used for assessing the overall personality make up, traits or attributes of the individual.
11. ***Neuropsychological tests:*** Used in assessing deficits in cognitive functioning (*i.e.* ability to think, speak, reason, etc.) that may result from some sort of brain damage such as stroke or brain injury.
12. ***Specific clinical tests***: Used to assess specific matters of clinical concerns such as level of anxiety, depression, mental retardation, emotional disturbance, etc.

Characteristics of psychological tests

Psychological tests used for the psychological assessment of the individuals have some unique characteristics like below:

1. **Provision for stimuli to generate responses or sample of behaviour:** All psychological tests require the respondents to do something. For this purpose, in every psychological test, there is a provision of certain stimuli in the form of open-ended/closed questions or structured/ unstructured situations to evoke responses on the part of the subjects for generating a sample of behaviour related to one or the other psychological attributes such as intelligence, aptitude, attitude adjustment, etc.
2. **Standardization of the test:** Every psychological test for serving its objectives has the need of being standardized on a given population. Standardization of the test is aimed to achieve the following:
   - **Uniformity in administration**
   - **Uniformity and objectivity in scoring**
   - **Uniformity and objectivity in interpretation**

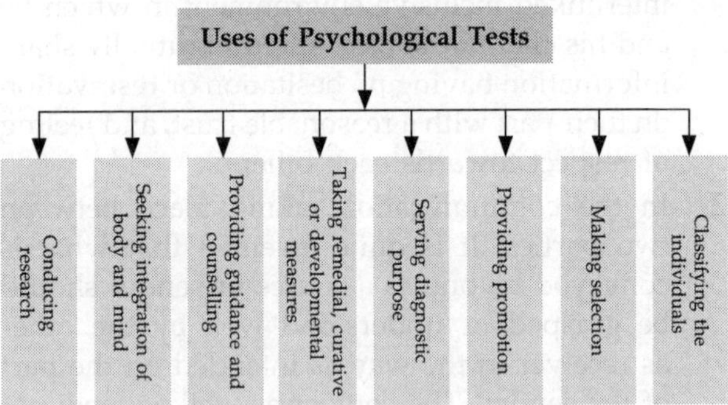

Fig. 18.2: Uses of the psychological tests

Skills needed to be acquired for the use of psychological tests

Psychological testing is a very skilled and professional task. Therefore, it needs on the part of professional psychologists and researchers to get them imbibed with certain essential skills and know-how regarding the use of psychological tests. Imbibed with these skills, they are required to proceed or take care of the following in the execution of a task related to psychological testing.

- First of all they should be quite specific about the objectives or purposes being served through the psychological testing being done on their part and decide well that they will remain quite objective, scientific and ethically fair to all the subjects during the whole course of psychological testing.
- Then they should search for an appropriate well standardized psychological test for assessing the psychological attribute in question such as intelligence, aptitude, adjustment etc. In such a selection, they should try to analyze properly its appropriateness for its use on the individuals or sample of their study, along with its worth in terms of its reliability and validity, objectivity in scoring, suitability in terms of norms providing an ease in interpretation and drawing conclusion about the needed assessment of the subjects under testing.
- The third stage of the use of psychological test is the test administration. The professional psychologists are needed to have essential

expertise in the administration of psychological tests in a proper way as needed and provided in the manual of the test developed by the test developer. Here they should be quite specific and particular about the maintenance of uniformity required in connection with the environmental conditions, seating arrangement, noise levels, ensuring or responding to the structured or unstructured stimuli, time or duration of the test, etc.

- The next is the task of scoring and interpretation of the individual responses of the subjects available separately on their test sheets. The psychologists as the administrator of the test should try to acquire necessary expertise in this technical task of scoring and interpretation. They should strictly follow the procedure laid down in the manual for the scoring of the responses and their interpretation in the light of the standardized age, grade, or sex-wise norms given in the manual.
- The task of interpretation of the individual responses, however, needs more caring and expertise on the part of professional psychologists and researchers. They need to be better acquainted and skilled in this task by knowing more about it in details as below.

Two different approaches, namely criterion-referenced and norm-referenced approaches may be employed for the interpretation of the test score of the individuals.

A criterion-referenced approach for the interpretation of the scores asks for comparing an individual's performance to some criterion other than the performances of the other individual. This criterion is almost fixed before the administration of the test such as giving satisfactory or affirmative answers to so many items will be enough to label the individual concerned in such and such way. For example, providing correct answers to 9 problems out of 10 will be the criterion of declaring him passed in the test of mathematical ability. Showing agreement to a specified number of adjustment related items will be accepted as the criterion for their better adjustment, adjustment or poor adjustment, etc.

In the norm referenced approach for the interpretation of the scores, on the other hand, one goes with the norms laid down in the test manual by the test developer at the time of the standardization of his test. Norm referenced interpretation is based on the comparison of the examinee' scores with the scores earned by the majority of the individuals acting as subjects at the time of the standardization of the test on a given population. The test developer thus sets a standard of performance, *i.e.* by stating that the scores within this range will indicate average adjustment, poor adjustment or good adjustment or he may provide norms in terms of percentile (age, grade or sex-wise) showing that a certain score earned by an individual will place him on certain percentile rank (*i.e.* the specific percentages of the individual in the group comprising the population of the standardized test lies below him in relation to the performance or ability in question). Such interpretation of one's scores on a psychological test thus provides a clue for his relative strengths and weaknesses in relation to other members of the population of the standardized test on a psychological attribute in question.

Interviewing Skills

There are a number of occasions before the professional psychologists when they have to get engaged in the task of interviewing people for deriving useful information from them on a direct personal basis about something they are familiar or the things concerning their own self such as their interests and likings, attitudes and beliefs, norms and values, hopes and desperations etc. Such need of interviewing people may be felt much on the part of psychologists working in the field of sociology and anthropology, education, sports, health and environmental protection, guidance and counseling, market management, providing consultancy for hiring or promoting individuals for specific tasks, medicine, clinical setup, etc.

As a technique, interview may be defined as a way or mode of collecting information from a person or group of persons in a face-to-face direct contact on the basis of the questions put and responses received by us from them on this account.

For acquiring proficiency in the art of taking interview of the target individuals or group of individuals, the professional psychologists are needed to have a thorough knowledge of the mechanism or processing of interviewing with the things needed to be cared on their part in handling this process in a successful way. In this connection, the beginning may be made by getting acquainted with the formats used for interviewing the people.

Formats of the Interview

Interview in view of its structural organization may be shaped in the following two forms.

(*i*) Structured and standardized.

(*ii*) Unstructured and non-standardized.

Structured and Standardized Interview

In such a format the interview is structured as well as standardized well in advance before it is put to use for getting information from individuals as per the need of the situation or purpose served through the interview. This is done by taking care of the following:

- Selection of appropriate questions to be put to the individuals.
- Deciding about the order and sequence of the asked questions.
- To decide on the type of answer or responses for an asked question that will be able to provide the required information in the light of the objectives of the interview.

Hence, by taking proper definite decisions about the mode, procedure and outcomes of the interview, the desired control can be effectively exercised over the total operation of the interviewing process. Such control and effective organization of the interview then automatically makes it more objective, reliable and valid. The path of the psychologists here thus becomes totally clear as they have all the material with them (pre-planned, structured and standardized) for the achievement of the interview objectives.

Unstructured and Non-standardized Interview

In this type of an interview, the interviewer neither possesses the pre-prepared set numbers of questions with him for getting the individual's response nor does he have a set of prior decision about the evaluation of their responses in terms of the objectives of the study. The interviewer is totally free to ask any type of questions to the subject to get the desired information. He may go to any depth to seek such information. This unstructured, unplanned and non-standardized format of the interview may result in losing control over the systematic schedule of the interview. The interviewer may put up unnecessary questions after questions for going deep into a single direction, digging out a single aspect of one's knowledge or personality attribute. The subject may also go on elaborating his response and focusing on an irrelevant theme. Thus, this type of interview is regarded as less objective, reliable and valid in comparison to the structured interview. However, it scores a merit point over the structured interview in its characteristic of providing complete freedom to the interviewer and the subject for setting the direction of the interview as per their wish and the needs of the situation. The subject gets enough opportunity for self-expression through the spontaneously formed questions of the interviewer and hence there lies greater opportunity for the expression and assessment of the spontaneous behaviour in such kind of unstructured interview.

Processing of the interview

After going through the task related to the format of interview, the psychologist needs to go through the actual task of interviewing the target individuals by following some systematic steps discussed as below.

Pre-preparation for the Interview

The following pre-preparation on the part of interviewer may prove quite helpful in the proper application of the interview instrument in realizing the objectives of the interview.

- Be definite about the objectives of the interview and then plan accordingly what is to be asked and observed.
- Locate the individuals to be interviewed and try to enlist their cooperation in conducting the interview.
- Motivate respondents by convincing them about the importance of the interview well in advance.
- Acquire enough knowledge and training about using interview as a technique for collecting the required information.
- Ensure that the physical and psychological conditions in which the interview is to be held are properly checked so that the respondent and interviewer do not feel uncomfortable.
- Ensure that the respondent feels as natural and spontaneous as possible for providing desired information.
- Have proper arrangement for recording the responses of the individuals interviewed.

Taking an Interview

The following essential points should be kept in mind while taking an interview on the part of the concerned psychologist:

- Introduce himself with necessary legitimate identification as an interviewer to the subject/client.
- Explain the purpose of his study by being as definite and short as possible.
- Giving proper time to the subject/client to get ready to be interviewed for the interview questions.

- Asking the questions very carefully but in a spontaneous and informal way, surely in the manner and order as planned in the interview schedule.
- Avoiding dominating or monopolizing the conversation during the interview. He should not put words unnecessarily into the mouth of the respondent. During the course of interview he should try to be a patient listener and never feel disappointed, irritated or surprised by what the respondent says.
- Using the silent probe technique for getting adequate responses by just pausing and waiting. It really works by suggesting to the respondent that the interviewer is waiting for his response.
- Motivating the client/subject by providing direct encouragement. However, this does not imply that the interviewer approve or disapprove his responses. It may be as simple as saying OK or nodding head on his part.
- Trying to get more desired information by asking for elaboration, *e.g.* Is there anything else you would like to say?
- Asking for the desired clarification, if needed, by putting questions in some other ways or repeating his question.
- Demonstrating warmth and respect towards the respondent. In addition, he should also try to have a rapport by winning his confidence and assuring him of the secrecy of his thoughts and feelings.
- Trying to accept the responses and reactions of the respondent in their original form and have its record as adequately as possible.

Closure of the interview

The following things may be kept in mind by the psychologists at this final stage:

- Ensuring optimum realization of the objectives of the interview, as decided before holding the interview.
- The information collected should be as complete as possible.
- Thanking the respondent for allowing him to take his interview.
- Assuring the respondent for getting benefited through the interview.
- Making the respondent feel natural and satisfied with the conversation held at the time of the interview.
- Trying to draw necessary conclusion from the recorded information and responses of the interview for realizing the objective of the interview.

In this way, the professional psychologists working in the various fields are required to gain necessary proficiency in acquiring necessary skills in the art of interviewing particularly related to the structuring of the format of the interview and then making use of this interview schedule for executing the task of interview in a successful way by following the needed systematic steps in the name of pre-preparation, taking interview and closure of the interview.

Counseling Skills

Counseling skills falling in the category of special skills are needed on the part of professional psychologists to counsel individuals or group of individuals for rendering help or assistance to them at the time of their need. For knowing about the counseling skills and their acquisition, let us first try to understand the term counseling.

What is counseling?

The word counseling in its general interpretation stands for the act of giving advice, providing suggestion and consultation, expressing opinion, etc. In our day-to-day life generally, we make use of this term in the above-referred sense. When we are confronted with a personal or family problem, we approach our friends, relatives, or an experienced and respectable aged person in our neighborhood or community for seeking necessary counseling (his valuable suggestions, opinions or piece of advice) for solving our problem. In this way, in our day-to-day life, counseling is asked or provided by each of us at different occasions for taking or providing help to somebody in the hour of need. However, as far as the use of the term counseling provided by professional counselors is concerned, it is not done in such a simple way as referred above. A few definitions of this term put forward by eminent authors and psychologists may be cited as a support for such observation:

1. **Rogers (1942):** Counseling may be defined as a series of direct contacts with the individual which aims to offer him assistance in changing his attitudes and behaviour.
2. **Shostrom and Brammer (1952):** Counseling is a self-adjustive process which helps the client become more self-directive and self-responsible.
3. A comprehensive definition cited in the textbook published by NCERT (1998) may certainly help us understand the meaning and concept of the

term counseling. This definition given by E.G. Vedanayagam runs as under:

"Counseling is an accepting, trusting and safe relationship in which clients (or the counselees) learn to discuss freely what upsets them, to define their goals, to acquire the essential social skills, and to develop the courage and self-confidence to implement desired new behaviour."

The above-cited three definitions, now, may substantially help us arrive at the following conclusions about the meaning and nature of the term counseling.

(i) Counseling is that behavioural process which involves at least two persons, namely counselee and counselor.

(ii) The two persons, counselee and counsellor, must have a very cordial and satisfying relationship based on mutual understanding, acceptance, faith and trust.

(iii) In counselling the counsellee must be provided with the essential facilities and opportunities for clearly putting up his problem before the counselor or the counselor should have such guts, courtesy and skills to know about the problem of his counsellee.

(iv) It is essential to have a continuous and direct contact between the counselor and the counselee for the proper give-and-take of required counseling.

(v) Counselling should not be misunderstood as a task of providing some immediate solution or accepting the burdens of the problems of counsellee by the counsellor himself. His task is only to help him by providing valuable suggestion, in the form of ideological and psychological support for equipping him to gain proper insight and strength for the solution to his problem.

(vi) Counseling, in this way, provides the way for self-adjustment by enhancing the abilities and capacities of the counsellee for facing the problems and challenges at his own. Counselling thus aims for the development of self-dependence in the counsellee instead of remaining dependent on the counsellor.

(vii) In counselling, all possible attempts are made to bring such desirable modification in the interests, attitudes, abilities and overall behaviour of the counsellee so that he may be able to develop his abilities and capacities for gaining proper confidence in solving his problem and proceeding further on the path of his personal and social development.

In this way as a conclusion, *we may consider counselling as a help and assistance provided by a counsellor (through a cordial and satisfying relationship) to bring desirable modification in the behaviour of the counselee for making him/her quite independent in solving his/her immediate problems and proceeding properly on the path of self and social progress.*

Counseling: Process of giving expert advice to the client on the basis of trusted relationship for enabling him to do his self efforts for his needed adjustment and development.

Task of counseling

The task of counseling, existing in its various forms and shapes as shown in figure 18.3 needs to be carried out by some efficient and trained persons known as counselors to help those who are in need of such assistance for helping themselves.

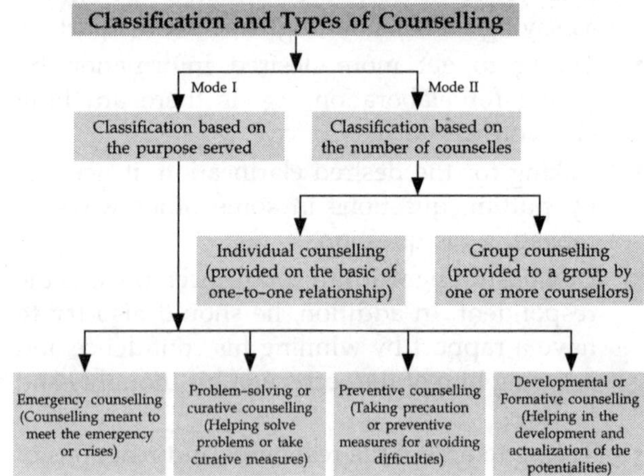

Fig. 18.3: Classification and Types of Counselling

For execution of the task of counseling rendered in varying situations and forms shown in the above figure, needs to be done on the part of the persons who are quite skilled in terms of its proper execution. These skilled persons known as counselors are supposed to be equipped with certain essential skills for carrying out their task of counseling. These skills may be named and grouped into the categories mentioned below (Hopsons, 1982: 258):

1. Relationship building skills
2. Exploring and clarifying skills
3. Objective setting and action planning skills

Let us try to know about the role played by these skills in carrying out the task of counseling on the part of a counselor in the subsequent three phases discussed below.

Phase I. Relationship Building

The task of counseling begins with the use of relationship building skills on the part of the counselor. By using such skills, the counselor tries to win the confidence and trust of the counselee for establishing desired rapport with him. In building such rapports, the counselor tries to keep in mind that the desired relationship and rapport can be maintained.

- If one has and conveys respect for another
- If one is genuine to oneself
- If one attempts to see things from the other's point of view and
- If one endeavours not to pass judgement

Phase II. Exploring and Clarifying

After establishing good rapport with the counsellee, the counsellor tries to persuade the counsellee to open himself before the counsellor about his felt problem. The counsellor makes him explore and understand more about how he feels and why he feels so. The cousellor helps him to be clearer about his thoughts and feelings and persuades him to examine options for the solution to his felt problem or ways and means of better adjustment and development in the present situation. The counsellor here in this phase tries to make use of his exploring and clarifying skills (e.g. putting open-end questions, summarizing, focusing, reflecting, clarifying, confronting, etc.).

Phase III. Objective Setting and Action Planning

As a result of work done in phase II, the counsellee becomes clear about his problem or developmental/ adjustment target. In the third phase now, the counsellor makes him set objectives, plan actions for achieving his target and act to help him at his own. In doing so the counsellee thus becomes clear about his felt difficulties or uncertainties and can explore options and alternatives, in terms of what he might do to change what he is not happy about. By getting the timely support from the counsellor he becomes adequately prepared and capable dealing with his felt problems or difficulties. In this way, as a result of counselling, he is adequately helped for helping himself regarding his needed adjustment, development and progress. The skills utilized by the counsellor for helping the counsellee in this phase are named as objective setting, action planning and problem-solving skills helpful in persuading the counsellee to set clear objectives, build specified plans and act with a little support to achieve what he needs to achieve.

In this way, it should be well understood on the part of professional psychologists desirous to play the role of a counselor in one or the other situations emerging during executing their responsibilities towards their clients or subjects to get them well equipped with the necessary knowledge and skills needed for doing their best in this concern. For this purpose, they need not only have a workable knowledge of the meaning and nature of the task counseling but should also acquire the required proficiency in the use of the skills related to the processing of the task of counseling in its proper way.

To Sum Up

The skills known as special skills to be acquired on the part of psychologists represent the skills that are quite specific and special in nature for helping them in their specific professional activities in an appropriate way. We may name them as Communication skills, Psychological testing skills, Interviewing skills, and Counselling skills.

Communication skills are the skills, the acquisition of those help the psychologists to get engaged in their interaction with the subjects of the study for gathering information from them of one or the other particular nature through a well meaning process named communication. The acquisition of the psychological testing skills on the other hand, helps the professional psychologists to make use of one or the other types of psychological tests for assessing or knowing about one or the other things related to the psychological potential, abilities and behavioural functioning of their subjects for one or the other purposes.

Interviewing skills acquired by the psychologists help them in performing the quite important and essential task of interviewing the subjects of their study for deriving useful information from them on a direct personal basis about something they are familiar or the things concerning their own self in a proper way. For serving this purpose, they need to learn the way of structuring the format of interview and conducting the interviews in a desired needed way.

Counselling skills acquired by psychologists perform the role of getting them equipped with the necessary abilities and capacities of providing expert advice to the client on the basis of trusted relationship for enabling him to do his self efforts in solving his one or the other problems. The skills like establishing rapport with the client, understanding his problem, knowing about his ability to deal with his problem and helping him develop his capacity to deal with his problem are some of the skills that are part and parcel of one's counselling skill.

ASSIGNMENT QUESTIONS

Section I: Essay Type Questions

1. A professional psychologist needs to acquire certain psychological skills. What are these skills? Name and discuss them in brief.
2. Discuss in detail about the following types of general psychological skills.
3. Intellectual skills, (ii) Personal skills and (iii) Observational skills.
4. What are the skills designated as special psychological skills? Name and discuss them in brief.
5. Describe and discuss about any two of the following types of psychological skills.

(i) Communication skills, (ii) Psychological testing skills,(iii) Interview skills and (iv) Counselling skills.

6. What is communication? Throw light on the nature and use of communication skills on the part of professional psychologists.
7. What are observational skills? Discuss their employment on the part of the professional psychologists.
8. What is psychological testing? What types of skills are needed for the task of psychological testing carried out on the part of professional psychologists? Discuss.
9. Discuss about the use of observational skills on the part of the psychologists in detail.
10. What is counselling? Discuss the nature and use of the counselling skills employed by the professional psychologists for providing counselling to the clients.

Section II: Short Answer Type Questions

1. What are the skills designated as psychological skills?
2. What are intellectual/personal/ observation skills?
3. Name any two skills named as intellectual/ personal/ observation/ communication/ psychological testing skills/interview skills.
4. What are personal skills? Why are these referred to as personal?
5. Name any three types of psychological tests employed on the part of professional psychologists.
6. Explain any two characteristics or uses of psychological tests.
7. Name the different formats of the interviews of the subjects taken on the part of professional psychologists.
8. What is counseling?
9. Which relationship building skills are needed on the part of counselors?

Section III: Objective Type Questions

1. Which one of the following is not included in the category of personal skills?
   (a) Awareness about the self
   (b) Habits and lifestyles
   (c) possession of the needed sensitivity to diversity
   (d) ability to provide guidance to others
2. Which one of the following is not included in the category of communication skills?
   (a) Ability testing skill
   (b) Verbal communication skill
   (c) Non-verbal communication skill
   (d) Skill of establishing proper link with people in communication
3. What is not possessed as one of its attribute on the part of a psychological test or the process of psychological testing?
   (a) Provision for stimuli to generate responses or sample of behaviour
   (b) Being standardized on a given population
   (c) Uniformity and objectivity in scoring
   (d) Freedom to interpret the result

Answers

1 (d) 2 (a) 3 (d)

19

Psychology Practical Work

Chapter Composition

- Introduction
- Measurement of Intelligence
- Aptitude Measurement
- Assessment of Personality
- Measurement of Adjustment
- Measurement of Attitudes
- Measurement of Creativity
- Case study of a Problem Child

Introduction

There is no exaggeration in Kant's saying that "experiment without theory is blind and theory without experiment is lame." Theory and practice, related to any field of knowledge, present idea and action. One is necessary for the other, not only for their survival but also for rendering some service to humanity. Therefore, in any scheme of study there should be a close integration of theory with practice. Psychology is not an exception. Here too we must pay due emphasis on practical work besides theoretical insight into the subject. Being a student of psychology you must be well-versed in using and employing the theory and contents of psychology in a practical way. You may yourself be curious to know your intellectual level, your interests and aptitudes, your personality make up, your adjustment to the self and the environment etc. You can know such things through measurements, possible with the relevant psychological tests. Many of these tests have been constructed and standardized by psychologists and researchers in India as well as abroad. In their test manuals, they have described their tests, their usability, methods of administration, scoring and interpretation etc, for the benefit of their users. In your interest here, we have selected a few psychological tests related to your syllabus. In this chapter, we are going to discuss the methodology of conducting and reporting these tests.

Besides, knowing about the use of one or the other types of psychological tests, you are also required to be acquainted with the process of conducting and reporting of the case study of some individuals having exceptionality on one or the other accounts such as delinquent or problematic behaviour. Accordingly, for your help, here in this chapter we are also having discussion on this issue with the presentation of a case study report of a problem child.

Measurement of Intelligence

Introduction

What is intelligence? It has been discussed and interpreted by psychologists and scholars in their own ways. While some have described it as an ability to learn, or ability to adopt or adjust, others have accepted it as the ability to think, reason, imagine or problem solving. While agreeing with all such views about one's intelligence, we can globally consider it as a complex blend of all the mental abilities and capabilities of an individual which help him perform all the tasks needing the use of such mental abilities and capacities of an individual. Hence, one's intelligence is nothing but his intellect put to use.

Nothing definite can be said about the number of different mental or cognitive abilities and capacities comprising one's intellect. Various theories of intelligence have tried to throw light on this aspect from their own angles. Factor theories have tried to point out a definite number of elements or factors present in human intelligence. The nature, degree and amount of such factors present in one's intelligence may thus become the measuring yardstick of one's intelligence in relation to other individuals belonging to his group.

Intelligence tests in this way are designed so as to find out the extent and level of these various elements or factors in one's intellectual performance.

The performance-related behaviour may be either verbal or non-verbal. Consequently, intelligence tests are mainly grouped into two main categories, verbal and non-verbal. These can be used for testing the intelligence of an individual one at a time or in group according to their nature.

While verbal tests are language dominated, the use of language is strictly prohibited or is limited in the non-verbal tests. Instead of language, we make use of pictures, signs and symbols to judge one's intelligence through his performance in activities requiring some use of his intellect.

Let us now discuss the process of using the intelligence tests with the help of two different tests, verbal as well as non-verbal in the present chapter.

Verbal Intelligence Test

The reporting work of the use of such a verbal intelligence test can be illustrated as below:

Objective

To test the intelligence of a subject by making use of a verbal intelligence test.

Needed test material and environmental situations

(i) A copy of the Group Test of General Mental Ability constructed and standardized by Dr. Shyam Sunder Jalota comprising test booklet, answer-sheet, scoring key and test manual.
(ii) A subject whose intelligence is to be tested.
(iii) The arrangement of proper environmental conditions and material facilities for conducting the test.
(iv) A table clock or stopwatch.

Identifying Data of the Subject

Name of the Subject: Ramesh	Name of the School: Model School, Rohtak
Class: VIII	
Date of Birth: 5.7.1993	Date of testing: 5.1.2006

Description of Test Material

This verbal intelligence test has been constructed and standardized by Dr. S.S. Jalota. It can be used to test the intelligence of the Hindi-speaking students of VIII, IX and X classes. It is a group test meaning thereby that we can test the intelligence of a group of students at a time by using this test. It can also be used for testing the intelligence of a single student like in the present case where we are testing the intelligence of our subject Ramesh studying in class VIII. Its test material can be divided into four parts for its proper description.

Test Booklet

It is a reusable booklet. The testees are instructed not to write anything in it or damage it in any way.

The starting page contains all the necessary instructions regarding the administration of the test. The examinees are asked to read them carefully. On the second page, there are 20 questions given for illustration purpose to let the examinees know how to answer the test items. On the third page, there is an instruction which reads as "Unless asked, do not turn this page." From fourth page onwards, there are test items in the form of verbal questions. Every page contains 20 questions and there are 100 questions in all in this test. Most of these questions are multiple choice-type. Out of the given four alternatives, only one is correct. The examinees are required to search for this correct response. A few questions are not the multiple choice type and the examinees are required to provide their answer by writing a number or digit. The examples of both these types of questions included in this test are as follows:

1. तट का अर्थ है - (i) गंगा (ii) किनारा (iii) बाँध (iv) पर
2. 19, 17, 15, 13, 11 इन संख्याओं के क्रमानुसार आगे की एक संख्या उत्तर पत्र (Answer Sheet) पर लिखें।

Answer Sheet

This sheet is given to the subject for writing the answers of the 100 test items. The top of the sheet contains columns to write name, class, school, date of birth, date of the testing etc. for ascertaining the identity of the subject. This information is to be furnished by the examinee. Then, there is blank space for answering the 100 test items. In each column, there is a serial order of 20 items page wise and in front of it in the next column there is a blank space. The subject has to write his response either by writing the serial number of the chosen alternative or by writing the number or digit in the blank space provided adjacent to the test item.

Scoring Key

Scoring key lies with the examiner or administrator of the test. He provides numerical scores to the student's responses by checking their correctness through this key. Every question or test item is scored as 1 if correct and 0 if incorrect. In this way, the maximum and minimum score in the test ranges from 100 to zero.

Test Manual

It also lies with the examiner. It contains all the essential details about the test like how the test items have been selected? How the test has been standardized? What type of subjects can be tested through this intelligence test? How can this test be administered? How is the scoring done? How can we interpret the intelligence of the subjects with the help of the computed scores? This manual also contains a conversion table which helps the examiner convert the test scores of the students into their mental age scores. This manual contains another table meant for converting original test scores of the subjects into the respective stanine scores. It also contains the norms for the VIII, IX and X class of students which may help in grading a subject on the basis of their stanine scores as poor, very dull, superior, very superior and excellent etc.

Administration of the test

For the administration of the test, the following procedure was followed:

(i) The environmental situations and seating arrangement etc, were so arranged that the examinee feels quite at home. The necessary rapport was established and he was told that the objective of this test is to measure his intelligence.

(ii) He was given a test booklet and an answer sheet. He was told that nothing should be written on the test booklet. He is to use it as a question paper and return it safely along with his answer-sheet.

(iii) He was then asked to carefully read all the instructions given on the first page of the test booklet. All these instructions were also explained to him verbally and he was clearly told that there is a time limit of 20 minutes for answering all the 100 items of the test.

(iv) He was then given full opportunity to go through all the 20 examples for letting him know the way of answering the test items. These illustrations were also properly explained verbally to the subject.

(v) Now the subject was asked to start responding to the test items. It was properly taken care of that the subject provides answers correctly on the answer-sheet, items and page wise as per the instructions. After 20 minutes, he was asked to submit his answer sheet along with the reusable booklet.

Scoring of the test items

For scoring the responses of the subject of all the 100 items, proper help was taken from the scoring key. Every correct answer was scored as 1 and incorrect as zero. Since our subject Ramesh provided correct responses for 53 test items, he was awarded 53 marks.

Interpretation of the result

For the necessary interpretation and drawing conclusion about the intelligence of the subject from his earned scores, following procedure was adopted.

(i) First of all this score was used to determine his mental age. The help of the conversion table provided in the test manual was taken for this purpose. It was read as 15 years for his scores of 53. Next his chronological age was computed with the help of his date of birth furnished by him in his identifying data. It was 12 years and 6 months. Now his I.Q. was computed as below:

Mental Age = 15 years = 180 months.

Chronological age = 12 years 6 months = 150 months.

$$IQ = \frac{\text{Mental age}}{\text{Chronological age}} X\,100 = \frac{180}{150} X\,100 = 120$$

(ii) Now to know about the nature and degree of the intellectual potential of our subject on the basis of his so computed I.Q., necessary help was taken from the classification table given by Terman (given earlier in this text). It can be inferred from this table that Ramesh with his I.Q. of 120 can be adjudged as superior.

(iii) For interpreting in another way, Ramesh's original score of 53 was converted into stanine score. Ramesh is the student of VIII class, hence for his scores of 53, his stanine score was computed as 6. Now this stanine score of 6 was converted into grade and it was bright according to the interpretation given in the test manual (It has been also mentioned right on the page of answer sheet). Judging on this line of interpretation also, Ramesh can be adjudged as superior or bright.

Conclusion

Ramesh may be adjudged as a bright superior child in terms of his intellectual capacities on the basis of the present test. This fact may be further ascertained with the help of some other measure of intelligence.

Non-Verbal Intelligence Test

The non-verbal intelligence test can be used for testing the intelligence of a subject in the following way.

Objective

To test the intelligence of a subject with the help of a non-verbal intelligence test.

Needed test material and environmental situations

(i) A copy of the (CIE) Non-verbal Group Test of Intelligence containing practice booklet, test booklet and test manual.

(ii) A subject under testing.

(iii) Appropriate and conducive environment and facilities for the administration of the test.

(iv) A stop watch.

Identifying data of the subject

Name of the Subject :	Satish
	Name of the School
Date of Birth : 15.8.2002	Govt. High School,
Class : VII : Age : 11 years	Rohtak

Description of the test

This test was originally designed and constructed by J.W. Jenkins. Here we are using its Hindi adaptation prepared and standardized by Central Institute of Education (CIE), New Delhi. It can be used only with the Hindi speaking, school-going Indian children. This test contains the pictorial items as given below:

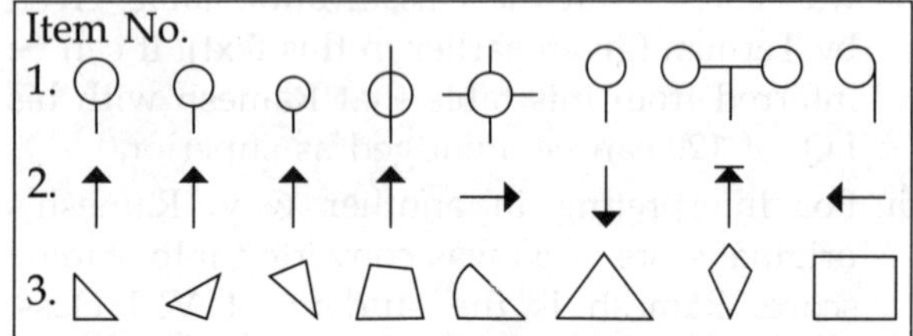

For responding to these items, instructions like below are issued to the examinees.

"The three figures in each lines (rows) given on the left hand side are somewhat similar. On the right hand side, there lie five figures. One of these five belongs to the family of the three given on the left hand side. You have to locate and mark its serial no. (i), (ii), (iii), (iv) or (v) on the answer-sheet against the S. No. of the item."

The test material used in this test can be divided into three main components: (i) Practice Booklet, (ii) Test Booklet, and (iii) Test manual.

Administration of the test

The subject was made to feel comfortable and a good rapport was established with him and he was made acquainted with the objective of the testing. The administration of this test was done in the following two phases:

(a) Preliminary practice test.

(b) The main proper test.

Administration of the Preliminary Practice Test

It was done in the following steps:

(i) The subject was given the preliminary practice test booklet and instructed not to open it unless asked to do so.

(ii) He was then asked to carefully read the instructions given in this booklet. The same was again well-explained to him and he was instructed to follow them carefully. He was also told that he should strictly follow the time schedule. He must begin and end the moment he is asked to do so.

(iii) The subject was then asked to begin responding to questions related to Group 1. After two minutes he was asked to stop responding. For moving further he was asked to respond to the questions related to group II, III, IV and V one by one by following the time schedule to the questions related to a single group.

(iv) Thus, after 10 minutes, the practice test booklet was taken back from him. It was not scored but the subject was not told that practice test is not scored.

Administration of the Proper Test

The proper test was administered by keeping the following points in consideration:

(i) After 10 minutes the subject was given proper test booklet. He was instructed not to open it unless asked to do so.

(ii) He was then asked to carefully read the instructions given on the first page of the booklet. The same was explained to him again verbally.

(iii) He was then asked to begin with responding to questions belonging to different groups starting from group I to V by strictly sticking to the following time schedule for responding to the questions of a particular group.

Sub-tests of Group	*Page*	*Time*
I	2 pages	5 minutes
II	2 pages	5 minutes
III	2 pages	5 minutes
IV	2 pages	5 minutes
V	3 pages	10 minutes
	Total Time = 30 minutes	

(iv) After 30 minutes, he was asked to hand over the proper test booklet to the examiner.

Scoring of the response

The responses of the subject were scored with the help of the scoring key by assigning one mark to correct responses and zero for the incorrect, incomplete and ambiguous answers, i.e. providing no or more than one answer. The total scores were thus computed as under:

Sub-test or group	I	II	III	IV	V	Total score
Scores	10	11	13	13	8	57

These test scores were then converted into standard scores with the help of the conversion table provided in the manual. (This table provides the standard scores for the scores earned in the test separately for boys and girls in view of their different ages and grades with a mean of 100 and S.D. as 15).

Summary of Results

The total scores	Age-wise	Grade-wise
Obtained in the test	Standard Scores	Standard Scores
57	125	130

Interpretation of the results

By comparing the standard scores of 125 and 130 with the mean and S.D. of the standardized group, we can come to the conclusion that our subject Satish is quite an intelligent boy. By taking into consideration the percentile values of 125 and 130, we can have some more ground for the verification of his good intelligence.

Aptitude Measurement

Introduction

We usually come across individuals who are found to excel in one or the other sphere of everyday life. It may be attributed on account of many factors or reasons. One such important reason may lie in their possession of certain specific abilities or aptitudes more than others due to which they acquire more success in certain fields.

Therefore, simply put, aptitude may be considered as the special ability or specific capacity of an individual, other than his general intellectual capacities, interests, life opportunities, hard work, etc., which help him acquire a required degree of proficiency or achievement in a specific field.

So, if we can determine the range of aptitudes of our children, in different fields, it may help us a lot in planning and organizing proper educational and vocational guidance and counseling services to them. We can surely predict that a particular child has abilities or aptitude for doing a particular job or judging a particular subject. Hence, it will be quite beneficial for him if he chooses that particular subject or vocation.

Judging in this way, the measurement of the aptitudes of the children becomes a necessity in the field of education, psychology and guidance. As a student of psychology you must also be well-versed in the measurement of aptitudes.

Measurement of Aptitude

The students may possess different types of aptitudes like mechanical aptitude, musical aptitude, artistic aptitude, aptitude for learning a particular subject and getting success in a particular profession or vocation etc. These aptitudes can be measured through various types of specific aptitude tests. For example, if we intend to know for a student of XII class about his level of teaching, we have to take the help of suitable standardized teaching aptitude test for this purpose. Such measurement of his teaching aptitude may then help us to take a judgement about whether or not he should take admission in a teacher-training course. Similar guidance can also be provided to other students choosing engineering, medical, computer or management courses on the basis of the measurement of their aptitudes with the help of relevant aptitude tests.

Measurement of Aptitude with the Help of an Aptitude Test

To illustrate the process of measurement of aptitude, we would like to use a teaching aptitude test for measuring teaching aptitude of a subject here. The use of the test along with its reporting can be done in the following way.

Objective

To find about the teaching aptitude of a subject with the application of a teaching aptitude test.

Test material and environmental situations:

(i) A copy of the teaching aptitude test constructed and standardized by Dr. R.P. Singh and Dr. S.N. Sharma containing test booklet, answer-sheet and test manual.

(ii) A subject whose teaching aptitude is to be measured.

(iii) Proper environmental situations and facilities for conducting the test.

Identifying data of the subject

Name : Arti Sharma	Age : 17 years
Name of the School :	Date of Testing : 8.9.2005
Govt. Girls Hr. Sec. School, Rohtak	Class : XII

Description of the test

The present test named as Teaching Aptitude Test Battery has been constructed and standardized by Dr. R.P. Singh and Dr. S.N. Sharma of Patna University, Patna (Bihar). It has been published by National Psychological Corporation, Agra. This test can only be employed with the Hindi speaking testees. Its objective is to test the teaching aptitude of teachers working in elementary schools or those who wish to intend to become elementary school teachers in the near future. In this sense, it can be used as a measure of selecting trainees for the J.B.T. or Diploma in Education Teacher's training course. Test material of this test can be divided into three sections for the necessary description.

Test Booklet

It is meant to provide necessary instructions to the examinee regarding answering the questions (test items) given in this test booklet on a separate answer sheet. The title page of this booklet contains the names of the test, author and the publisher along with the necessary instructions regarding the test. The next 16 pages of this booklet contain test item. This test has its five sub-tests each having a special type of test item. In the first sub-test, there are 32 items, in the second 20, 28 each in third and fourth and 12 in the fifth. In this way, there are 120 total test items (questions) in this aptitude test. In the beginning of the each section (sub-test), the necessary instructions for responding to the items in the sub-test are given for the benefit of the examinees. The nature of the items and instruction related to each sub-test or section is hereby illustrated by reproducing some sample items from this aptitude test.

खंड 1. प्रश्न 1 सूची 'क' में रिक्त स्थान की पूर्ति हेतु सूची 'ख' में अंकित शब्दों में से किसी एक उपयुक्त शब्द को उत्तर पर लिखें -

सूची क   सूची ख

पान : हरा दूध : ? गाय, बकरी, उजला, मीठा

प्रश्न 25 एक बिजली की गाड़ी पूना से मुम्बई जा रही है। हवा पश्चिम की ओर बह रही है तो गाड़ी का धुआँ किस ओर उड़ेगा?

खंड 2: प्रश्न 2 यदि आप प्रश्न से बिल्कुल सहमत हैं तो उत्तर में 5 को यदि सहमत हैं तो 4 को यदि उदासीन हैं तो 3 को, यदि असहमत हैं तो 2 को तथा बिल्कुल असहमत हों तो 1 को गोले से घेरें।

शिक्षकों के स्नेह के कारण बच्चे बिगड़ सकते हैं।

खंड 3: प्रश्न 4 मान लीजिए कोई शिक्षक प्रतिदिन देर से आता है। क्या आप,

(क) उन्हें समय पर आने की राय देंगे?

(ख) विद्यालय प्राचार्य को सूचित करेंगे?

(ग) अन्य शिक्षकों के सामने उन्हें लज्जित करेंगे?

(घ) छात्रों तथा अभिभावकों में इसका प्रचार करेंगे?

खंड 4: प्रश्न 2 शिक्षक में विज़य का अच्छा ज्ञान आवश्यक है, इसलिए कि-

(क) वे छात्रों को अपने बस में रख सकें।

(ख) वे छात्रों की शंकाओं का समाधान कर सकें।

खंड 5: प्रश्न 2 आपने अध्यापन पेशा अपनाया है, क्योंकि

(क) आपके पिता शिक्षक थे।

(ख) आपके कॉलेज (प्रशिक्षण संस्थानों) में पढ़ने का साधन था।

(ग) आप शिक्षक बनना चाहते थे।

(घ) आपको कोई अन्य नौकरी नहीं मिली।

Answer-Sheet

There are two pages in the answer-sheet. On the top of the Ist page, there are various columns meant for collecting identifying data of the subject. It is to be filled by the subject before responding to the test items. The remaining space of the Ist page contains the serial number of the test items or questions related to sections or sub-items I and II, alongwith the spaces for writing responses to these items. (Questions in one column and the space for answers in the other). On the second page of this answer sheet, there is appropriate provision for the serial no. of the questions related to section III, IV and V and the needed space for writing responses of these questions by choosing one alternative out of the given four.

Test Manual

It is meant for the examiner or test administrator. It mentions all about the need of constructing this test, procedure for construction, its standardization, reliability and ability and validity of the test, its main objectives, purposes and all about the application and administration of this test. It clearly explains the process of administration, scoring, interpretation and drawing conclusions on the basis of one's scores in this test. There is a scoring key for marking the responses of the examinees in this manual. Besides this, it also contains the necessary norms for converting original scores into standard scores and percentiles.

Administration of the test

The test was administered in the following ways:

(i) Environmental situations were so arranged as to provide quite congenial environment for the administration of the test. The subject was made to feel quite at home and comfortable. The essential rapport was established and he was made aware of the objective of testing.

(ii) He was then given test booklet and answer-sheet. It was clearly told to him that he was not to write anything on the booklet or damage it in any way.

(iii) Then, he was asked to carefully read the instructions given in the test booklet. These were also clearly explained to him by the examiner.

(iv) The subject was clearly told that the five sub-tests of this aptitude test are not all alike. They contain items of different nature. They have to be responded in different ways. For understanding the nature of these items and the method of providing responses, illustrations were given in the beginning of the each sub-test or section. The subject was instructed to read all the instructions carefully and then respond accordingly. Although there is no time limit for the completion of this test, subject should finish his work as early as possible. On an average, this test takes about 90 minutes.

(v) During the administration of the test, it was ensured that the subject provided all information related to identifying data and gave responses to all the 120 items of the test on the given answer-sheet. It was also seen that he gave only one response to each test item. The incompleteness in any way was removed by asking him to do so. After such thorough inspection, the answer-sheet and test booklet were taken from the subject.

Scoring of the responses

Help was taken from the scoring key given in the test manual for scoring the responses of the subject. The scoring work so done can be presented as below:

Sub-tests	I	II	III	IV	V	Whole test
Raw Scores	19	13	16	15	8	71

Interpretation of the test scores

For the interpretation of the test scores, help was taken from the norms given in the form of standard scores and percentiles in the manual. Our subject scored 71 marks in the present aptitude test. These original scores were subjected to conversion as below:

Raw Scores	Standard Scores	Percentile
71	116.42	P80

The level of the teaching aptitude of our subject can now be properly interpreted with the help of his standard scores and percentile.

Our subject has 116.42 as his standard scores. The similar standard scores can be computed for other candidates. It may then help to prepare a merit list for selecting the candidates for a teacher training course or their recruitment as a teacher.

Our subject's percentile is P80. This knowledge can help us locate where does this boy stand in the group in relation to other candidates. The percentile P80 clearly indicates that only 20 per cent of the boys from the whole group possess more teaching aptitude potential in comparison to him. In this respect, he is superior to 80 per cent candidates of the group.

Assessment of Personality

Introduction

In general, we have quite a lot of misconception about the term 'personality'. We often say 'poor' or 'magnetic' personality on the basis of one's outward appearance or behaviour. It is a very superficial approach. We must have a total picture of a person for the assessment of his personality. This picture should include all the aspects of his personality in physical, mental, social, emotional, moral and aesthetic dimensions, and the nature of his total behaviour, inner and outer, conscious and unconscious, in all the three cognitive and affective domains. Consequently, it is proper to say that personality is all that a person is in his total self.

To throw light on its meaning and nature, various scholars and psychologists have tried to define the term 'personality' in their own ways. The definitions given by Allport, Cattle and Eysenck are quite mentionable and popular among these definitions. Through the study of these popular definitions, we can reach the conclusion that personality is such a complex blend or organization of one's psychophysical systems—body, mind and soul, which provides him an identity of his own through his unique style of living and making adjustment with his self and the environment.

Here question may arise as to how can we know about one's personality for labeling or describing it as good or poor. It can be done through various methods and techniques available for the assessment of one's personality like observation, questionnaire and inventories, interview and various other projective techniques and tests. How these tests and techniques may be employed for the assessment of one's personality can be understood through an example given in the following text. Here we are making use of a personality inventory for the assessment of a subject.

Assessment of the personality of an individual through personality test

The administration and reporting work of the assessment of the personality of an individual can be done by the following steps discussed below:

Objectives

To assess the personality of a subject with the help of a written verbal test of personality

Required Test Material and Environmental Situations

(i) A copy of the Personality Dimensional Test constructed and standardized by Dr. S.P. Kulshrestha and R.P. Kothiyal containing test booklet, answer-sheet, scoring key and test manual.

(ii) The subject whose personality is to be assessed.

(iii) The appropriate and congenial environmental situations for the proper administration of the test.

Identifying data of the subject

Name of the Subject : Arun	Name of the School
Age : 15 years	DAV School, Rohtak
Date of the testing : 10.8.2005	Class : X

Description of the test material

This test named as Personality Dimensional Test has been devised and standardized by Dr. S.P. Kulshrestha and R.P. Kothiyal for the assessment of the personality of Hindi speaking, school-going students of not more than 16 years old. It has been published by ISPT, Dehradun and can be employed both in individual or group tests for testing one's personality in 12 dimensions. The main components of the test material can be divided and explained as under:

Test Booklet

The title page contains the name of the test, the authors of the test, the name and address of the publisher, and so on. On the second page, there are 10 instructions meant for the examinees regarding the test. In the third page, there is an illustration to explain the way of responding to the items of the test. In the pages four to seven, there are 122 test items or questions. Every question is in the form of a compound sentence containing contradictory statements joined by 'or'. The subject is to select any one of these statements (lying left or right) which appears true for describing his self and marking in the left or right boxes. Such test items (originally in Hindi) are of the following nature:

1. I easily get angry or I take the steps after careful consideration.
2. I usually remain happy or I become happy and sad quite soon.
3. I begin to weep soon or I live my life laughing.
4. The numbers 22, 25, 28 should be followed by 38 or 31.

Answer-Sheet

The top portion of this sheet is meant for collecting identifying data from the subject. In the remaining portion, there is a provision for writing responses for the all 122 items or questions. In the first column, there are serial numbers (from 1 to 122) of the test items and in the second, there is a provision of two blank rectangles. The subject has to tick in the left or right box to specify telling whether he considers the left or right statement of the item as true description of his self.

Answer Key

Every response is marked as one or zero in the way as shown in the given answer key or sheet. It is of the following nature:

0	1
□	□
1	0
□	□

In case the subject marks the left box, he will earn zero score but if he puts it in the right box he will be awarded a score of 1. In Q. No. 2, the scoring will be just reverse. The test has a total of 122 items or questions to assess 12 personality dimensions. To facilitate the process or computation, scoring is not made for two questions (S. No. 31 and 32). Remaining 120 questions are scored and divided into 10 groups. Each group consists of 10 items. The total scores of these 10 items called factor score provide assessment for one of the factors or dimensions associated with one's personality.

Test Manual

In the test manual, the authors of the test have mentioned the objectives and purposes of the construction of the test, the procedure of construction and standardization, the ways of the test administration, scoring and interpretation etc. This test manual is meant for the examiner.

Administration of the Test

The following steps were taken for the proper administration of the test.

(i) The subject was made to feel quite at home by providing congenial environment and establishing a proper rapport. He was made to realize that it was not a testing or examination for ascertaining something good or bad about his personality but to know about his liking or disliking about certain behaviour acts. He was to show his liking by marking the statements written on the left and right sides of the word 'or'.

(ii) The subject was asked to carefully read all the instructions about the test and he was also helped to understand the way of responding to all the 122 test items through the help of an illustration.

(iii) He was allowed to respond freely to all the 122 items. It was well assured that he had responded to all these items by putting mark on the assigned places. It was also examined that he had not written anything on the test booklet or damaged it in any way. Once completed, both the test booklet and the answer-sheets were taken back from the subject.

Scoring of the responses

Scoring was done with the help of the scoring key. Score of 1 or 0 was awarded to the mark put up by the subject in the left or the right rectangular box strictly on the basis of what was written on the top of the mark. The scores of 10 questions were then totaled for computing the total scores of the Dimension or Factors. In this way 10 Factor Scores were computed and tabulated as under:

S. No. questions and the total of their responses		*Name of the Factor*
Total for the responses of the questions 1 to 10 =	5	A
Total for the responses of the questions 11 to 20 =	6	B
Total for the responses of the questions 21 to 30 =	5	C
Total for the responses of the questions 33 to 42 =	8	D
Total for the responses of the questions 43 to 52 =	7	E
Total for the responses of the questions 53 to 62 =	8	F
Total for the responses of the questions 63 to 72 =	5	G
Total for the responses of the questions 73 to 82 =	5	H
Total for the responses of the questions 83 to 92 =	6	I
Total for the responses of the questions 93 to 102 =	7	J
Total for the responses of the questions 103 to 112 =	8	K
Total for the responses of the questions 113 to 122 =	5	L

Interpretation of the Test Scores: It was done as under:

(i) The factor scores were converted into stanine scores. In this task due help was taken from the conversion table provided in the manual.

Table for converting factor-wise Raw Score into Stanine

Stanine Scores	*Factor*	*I*	*II*	*III*	*IV*	*V*	*VI*	*VII*	*VIII*	*IX*
5	A	0	1	2	3	4	5	6	7	8–10
6	B	0–1	2	3	4	5–6	7	8	10	10
5	C	0	1	2–3	4	5	6	7	8–9	10
8	D	0	1	2	3	4	5	6	7–8	9–10
7	E	–	0	1	2	3	4–5	6	7	8–10
8	F	0–2	3	4	5–6	7	8	9	–	10
5	G	0–1	2	3	4	5	6	7	8–9	10
5	H	0–1	2	3	4	5	6	7	8	9–10

6	I	0–2	3	–	4	5	6–7	8	9	10
7	J	0	1	2	3–4	5	6	7–8	9	10
8	K	0	1	2	3–4	5–6	7	8	9	10
5	L	0–1	2	3	4	5	6	7	8–9	10

In this way, the stanine scores of our subjects along with their original factor scores can be tabulated as under:

Stanine Scores Average

I	II	III	IV	V		VI	VII	VIII	IX
...	...	...	...	...	A	...	..	..	..
...	...	...	...	...	B	...	..	..	..
...	...	...	...	...	C	...	..	..	..
...	...	...	...	...	D	...	..	..	..
...	...	...	...	...	E	...	..	..	..
...	...	...	...	...	F	...	..	..	..
...	...	...	...	...	G	...	..	..	..
...	...	...	...	...	H	...	..	..	..
...	...	...	...	...	I	...	..	..	..
...	...	...	...	...	J	...	..	..	..

Factor	*A*	*B*	*C*	*D*	*E*	*F*	*G*	*H*	*I*	*J*	*K*	*L*
Total Scores	5	6	5	8	7	8	5	5	6	7	8	5
Stanine Score	VI	V	V	VIII	VIII	VI	V	V	VI	VII	VII	V

(II) These stanine scores were then used to describe the personality traits of the subject on the following pattern as suggested in the manual. This pattern is being produced below:

Low Score Description	**I**	**II**	**III**	**IV**	**V**	**Stanine Scores Average**	**VI**	**VII**	**VIII**	**IX**	**High Score Description**
Emotionally Less stable	...	...	...	...	...	A	...	...	...	...	Emotionally More stable
Submissive	...	...	...	...	...	B	...	...	...	...	Dominant
Inactive	...	...	...	...	...	C	...	...	...	...	Over active
Less Intelligence	...	...	...	...	...	D	...	...	...	...	More Intelligence
Introvert	...	...	...	...	...	E	...	...	...	...	Extrovert
Tensed	...	...	...	...	...	F	...	...	...	...	Relaxed
Poor Mental Health	...	...	...	...	...	G	...	...	...	...	Good Mental Health
Poor Adjustment	...	...	...	...	...	H	...	...	...	...	Good Adjustment
Insecured	...	...	...	...	...	I	...	...	...	...	Secured
Superstitious	...	...	...	...	...	J	...	...	...	...	Non-Superstitious
Less Creative	...	...	...	...	...	K	...	...	...	...	More Creative
Low Moral ability	...	...	...	...	...	L	...	...	...	...	High Moral ability

Now with the help of the above pattern, we can use the stanine scores (for the original factor scores) of our subject for describing personality traits factor-wise, as below:

Factor	*Stanine Score*	*Personality Traits*
A	VI	Emotionally more Stable
B	V	Dominant and Assertive
C	V	Over active
D	VIII	More Intelligent
E	VIII	Extrovert
F	VI	Relaxed
G	V	Good Mental Health
H	V	Good Adjustment
I	VI	Secured
J	VII	Non-Superstitious
K	VII	More creative
L	V	High Moral ability

Measurement of Adjustment

Introduction

What is known as 'adaptation' in biological sciences is termed as 'adjustment' in the subject psychology. According to Darwin's theory of evolution, our life represents a continuous chain of struggle for our existence and survival. In this struggle only the species, which tried to adapt to the changing demands of the environment, were able to survive while others who did not adapt completely suffered their extinction. In this way, if we want to live or live in a better way in this physical world, we have to adapt ourselves all the demands of our physical environment. However, man is somewhat different from other species. He needs to live well physically as well as socially and psychologically. For him the psychological survival is as much essential as his physical survival. Therefore, the term adaptation used for biological or physical survival is somewhat small and narrow for the description of the physical, social and psychological survival of the human being. Therefore, it has been now replaced by a more comprehensive term 'adjustment'.

Adjustment, in this way, refers to the state of one's body and mind in which he remains adapted to the physical and socio-psychological demands of his self and the environment. In this way, for one's adjustment, the satisfaction of his self and his environmental needs are quite essential. One remains adjusted as long as his basic needs are gratified or he has a hope for their gratification. Once this balance is disturbed or seems to be in danger, the individual gets maladjusted resulting in the deterioration of his mental health.

In this way, while a good adjustment to one's self and the environment is the key to one's good mental and physical health and the overall well-being of the individual, the maladjustment may drift him towards abnormal behaviour and poor mental health. The welfare of our children thus lies in seeking proper adjustment with their self and the environment. Since prevention is said to be better than cure, our efforts should be directed towards knowing well about the adjustment level of our children well in time. It is equally true for the children. They must also know their adjustment level with their self and the environment.

Hence, we must be acquainted with the measures of adjustment. The use of adjustment inventories in this direction has been found quite practicable. There are various inventories available for measuring the adjustment of the individuals belonging to different ages, grades, professions, and categories. For example, we have inventories for measuring the adjustment of school-going children, college-going students, adults, teachers, and so on. We are illustrating here the task of the measurement of adjustment with the help of an inventory meant for measuring the adjustment of college students.

Measurement of Adjustment by Using Inventory

The measurement of adjustment with the help of a suitable adjustment inventory can be done and reported through the following steps:

Objective: To measure the adjustment of a college student with the help of an adjustment inventory

Needed test material and environmental situations

(i) A subject (studying in a college) whose adjustment we want to measure.

(ii) A copy of the adjustment inventory (meant for college students) divised by Dr. A.K.P. Sinha and Dr. R.P. Singh which includes a test booklet, answer-sheet and test manual.

(iii) The proper congenial environment and facilities for the administration of the test.

Identifying data of the subject

Name : Somesh Institution : Vaish College, Rohtak
Age : 17 years Class : XII
Sex : Male Date of Testing : 10th September, 2005
Occupation of Father : Service
Income : Rs. 4,000 per month

Description of the test material

This inventory has been devised by Dr. A.K.P. Sinha and Dr. R.P. Singh. It has been published by National Psychological Corporation, Agra. It can be used for measuring the adjustment of Hindi as well as English speaking college students. It measures their adjustment in five areas related to home, health, social, emotional and educational adjustments. The test material of this inventory can be divided and described as under:

Test Booklet

It contains 8 pages. The title or front page contains the name of the test, name of the authors and name and address of the publisher. Besides, there are instructions related to the administration of the test on the page. Nothing is written on the back of the front page. Similarly, the back cover page also does not have any thing written on it. In this way, the test items are given only on the pages 3 to 7. These are 102 in number. All the 102 items have been identified and marked with either of the five bracketed letters as (a), (b), (c), (d) or (e) written in front of them. Such identification is done for indicating that a particular item aims to measure one's adjustment in a particular area symbolized by that bracketed letter like home, health, social, emotional or educational. This booklet is a reusable one and hence examinees are instructed not to write anything on it. For response, they are provided an answer sheet. The test items are available in Hindi as well as in English.

Answer Sheet

It is given to the subject along with the test booklet. The top of this sheet is meant for collecting the identifying data from the subject. The rest of this sheet is meant for the responses of the subject. For this purpose, there are S. Nos. of the 102 test items in the left column and in the second column, there are two rectangular boxes printed in front of each item. On the top of these boxes, ye s or no is already written and one has to simply put mark in either of the boxes depending upon his response. The bottom of this answer sheet contains scoring table meant for the use of the examiner.

Test Manual

In this test manual, the authors of this inventory have described the need and objective of this inventory, the way of its preparation and standardization, the methods of administration, scoring and interpretation etc. Every examiner should carefully read this manual for the required success in his task.

Administration of the test

This inventory was administered to the subject in the following way:

(i) First of all care was taken for proper and congenial environment needed for the administration of the test. Then the subject was made to feel relaxed. A good rapport was established with him and he was made aware of the objective of the testing.
(ii) Then he was given a copy of the test booklet and an answer sheet.
(iii) Then he was asked to fill the columns meant for his identifying data. It was observed and assured that he had completed this work in a desired way.
(iv) Then he was asked to read the instructions given in the test booklet carefully. These were again well explained to him so that he might not feel any difficulty in responding to the test items.
(v) He was allowed to work at his own speed. It was fully taken care of that he provides his answer in yes or no by marking in the appropriate column. After the completion of the work, the test booklet and answer sheet were taken back from him. It was again ensured that he had not written anything on the test booklet and provided responses to all the test items.

Scoring of the responses

The responses of the subject were scored with the help of five transparent scoring keys provided in the test material of this inventory. Each of these scoring keys is used for scoring the responses of the items meant for measuring one's adjustment in a particular area. Hence the respective keys were employed for scoring the responses of the items identified and marked as (a), (b), (c), (d), or (e). For this purpose, we first made use of a key meant for scoring the items related to home adjustment. This transparency was placed on the answer sheet of the subject. We counted all the marks with the help of the circles of the key. The counting of these marks then provided us the home adjustment scores of our subject. Similar practice was adopted for the computation of the scores related to the other four adjustment areas.

The scores so computed were tabulated as under:

Areas of Adjustment	*Scores*
(a) Home Adjustment	7
(b) Health Adjustment	6
(c) Social Adjustment	10
(d) Emotional Adjustment	15
(e) Educational Adjustment	11
(f) General Adjustment	49

Interpretation of the test scores

It was done in the following two ways:

Interpretation through percentile norms

In the manual percentile norms tables were given separately for males and females. With their help, we converted the original scores of our subject (both Area wise and General Adjustment Scores) into percentiles. Percentiles thus computed and conclusions then derived for our subject can be summarized as under. It is also to be remembered that this inventory provides one's maladjustment scores meaning thereby that more the scores one gets, more maladjusted he is.

- Our subject Somesh scored 7 in the area of home adjustment. By consulting table 3 of the manual, we converted his raw scores of 7 into the percentile value P80. The percentile value P80 clearly reveals that in this area of adjustment, there are only 20% students who are more maladjusted than him.
- The same is true for his adjustment in the area of health adjustment, social adjustment and educational adjustment where our subject has earned the same percentile value i.e. P80 (on the basis of his original scores in these area as 6, 10 and 11 respectively).
- In the area of emotional adjustment, the original scores of our subject is 15. The percentile value of this score is P80. It means that he has somewhat less maladjustment in this area is comparison to all the other areas of adjustment. However, in this area also, only 30% students are more maladjusted than him.
- In terms of total general adjustment, our subject's score is 49. The percentile value of this score, known from the conversion table, is more than P80. In this way, he may be adjudged as quite maladjusted even in terms of his total general adjustment.

Interpretation through Adjustment Categories

Tables of the manual help in converting the raw scores (Total General Adjustment Scores and Areawise Adjustment Scores) of the male and female subjects into some specific adjustment categories for describing them as Excellent, Good, Average, Unsatisfactory or Very Unsatisfactory in terms of their level of adjustment. We took the necessary help from both these tables for the interpretation of the respective original scores of our subject. The results may be summarized as below:

	Adjustment Area	*Raw Scores*	*Adjaustment Description*	*Adjustment Categories*
(a)	Home Adjustment	7	C	Average
(b)	Health Adjustment	6	D	Unsatisfactory
(c)	Social Adjustment	10	D	Unsatisfactory
(d)	Emotional Adjustment	15	C	Average
(e)	Educational Adjustment	11	D	Unsatisfactory
General Adjustment		49	D	Unsatisfactory

Discussion

Somesh is average and normal in terms of his adjustment in the areas of home and emotional adjustment. However, in all the other three areas of adjustment—health, social and educational—his level of adjustment is unsatisfactory. In terms of total general adjustment also, his level of adjustment is unsatisfactory. In this way, it may be concluded that he is not properly adjusted with his self and the environment.

Conclusion

With the result of the administration of the present adjustment inventory, it can be concluded that our subject Somesh is not properly adjusted with his self and the environment. He is the victim of maladjustment. Therefore, attempts should be made to help him in his proper adjustment by finding out the root causes of his maladjustment.

Measurement of Attitudes

Introduction

Our attitudes play quite a significant role in shaping our behaviour and personality make-up. The nature of our reactions and responses towards things, ideas or persons depends much on the formation of our attitudes towards them. As a matter of definition, we may understand by the term attitude a determining acquired tendency which prepares us to behave in a certain way towards a specific object or class of objects, subject to the conditions prevailing in the environment. Consequently if we keep positive and favourable attitude towards an object, we will be attracted towards it, admire it and try to achieve it. On the other hand, if we have a negative or unfavourable attitude towards it, we will try to avoid it and even feel hostile towards it. Summing in this way, we can conclude that attitudes are, to a great extent, responsible for the particular behaviour of a person towards an object, idea or person.

Measurement of Attitudes

Attitudes are learned behaviour. What type of attitude, favourable or unfavourable, positive or negative one possess towards an object, idea or person is a thing of investigation. Its objective assessment needs a type of measurement that can help us to determine to some extent in a reliable and accurate way the nature of one's attitude towards a given object, idea or person. It needs the administration of a properly constructed and standardized attitude scale. Research workers and investigators have devised a number of attitude scales for the measurement of one's attitude towards a number of objects, ideas or persons. Let us learn the way of measuring one's attitude towards a thing with the help of a practical illustration given ahead.

Measurement of Attitude with the Help of an Attitude Scale

To illustrate the process of measurement of attitude, we would like to use an attitude scale here for measuring one's attitude towards science. The use of this test alongwith its reporting can be done in the following way.

Objective

To find out the attitude of a subject towards science with the help of an attitude scale.

Test material and environmental situation

(i) A copy of the Science Attitude scale constructed and standardized by Mrs. Avinash Grewal, containing test manual and test booklet cum answer sheet.

(ii) A subject whose attitude towards science we want to measure.

(iii) Proper environmental situations and facilities for conducting the test.

Identifying data of the subject

Name :	Aruna Verma
Age :	16 years
Name of the School :	Girls Hr. Secondary School, Rohtak
Date of Testing :	8-2-2006
Class :	X

Description of the test

The present test named as Science Attitude Scale has been constructed and standardized by Mrs. Avinash Grewal, Lecturer Regional College of Education, Bhopal. It has been published by National Psychological Corporation, Agra. It has both English and Hindi version and thus can be used with the English as well as Hindi speaking testees. Its objective is to measure the attitude of the individual students towards science so that we can guide them in their selection of the subjects for their future study or professions.

The test material of this attitude scale may be divided into two sections for the necessary description.

Test Booklet cum Answer Sheet

It consists of two pages (one for English speaking and the other for Hindi speaking testees). The top contains space for the identifying data of the subject like his name, class, age, sex, school or college etc. It is followed by necessary directions regarding getting response of the test or scale items from the testees. Below, there are 20 statements for measuring one's attitude towards science. One has to provide one's degree of agreement or disagreement through the five alternatives ranging from strongly agree to strongly disagree by encircling his chosen option. These directions along with 12 statements (out of 20) are reproduced below to give an idea about the nature of the material of the test booklet cum answer-sheet of the Science Attitude Scale.

Directions

Given below are some statements about science. Some of these statements describe how you might feel about science. We are interested in knowing your valuable opinion about science as a subject of study. You may agree with some of the statement, carefully decide whether or not you agree with the statement.

If you agree strongly with a statement, put a circle (O) around the category SA (Strongly Agree); if you agree, put a circle around A (Agree); if you undecided, put a circle around U (Undecided); if you disagree, put a circle around D (Disagree); and if you strongly disagree, put a circle around SD (Strongly Disagree).

You are requested to give your free and frank opinion.

1.	Scientists are persons without human considerations.	SA	A	U	D	SD
2.	Scientific careers are more useful to the society than other careers.	SA	A	U	D	SD
3.	Study of science subjects is rather a dull affairs.	SA	A	U	D	SD
4.	Other subjects cannot be properly understood without the knowledge of science.	SA	A	U	D	SD
5.	Science subjects are very difficult to study.	SA	A	U	D	SD
6.	Science subjects are more exact than others.	SA	A	U	D	SD
7.	Science is bound to lead our society to Godlessness.	SA	A	U	D	SD
8.	Science subjects provide more recreation than other subjects.	SA	A	U	D	SD
9.	Scientific knowledge alone cannot improve a man's life.	SA	A	U	D	SD
10.	Science sharpens our reasoning power and logical thinking.	SA	A	U	D	SD
11.	Science fails to solve all our problems.	SA	A	U	D	SD
12.	Science subjects are useful for getting success in competitive examinations.	SA	A	U	D	SD

Test Manual

It is meant for the examiner or test administrator. It mentions all about the need of constructing the attitude scale, procedure for its construction, and standardization, reliability and validity of the measurement through this scale, its main objectives, purposes and all about the application of this scale etc. It clearly explains the process of administration scoring interpretation and drawing conclusion on the basis of one's score on this scale. It provides guidance for scoring each item of the scale on the basis of one's degree of agreement or disagreement to the given 20 items. Besides this, it also contains the necessary norms for converting original raw scores into standard scores and percentiles.

Administration of the test

The Test was administered in the following way:

(i) Environmental situations were so arranged that provided quite a congenial environment for the administration of the test. The subject was made to feel quite at home and comfortable. The essential rapport was established and she was made aware of the objective of testing.

(ii) She was then given test booklet cum answer-sheet. She was asked to first fill up the identifying data and then carefully read the given instruction carefully before responding to the 20 statements of the scale. The same was also verbally explained to her. The procedure of encircling her choice out of the five alternative was clearly emphasized and demonstrated to her.

(iii) She was told that she had to respond to each and every statement given in this scale. Although there is no time limit for the completion of the test, subject was asked to finish her work as early as possible. On an average it takes about 5 minutes to explain the test and the subject required about 15 minutes for giving responses to the 20 times of the scale.

(iv) During the administration of the test, it was ensured that the subject provided all information related to the identifying data and gave responses to all the 20 items of the scale by properly encircling her choice. It was also seen that she gave only one response to a scale item. The incompleteness in anyway was removed by asking her to do so. After such thorough inspection, the test booklet cum answer sheet was taken from the subject.

Scoring of the responses

Scoring work of the responses of the subject was carried out by observing the following procedure given in the manual.

Each of the even numbered positive items (No. 2, 4, 6, 8, 10, 12, 14, 16, 18, 20) of the scale were assigned a weight ranging from 4 (strongly agree) to zero (thoroughly disagree). In the case of the remaining ten odd numbers negative items (S. No. 1, 3, 5, 7, 9, 11, 13, 15, 17, 19) the scale scoring was reversed ranging from zero (thoroughly agree) to 4 (strongly disagree). In this way, for our subject her total score on this science attitude scale was obtained by summating her scores for the individual items. Computing in this way, our subject Aruna got her individual and total scores on the attitude scale as below:

Item No.	1	2	3	4	5	6	7	8	9	10
Scores	(4)	(1)	(3)	(3)	(1)	(3)	(3)	(1)	(1)	(4)
Item No.	11	12	13	14	15	16	17	18	19	20
Scores	(3)	(1)	(4)	(4)	(3)	(1)	(4)	(4)	(3)	(4)

Total of all individual items Scores = 55.

Interpretation of the test scores

For the interpretation of the test scores, help was taken from the tables 1 and 2 given in the test manual. Table 1 helped in converting the raw score (original total score earned by our subject on the scale) into percentile rank (PRS). The table 2 provided norms for interpreting the attitude of our subject towards science in terms of her position in the standardized population along with a verbal description of her behaviour (related to her attitude towards science).

Both the tables are presented here for the purpose of required information and illustration.

Table 19.1: Percentile Rank (PRS) Equivalent to the Raw Scores

Percentile Rank	*Raw Score*	*Percentile Rank*	*Raw Score*
Above 99	*Above 65*	*Rank 33*	46
99	64	30	45
98	63	25	44
97	62	22	43
96	60–61	18	42
89	59	14	41
87	58	10	40
86	57	6	39
85	56	5	38
84	55	4	36–37
72	54	3	35
70	53	2	31–34
65	52	1	27–30
63	51	Less than 1	25–26
43	49		
40	48		
36	47		

Table 19.2 gives the complete norms of the scale in Percentile Ranks, Standard Scores and Stannic. Verbal description and interpretation of the rank obtained by a subject is also given in this table.

Table 19.2: The Various Norms of the SAS and Their Interpretation

Attitude Scores	*Range of PRS and standard scores (in brackets)*	*% of cases includeed*	*Stanine*	*Verbal Description*	*Interpretation*
65–64 and above	99 and above (+2.29 to +2.85)	1%	9	Superior	Extremely Favourable
60–64	96.28 – 99 (1.59 to +2.15)	5%	8	Above Average	Decidedly Favourable
55–59	84.08 – 89.20 (+0.89 to +1.45)	12%	7	Above Average	Fairly Favourable
50–54	60.12 – 72.72 (+0.18 to + 0.75)	24%	6	Average	Somewhat Favourable
45–49	30.24 – 42.40 (–0.52 to + 0.5)	30%	5	Average	Just Favourable
40–44	10.28 – 5.50 (–1.22 to – 0.66)	18%	4	Average	Somewhat Favourable
35–39	3.18 – 5.50 (–1.92 to – 1.36)	7%	3	Below Average	Unfavourable

30-34	1.16 - 1.96 (-2.63 to - 2.06)	2%	2	Below Average	Decidedly Unfavourable
25-29	0.0 - 1.0 (-3.33 to - 2.77)	1%	1	Low	Extremely Unfavourable

The attitude of our subject can now be interpreted in the light of her total scores earned on the Science Attitude Scale as below:

- Our subject earned 55 as the raw scores. Similar scores can be computed for other students desiring to seek admission to science section or any science subject related professional course. It may then help to prepare a merit list for their selection or providing vocational and educational guidance.
- The percentile rank (PRS) of our subject equivalent to her raw scores 55 is 84. The knowledge can help us to locate where our subject stands in the group in relation to other students. The percentile P84 clearly indicates that only 16 per cent students from the whole group possess more favourable attitude towards the science subject in comparison to her. She is superior in this respect to 84 per cent students of the group.
- The range of her standard scores (for the raw scores of 55) as read from the table is 0.89 to 1.45. The further interpretation of these standard scores reveals the following things about our subject.

She is above average in terms of her total scores earned on this science attitude scale and her attitude towards the subject science is fairly favourable.

Measurement of Creativity

Introduction

All of us possess creative abilities whether in lesser or greater amount. The creative process and its output is linked with creative thinking. One who can think creatively and constructively is sure to lead and progress well on the path of creativity. However, we may find wide individual differences regarding the abilities and capacity to think creatively and constructively and that is why only a few of us are recognized as creative, the one who can create, discover or produce a new idea or object (including the re-arrangement or reshaping of what is already known to us). The question then arises is that how can we identify the students or persons who can be labelled as creative? How can we say that a particular child possesses so much creativity? This is done through some tests or measures available for assessing the degree of the creativity level among the testees. Through these tests, we try to make an assessment of creativity like originality, fluency, inventiveness, flexibility, elaboration, divergent thinking, etc. Both verbal as well as non-verbal tests are available for the measurement of creativity. In the following pages, we would be illustrating the use of a creativity test for measuring the creativity level of a subject.

Illustrating the Use of Creativity Test

Objective

To determine the level of a subject by using a creativity test.

Identifying Data

Name of the subject :_________

Age :_________

Class : __________

School : ____________________

Name of the Experimenter : _______________

Dated : __________

Required Test Material and Environmental Situations

(i) The subject whose creativity level is to be identified.

(ii) A copy of creativity test standardized by Dr. Baquer Mehdi including a test booklet, scoring sheet, scoring guide and test manual.

(iii) The desirable situation and environment conductive to the administration of the test.

Description of Test Material

The present test has been prepared by Dr. Baquer Mehdi. It is a verbal test that attempts to measure the level of creativity held by an individual. It has been published by National Psychological Corporation, Agra. Its test material can be well understood by making a three-fold division like below:

Test booklet

The introductory page of the test booklet contains the essential directions regarding the administration of the test. The pages to follow contain problematic questions (along with the space for the responses) based on four different types of activities as below:

Activity I. If it happens, then

The following three problems are mentioned under this title.

1. What will happen if men begin to fly like birds?
2. What will happen if your school gets wheels?
3. What will happen if the need to consume food vanishes among human beings?

Enough space is provided for responses to each of these three unprobable events. If needed, the responses can be extended on extra sheets.

Activity II. Innovative use of the objects

The following three objectives have been mentioned and subjects are required to think and write the types of noble, strange and innovative unusual uses they can make of these three objects.

(i) A piece of the stone
(ii) Wooden stick
(iii) Water

Activity III. Discovering new relationships

The following three pairs are mentioned and subjects are required to discover new, noble and unusual relationships existing between them.

(i) Tree and house
(ii) Chair and the stair
(iii) Air and water

Activity IV. To make a given product or object more interesting, strange and playful

Here in this problematic task, the subject is given a horse play toy and asked to suggest how can it be made more interesting, strange and playful. The responses are to be written in the space provided in the test booklet.

In this way this test booklet serves the function of a question paper as well as the answer sheet and thus can be used only once.

Scoring sheet

This one page scoring sheet remains with the experimenter. Here he writes the scores of the subject's responses computed with the help of scoring guide (provided in the manual) in three different categories namely fluency, flexibility and originality separately and then compute their total for getting category-wise and composite scores.

Scoring guide

It is that part of the test manual which helps an experimenter to score the responses of the subject. With its help, the responses can be scored in terms of three categories namely, fluency, flexibility and originality.

Administration of the Test

It was conducted as under:

(i) The subject was allowed to sit comfortably and was told about the objective of the test.

(ii) He was given a test booklet and asked to go through the given instructions carefully.

(iii) The four types of tasks mentioned in the test were explained to him with regard to their problematic nature and type of responses required from the subject with the help of the illustrations given in the booklet.

(iv) He was specifically told about the time limit required for giving responses to the problems related to the four types of activities, *i.e.* 15 minutes for activity I, 12 minutes for activity II, 15 minutes for activity III and 6 minutes for activity IV.

(v) He was asked to hand over the test booklet after the expiry of the total time, *i.e.* 1 hour 18 minutes.

(vi) He was also given two or three extra sheets in case he required more space for responding to the test problems.

Scoring of the Test

It was done as per provision of the scoring guide by computing three types of scores: (i) Originality scores (ii) Fluency scores and (iii) Flexibility scores. The task was carried out as under:

Computation of originality weight for each response

In the scoring guide, all the probable responses of the given problems related to the four activities have been provided separate alphabetical categories as A, B, C, D, E, F ...and also given the name as (i) Effect on Transport and Travel (ii) Thrill of new experience (iii) Effect on Economy (iv) Effect on Sanitation (v) Saving of Life (vi) Destructive use etc. Therefore, at the time of scoring, the task of the scorer is to first find out the category (alphabet and title of the category) in which a particular response is falling and then read out the originality weight given to that category from the last column of the scoring guide table. A portion of the specimen of such scoring guide for the calculation of originality weight is reproduced as follows:

Table 19.3: Scoring Guide (List of Categories and the Responses on Verbal Test of Creativity)

Activity No.	*Item No.*	*Category Alphabet Serial*	*Category*	*Responses*	*Originality Weight*
I	1	A	Effect on	1. Disuse of vehicles	
Conse-			Transport	2. Disuse of aeroplanes	
quences			and Travel	3. Disuse of parachute	4
				4. Ease in travel	
If it	If man is	B	Effect on	1. Disuse of telephone	5
happens	able to		Communi	2. Disuse of postal	
then....	fly like		cation	communication	
	birds				
		C	Effect on	1. No walking	
			Living	2. Less privacy	1
			Habits	3. No use of stairs	2
				4. Living on trees possible	
				5. Need for tight clothes	
		D	Thrill of	1. Moon travel	4
			New	made easy	
			Experience	2. Travel to fairy	3
				land	
				3. Meeting with angels	
		E	Man-Bird	1. Competition	
			Relationship	between species	
				2. New friendships	2
				3. Hostility with birds	

The originality weight thus read from the scoring guide for each response of our subject were in this way entered on the score sheet. For the responses which were not present in the scoring guide for the computation of originality weight, the following procedure was adopted.

(i) Since originality is defined as uncommonness of a given response hence responses given by less than 5% of the group were to be treated as original (as per instructions given in the manual).

(ii) Then original weights were assigned as below:

Nature of ResponseOriginality weight

Responses given below 1% 5

Responses given below 2% 4

Responses given below 3% 3

Responses given below 4% 2

Responses given below 5% 1

Responses given by 5% or more 0

Scoring for fluency

Fluency in this test refers to the number of relevant and unrepeated ideas reflected through the responses of the subject. Consequently from the responses, an item found irrelevant and repeated was struck off and the ones remaining were counted and entered on the scoring sheet as the fluency score.

Scoring for flexibility

From the scoring guide, alphabetical serial of the category awarded to each response just as A, B, C, D, E etc. was noted down (for a response belonging to an entirely new category a new alphabet serial was given). Then flexibility score was computed by using the following formula.

Flexibility score = Total number of different alphabet serials used

Now proceeding as above, the originality, fluency and flexibility scores for different items belonging to each of the four activities or task I, II, III and IV were noted down on the scoring sheet. The specimen of the scoring sheet is given below:

Table 19.4: Scoring Sheet used in Creativity Test

	Fluency	Flexibility	Originality
Task or Activity I			
Item 1.	....	....	....
Item 2.	....	....	....
Item 3.	....	....	....
Total			
Task or Activity II			
Item 1.	....	....	....
Item 2.	....	....	....
Item 3.	....	....	....
Total			
Task or Activity III			
Item 1.	....	....	....
Item 2.	....	....	....
Item 3.	....	....	....
Total			
Task or Activity IV			
Item 1.	....	....	....
Item 2.	....	....	....
Item 3.	....	....	....
Total			
Score Summary			
Task of Activity I.	....	....	....
Task of Activity II.	....	....	....
Task of Activity III.	....	....	....
Task of Activity IV.			
Grand Total			

Interpretation of the Test Scores

Thus, we obtained three types of factor scores namely originality scores. Fluency scores and Flexibility scores of the subject along with the total creativity scores by summing up these three factor scores. These scores can now help us derive the desired conclusions regarding the creativity level of the subject in the manner detailed below:

1. The test manual contains the norms for interpreting the scores earned by a subject in the creativity test. We can safely interpret the earned scores of the subject in terms of these given norms and conclude about the creativity level of our subject.
2. In case we are administrating this creativity test to a subject or group of subjects not covered in the norms given in the test, e.g. a group of B.Ed. students, then you as an experimenter should yourself build up the required norms for the interpretation of the derived creativity scores. The adopted procedure for this purpose may be laid down as under:
   (i) Suppose you have administered this creativity test on a group of 100 B.Ed. students, then the first task is to compute three factors scores namely Originality scores, Fluency scores and Flexibility scores for the responses of all the students separately and enter them into respective score sheets.
   (ii) These raw scores on originality, fluency and flexibility are then converted into T scores (standard scores) by using the formula

$$T = \frac{10\ (X-M)}{\sigma} + 50$$

Here X means raw scores, M and σ stand for the mean and standard deviation of the scores earned by 100 students. (For computing s you may use the formula $\sigma = \sqrt{(X - M)^2/N}$.

   (iii) Now these three T scores belonging to originality, fluency and flexibility factors are added for providing composite creativity scores on the creativity test.
   (iv) The composite creativity scores of the students can be used for making comparison of the creativity level of the students within the examined group. For this purpose we can also compute percentile rank.

We can also employ an alternative method for the required interpretation in which we can make use of raw scores directly without converting these into T scores. It is based on high and low scores earned in the test. For this purpose we have to compute mean and standard deviation (SD) of the scores of the group and then use the following rule.

"Scores which are 1 σ or SD above the mean are taken as high creativity group and those which are 1 σ or SD below the mean are designated as low creativity group."

Therefore in case your group is your own class group and norms are not available in the manual you can employ this alternative method for the interpretation of the creativity scores and then may be able to determine the creativity levels of the students of your class.

Case Study of The individuals

The term 'case' is used in a number of ways conveying different meanings in our day-to-day life. A lawyer helps his client by arguing his *case* in a court of law. A doctor attending a *case* diagnoses the disease of his patient and prescribes appropriate medicines. A Judge decrees after hearing and studying the *case* file of an offender. An officer disposes of a number of *cases* put up by his subordinate clerks.

In all such situations, the term 'case' is used for a person or matter put to examination, observation or investigation for the purpose of helping the concerned individual in deciding or solving the problem related to him. In the subject psychology, the term case is also used almost in the similar sense. Here the individual who is confronted with an educational, vocational, socio-psychological or personal problem is termed as a 'case' and is subjected to proper study. Investigation, diagnosis and remedial or treatment measures go on the similar lines as happen with the cases of the doctors or lawyers. Such investigation and study of one's behaviour related with the task of finding a solution of his problem is termed as 'Case Study' in the subject of psychology. This investigation or study is quite comprehensive as it covers the subject's past history related to the problem, the present status of the problem and the future possibilities of dealing with the problem.

Purposes or Objectives of the Case Study

Case study is carried out mainly to serve the following two purposes:

1. **Diagnosis and treatment of behavioural problems:** Some individuals may suffer from one or the other behavioural problems on account of their lack of adjustment to their self or the environment. For example, children may have emotional or social maladjustment or may be lagging behind in their studies or normal mental functioning. Such type of problem children, backward, slow learners, delinquents or anti-social personalities, need quite careful attention and it is done here by studying them as individual and unique cases. The case study method thus aims at going into the depth of the nature of the problem, search for the probable cause of the eruption of this behaviour and then suggests the possible remedial or treatment measures for helping the sufferer get rid of the problem.
2. **To provide better guidance and counseling:** The case study methods and techniques are quite helpful to guidance personnel and counsellors in exercising their responsibilities in an effective way. Whether it is the field of educational guidance or vocational and personal guidance, the assistance to the guidance seeker is given by treating him as a case, studying him in relation to his environment and his problem and then providing appropriate guidance. In this way whatever guidance or counselling is given to a guidance seeker or counsellee depends to a great extent on the results of his case study, much in the same way as a doctor has to carry out the proper diagnosis of his patient's problem before subscribing any medicines for the treatment.

Subjects of the Case Study

It must be clear by now that whosoever feels any kind of difficulty and problem in his adjustment, development or progress, or due to one reason or the other, if we as investigators are interested in the investigation or study of one's behaviour, then such individual may be treated as a case for carrying out the study in a quite professional and technical way. Thus all individuals, whether normal or abnormal, average, above average or below average in the possession of the abilities or capacities related to their growth and development, personality traits or adjustment, may be taken as a subject for the case study. However, in general, the case study is more particularly applied for those in search of any assistance or help for solving their felt problems or for those whose behaviour we want to study in bringing desirable modification for their necessary adjustment, development and progress. This is why case studies of the following types of children or individuals are more commonly carried out in the field of education and psychology–(i) Creative person; (ii) Gifted or Genius; (iii) Backward or Slow learners; (iv) Delinquents or Criminals; (v) Persons suffering from emotional, social psychological and educational problems or maladjustment; (vi) Addicted individuals; (vii) Anti-social personality, etc.

How to Conduct a Case Study

In carrying out the case study, any individual who is under study, is treated as a unique or individual case in himself. Thus the study of his behaviour begins by giving due recognition and respect to his individuality. The next task is concerned with the establishment of a good rapport with him. He must be taken in confidence by winning over his trust and faith in the investigation. Henceforth all attempts are made to know him in relation to his personal identity, past history particularly regarding his felt problem of development and adjustment, all relevant information about the present status, circumstances and situations concerning his behaviour, development and adjustment, and so on. Truly speaking, case studies aim to study the past and present of the subject thoroughly in all its aspects of behavioural or personality dimensions vis-a-vis his environment. In this way, it deeply studies the investigation of all the essential things related to the subject's case in a very comprehensive way. Technically it is quite proper to use a pre-prepared format for such a study. It may provide more objectivity, reliability and validity to the case study work. The use of such a format may be illustrated through the case study of a problem adolescent.

Case Study of a Problem Adolescent

1. Identifying Data

(i)	Name	*Narender Chawla*
(ii)	Sex	*Male*
(iii)	Father's Name	*Sh. R.K. Chawla*
(iv)	Address	*House No. 150, Model Town, Delhi*
(v)	Date of Birth	*10.1.1989*
(vi)	Name of the School	*Govt. Sr. Sec. School, Delhi*
(vii)	Class	*X*
(viii)	Problems	
	– Emotional:	*Extremely Aggressive*
	– Social:	*Excessive sex interests, teasing girls*
	– Education:	Little interest in studies.

Source of identification: The parents and teachers have identified these problems and told about these in their own way to the investigator.

2. Birth Information

(i)	Place of birth:	*Delhi*
(ii)	The health of the mother at the time of his birth:	*Normal*
(iii)	The health of the subject at the time of birth:	*Normal*
(iv)	Any mishappening at the time of the birth:	*No mishap*

3. Health Record

(i)	General Health	Good/Average/Poor	*Good*
(ii)	Height		*5'4"*
(iii)	Weight		*50 kg*
(iv)	Eyesight	Normal/Defective	*Normal*
(v)	Power of Hearing	Normal/Defective	*Normal*
(vi)	Power of Conversation	Normal/Defective	*Normal*
(vii)	Condition of Teeth	Normal/Defective	*Normal*
(viii)	Condition of Throat	Normal/Defective	*Normal*
(ix)	Does the subject perform daily exercise for health.	Yes/No	*No*

4. Family Data

(i)	Tell, if		
	(a) Father is alive or dead		Alive
	(b) Mother is alive or dead		Alive
(ii)	If both alive, do they live together/ live separately/are divorced		Live together
(iii)	Education of the Father		M.B.B.S., M.D.
(iv)	Occupation of the Father		Doctor
(v)	Education of the Mother		M.B.B.S., M.S.
(vi)	Number of real brothers with their age		No Brother
(vii)	Number of real sisters with their age		Two (18 & 13 years)
(viii)	Total Members in the Family		Five
(ix)	Joint Family	Yes/No	No
(x)	The birth order of the Subject First/ Second/Third/Fourth etc.		Second
(xi)	Has the subject been brought up in the family	Yes/No	No
(xii)	Does the subject get proper love and affection from his parents?	Yes/No	No, lack of love and affection
(xiii)	Does the subject get proper recreational facilities at home?	Yes/No	No
(xiv)	Does the subject get proper education?	Yes/No	No
(xv)	Do the parents meet all the basic needs of the subject?	Yes/No	His psychological needs are not satisfied
(xvi)	Do the parents provide due encouragement to the subject?	Yes/No	No
(xvii)	Is the relationship between father and mother quite satisfactory?	Yes/No	No
(xviii)	Is the relationship between the subject and parents quite satisfactory?	Yes/No	No
(xix)	How does the subject spend his leisure time?		
	(a) Mostly with members of the family	Yes/No	No
	(b) Mostly with friends	Yes/No	No
	(c) Anywhere outside family	Yes/No	Yes
(xx)	His attitude towards siblings	Positive/Negative Negative	
(xxi)	The attitude of siblings towards the subject	Positive/Negative	Negative
(xxii)	The discipline in the home	Strict/Loose	Loose

5. Socio-Economic Status

(i)	The total monthly income of the family	*More than Rs. 20000*
(ii)	The source of the income Salary and some private practice	
(iii)	Does the family own a house? *Yes/No*	*No*
(iv)	The source of entertainment within the family environment – Radio/ Television/ Magazines/ Indoor games etc.	*Radio/Television* *Magazines*
(v)	The surroundings where family is residing Lonely/Crowdy	*Not so crowdy*
(vi)	The type of society in which the family resides : High/Middle/ Low	*High, Middle class*
(vii)	The status of the family in the society High/Middle/ Low	*Middle*

6. (i) Level of Intelligence

(a) The opinion of the teachers	Above average intelligence
(b) The opinion of the parents	Average Intelligence

(ii) Level of creativity

(a) The opinion of the teachers	Demonstrates creativity in his work and adjustment
(b) The opinion of the parents	Nothing creative can be expected from him.

7. Educational Record

(i) Academic Achievements (Last three years)

Subjects	*Class VII* *Year 1998*	*Class VIII* *Year 1999*	*Class IX* *Year 2000*
Hindi	55/100	40/100	34/100
English	60/100	50/100	35/100
Mathematics	80/100	40/100	30/100
General Science	70/100	35/100	33/100
Social Sciences	65/100	35/100	33/100
Art	75/100	38/100	34/100
Total	405/600	238/600	199/600
The position in the class	II positon	30th out of 50	Passed with Grace marks 46th out of 50

(ii) The subjects he likes most	*English and Art*
(iii) The subjects he does not like	*Maths and Science*
(iv) The relationship with the teachers Good/Satisfactory/ Not satisfactory	*Not satisfactory*
(v) The relationship with the colleagues Good/Satisfactory/ Not satisfactory	*Not satisfactory*
(vi) The opinion of the teachers about the subject	*Careless*
(vii) The status of his attendance in the school Satisfactory/ Unsatisfactory	*Unsatisfactory*
(viii) Has he ever failed in the school examination?	*He has passed IX class with the grace marks*
(ix) If yes, the name of the subject in which failed	*Mathematics*

8. Areas of Interests

(i) Co-Curricular Activities

	The name of the activity	*Participated or not participated*	*The distinction if achieved*
(a)	Drama/Play	Participated	–
(b)	Music	Not participated	–
(c)	On the spot painting	Participated	–
(d)	N.C.C.	Not participated	–
(e)	Social Sciences	Not participated	–
(f)	Declamation/ Debate	Not participated	–
(g)	Games and Sports	Participated	*Won some prizes*
(h)	Literary	Not participated	–
(i)	Any other	Participated in excursion	–

(ii) What type of books does he want to read? *Film magazines, love stories and detective novels*

(iii) His specific interests:

(a) Reading novels and film magazines

(b) Watching films

(c) Having friendship with girls and teasing them.

9. Adjustment

(i) Home Adjustment

(a) Does the subject feel that his parents are disappointed with him?	Yes/ No	Yes
(b) Does the subject enjoy the family environment?	Yes/ No	No

(ii) Emotional Adjustment

(a) Does the subject feel difficulty in talking to strangers?	Yes/ No	No
(b) Does the subject usually remain anxious?	Yes/ No	No

(iii) Social Adjustment

(a) Does the subject make friendship easily with others?	Yes/ No	Yes
(b) Does he take interest in social work?	Yes/ No	Yes

10. Behaviour in the Classroom

(i) Does the subject behave properly with his teachers?	Yes/No	No
(ii) Does the subject take interest in classroom activities?	Yes/No	No

11. Behaviour in the Classroom

(i) Does the subject demonstrate a socially responsive behaviour on the playground?	Yes/No	No
(ii) Does the subject remain aggressive and assertive on the playground?	Yes/No	Yes

12. Personality Traits

Traits	*High level*	*Middle level*	*Low level*
Self-confidence	H	M	L
Emotional stability	H	M	L
Stability	H	M	L
Leadership	H	M	L
Persistence	H	M	L

Note: The encircled M and L here are indicating the middle and low levels respectively of the possession of the related personality traits. The subject has not reached a high level in respect of the demonstration of any of the mentioned traits in his behaviour.

13. Educational and Vocational Plan or Ambitions

(i) What subjects would the subject prefer for his further studies after class X?

First choice	Dramatics
Second choice	Fine Arts
Third choice	Tourism

(ii) What profession or occupation would the subject prefer to enter after his studies?

First choice

Second choice

Third choice

14. Follow up Work

After collecting relevant information in the above form by using a pre-structured pro forma through various sources, attempts were again made to seek interview with his parents, colleagues, family members and friends for bringing more objectivity, reliability and validity to the collected data. The observation of their behaviour was also subjected to repetition for arriving at more appropriate conclusions. All these above-mentioned efforts related to the case study of our subject Narendra Chawla has finally led us to conclude about him as under:

Subject and His Problem. Narendra is enjoying a good physical health. He is above average in intelligence. He is ill tempered, emotional and aggressive in his behaviour. He faired well in his studies till class VII. His downfall began from class VIII. It was at this time when his mother joined a service and both his parents were quite occupied in their respective professions. The higher social status made them quite busy at the cost of looking after their home and children. Now there is free-for-all in the home environment. The impact of western culture is clearly reflected in the lifestyle of all the family members. The elder sister has developed unhealthy heterosexual relationships. Following her lines of behaviour, Narendra has developed an unusual excessive interest in girls to the extent of teasing and molesting them. He is maladjusted in the class and school and it has led to his truant behaviour. He has no attraction for the school life except taking part in dramatics or excursion activities for the sake of fun and enjoyment.

Probable Causes of His Present Behaviour: The more probable causes leading him to the present status may be listed as below:

(a) He is not receiving the desired emotional support from his parents.

(b) His sexually deviant behaviour may be the result of the impact of the sex behaviour of his parents and elder sister. There is no co-education in his own school and this has led him not to pay proper respect to the opposite sex. His interest in heterosexual behaviour has directed him to tease and harass girls.

(c) There is no proper provision and opportunities for the co-curricular and social activities in the school curriculum. Teachers are also indifferent to the children's need and there is no proper arrangement for the guidance and counselling services in the school.

Remedial Work and Suggestions

1. The parents should come to the reality. They must try to bring desirable changes in their attitude especially in dealing with their children. They must not neglect their children for their own enjoyment, professionalism and social life. Narendra should get the essential moral, emotional and educational support from his parents.
2. There is need of proper change in the attitudes, behaviour and inter-personal relationships on the part of every member of the family. The parents should produce better examples before the youngsters. The over indulgence in sex behaviour, especially in the presence or awareness of the children should be altogether avoided by the parents.
3. The school environment also needs to be restructured in terms of suitable modifications in the methods of teaching, individual attention and care, proper organisation of appropriate cocurricular activities and social work, group activities, tours and excursions, and the maintenance of proper discipline in classrooms and school etc. Narendra, for his behaviour modification, needs some extra care and attention from the teachers and school authorities. He should be properly attended to and given due recognition and appreciation for the goodness shown in any ongoing curricular or extra-curricular activities.

References and Suggested Readings

Adler, A. (1927), Practice and Theory of Individual Psychology, New York: Harcourt Brace and world.

Alexander, Luria (1966), *Human Brain and Psychological Processes*, New York: Harper & Row.

Alexander, Luria (1973), The Working Brain, New York: Basic Books

Allport, G.W. (1948), Personality—A Psychological Interpretation, New York : Holt.

Allport, G.W.(1961), Pattern and Growth in Personality, New York :Holt.

Allport, G.W. (1954), *The nature of prejudice*, Cambridge, MA: Harvard University Press.

American Psychiatric Association (2013), *Diagnostic and Statistical Manual of Mental Disorders* (5th ed.), Washington, DC: American Psychiatric Association.

American Psychological Association, (2007), Compliance, In: *APA Dictionary of Psychology*. Washington, D.C.: American Psychological Association.

Anderson, C.A. & Bushman, B.J. (2002) Human Aggression, *Annual Review of Psychology*, 53, 27-51.

Aronson, E. Wilson, T.D. and Akert, R.M. (2014), *Social Psychology*, New Delhi: Pearson.

Asch, S.E. (1952), *Social Psychology*, New York: Prentice Hall.

Asch, S.E. (1951), Effects of group pressure upon the modification and distortion of judgments, In H. Guetzkow (ED.), *Groups, leadership, and men: Research in Human Relations* (177-190), Oxford: Carnegie Press

Ausubel, D.P. (1952), *Ego-involvement and Personality Disorders*, NY: Grune and Strattons.

Avermaet, E.V. (2004), Social influences in small groups, In M. Hewstone and W. Stroebe (Eds.), Introduction to Social Psychology, U.K.: Blackwell Publishing.

Bandura, A. (1986), *Social foundations of thought and action: A social cognitive theory*, Englewood Cliffs, NJ: Prentice-Hall.

Bandura, A. (1994), Self-efficacy. In V. S. Ramachaudran (Ed.), *Encyclopedia of human behaviour* (Vol. 4, pp. 71-81), New York: Academic Press.

Bandura, A. (1977), *Social Learning Theory*, Englewood Cliffs, N.J.: Prentice-Hall.

Bandura, A. and Walters, R.H.(1963), *Social Learning and Personality Development*, New York: Holt.

Bandura, Albert (1973), *Social learning Theory*, Englewood Cliffs, NJ: Prentice-Hall.

Bandura, A. (1969), Principles of Behaviour Modification, New York: Holt Rinehart &Winston.

Bandura, A.(1973), *Aggression: A social learning analysis*, Englewood Cliffs, NJ: Prentice-Hall.

Baumeister, R. F., DeWall, C. N., Ciarocco, N. J., & Twenge, J. M. (2005). Social exclusion impairs self-regulation. *Journal of Personality and Social Psychology, 88*(4), 589-604.

Barney, Katz and Lehner, G.F. (1953), Mental Hygiene in Modern Living, New York: The Ronald Press Company.

Bar-on Reuven, (1996),*The Emotional Quotient Inventory (EQ-i), A test of emotional intelligence*, Toronto: Multi-Health System.

Baron, R.A. and Byrne, Donn (2001), Social Psychology (8th edition), New Delhi: Prentice-Hall.

Baron, R.A., Byrne, D. and Brans combe, N.R. (2006), *Social Psychology*, New Delhi: Prentice -Hall of India.

Baron, R.A., Byrne, D. and Brans combe, N.R. (2008), *Social Psychology*, New Delhi: Prentice -Hall of India.

Baron, R.A. & Byrne, Donn (2004), *Social Psychology* (8th ed.), New Delhi: Prentice- Hall of India.

Barrett, D.W. (2017), *Social Psychology: Concept and emerging trends*, New Delhi: Sage Publications.

Baumeister, R.F. (1998), The self, In D.T. Gilbert, S.T. Fiske and G. Lindzey (Eds.), *The handbook of social psychology,* (vol.1, 4th ed., pp.680–740), New York: McGraw-Hill.

Beck, A. T. (1967), *Depression: Causes and treatment.* Philadelphia: University of Pennsylvania Press.

Bellack, K.L. and Seigel, H. (1889), The Children Apperception Test, Needham Heights, MA: Allyn & Bacon.

Berkowitz, L. (1978), Whatever happened to the frustration-aggression hypothesis?, *American Behavioural Scientists,* 21:691–708.

Berkowitz, L.(1989), Frustration-aggression hypothesis: Examination and reformation, *Psychological Bulletin,* 106, 59–73.

Berkowitz, L.(1993), *Aggression: Its causes, consequences, and control,* Philadelphia: Temple University Press.

Bhatia, H.R.(1968), *Elements of Educational Psychology* (3rd ed.) Calcutta: Orient Longman.

Bingham, W.V.D. (1973), *Aptitudes and Aptitude Testing,* New York: Harper & Brothers.

Binnet, A. and Simon, T. (1916), *The Development of Intelligence in Children,* Baltimore: Williams & Wilkins.

Branden, Nathaniel (1987), *Honoring the Self, Personal Integrity and the Heroic Potential of Human Nature,* LA: J.P. Tarcher, Inc.

Branscombe, N.R. & Baron, R.A. (2017), *Social Psychology,* (14th edition), New Delhi: Pearson India Education.

Brown, F.J., (1960), 'Educational Sociology', (5th Printing), New York: Prentice Hall.

Burger, J.M. and Cornelius, T. (2003), Raising the price of agreement: Public commitment and the law-ball compliance procedure, *Journal of Applied and Social Psychology,* 33: 923–934.

Carrol, H.A., Mental Hygiene—The Dynamics of Adjustment, Prentice-Hall, New Jersey, 1967.

Carron, A.V. (1988), *Group dynamics in sport,* London: Ontario: Spodym.

Cartwright, D and Zander A, Group Dynamics, New York: Harper and Row, 1968 (International edition.)

Cattell, R. B. (1946), *Description and Measurement of Personality,* New York: World Book.

Cattell, R. B. (1950). *Personality: A systematic theoretical and factual study* (1st ed.), New York: McGraw-Hill.

Cattell, R. B. (1963). Theory of fluid and crystallized intelligence: A critical experiment. *Journal of Educational Psychology, 54,* 1–22.

Christenson, A., Doss, B. & Jacobson, N.S. (2014),*Reconcilable Differences,* (2nd ed.), New York: Guilford Press.

Cialdini, R.B. (1994), *Influence: Science and Practice,* (3rd ed.), New York: Harper Collins.

Ciccarelli, Saundra K. and White, J Noland (2012), *Psychology,* New York: Pearson Prentice Hall

Cohen, F. and Lazarus, R.S., "Coping with the Stress of Illness", In Stone, C.G., Cohen, F. Adler, N.E. (Eds.), Health Psychology, A Hand Book, San Francisco, CA: Jessy-Brass, 1979.

Coleman, James C. (1970), Abnormal Psychology and Modern Life (3rd Indian ed.), Bombay: Tarapore Wala & Sons.

Cooley, CH; Quoted by Brown F.J., *Educational Sociology,* New York: Prentice Hall, 1960

Cox, Richard H. (2007), *Sport Psychology: Concepts and Applications* (Sixth Ed.), New York: McGraw-Hill.

Crisp, Richard J. and Turner, Rhiannon N. (2014), *Essential Social Psychology* (3rd ed.), New Delhi: Sage Publications.

Crow, L.D. and Crow, Alice (1973), *Educational Psychology ,New Delhi:* Eurasia Publishing House.

Dale, Edgar, (1961), Audio-Visual methods in Teaching, New York: Dryden Press.

Das, J. P., Naglieri, J. A., & Kirby, J. R. (1994), *Assessment of cognitive processes: The PASS theory of intelligence, Boston:* Allyn & Bacon.

Davision, Gerald C. and Naele, John, M. (1978), *Abnormal Psychology,* (2nd ed.), New York: John Wiley.

Dollard, J. and Miller, N.E.(1950), *Personality and Psychotherapy,* New York: McGraw-Hill.

Dollard, J., Miller, N., Doob, I., Mourer, O.H., & Sears, R.R.(1939), *Frustration and aggression,* New Haven, CT: Yale University Press.

Douglas, O.B. and Holland, B.F. (1947), *Fundamentals of Educational Psychology,* New York: The Macmillan Co.

Drevdahl, J.E. (1956), "Factors of Importance for Creativity", *Journal of Educational. Psychology,* Vol. 12.

Driscoll, M. (2001), *Psychology of Learning for Assessment*, (2nd Edition), Boston: Allyn & Bacon.

Durand, V. Mark and Barlow, David H. (2013), *Essentials of Abnormal Psychology*, (6th ed.), Belmont CA: Wadsworth

Ellis, A. (1957). Rational Psychotherapy and Individual Psychology, *Journal of Individual Psychology*, 13: 38-44.

Eysenck, H.J. (1947), *Dimensions of Personality*, London: Methuen.

Eysenck, H.J.(1971), *The Structure of Human Personality* (3rd ed.), New York: Methuen.

Eysenck, H.J. (1960), *Handbook of Abnormal Psychology*, Oxford: Isaac Pitman & Sons Ltd.

Fairchild, Henry Pratt (1944), *Dictionary of Sociology*, New York: Rowman & Littlefield Publishers.

Feldman, Robert S. (2016), *Child Development* (7th edition), Boston: Sage

Fisher, R.J. (1982), *Social Psychology: An applied approach*, New York, NY: St. Martin's Press, Inc.

Fredman, M. and Rosenman, R. (1974), Type A Behaviour and Your Heart, New York: Knopf.

Freeman, F.S. (1971), *Theory and Practice of Psychological Testing*, (3rd Ind. ed.), Bombay: Oxford & IBH, Bombay.

Freud, S. (1939), *An Outline of Psychoanalysis*, New York: Norton.

Freud, S., (1935), *A General Introduction to Psychoanalysis*, New York: Liveright,

Freud, S. (1900). The interpretation of dreams, In Strachey, J. Trans. & Ed., The standard edition of the complete psychological works of Sigmund Freud (Vols. 4-5, pp. 1- 28), Hogarth Press/ Institute of Psychoanalysis London, UK. (Original work published 1886-1939)

Gardner, Howard,(1983), *Frames of Mind: The theory of multiple intelligence*, New York: Basic Books..

Good, Carter, V., (1959), *'Dictionary of Education'*, New York: McGraw Hill.

Goode and Hatt (1952), Methods of Social Research, New York: McGraw-Hill.

Goleman, Daniel (1995), *Emotional Intelligence: Why it can matter more than IQ*, New York: Bantam Books, 1995.

Goleman, Daniel (1998), *Working with Emotional Intelligence*, New York: Bantam Books.

Gross Richard & Kinnison, Nancy (2007), *Psychology for Nurses and Allied Health Professionals; Applying Theory to Practice*, London: Hodder Arnold.

Guilford, J.P. (1967), *The Nature of Human Intelligence*, New York: McGraw-Hill.

Guilford, J.P. (1982). Cognitive psychology's ambiguities: Some suggested remedies. *Psychological Review*, 89, 48-59.

Hall, C.S. and Nordby, V.J.(1973), A Primer of Jungian Psychology, New York : New American Library.

Hall, C.S. and Lindzey, G (1978)., Theories of Personality, (3rd ed.), New York: John Wiley.

Higgins, E.J. (2000), Social cognition: Learning about what matters in the world, *European Journal of Social Psychology*,30:3-39.

Hopson, B., (1982), *Counselling and Helping, Psychology for Nurses and Health Visitors*, London: The British Psychological Society

Horn, J.L. (1965), *Fluid and Crystalized intelligence: A Factor analytical and developmental study of the structure among primary mental abilities*, unpublished doctoral dissertation, Champaign: University of Illinois.

Horn, J.L. & Cattell, R.B. (1966), "Refinement and test of the theory of fluid and crystalized intelligence", *Journal of Educational Psychology*, 57, 253-270

Insko, C.A., Dreenan, S., Soloman, M.R.,Smith R., and Wade, T.J. (1983), Conformity asafunction of consistency of positive self-evaluation with being liked and being right, *Journal of Experimental Social Psychology*, 19: 341-358.

Janis, I. L. (1982), *Groupthink: Psychological Studies of Policy Decision and Fiascos*, Boston: Houghton Mifflin.

Jellinek, E.M. (Ed.), (1942), *Alcohol Addiction and Chronic Alcoholism*, New Haven: Yale University Press

Judd, Charles M. and Park, Bernadette (1993), "Definition and Assessment of Accuracy in social stereotypes" *Psychological Review*, 100(1): 109-128.

Keinan, G. (1994), Effects of stress and tolerance of ambiguity on magical thinking, *Journal of Personality and Psychology*, 67, 48-55.

Kirkpatrick,I.A., & Epstein, S. (1992), Cognitive-experimental self-theory and subjective probability: Further evidence for two conceptual systems, *Journal of Personality and Social Psychology*, 63, 534-544.

Kisker, George W. (1964), *The Disorganized Personality*, (3rd International Students Edition), New York: McGraw-Hill.

Knight, Rex and Knight, Margaret (1952), *A Modern Introduction to Psychology*, London: University Tutorial Press

Krech, D. And Crutchfield, R.S. (1948), Theory and Problems of Social Psychology, New York: McGraw Hill.

Kretch D. Crutchfield R.S. and Ballachey E. (1950), *Individual in Society*, Tokyo: McGraw Hill (International Student edition).

Kretschmer, E.(1925), *Physique and Character*, New York: Harcourt Brace.

Lautenschlager, Yetta (1997), *The Four A's of Emotional Intelligence*, paper submitted at the ISNIP Conference, U.S.A.

Lazarus, R.S., Psychological Stress and the Coping Process, New York: McGraw-Hill, 1961.

Lazarus, R.S. and Folkman, S., Stress Appraisal and Coping, New York: Springer, 1984.

Likert, R. (1932), A technique for measurement of attitude, *Archives of Psychology*, 22:40.

Luthans, F. (2010), Organizational Behaviour: An evidence based approach (12th ed.), New York: McGraw Hill

Malot, R.W. and Whaley, D.L., Psychology, Holmes Beach, F.L.: Learning Publications, 1983.

Maslow, A.H.(1962), *Toward a Psychology of Being*, Princeton N.J.: Van Nostrand.

Maslow, A.H. (1970), *Motivation and Personality* (2nd ed.), New York: Harper & Row.

Mayer John D. and Salovey Peter (1995), *Emotional intelligence and the construction and regulation of feelings*, Applied & Prevention Psychology, 4(3), 197-208

Mayer, John D., Caruso, D.R. and Salovey, P., Mayer-Caruso- Salovey, (1998), *Emotional Intelligence Test (MSCEIT),Version 2.0*, Toronto Canada: Multi Health Systems, Inc.

McKeachie, W.J. and Doyle, C.L. (1966), *Psychology*, New York: Addison-Wesley.

Mehdi, Baqer (1989), *Verbal and Non-verbal Tests of Creative Thinking*, Agra: National Psychological Corporation.

Meier, C.N. (1963), Meier Art Tests of Aesthetic Perception, IOWA: University of Iowa.

Messer, David & Meldrum, Claire (Eds.), Psychology for Nurses and Health Care Professionals, London: Prentice-Hall, 1955.

Milgram, S. (1963), Behavioural study of obedience, *Journal of Abnormal and Social Psychology*, 67, 371-378

Milgram, S. (1965), Some conditions of obedience and disobedience to authority, *Human Relations*, 18:57-76.

Morgan, C.T., Introduction to Psychology, 2nd ed., McGraw-Hill, New York, 1961.

Moskowitz, G.B. (2005), *Social Cognition: Understanding self and others*, New York: Guilford Press.

Munn, N.L. (1967), *Introduction to Psychology*, (Indian ed.), Delhi: Oxford & IBH.

Murphy, Gardner (1968), *An Introduction to Psychology*, New Delhi: Oxford & IBH, New Delhi.

Murry, H.A.(1943), *The Thematic Apperception Test*, Cambridge (Mass.): Harvard University Press.

Myers, David G. (2014), *Exploring Psychology*, New York: Wordsworth

Ormrod, Jeanne Ellis,(2009), *Essentials of Educational Psychology*, New York: Pearson Education Inc.

Oxford Advanced American Dictionary on line, retrieved on 08/04/2020 from https://www.oxfordlearnersdictionaries.com/definition/american english/cognition

Page, James D. (1976), *Abnormal Psychology*, New Delhi: Tata McGraw-Hill.

Paris, S., Paris, A. (2001), Classroom Applications of Research on Self-Regulated Learning, *Educational Psychologist*. 36 (2), 89-101.

Park, Claria Claiborne, (1998), "Existing Nirvana", *The American Scholar*, 67:2

Prince, Morton (1929), *The Unconscious* (2nd ed.), New York: Macmillan.

Rogers, C.R. (1959), A theory of therapy, personality and inter-personal relationships, *in* S. Koch (Ed.), *Psychology: A study of science*, Vol. III, New York: McGraw-Hill.

Rogers, Karl (1983), *Freedom to Learn for the 80s*, Columbus, Ohio: Charles Merrill.

Rogers, C.R. (1951), Client- centered Therapy, Boston: Houghton Mifflin.

Rogers, C.R., (1970), Carl Rogers on Encounter Groups, New York: Harper & Row.

Rogers, C.R. (1961), *On becoming a person: A therapist's view of psychotherapy*, Boston: Houghton Mifflin.

Rogers, C.R. (1980), *A way of being*, Boston: Houghton Mifflin.

Rogers, Cart, R. (1942), Counseling and Psychotherapy, Boston: Houghton Mifflin.

Rorschach, H.(1927), Rorschach Test-Psycho-diagnostic Plates, Cambridge MA: Hogrefe Publishing Corporotion.

Rozin, P., & Nemeroff, C. (1990), The laws of sympathetic magic: A psychological analysis of similarity and contagion, In W. Strigler, R.A. Shweder & G. Herdt (Eds.) *Cultural Psychology: Essays in comparative human development* (pp.205-232), Cambridge, England: Cambridge University Press.

Ruch F.L.(1970), Psychology and Life, Bombay: D.P. Taraporewala Sons & co.

Salovey, Peter & Mayer, John D (1990), *Emotional Intelligence, Imagination, Cognition and Personality,* Vol.9 (3), 185-211, Amityville, NY: Baywood Publishing Co.

Schachter, S. & Singer, J.E. (1962), Cognitive, social and physiological determinants of emotional states, *Psychological review,* 69, 379-399

Sears, D.O., Peplau, A.L., and Taylor, S.E. (1991), *Social Psychology,* Englewood cliffs, N.J.: Prentice Hall.

Seashore, C.E. (1960), *Seashore Measures of Musical Talents,* New York: Psychological Corporation.

Secord, P.F. and Backman, C.W. (1964), *Social Psychology* (International Student Edition), New Delhi: McGraw Hill.

Shaffer, L.F. (1961), L.S. Shaffer's Article in Foundations of Psychology (Ed.), Boring, Langfield and Weld, New York: John Wiley.

Sheldon, W.H.(1942), *The Varieties of Temperament: A Psychology of Constitutional Differences,* New York: Harper.

Shepperd, J.A., Ouellette, J.A., and Fernandez, J.K. (1996), Abandoning unrealistic optimistic performance estimates and the temporal proximity of self- relevance feedback, *Journal of Personality and Social Psychology,* 70:844-855

Sherif, M. (1935), A study of some social factors in perception, *Archives of Psychology,* 27: 1-60.

Sheriff, M. (1966), *Group Conflict and Cooperation: Their Social Psychology,* London: Routledge and Kegan Paul.

Shostrom, Everett, L. and Brammer, Lawrence M. (1952), The Dynamics of the Counseling Process, New York: McGraw-Hill.

Skinner, C.E. (Ed). (1968), *Essential of Educational Psychology,* New York: Prentice-Hall.

Sorenson, Herbert (1977), *Psychology in Education,* (7th ed.), New Delhi: Tata McGraw-Hill.

Spearman, C. (1904),"General Intelligence objectively determined and measured", *American Journal of Psychology,* 15, 201-293.

Spearman, C. (1927), *The abilities of man,* London: Macmillan.

Stern W, (1914), *Psychological Methods of Testing Intelligence,* Baltimor.

Stagner, R., & Karwoski, T.F (1973), Educational Psychology, New Delhi: Eurasia Publishing House.

Stagner, R., (1948). *Psychology of Personality,* New York: McGraw Hill Book Company.

Sternberg, R.J. (1977), *Intelligence, Information Processing and Analytical Reasoning,* Hillsdale, N.J.: Erlbaum,.

Sternberg, R. J. (1985), *Beyond IQ: A Triarchic theory of human intelligence,* London: Cambridge University Press.

Sternberg, R.J., (1986), *Intelligence applied.* New York: Harcourt Brace Jovanovich, Publishers.

Sumner, W.G., Quoted by Brown F.J.; (1960) *Educational Sociology,* New York: Prentice Hall (5th printing)

Taylor, S.E., Peplau, L.A., and Sears, D.O. (2006), *Social Psychology,* New Delhi: Pearson Prentice-Hall.

Taylor, D.A. (1984), Race Prejudice, discrimination and racism, In A.S. Kahn (Ed.), *Social Psychology,* IOWA: Wm C. Brown Publishers, College Division.

Terman, L. M. (1921). Intelligence and its measurement: A symposium--II. *Journal of Educational Psychology, 12*(3), 127-133

Terman, L.M. and Merrill, M.A. (1937), *Measuring Intelligence,* Boston: Houghton Mifflin.

The American Heritage New Dictionary of Cultural Literacy (Third Edition), (2005), New York: Houghton Mifflin Company

Thurston, L.L. (1938), *Primary Mental abilities,* Chicago: University of Chicago Press.

Thurstone, L.L. (1929), Theory of attitude measurement, *Psychological Bulletin* 5: 221-241.

Torrance, E.P. (1974), *Torrance Tests of Creative Thinking: Norms Technical Manual,* Bensonville, Illinois: Scholastic Testing Service.

Travers, Robert, M.W. (1973), *Educational Psychology,* New York: Macmillan.

Traxler, A.E. (1957), *Techniques of Guidance,* (Rev. ed.), New York: Harper & Brothers.

Tuckman, B.W. (1965), Developmental sequence in small groups, *Psychological Bulletin,* 63:384-399.

Tversky, A., & Kahneman, D. (1974), Judgment under uncertainty: Heuristic and bias, *Science*, 185, 94157)1124–1131.

Retrieved from http: psiexp.ss.uci.edu/research. teaching.Tvesky_1974.pdf

Tversky, A., &Kahneman, D. (1982), Judgment under uncertainty: Heuristic and bias, In D.Kahenman, P. Slovic and A. Tveisky (Eds.) *Judgment Under Uncertainty: Heuristics and biases*, 3–20, NY: Cambridge University Press.

Vinokur, A. & Burnstein, E. (1974), Effects of partially shared persuasive arguments on group-induced shifts: A group problem-solving approach, *Journal of Personality and Social Psychology*, 29: 305–315.

Wagnon, M.J. (Ed.) (1937),, *Readings in Educational Psychology*, New York: Houghton Mifflin.

Watson, J.B.(1930), *Behaviourism*, London: Kegan Paul.

Webster's Seventh New Collegiate Dictionary (1970), Springfield, Massachusetts, G.C. Merriam Company, Publisher

Wechsler, D. (1944), *The Measurement of Adult Intelligence*, New York: Williams & Wilkins.

Wegner, D.M. (1992), You can't always think what you want: Problems in the suppression of unwanted thoughts, In M. Zanna (Ed.) *Advances in Experimental Social Psychology*, 25: 193–225, San Diego, CA: Academic Press.

Weiten, W., Dunn, D., & Hammer, E. Y. (2012), *Psychology Applied to Modern Life: Adjustment in the 21st Century*, (10th Ed.), Boston: Cengage Learning.

Whitley, B.E. Jr., & Kite, M.E. (2006), *The psychology of prejudice and discrimination*, Belmont, CA: Thompson Wadsworth.

Wilson, R. C., Guilford, J. P., & Christensen, P. R. (1953), The measurement of individual differences in originality. *Psychological Bulletin*, *50*(5), 362–370.

Winne, PH, and Perry NE.(2000), Measuring self-regulated learning. In: Boekaerts M, Pintrich PR, Zeidner M, (editors), *Handbook of Self-regulation*. San Diego: Academic Press. pp. 531–566.

Wittakar, J.O. (1970), *Introduction to Psychology* (International Students Edition), New York: W.B. Saunders, International Students Edition.

Woodworth, R.S., and Marquis, D.G. (1948), *Psychology*, New York: Henry Holt.

World Health Organization (2010), *The ICD-10 Classification of Mental and Behavioural Disorders: Clinical Descriptions and Diagnostic Guidelines*, 10th ed. Geneva: World Health Organization.

Wyer, R.S. (1976), *The Hand book of Attitudes, Vol.1, Basic principles* (2nd ed.), London: Routledge.

Yinger, J.M. (1971), Personality, character and the self, In E.P. Hollander and R.G. Hunts (Eds.), *Current Principles in Social Psychology*, (3rd ed.), New York: Oxford University Press.

Young, Kimble (1953), *Hand Book of Social Psychology*, London: Routledge.

Zusne, L. & Jones, W.H. (1989), *Anomalistic Psychology: A study of magical thinking* (2nd ed.), Hillsdale, NJ: Erlbaum.